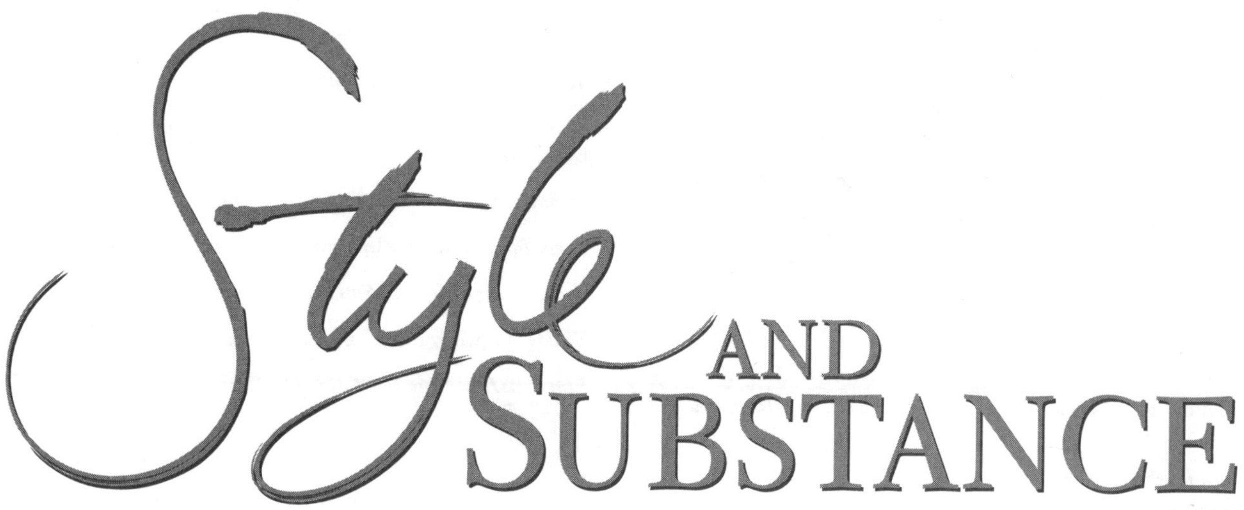


**A MULTIMEDIA APPROACH TO LITERATURE AND COMPOSITION**

**Pearson Education ESL**
Canadian Titles and Authors

***Canadian Stories*** by Eleanor Adamowski

***The Longman Picture Dictionary***, Canadian ed., Julie Ashworth & John Clark

***Reading for the Write Reasons: English Reading and Writing for Advanced ESL Students*** by Donna Aziz-Canuel, Lynne Gaetz & Richard Pawsey

***Amazing! News Interviews & Conversations*** by Susan Bates

***Amazing Canadian Newspaper Stories*** by Susan Bates

***Amazing 2! News Interviews & Conversations*** by Susan Bates

***Amazing 2! Canadian Newspaper Stories*** by Susan Bates

***Canadian Concepts***, 2nd ed., Books 1-6 by Lynda Berish & Sandra Thibaudeau

***English Fast Forward 1***, 2nd ed., by Lynda Berish & Sandra Thibaudeau

***English Fast Forward 2***, 2nd ed., by Lynda Berish & Sandra Thibaudeau

***English Fast Forward 3***, 2nd ed., by Lynda Berish & Sandra Thibaudeau

***Grammar Connections***, Books 1, 2 & 3, by Lynda Berish & Sandra Thibaudeau

***On Target*** by Keith L. Boeckner & Joan Polfuss Boeckner

***On Target Too*** by Keith L. Boeckner & Joan Polfuss Boeckner

***Target Practice*** by Keith L. Boeckner & Joan Polfuss Boeckner

***Classics Canada: Authentic Readings for ESL Students***, Books 1-4, by Patricia Brock & Brian John Busby

***Coming to Canada: Authentic Reading for ESL Students*** by Patricia Brock & Brian John Busby

***Contemporary Canada: Authentic Readings for ESL Students*** by Patricia Brock & Brian John Busby

***Being Canadian: Language for Citizenship*** by Judy Cameron & Tracey M. Derwing

***Focus 2: Academic Listening and Speaking Skills*** by Ranka Curcin, Mary Koumoulas, & Sonia Fiorucci-Nicholls

***Focus 2: Academic Reading Skills*** by Ranka Curcin, Mary Koumoulas, & Sonia Fiorucci-Nicholls

***Focus 2: Academic Writing Skills*** by Ranka Curcin, Mary Koumoulas, & Sonia Fiorucci-Nicholls

***Writing for Success: Preparing for Business, Technology, Trades and Career Programs*** by Dale Fitzpatrick & Kathleen Center Vance

***All Right!: A Guide to Correct English*** by Paul Fournier

***English on Demand***, 2nd ed., by Paul Fournier

***English on Line***, 2nd ed., by Paul Fournier

***English on Purpose***, 2nd ed., by Paul Fournier

***This Side Up*** by Paul Fournier

***This Way Out*** by Paul Fournier

***Before Brass Tacks: Basic Grammar*** by Lynne Gaetz

***Before Brass Tacks: Basic Skills in English*** by Lynne Gaetz

***Brass Ring 1: Basic English for Career-related Communication*** by Lynne Gaetz

***Brass Ring 1: Basic Grammar Review*** by Lynne Gaetz

***Brass Ring 2: English for Career-related Communication*** by Lynne Gaetz

***Brass Ring 2: Grammar Review*** by Lynne Gaetz

***Brass Tacks Grammar*** by Lynne Gaetz

***Brass Tacks: Integrated Skills in English*** by Lynne Gaetz

***Bridge to Fluency*** by Elizabeth Gatbonton

***Links: ESL Writing and Editing*** by Carolyn Greene & Claudia Rock

***A Beginning Look at Canada*** by Anne-Marie Kaskens

***A Canadian Conversation Book: English in Everyday Life, 2nd ed., Book 1***, by Tina Kasloff Carver, Sandra Douglas Fotinos & Clarice Cooper

***Reading Matters: A Selection of Canadian Writing*** by Jane Merivale

***Word-by-Word Beginning Workbook***, Canadian ed., by Steven Molinsky & Bill Bliss

***Word-by-Word Intermediate Workbook***, Canadian ed. by Steven Molinsky & Bill Bliss

***Word-by-Word Picture Dictionary***, Canadian ed. by Steven Molinsky & Bill Bliss

***Take Charge: Using Everyday Canadian English*** by Lucia Pietrusiak Engkent

***Take Part: Speaking Canadian English***, 2nd ed., by Lucia Pietrusiak Engkent & Karen P. Bardy

***Technically Speaking . . .: Writing, Reading and Listening, English at Work*** by Susan Quirk Drolet & Ann Farrell Séguin

***Style and Substance: A Multimedia Approach to Literature and Composition*** by Claudia Rock & Suneeti Phadke

***Read on Canada*** by Paul Sharples & Judith Clark

***Getting it Together, Books 1 & 2***, by Véra Téophil Naber

***A Grammar Manual, Volumes A & B***, by Véra Téophil Naber & Savitsa Sévigny

***Advanced Half-Hour Helper: Puzzles and Activities for ESL Students*** by Joan Roberta White

***Half-Hour Helper: Puzzles and Activities for ESL Students*** by Joan Roberta White

***Making the Grade: An Interactive Course in English for Academic Purposes*** by David Wood

Claudia Rock
Suneeti Phadke

# A Multimedia Approach to Literature and Composition

ERPI
Éditions du Renouveau Pédagogique Inc.
5757, rue Cypihot
Saint-Laurent (Québec)
H4S 1R3
Téléphone : (514) 334-2690
Télécopieur : (514) 334-4720
Courriel : erpidlm@erpi.com

## Credits

**The following authors, publishers, and photographers have generously given permission to reproduce copyright material.**

**UNIT 1.** Edgar Allan Poe photograph courtesy of Sipa Press / Ponopresse. "Hills Like White Elephants" by Ernest Hemingway. Reprinted with permission of Scribner, a division of Simon & Schuster, from *Men Without Women* by Ernest Hemingway. Copyright 1927 by Charles Scribner's Sons. Copyright renewed 1955 by Ernest Hemingway. Ernest Hemingway photograph courtesy of Sipa Press / Ponopresse. "The Lottery" from THE LOTTERY by Shirley Jackson. Copyright 1948, 1949 by Shirley Jackson. Copyright renewed 1976, 1977 by Laurence Hyman, Barry Hyman, Mrs. Sarah Webster and Mrs. Joanne Schnurer. Reprinted by permission of Farrar, Straus and Giroux, LLC. "The Veldt" by Ray Bradbury. Permission granted by Don Congdon. Ray Bradbury photograph courtesy of Ulf Andersen / Sipa Press / Ponopresse. "The Yellow Sweater" by Hugh Garner. Permission granted by McGraw-Hill Ryerson Limited. Hugh Garner photograph courtesy of Barbara Wong. Stephen Leacock photograph courtesy of Topham / Ponopresse. "Bread" by Margaret Atwood. Reprinted with permission of McClelland and Stewart Inc. Margaret Atwood photograph courtesy of Ulf Andersen / Sipa Press / Ponopresse. "Old Habits Die Hard" by Makeda Silvera." Reprinted by permission of the author. "Newton" by Jeanette Winterson. Reprinted by permission of International Creative Management, Inc. Copyright © 1998 by Jeanette Winterson.

**UNIT 2.** Mark Twain photograph courtesy of Interfoto / Sipa Press / Ponopresse. "An Unquiet Awakening" by Mordecai Richler. Reprinted by permission of the author. Mordecai Richler photograph courtesy of Ulf Andersen / Sipa Press / Ponopresse. "Marilyn Monroe: The Woman Who Died Too Soon" by Gloria Steinem. Reprinted by permission of the author. Gloria Steinem photograph courtesy of Ponopresse. "Pretty Like a White Boy: The Adventures of a Blue Eyed Ojibway" by Drew Hayden Taylor. Reprinted by permission of the author. Drew Hayden Taylor photograph courtesy of the author. "Bending Spoons and Bending Minds" by Joe Schwarcz. Reprinted by permission of the author. Photograph of Joe Schwarcz courtesy of the author.

**UNIT 3.** A.E. Housman photograph courtesy of Housman Society. William Blake photograph courtesy of Topham / Ponopresse. Alfred, Lord Tennyson photograph courtesy of Topham / Ponopresse. William Shakespeare photograph courtesy of Topham / Ponopresse. John Donne photograph courtesy of Topham / Ponopresse. William Wordsworth photograph courtesy of Topham / Ponopresse. John McCrae photograph courtesy of Veterans Affairs Canada http://www.vac-acc.gc.ca. "Stopping By Woods on a Snowy Evening" by Robert Frost. From the poetry of Robert Frost, edited by Edward Connery Lathem. Copyright 1923, Copyright 1969 by Henry Holt and Co., copyright 1951 by Robert Frost. Reprint by permission of Henry Holt and Company, LLC. Photograph courtesy of Topham / Ponopresse. "Treblinka Gas Chamber" by Phyllis Webb. Reprinted by permission of the author. Phyllis Webb photograph courtesy of the author. "Calamity" by F.R. Scott. Reprinted with the permission of William Toye, literary executor for the Estate of F.R. Scott. F.R. Scott photograph courtesy of William Toye, literary executor for the Estate of F.R. Scott. "Meditation on the Declension of Beauty by the Girl with the Flying Cheek-bones" by M. Nourbese Philip. Reprinted by permission of the author. M. Nourbese Philip photograph courtesy of the author.

**UNIT 4.** Susan Glaspell photograph courtesy of Topham / Ponopresse. "The World of Mary Hunter" by Martin Kinch. Radio play reprinted by permission of the Canadian Broadcasting Corporation.

Registration of copyright: 2nd quarter 2001
Bibliothèque nationale du Québec
National Libary of Canada
Imprimé au Canada

ISBN 2-7613-1210-4
1234567890 IO 0987654321
131210 ABCD OF-10

# OVERVIEW

We have designed *Style and Substance* for the teaching of literary analysis and essay writing at the college level in contexts such as advanced ESL or remedial native language courses where students would benefit from a stimulating but in-depth, step-by-step approach. We have included a wide variety of texts (from many different periods) and activities to allow instructors teaching 45- or 60-hour courses to tailor their course to the specific needs of their students. *Style and Substance* consists of not only a textbook but also an audio CD, an instructor's manual, and a complementary website that will offer yet more texts, more practices (exercises and activities), and more information to teachers and students (including authors' biographies).

The textbook is divided into four units: Short Stories, Essays, Poetry, and Drama. The first two units comprise the true heart of the book. These units contain historical and cultural backgrounds (where pertinent), analytical exercises aimed at increasing the student's interpretative abilities, writing activities designed to develop the student's composition skills, and oral activities geared at preparing the student to make a finely honed oral analysis by the end of the term. Moreover, one chapter in the short story section provides students with a practical, step-by-step approach to the preparation of an oral presentation. Glossaries of literary and grammatical terms are included at the end of the book.

*Style and Substance* has been designed to teach writing in response to different kinds of literary works. Not only have texts been chosen for their excellence and style, but also for their representations of different epochs, themes, groups of people, and points of view. We believe that the texts included in the book and on the accompanying website will appeal to a wide variety of readers. First and foremost, we hope that students will enjoy their initial direct contact with each piece. Then, as the readers work through the exercises and activities, we hope the book will help stimulate them to delve deeper to find other levels of meaning and to appreciate how different authors use words and language in effective ways. As students become more sensitive to both "style and substance," they in turn will sharpen their own writing skills.

The authors feel, too, that it is very important for students to experience poetry and drama aurally. Both of these genres have much more impact when they are heard, and often they seem very flat in the written mode. We have, therefore, included audio recordings of the poems and a radio play that we believe will bring these works to life. Moreover, whenever possible, we have suggested sites on the Internet where recordings of some of the other works can be found.

All the supplementary on-line texts will be available in pdf format (pre-formatted for immediate printing) and may be either printed on paper or used online. The teacher's guide offers practical teaching suggestions (including on integrating new technology to advantage in a literature class), answer keys, and electronic transparencies (that can be used with a computer and video projector or that can be printed off and used with an overhead projector) for teaching literary elements and doing in-class error analysis. The e-transparencies can either be printed on acetates for use with an overhead projector or may be used electronically as Power Point presentations.

In a nutshell, *Style and Substance* features the following:

- 15 short stories (10 in textbook, 5 on website), 8 essays (5 in textbook, 3 on website)
- 21 poems (13 in textbook, 8 on website), 3 plays (2 in textbook, one a radio play recorded on the accompanying audio CD, 1 on website)
- key background information on authors, historical periods, literary movements, and the evolution of various genres
- detailed explanations on analysing literature both orally and in writing and on using literary terminology effectively
- written and oral exercises and activities to develop appropriate writing and speaking skills
- step-by-step approaches to making oral presentations and writing different types of essays: narrative, descriptive, persuasive, journalistic
- recordings of all poems and one of the plays
- teaching suggestions
- answer keys
- assessment grids and suggestions for evaluation activities
- electronic transparencies
- hypertext link references to relevant sites on the Internet as well as references to pertinent books and articles.
- a literary and a grammatical glossary

In conclusion, we believe that *Style and Substance* offers both teachers and students a very comprehensive and stimulating introduction to literary analysis and essay writing.

# To the Student

*"Ye who read are still among the living, but I who write shall have long since gone my way into the region of shadows. For indeed strange things shall happen, and many secret things be known, and many centuries shall pass away, ere these memorials be seen of men. And, when seen, there will be some to disbelieve, and some to doubt, and yet a few who will find much to ponder upon in the characters here graven with a stylus of iron."*

— from "Shadow — a Parable" (1835) by Edgar Allan Poe

You are about to embark upon a journey of discovery in which you will enter different realities that various authors have crafted just for you, the reader. Along the way you will meet fascinating and strange characters and enter into lives and times that may be very different from your own. As you approach a text for the first time, we invite you to open your mind and imagination to the experience the author is inviting you to explore. Let yourself be carried away by the power of words and story. Let your thoughts and feelings flow where they will.

Next, we will ask you to stand back and reexamine each piece you have read from various angles in a more formal fashion. You will look for meanings on different levels and interpret the work using appropriate terms as well as your own insights and experiences. You will present your response and analysis both orally and in writing. At the end of the term, you will be able to write an analytical essay and express your thoughts orally in a logical, concise fashion.

We hope that you will be able to say that not only did you enjoy reading and listening to the texts, but that you also learned and thought about many new things while improving your writing and speaking skills, too. Now you will surely speak and write with more "style and substance."

# Acknowledgements

The production of this book and its accompanying website was only made possible through the combined efforts and support of many people, and the authors extend thanks to them all. We would like to thank our students for providing the basic motivation for this work and for responding enthusiastically to our first tentative efforts of using the materials and methodology in their embryonic form. In particular, we thank Alexandra Deschamps-Sonsino and Josée Bissonnette for allowing us to use essays they wrote as students. Many thanks also go to Jean-Pierre Albert for believing in the project in the first place and to Jeanine Floyd for always being there to oversee everything and to tie up any loose ends. Our editor, Joyce Rappaport, provided sound advice concerning content and did a magnificent job polishing the text. Thanks must also go to Daniel Paquet for designing and overseeing the production of the website and to the excellent staff of Flexidée for their expertise in graphics and page layout.

We would also like to thank the following reviewers for their judicious comments at various stages of the project: in particular, Elaine Bander, Dawson College, who was involved in the project from its inception to its completion; also, Lise Ouellet and her team, CEGEP de Rimouski; Robert Walsh, CEGEP de Trois-Rivières; and Mary-Louise Taylor, CEGEP Ahuntsic. Last of all, we thank our husbands, families, friends, and colleagues for their continued support of this project as we worked through its many stages.

# TABLE OF CONTENTS

## UNIT 3 POETRY



## UNIT 4 DRAMA

# Literary Elements

**This section comprises both a theoretical and practical introduction to literary elements. A familiar fairy tale is used to illustrate many of the facets of literary analysis.**

Just as there are many different ways to read a literary piece, there are also many ways to respond to it. You may enjoy discussing it with a friend or using it as a trigger for your own artistic creativity. Perhaps you prefer to think about its meaning and how it connects to your own experience. In higher-level literature classes, you will be invited to respond to a short story (or novel, poem, or play) in an analytical fashion both orally and in writing. That is, you will examine the piece carefully from different perspectives, and both talk and write about your discoveries and observations. There is much more to this than simply retelling a story or stating your opinion about the piece. You will first be encouraged to enter into the author's fictional world, and then to read between the lines, drawing inferences and making deductions, much like a detective. Learning to look at literature in an analytical way often increases the pleasure and appreciation a reader derives from a literary work while honing his or her own writing skills at the same time.

One of the most traditional ways of analysing meaning in a work of fiction is to look at it in terms of its different parts or elements. The elements of a work of prose fiction have been traditionally called the plot, setting, characterisation, theme, narration and point of view, and style. As you read the short stories in this book, we will draw your attention to the ways in which these elements interact to make each story effective and meaningful. Our focus will vary for each story in accordance with its own unique mix of elements.

To illustrate the elements of a short story, let us look at an English version of a tale told to many children the world round since its publication in 1697: the story of Little Red Riding Hood.

# LITTLE RED RIDING HOOD

CHARLES PERRAULT

Once upon a time there was a little girl, the prettiest one of all the village. Her mother loved her dearly. Her grandmother loved her even more, and made her a little red hood that looked so good on her that everyone called her Little Red Riding Hood.

One day, her mother, who had just baked some cakes, called her and said: "Go and see how your grandmother is. I've heard that she is sick. Take her a cake and this little pot of butter."

Little Red Riding Hood set off at once for her grandmother's cottage, located in another village. On her way through the forest she met a wolf. He would have very much liked to eat her on the spot, but dared not do so because of some wood-cutters who were in the forest. He asked her where she was going. The poor child, not knowing that it was dangerous to stop and talk to a wolf, said: "I'm on my way to my grandmother's. I'm taking her a cake and a pot of butter from my mother."

"Does she live far away?" asked the wolf.

"Oh, yes," replied Little Red Riding Hood, pointing; "far over there by the mill, the first house in the village."

"Well," said the wolf, "I think I'll go and see her, too. I'll take this path, and you take that one, and we'll see who gets there first." The wolf took off down the shorter road, running as fast as he could. The little girl continued happily on her way along the longer one, stopping from time to time to gather nuts, run after butterflies, and pick wild flowers.

The wolf soon arrived at the grandmother's house. Knock. Knock.

"Who's there?"

"It is your granddaughter, Red Riding Hood," said the wolf, in a thin, high voice, "and I've brought you a cake and a little pot of butter as a present from my mother."

The grandmother, who was sick in bed, called out, "Come on in. The door's not locked." The wolf flew in through the open door, sprang upon the poor old lady and gobbled her up in an instant, for he hadn't eaten in three days.

Then, he shut the door, lay down under the covers of the grandmother's bed, and waited for Little Red Riding Hood to arrive.

Knock. Knock.

"Who's there?"

Upon hearing the wolf's hoarse voice, Little Red Riding Hood felt frightened at first, but then thinking that her grandmother had a bad cold, she replied: "It's your granddaughter, Little Red Riding Hood. I've brought you a cake and a little pot of butter from my mother."

Speaking in a high voice, the Wolf called out to her: “Come on in. The door’s not locked.” Little Red Riding Hood came in through the open door. The wolf lay hidden under the covers in the bed. “Put the cake and the little pot of butter on the night table,” he said, “and come up on the bed nearer to me.”

Little Red Riding Hood took off her jacket, but when she climbed up on the bed she was astonished to see how her grandmother looked in her nightgown.

“Granmama!” she exclaimed, “what big arms you have!”

“The better to hug you with, my child!”

“Granmama, what big legs you have!”

“The better to run with, my child!”

“Granmama, what big ears you have!”

“The better to hear with, my child!”

“Granmama, what big eyes you have!”

“The better to see you with, my child!”

“Granmama, what big teeth you have!”

“The better to eat you with!” And, with these words, the wicked wolf jumped on Little Red Riding Hood and gobbled her up.

The End

*(translated from the original by C. Rock)*

## PLOT: DRAMATIC AND NARRATIVE STRUCTURE

One of the most fundamental elements of a traditional short story is its **plot**. The plot is what happens in the story. In our example, a young girl has been sent to another village by her mother to deliver a cake to her grandmother who is ill. On her way, she passes through a forest where she stops to talk to a wolf. He beats her to the grandmother’s cottage, eats the old lady, and then disguises himself and lays in wait for the girl to arrive. When she does, he eats her, too. The end. This is the story as seen on a first level of meaning.

When you do literary analysis, one aspect you examine is how the plot is constructed. Let us look at our example. First there is the **exposition** or description of the situation at the outset: the mother telling her daughter to take some food to her sick grandmother. This, in itself, would seem to be a simple task but a **complication** arises: the little girl runs into a wolf in the forest. The **tension** starts to rise at this point because the girl doesn’t realise that she is in danger. The reader knows that wolves are dangerous and wonders what is going to happen; it can’t be good. The tension continues to build as the unsuspecting girl arrives in the cottage and engages in a conversation with the wolf. As the dialogue continues, the reader feels the girl’s suspicions about the situation growing as she realises that it is not her grandmother in the bed. Every reader can relate to the sinking feeling she must be experiencing as she starts to recognise the truth about her predicament. The reader wonders if the little girl will react in time! No. Horror of horrors! The **climax** of the story occurs when the wolf gobbles Little Red Riding Hood up, too. Perreault's story ends abruptly right here with the finality of this awful act, and leaves the reader somewhat suspended in disbelief and hoping that there is more to come. In other words, the reader hopes for a happy ending, such as the one the Brothers Grimm added to this tale. However, the story really has ended and the tension has been released by our knowing the final outcome or **dénouement**.

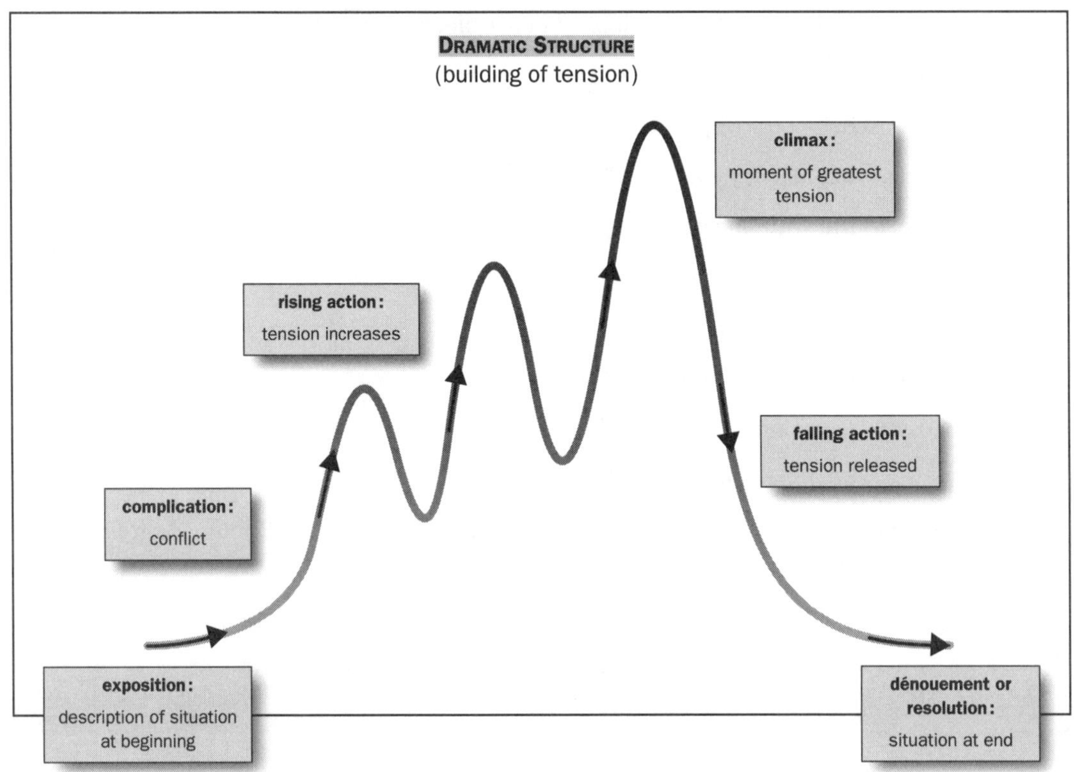


In summary, then, in its barest form, the **dramatic structure** of a short story very often entails the exposition of a situation, followed by a complication of some sort. The main character is faced with a conflictual situation that must be resolved. The tension rises until it reaches a climax, something happens to resolve it, and the story then ends. Of course, in reality, the dramatic structure of a short story is often more complex than this. The tension often rises and falls several times before coming to a climax. It is interesting to note that in many modern stories, the tension is sometimes only partly resolved, just as we learn to live with only half-solved problems and partial solutions (often there is no final, definite resolution).

The conflict experienced by the main character can be caused by an external agent, such as another character or a difficult situation, or by an internal one, such as his or her conscience or desire. The action in the story can often be interpreted on two levels at once; in other words, we perceive what is going on inside a person's mind as well as the external events taking place. In the story of Little Red Riding Hood, the **external action** — for example, the meeting of the girl with the wolf in the woods — is described explicitly, whereas the reader is left to imagine implicitly the **internal** action going on in the girl's mind as she begins to realise that she is in danger.

The **narrative structure** relates to the order in which the events of the story unfold. The events can be presented in a chronological order, one in which the action starts at one point in time and progresses forward in time. The action can also be presented in a non-chronological fashion, where the time sequences of the story are varied and do not progress forward in a linear way. Writers use literary devices such as **flashbacks**, a reference to an event in the past, or **foreshadowing**, a hint at what will happen in the future, in order to create an interesting effect in the plot of the story. Little Red Riding Hood is presented mainly in chronological order in terms of time. She meets the wolf, who hurries to the grandmother's house before the girl, and waits for her arrival. There is one powerful example of foreshadowing when the reader learns that the wolf would like to eat her on the spot. This, of course, is exactly what he does do at the end of the story. There is another less direct hint of what is to come in the future when the wolf asks her where she is going. The reader already knows that the wolf wants to eat the girl, but cannot do so in the forest. Therefore, the question is itself very ominous, and the reader guesses that the wolf is going to do something bad.

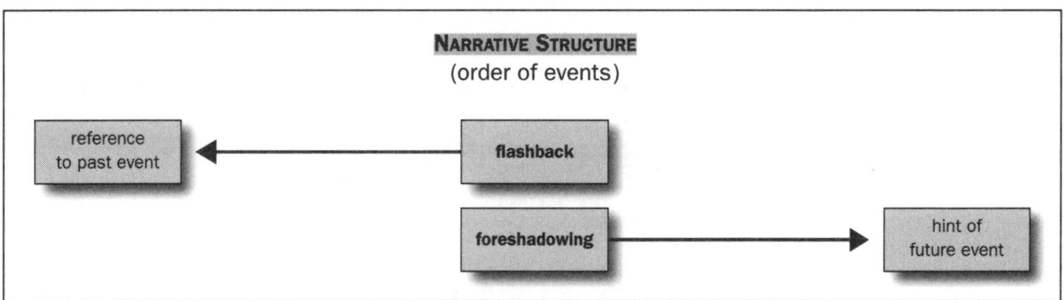


One last word about the importance of plot: the plot and dramatic structure are often the elements that move a story along, that make it exciting to read. However, these elements are always interwoven with the characters and setting in order to give an underlying meaning or theme to a piece. That is, if the story had a different plot, the characters would react differently and if it had different characters or a different setting, the plot itself would not be the same.

In conclusion, you may wish to use the following questions as a guide when discussing the element of plot for a literary analysis:

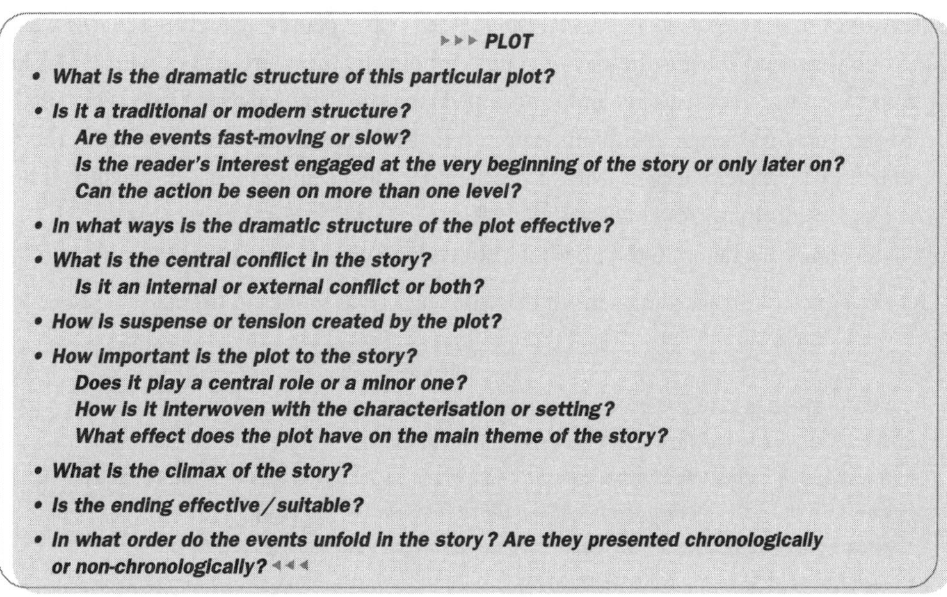

***PLOT***

- ***What is the dramatic structure of this particular plot?***
- ***Is it a traditional or modern structure?***
  ***Are the events fast-moving or slow?***
  ***Is the reader's interest engaged at the very beginning of the story or only later on?***
  ***Can the action be seen on more than one level?***
- ***In what ways is the dramatic structure of the plot effective?***
- ***What is the central conflict in the story?***
  ***Is it an internal or external conflict or both?***
- ***How is suspense or tension created by the plot?***
- ***How important is the plot to the story?***
  ***Does it play a central role or a minor one?***
  ***How is it interwoven with the characterisation or setting?***
  ***What effect does the plot have on the main theme of the story?***
- ***What is the climax of the story?***
- ***Is the ending effective/suitable?***
- ***In what order do the events unfold in the story? Are they presented chronologically or non-chronologically?***

## SETTING

When we talk about the **setting** of a short story, we refer to the time and place it occurred. A story can be set in the present, past, or future and the setting usually refers to a physical place, either real or fictional. Sometimes the **general** setting (epoch, historical period, on a continent, etc.) of a story is more significant than the **specific** setting (particular time and place). Usually, a setting is **external** (outside a character) but sometimes it can be **internal** (inside the head or imagination of a character) and sometimes the action shifts subtly between the two, for example in the story "An Occurrence at Owl Creek Bridge" (See the *Style and Substance* website for this story.)

The setting gives the story a certain concreteness and helps the reader connect with the characters and the plot. By using vivid imagery to describe elements in the setting, the author can create a **mood** for each scene and a general overall **atmosphere**. In the case of "Little Red Riding Hood," the story is set somewhere in Europe at an undetermined time in the past. The actual date or country of the story is irrelevant because historical significance is unimportant in the context. However, the main character must walk through a forest. The telling of this trek adds atmosphere, tension, and meaning to the story.

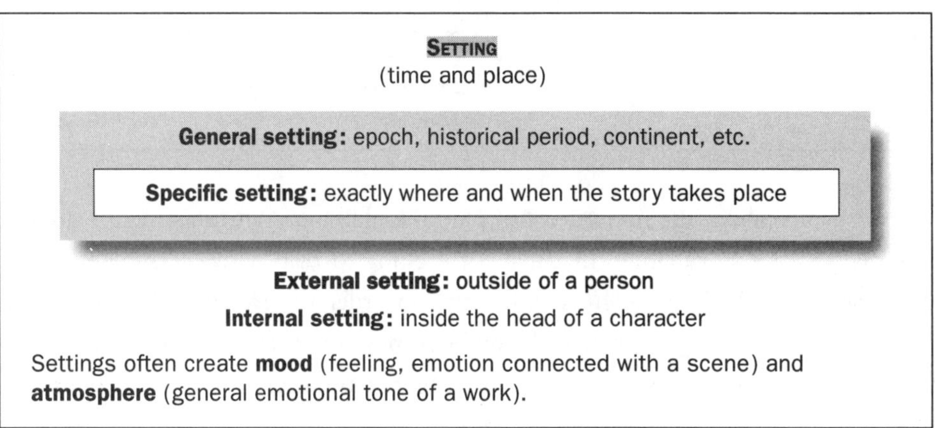


This particular setting has a direct influence on the plot, characters, and meaning (theme) of the story. Not only are forests dark, scary places for many people at night — places where you can lose your way even during the day — but symbolically, they are places where evil lurks in waiting to prey on the unsuspecting and innocent. Dangerous animals, such as wolves, lie hidden in wait. Moreover, forests can also be interpreted in Freudian terms as representing the human unconscious, filled with submerged fears of death and violence and repressed sexuality. Thus, this particular element of the setting in "Little Red Riding Hood" is absolutely central to the story. It not only determines the action in the plot but also lends an atmosphere of pregnant fear to the tale.

Here are questions regarding setting that you can use as guides in literary analysis:

***▸▸▸ SETTING***

- ***Does the setting have a historical or geographical significance?***
- ***How important is the setting in the story? (major or minor)***
- ***How does the setting affect other aspects of the story, such as plot, characterisation, and theme?***
- ***How does the setting influence the mood and atmosphere of the story?***
- ***Is the setting believable to the reader? Does it assist in establishing credibility?***
- ***Does the setting symbolise something?***
- ***Is the setting suggestive about the culture, the philosophy, or the spirit of the times?*** ◂◂◂

When reading fiction, the reader makes judgements about the story based on impressions of the characters. If a reader cannot identify or sympathise with a character, very often he or she will have a negative opinion of the story. Therefore, characterisation is a very important element in analysing a work of fiction. Characterisation has its root in the word *character*, and it means the technique with which a writer develops and portrays the characters in the story. There are different terms used for the different characters in a fictional work. The main character of a story is called the **protagonist** and the person who is in conflict or struggle with the protagonist is referred to as the **antagonist**. The terms *protagonist* and *antagonist* do not necessarily have positive and negative connotations. That is, the terms do not connote any value judgements, and therefore, a protagonist and an antagonist may or may not have heroic qualities. While the protagonist is easy to identify because the plot revolves around him or her, the antagonist is sometimes harder to identify. In "Little Red Riding Hood," the title of the story identifies the protagonist. The antagonist is not a human being in this case, but a wolf. In another story, Hemingway's "The Old Man and the Sea," the antagonist is a marlin with which an old fisherman struggles. Sometimes the antagonist might not be alive — it can be a difficult environment or social force such as a storm in the winter or war.

Character development is also another important consideration. A **round character** is well developed and multifaceted. These characters evolve and change as the story progresses. If they evolve, the characters are identified as dynamic. Opposite to round characters are characters who are **flat** or one-dimensional. These types do not grow or change and are also called **static** characters. Usually, such character types are **stereotypes.** It is important to mention that, as with the terms *protagonist* and *antagonist*, "flat" and "round" characters should not be cast in positive or negative terms. Each type serves a purpose in terms of the story as a whole. Even though Little Red Riding Hood and the wolf are the protagonist and antagonist, both are flat characters. She is a naïve little girl and he is the stereotypical villain who wants to eat her. They do not evolve or change.

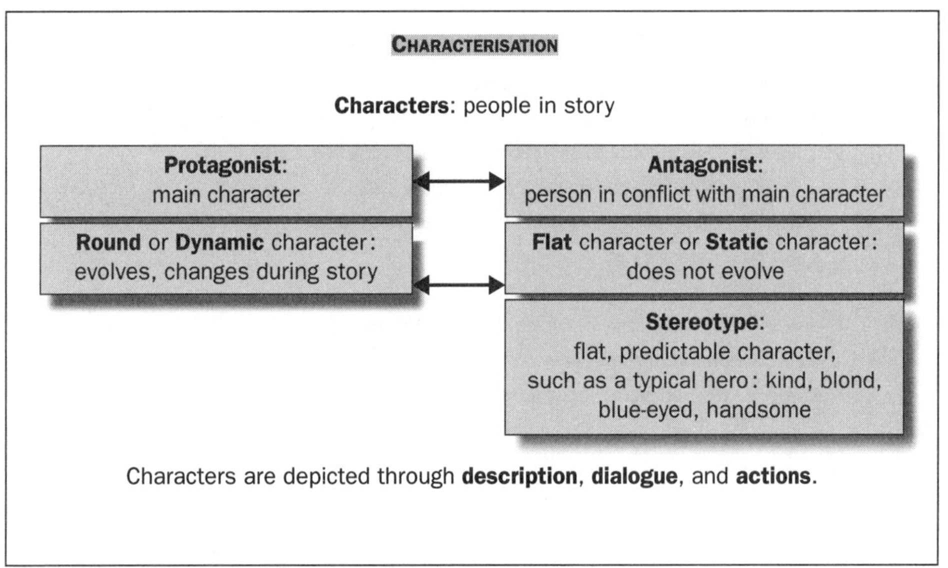

Writers reveal their characters in many different ways. For example, a writer can depict a character's physical appearance and personality through detailed **description**. Little Red Riding Hood obviously wears a red cape with a hood. She is also described as being very pretty and loved by her mother and grandmother. The reader can assume that she has a sweet and charming personality. Sometimes a name of a character can be symbolic and can reveal something vital about the character. For example, Old Man Warner and Mr. Graves are two characters in the short story "The Lottery" who are meant to be taken seriously.

Furthermore, a writer can establish a character through **dialogue**. The subject of the conversation and the tone convey a lot about a character. The reader should analyse the subject of the dialogue in terms of its importance. *Who* is participating in the conversation is also another important factor. *Where* and *when* the conversation is taking place are further considerations. Also, the *quality of the conversation*, and the *attitude of the speakers* are very important. In "Little Red Riding Hood," the conversation between the girl and the wolf in the woods gives clues as to the motive of the wolf. We know that he is trying to get as much information as possible from her about her grandmother. The dialogue at the grandmother's house has an ominous tone. Little Red Riding Hood's questions become pointed, revealing her growing alarm and suspicions about the wolf's answers.

In addition, a writer can depict characters through their **actions**. A character's behaviour in different circumstances gives clues to his or her personality. A character can act or react. Very often, as in real life, a character does both, either consciously or unconsciously. Little Red Riding Hood reacts to the threat of the wolf by trying to run away from him. The wolf behaves very predictably since he wants to eat the girl.

Above all, a character must be believable or credible. He or she must behave in a convincing manner. Any changes in his or her personality must be motivated. Characters are crucial in fiction. They make the story a story.

Here is a list of questions to guide you through character analysis:

**▸▸▸ CHARACTERISATION**

- ***Who is the protagonist in the story?***
- ***Who or what is the antagonist?***
- ***What are the main actions of the protagonist and antagonist?***
- ***What are their character traits or personalities?***
- ***What methods does the writer use to depict characters?***
- ***Are the characters round or flat?***
- ***Who are the secondary characters?***
- ***What is their importance or relevance to the story?***
- ***Are the characters interesting and credible?***
- ***How do the setting and plot influence the characters?*** ◂◂◂

The **theme** of a piece expresses the underlying meaning a reader derives from it. The main theme, in other words, concerns the unifying philosophy on life that the author wishes to convey. What the author wishes to tell the reader, whether it is a universal human truth or a specific observation, must be regarded as theme.

The complexity of a theme can vary from work to work. Readers might interpret the main theme of a work differently because important secondary themes may be present. In certain works, themes are explicitly stated, while in others, they are often implied. Different literary elements such as plot and setting interact and complement each other in order to develop the theme(s) of a work.

To discover the theme of a work, it is often useful to search out the ideas derived from the observations of the author. It is important not to confuse the **subject** of the work with the author's ideas or observations. Usually the subject of a work can be expressed in one word such as love, marriage, or hatred. Ideas and observations are judgements that express the values of the writer. The reader is also able to interpret the ideas of the work and make a value judgement based on his or her life experiences. The theme of a work should be expressed in terms of not just an idea, but a value statement that offers opinion or judgement for discussion. For example, the conflict in this story can be interpreted as the classic duel between good (the child) and evil (the wolf) or between male and female (the male preys on the female!). If you carefully reread the story with an eye open to signs of the latter, you will notice quite a lot of sexual imagery, such as the dark forest, the red colour (blood, passion, menstruation) of a young virgin's "hood," the females being devoured by the wolf in a bed, and so on.

**THEME**
(meaning)

**Theme:** underlying message or meaning

The theme of a piece is a value statement, such as "Love is wonderful", "Growing old is difficult", etc. In other words, it is the expression of an opinion or point of view.

*(not to be confused with the* subject *of a work: general topic, such as love, growing old, etc., in which no opinion is implied or expressed.)*

Here are some questions to ask when evaluating the theme of a work:

***THEME***

- ***What is the work about?***
- ***What are the ideas and values demonstrated in the work?***
- ***Are these implied or explicitly stated?***
- ***Do all the other elements convey the same ideas and values? (Look at what the characters say and think.)***
- ***Do the other elements (such as characters or setting) symbolise an idea?***
- ***Are the ideas and values universal?***
- ***Does the work contain any secondary themes?***
- ***In what ways do the secondary themes relate to the main theme?***

The **narrator** is the person or voice who tells the story. **Point of view** is the perspective from which the story is told. It is important not to confuse the author with the narrator or the author's opinion about a particular subject with the point of view.

Fiction abounds with different types of narrators. When a story is told by a character who participates either directly or indirectly, the narrator is referred to as the **first-person** narrator; the story is told from his or her point of view. The first-person pronoun "I" is used to relate the story. The first-person point of view has advantages and disadvantages. Because the narrator, "I," is a direct participant in the story, the events and actions in the story seem much more immediate or intimate. However, this type of narrator can give only incomplete information about the actions and thoughts of the other characters because he or she can only interpret them from a personal perspective. The reader receives interpretations and judgements of other characters from the first-person narrator. The reader then has to decide for himself or herself if the information and interpretation of the actions are accurate. Writers often use the first-person narrator when writing thrillers or detective novels because they want to give readers only select information.

When a narrator does not directly or indirectly participate in a story, but is an observer, he or she is called the **third-person narrator**. This type of narrator can tell the story from two points of view: the **omniscient point of view** or the **limited point of view.** In the first point of view the narrator knows everything about characters and the events; he or she is all-seeing and all-knowing. However, an omniscient narrator can relate the story **objectively** or can offer judgements. In other words, the third-person narrator can be **intrusive**. In the second point of view the narrator can limit himself or herself to telling the story from the point of view of one character in the story. The **first-person plural narrator** is rare in fiction. This narrator tells the story as part of a group or "we."

In "Little Red Riding Hood," the story is told by a third-person omniscient narrator who knows what is going on in the minds of each character. For example, the narrator tells us what the wolf is thinking in the forest when he meets Red Riding Hood (he'd love a snack!) and we learn that she is feeling frightened when she first hears his voice when she knocks on the door of her grandmother's house. This type of narration serves to distance the reader from the characters. The reader becomes a spectator who often knows more than the protagonist as the action unfolds.

Many novels written in the latter half of the twentieth century contain **multiple narrators**. That is, parts of a story are told from the point of view of one character; other parts are told from the points of view of other characters. This interesting technique gives the reader two or more points of view about the direction of the story.

**Narration and Point of View**
(how the story is told)

**Narrator**: person or voice telling the story

**Point of View**: perspective from which story is told

**First person**: narrator *directly involved* in a story; tells it using "**I**" (first-person singular narrator) or "**we**" (first-person plural)

**Third person**: narrator *not involved* in a story, is only an observer; the story is told in the third person using "**he**," "**she**," "**they**"

**Omniscient** point of view: narrator knows everything; is all-seeing and all-knowing

- **Objective**: narrator reports only the facts
- **Intrusive**: narrator offers opinions and judgements

**Limited** point of view: narrator can only give incomplete information

**Multiple** narrators: story told from several different points of view

Narration and point of view often affect how close the reader feels to the people and events in the story.

The following are some questions to ask in order to understand narration and point of view:

***▸▸▸ NARRATION AND POINT OF VIEW***

- ***Who is the narrator of the story? Is there only one narrator or are there multiple narrators?***
- ***Is the narrator credible or reliable as an interpreter of the action?***
- ***How does the narrator have access to the information in the story?***
- ***Does the narrator have a positive or negative opinion of the characters?***
- ***What is the point of view of the work?***
- ***Is the story told from only one point of view or many points of view?***
- ***How does the point of view affect the reader's sense of involvement in the story?*** ◂◂◂

## STYLE

**Style** refers to the techniques of language a writer uses in a specific work. When analysing style, it is common to consider two aspects. The first aspect is **diction**. Diction refers to a writer's (or a speaker's) choice and use of words and to the words' characteristics. Usually a writer controls and manipulates language very carefully for effect since it is language through which he or she conveys ideas. Diction consists of several levels of analysis. The reader should look at the relationship between the **denotation** or literal meaning and **connotation** or suggested meaning of the words. Also, the level of **concreteness** (perceptible by the senses) or **abstractness** (not perceptible by the senses, but only by the mind) should be taken into account.

**Figurative devices** or **figures of speech** are expressions used in a nonliteral way that create a special effect or extend meaning beyond the limits of ordinary usage. The most common figures of speech are **similes**, which compare two things using *like* or *as* (for example, his eyes were like deep pools) and **metaphors**, which comprise an implied comparison of two things without using like or as (for example, the deep pools of his eyes). Other common devices are **personification**, which gives human qualities to inanimate or abstract objects (the sighing wind); **imagery**, which consists of descriptive word pictures appealing to one of the senses (the golden rays of the setting sun); and **irony**, which consists of a statement or event that is the opposite to what is intended, expected, or expressed (she died just at the moment she had the most to live for). These figurative devices are important elements of style. Also, the **rhythm** or sound patterns of the sentences can make use of **alliteration** (repetition of the initial letter or sound in words), **assonance** (repetition of identical vowel sounds), **consonance** (repetition of identical consonant sounds) and the **repetition** of other sentence elements such as words and structure. Finally, the **level of language** (language for a specific social setting) such as **formal speech** (Good morning, how do you do), **informal speech** (hi), **slang** (howdy), and use of **dialogue** (conversation between two characters) should be considered.

**STYLE**
(techniques of language usage)

**DICTION:** a writer's (or a speaker's) choice and use of words and the words' characteristics

**Denotation**: literal or dictionary meaning

**Connotation**: associated or suggested meaning

**Level of Concreteness**: perceptible by the senses

**Level of Abstractness**: not perceptible by the senses but only by the mind

**Figures of Speech**: expressions used in a nonliteral way to create special effect or extend meaning
- **Simile**: comparison of two things using like or as
- **Metaphor**: implied comparison of two things without using like or as
- **Personification**: giving human qualities to inanimate or abstract objects

**Imagery**: descriptive word pictures appealing to one of the senses

**Irony**: the opposite of what is intended, expected, or expressed

**Rhythm**: sound patterns
- **Alliteration**: repetition of the initial letter or sound in words
- **Assonance**: repetition of identical vowel sounds
- **Consonance**: repetition of identical consonant sounds
- **Repetition**: of other sentence elements such as words and structure

**Level of language**: language for a specific social setting
- **Formal speech:** conventional language that respects the rules
- **Informal speech:** everyday, unofficial language
- **Slang:** casual speech

**Use of dialogue:** conversation between two characters

**SYNTAX:** the way in which the words, phrases, and sentences are arranged

**Sentence length:** long, short

**Word order**: subject, verb, complement

**Sentence types:** simple, compound, complex

Diction and syntax contribute to **tone** or **mood**.

The second aspect to look at is called **syntax**. Syntax refers to the way in which the words, phrases, and sentences are arranged. Important factors to consider are **length of sentences** (long or short), **word order** (arrangement of subject, verb, complement) and **sentence types** (simple, compound, complex). These aspects of style contribute to the **tone** or **mood** of the work. Tone refers to the attitude of the writer to the subject of the prose piece. Attitude can reflect irony, anger, sentimentality, humour, or can be objective or neutral.

In our "Little Red Riding Hood" example, the author uses language associated with fairy tales ("once upon a time" and "one day"). This leads the listener to anticipate that something bad is going to happen, as occurs in most fairy tales. Moreover, the appearance of the wolf in the forest brings forth connotations of fear and evil in the listener's mind. The instance of foreshadowing (when the wolf states that he would like to eat the girl when he first meets her) also helps set the tone of growing dread that culminates in the repeated elements of the final dialogue between the girl and the wolf in disguise: "Granmama! What big… you have!" followed by "The better to… my child!" The fact that the wolf is personified (he can talk) and that he disguises himself as an innocent grandmother reinforces the good-versus-evil theme of the story and reminds us all that we must beware of evil people lurking in the most surprising guises.

Throughout the story, the author uses concrete language ("gather nuts, run after butterflies, and pick wild flowers"). This enables young listeners to visualise the scenes. The story is told objectively by a third-person omniscient narrator using simple, straightforward vocabulary, but the language strikes the contemporary reader as fairly formal. This formality is enhanced because the tale was written in 1697 in Europe in the language of the times. The style fits the content and purpose of the piece.

Consider the following questions when analysing the writer's style:

▸▸▸ ***STYLE***

- ***What type of diction is found throughout the work? Consider the meaning of words in terms of their denotations and connotations.***
- ***Are the words concrete or abstract?***
- ***Is the language formal or informal? Slang or dialect?***
- ***What are the figurative devices such as similes, metaphors, and personifications?***
- ***How does the writer use imagery?***
- ***Is there a particular sound to the language, accomplished by the use of repetition, alliteration, assonance, or consonance?***
- ***What types of sentences are found in the work?***
- ***What is their length?***
- ***Does the sentence structure vary or is it always the same?***
- ***What is the overall tone or atmosphere of the work?***
- ***How is this tone or atmosphere created?*** ◂◂◂

This brings to a close our presentation of the traditional elements comprising literary analysis. As you work through the book, you will note that not only do these elements serve in the analysis of short stories but many of them are also useful for interpreting essays, plays, and poems. Although analysing a work may seem an arduous task at times, you will not be wasting your time. In fact, you will be developing a new awareness of the English language and the many ways it can be used. Your own composition skills will most certainly benefit. Moreover, your new analytical skills and heightened sensitivity will make you a better reader and no doubt increase your appreciation of the excellent texts you will read in the future, be they newspaper articles or novels.

In conclusion, we leave you with these thoughts penned by two famous writers, one a seventeenth-century playwright and the other a famous nineteenth-century humorist, essayist, and novelist.

**"For a man to write well, there are required three necessaries: to read the best authors, observe the best speakers, and much exercise of his own style."**

— Playwright Ben Johnson in *Discoveries*.

**"The difference between the almost right word and the right word is really a large matter — 'tis the difference between the lightning bug and the lightning."**

— Humorist Mark Twain in *The Art of Authorship*.

# UNIT 1

# SHORT STORIES

UNIT 1

# SHORT STORIES

**THE SHORT STORY SECTION COMPRISES AN INTRODUCTION AND EIGHT CHAPTERS CONTAINING TEN VERY DIFFERENT SHORT STORIES. TO ILLUSTRATE THE EVOLUTION OF THE GENRE OVER THE LAST CENTURY AND A HALF, THE STORIES APPEAR, FOR THE MOST PART, IN CHRONOLOGICAL ORDER. THIS SECTION PRESENTS THE BASIC VOCABULARY AND TECHNIQUES NEEDED TO ANALYSE FICTION BOTH IN WRITING AND ORALLY.**

HISTORY OF THE SHORT STORY. The short story developed as a genre in English very gradually over the centuries. It was inspired and influenced by narratives that emanated from other parts of the world. Scholars suggest that the story had its origins in Middle Eastern narratives. With the dawn of spoken language, early peoples most surely began to tell tales of things that had happened. As early as 2000 B.C., the ancient Babylonians recorded one of the oldest narratives in the world, the *Epic of Gilgamesh*. At roughly the same time, Egyptians were writing down tales in prose on papyrus.

The earliest recorded tales from India date from around 700 B.C. About a century later, Aesop wrote his famous fables in Greece. Starting in the eighth or ninth century B.C., the Hebrews recorded the narratives that now make up part of the Old Testament in the Bible, stories such as those of Adam and Eve, Cain and Abel, David and Goliath, and many more. Later, the New Testament, which contains the numerous parables that Jesus was said to have told his followers, completed the Bible as we know it. The Bible had a huge influence on English and European culture and was the first book to have been printed by Johann Gutenberg using movable type in 1455. Before this revolutionary invention, books had been copied painstakingly by hand, and not many people had access to them. With the invention of movable type, books could be printed and put into circulation much more rapidly and widely. As a result, more and more people learned to read.

*"When a book, any sort of book, reaches a certain intensity of artistic performance it becomes literature. That intensity may be a matter of style, situation, character, emotional tone, or idea, or half a dozen other things. It may also be a perfection of control over the movement of a story similar to the control a great pitcher has over the ball."*

— Raymond Chandler (1888-1959), U.S. author. Letter, 29 Jan. 1946, to crime writer Erle Stanley Gardner.

Most of the ancient stories had a didactic purpose; they were aimed at teaching people important values. They taught people how to live a "good" life (and what would happen if you didn't!) and how to distinguish right from wrong. In his fables, for example, Aesop ascribed human characteristics to animals and then placed the animals in a conflict of some sort designed to teach a moral lesson. It was hoped that people would learn from these stories. In this tradition, tales about the lives of saints (called *exempla)* became very popular in the eleventh and twelfth centuries. An exemplum was meant to show and inspire model behaviour.

In late-fourteenth-century England, influenced by ribald, comic short narratives called fabliaux, Geoffrey Chaucer (c.1343-1400) composed his famous *Canterbury Tales*. Although the tales are primarily written in verse, they are considered to be stories nonetheless. Sir Thomas Malory (c.1400-1471) was another early writer of stories, called romances. His *Le Morte d'Arthur* represents the first complete account of the legends of King Arthur and the knights of the Round Table. At roughly the same time, short fiction was taking similar form in other parts of Europe, and it was at this time that the stories of Scheherazade and *The Arabian Nights* became famous.

> ***"The object of art is to give life shape."***
>
> —Jean Anouilh (1910-1987), French playwright. *The Rehearsal*

During the Elizabethan period from approximately 1550 to 1625, the English were generally far more interested in drama than in short stories. The existing short stories were often copies or translations of flowery Italian novellas and were considered too superficial for popular taste. During the reign of Elizabeth I, Shakespeare came to the height of his powers as a brilliant dramatist who provided audiences with one compelling tragedy after another.

Short fiction in the form of stories became a very popular genre in the second half of the eighteenth century because of growing interest in the oriental tale and the Gothic novel. The Gothic novel had characteristics of the dark, eerie, and the supernatural, and was the precursor to the modern horror tale. For example, Mary Shelley's *Frankenstein* has Gothic elements. Between 1780 and 1840, the modern short story emerged at almost the same time in France, Russia, Germany, and the United States. Tales of ghosts, horror, and the supernatural, written in German by E.T.A. Hoffman (1776-822) and Heinrich von Kleist (1777-1811) influenced the development of the genre in English.

In the United States, authors as such Washington Irving (1783-1859), Nathaniel Hawthorne (1804-1864), and Edgar Allan Poe (1809-1849) gave new forms to the short story and greatly accelerated its development by providing models for future writers. In fact, two basic types of short story developed at this time: one more realistic, focusing on the objective reality of events; and the other more impressionist, portraying the impressions left in a person's mind by reality (these impressions were often distortions of reality). Poe is considered by many to be the father of the modern short story in English. Not only did he define the most central characteristic of the genre, the "unity of effect," which implies that all the distinct elements of the short story such as plot, setting, and characterisation must create a united picture, but each of his stories is also structured so that an atmosphere of unity is conveyed to the reader.

The short story as a literary genre in English-speaking countries continued to appeal to both writers and readers during the latter half of the nineteenth and all of the twentieth century. Hundreds of excellent stories were written during these years. In the chapters presenting individual short stories, we will examine how each fits into the literary trends of its time.

UNIT 1.1

# THE TELL-TALE HEART

## CHAPTER CONTENTS

- **READING:** "The Tell-Tale Heart" by Edgar Allan Poe; author's biography; literary trends (Gothic novel, Romanticism)
- **WRITING:** dissecting and constructing sentences (clauses, sentence types, fragments, run-on sentences, comma splices); paragraphs
- **LITERARY ELEMENTS:** first-person narration and point of view; imagery, metaphor, simile; use of repetition and contrast; irony
- **GRAMMAR AND VOCABULARY:** vocabulary development: Latin and Germanic roots, prefixes and suffixes

## ABOUT THE AUTHOR

EDGAR ALLAN POE (1809-1849) is considered to be one of the founders of the modern psychological thriller and short story. He developed theories about the new genre, and was the author of many horror stories. The result of his work insured the popularity of narrative fiction and the short story in the nineteenth century, a popularity that has continued to the present day.

Poe was born and raised in Virginia. He established his writing career first as a poet and then started to write fiction, publishing his first set of short stories in 1832. By 1835, Poe had been appointed editor of *The Southern Literary Messenger*, a magazine, to which he contributed his own fiction as well as literary criticism. Poe's works show an overall predilection to the grotesque and macabre. His most famous works, "The Raven" (1845), "The Fall of the House of Usher" (1839), "The Pit and the Pendulum" (1842), and "The Tell-Tale Heart" (1843), make use of black elements such as murder, death, melancholy, madness, and torture. Controversy surrounds the circumstances of his death in 1849 in Baltimore.

## LITERARY TRENDS OF THE TIMES

When studying literature, students are often confounded about its meaning and utility. It is useful, therefore, to study literature within a context that takes into account its origins, theory, or criticism. With this type of approach to literature, we will try to establish a historical context to the fictional works we will be studying.

"The Tell-Tale Heart" was published in 1843 in the magazine *The Pioneer*. Many adjectives come to mind when one analyses this story. For example, *weird*, *grotesque*, *bizarre*, and *gross* are just some of the descriptions that can apply to this tale. All of these impressions are valid, and when put into a historical perspective, they become very understandable. Poe was writing narrative fiction in the first half of the nineteenth century. This period of time was referred to in European literature as the Romantic era. Romanticism was, first, a reaction against the earlier period in literature called Classicism, an age that viewed humanity as rational and enlightened creatures. Second, Romanticism had its origins in the English Gothic novel, a popular genre from about the 1760s to the 1820s. Stories in this type of novel were about mystery, terror, or the supernatural. Dark, horrific events, which drew upon the irrational nature of humanity, predominated. Mary Shelley's *Frankenstein* (1817) is an excellent example of a Gothic novel.

During the Romantic era, the theme of madness was quite often used to show the opposite of rationality. Furthermore, characters who were not part of mainstream society, such as robbers and hermits, dominated the literature of the time. Romantic literature was also saturated with subjects such as mysticism, good versus evil, the spirit world, hallucinations, the dream world, and the dark side of nature.

Today in contemporary horror novels, short stories, and films, we are still influenced by the tradition of Gothic novels and the elements of Romanticism. Modern writing is still fascinated by the supernatural and the dark side of nature. Stephen King is the most famous current writer whose works, such as *The Shining*, contain elements from this earlier period. Moreover, many young people worldwide refer to themselves as Goths. This movement started out as a punk subculture in the 1970s and is still popular today; its adherents wear black clothes and pale make-up, and have strange hairstyles and hair colours. Goth culture is represented in such films as *The Crow*, *Nosferatu*, and the *Cabinet of Doctor Caligari*, as well as in music played by bands such as Bauhaus, Siouxsie and the Banshees, the Sisters of Mercy, and Dead Can Dance.

## Warm-Up Discussion Topics

▸1 What are some stories, novels, or films you have read or seen that use Gothic and Romantic elements like the supernatural?

▸2 Did you find these literary works or films scary? Why or why not?

▸3 What makes scary stories or films so popular?

▸4 Have you ever read any works by Edgar Allan Poe? If so, which ones? Did you enjoy them?

**INITIAL READING ▸ Read the story for the first time for personal enjoyment. Don't look up each unfamiliar word in the dictionary. If you were to do that, you would break up the reading process and be distracted from the story. Instead, try to guess the word from clues contained in the paragraph in which the word is found. That is, look for meaning of unfamiliar words within context.**

STORY

1843

# The Tell-Tale Heart

Edgar Allan Poe

MAD→CRAZY

TRUE! — nervous — very, very dreadfully nervous I had been and am; but why will you say that I am ***mad***? The disease had sharpened my senses — not destroyed — not dulled them. Above all was the sense of hearing acute. I heard all things in the heaven and in the earth. I heard many things in hell. How, then, am I mad? Hearken! and observe how healthily — how calmly I can tell you the whole story.

It is impossible to say how first the idea entered my brain; but once conceived, it haunted me day and night. Object there was none. Passion there was none. I loved the old man. He had never wronged me. He had never given me insult. For his gold I had no desire. I think it was his eye! yes, it was this! He had the eye of a vulture — a pale blue eye, with a film over it. Whenever it fell upon me, my blood ran cold; and so by degrees — very gradually — I made up my mind to take the life of the old man, and thus rid myself of the eye forever.

Now this is the point. You fancy me mad. Madmen know nothing. But you should have seen *me*. You should have seen how wisely I proceeded — with what caution — with what foresight — with what dissimulation I went to work! I was never kinder to the old man than during the whole week before I killed him. And every night, about midnight, I turned the latch of his door and opened it — oh so gently! And then, when I had made an opening sufficient for my head, I put in a dark lantern, all closed, closed, that no light shone out, and then I thrust in my head. Oh, you would have laughed to see how cunningly I thrust it in! I moved it slowly — very, very slowly, so that I might not disturb the old man's sleep. It took me an hour to place my whole head within the opening so far that I could see him as he lay upon his bed. Ha! — would a madman have been so wise as this? And then, when my head was well in the room, I undid the lantern cautiously — oh, so cautiously — cautiously (for the hinges creaked) — I undid it just so much that a single thin ray fell upon the vulture eye. And this I did for seven long nights — every night just at midnight

— but I found the eye always closed; and so it was impossible to do the work; for it was not the old man who vexed me, but his Evil Eye. And every morning, when the day broke, I went boldly into the chamber, and spoke courageously to him, calling him by name in a hearty tone, and inquiring how he had passed the night. So you see he would have been a very profound old man, indeed, to suspect that every night, just at twelve, I looked in upon him while he slept.

Upon the eighth night I was more than usually cautious in opening the door. A watch's minute hand moves more quickly than did mine. Never before that night had I *felt* the extent of my own powers — of my sagacity. I could scarcely contain my feelings of triumph. To think that there I was, opening the door, little by little, and he not even to dream of my secret deeds or thoughts. I fairly chuckled at the idea; and perhaps he heard me; for he moved on the bed suddenly, as if startled. Now you may think that I drew back — but no. His room was as black as pitch with the thick darkness (for the shutters were close fastened, through fear of robbers), and so I knew that he could not see the opening of the door, and I kept pushing it on steadily, steadily.

I had my head in, and was about to open the lantern, when my thumb slipped upon the tin fastening, and the old man sprang up in bed, crying out — "Who's there?"

I kept quite still and said nothing. For a whole hour I did not move a muscle, and in the meantime I did not hear him lie down. He was still sitting up in the bed listening — just as I have done, night after night, hearkening to the death watches in the wall.

Presently I heard a slight groan, and I knew it was the groan of mortal terror. It was not a groan of pain or of grief — oh, no! — it was the low stifled sound that arises from the bottom of the soul when overcharged with awe. I knew the sound well. Many a night, just at midnight, when all the world slept, it has welled up from my own bosom, deepening, with its dreadful echo, the terrors that distracted me. I say I knew it well. I knew what the old man felt, and pitied him, although I chuckled at heart. I knew that he had been lying awake ever since the first slight noise, when he had turned in the bed. His fears had been ever since growing upon him. He had been trying to fancy them causeless, but could not. He had been saying to himself — "It is nothing but the wind in the chimney — it is only a mouse crossing the floor," or "It is merely a cricket which has made a single chirp." Yes, he had been trying to comfort himself with these suppositions: but he had found all in vain. *All in vain*; because Death, in approaching him had stalked with his black shadow before him, and enveloped the victim. And it was the mournful influence of the unperceived shadow that caused him to feel — although he neither saw nor heard — to *feel* the presence of my head within the room.

When I had waited a long time, very patiently, without hearing him lie down, I resolved to open a little — a very, very little crevice in the lantern. So I opened it — you cannot imagine how stealthily, stealthily — until, at length a simple dim ray, like the thread of the spider, shot from out the crevice and fell full upon the vulture eye.

It was open — wide, wide open — and I grew furious as I gazed upon it. I saw it with perfect distinctness — all a dull blue, with a hideous veil over it that chilled the very marrow in my bones; but I could see nothing else of the old man's face or person: for I had directed the ray as if by instinct, precisely upon the damned spot.

And have I not told you that what you mistake for madness is but over-acuteness of the senses? — now, I say, there came to my ears a low, dull, quick sound, such as a watch makes when enveloped in cotton. I knew *that* sound well, too. It was the beating of the old man's heart. It increased my fury, as the beating of a drum stimulates the soldier into courage.

But even yet I refrained and kept still. I scarcely breathed. I held the lantern motionless. I tried how steadily I could maintain the ray upon the eye. Meantime the hellish tattoo of the heart increased. It grew quicker and quicker, and louder and louder every instant. The old man's terror must have been extreme! It grew louder, I say, louder every moment! — do you mark me well? I have told you that I am nervous: so I am. And now at the dead hour of the night, amid the dreadful silence of that old house, so strange a noise as this excited me to uncontrollable terror. Yet, for some minutes longer I refrained and stood still. But the beating grew louder, louder! I thought the heart must burst. And now a new anxiety seized me — the sound would be heard by a neighbour! The old man's hour had come! With a loud yell, I threw open the lantern and leaped into the room. He shrieked once — once only. In an instant I dragged him to the floor, and pulled the heavy bed over him. I then smiled gaily, to find the deed so far done. But, for many minutes, the heart beat on with a muffled sound. This, however, did not vex me; it would not be heard through the wall. At length it ceased. The old man was dead. I removed the bed and examined the corpse. Yes, he was stone, stone dead. I placed my hand upon the heart and held it there many minutes. There was no pulsation. He was stone dead. His eye would trouble me no more.

If still you think me mad, you will think so no longer when I describe the wise precautions I took for the concealment of the body. The night waned, and I worked hastily, but in silence. First of all I dismembered the corpse. I cut off the head and the arms and the legs.

I then took up three planks from the flooring of the chamber, and deposited all between the scantlings. I then replaced the boards so cleverly, so cunningly, that no human eye — not even *his* — could have detected anything wrong. There was nothing to wash out — no stain of any kind — no blood-spot whatever. I had been too wary for that. A tub had caught all — ha! ha!

When I had made an end of these labors, it was four o'clock — still dark as midnight. As the bell sounded the hour, there came a knocking at the street door. I went down to open it with a light heart — for what had I *now* to fear? There entered three men, who introduced themselves, with perfect suavity, as officers of the police. A shriek had been heard by a neighbor during the night; suspicion of foul play had been aroused; information had been lodged at the police office, and they (the officers) had been deputed to search the premises.

I smiled, — for *what* had I to fear? I bade the gentlemen welcome. The shriek, I said, was my own in a dream. The old man, I mentioned, was absent in the country. I took my visitors all over the house. I bade them search — search *well*. I led them, at length, to *his* chamber. I showed them his treasures, secure, undisturbed. In the enthusiasm of my confidence, I brought chairs into the room, and desired them *here* to rest from their fatigues, while I myself, in the wild audacity of my perfect triumph, placed my own seat upon the very spot beneath which reposed the corpse of the victim.

The officers were satisfied. My *manner* had convinced them. I was singularly at ease. They sat, and while I answered cheerily, they chatted of familiar things. But, ere long, I felt myself getting pale and wished them gone. My head ached, and I fancied a ringing in my ears: but still they sat and still chatted. The ringing became more distinct: — It continued and became more distinct: I talked more freely to get rid of the feeling: but it continued and gained definiteness — until, at length, I found that the noise was *not* within my ears.

No doubt I now grew *very* pale; — but I talked more fluently, and with a heightened voice. Yet the sound increased — and what could I do? It was *a low, dull, quick sound — much such a sound as a watch makes when enveloped in cotton*. I gasped for breath — and yet the officers heard it not. I talked more quickly — more vehemently; but the noise steadily increased. I arose and argued about trifles, in a high key and with violent gesticulations; but the noise steadily increased. Why *would* they not be gone? I paced the floor to and fro with heavy strides, as if excited to fury by the observation of the men — but the noise steadily increased. Oh God! what *could* I do? I foamed — I raved — I swore! I swung the chair upon which I had been sitting, and grated it upon the boards, but the noise arose over all and continually increased. It grew louder — louder — *louder!* And still the men chatted pleasantly, and smiled. Was it possible they heard not? Almighty God! — no, no! They heard! — they suspected! — they *knew!* — they were making a mockery of my horror! — this I thought, and this I think. But anything was better than this agony! Anything was more tolerable than this derision! I could bear those hypocritical smiles no longer! I felt that I must scream or die! and now — again! — hark! louder! louder! louder! *louder!* —

"Villains!" I shrieked, "dissemble no more! I admit the deed! — tear up the planks! here, here! — It is the beating of his hideous heart!"

## READER'S RESPONSE

▸1 What were your first impressions of the story?

▸2 What did you like best about this story?

▸3 Was there anything you didn't like about the story? If so, what?

▸4 What kinds of feelings or emotions did this story evoke in you?

**CLOSE READING▸ Reread the story, paying particular attention to what the narrator feels and senses, to the colourful vocabulary, and to the pictures the story creates. Then answer the following questions, which are designed to help you explore the text and its various aspects in depth.**

▸1 Who is telling the story? What are his or her most prominent personality traits?

▸2 What is the narrator trying to prove to the reader throughout the story?

▸3 What is the relationship between the narrator and the old man? (Circle your answer.)

They are **a)** relatives **b)** friends **c)** enemies **d)** neighbours

▸4 What does the narrator want to do? Why?

▸5 How does the narrator react as he commits the crime?

He **a)** weeps **b)** smiles **c)** shrieks **d)** feels sorry for his actions

▸6 Why do the policemen come to his house?

▸7 Describe the narrator's initial reaction to the policemen's investigation.

▸8 Does his reaction to the policemen change? If so, how?

▶9 What is his emotional state at the end of the story?

▶10 How does he try to cover up the crime?

▶11 Which of the following adjectives could be used to describe the mood and atmosphere of this story?

**a)** serene **b)** terrifying **c)** nervous **d)** sensitive **e)** naïve

▶12 Explain the significance of the title of the story.

**WRITER'S CRAFT ▶ As preparation for the following questions, read the explanation on narration and point of view found in the literary elements section at the beginning of the book.**

***▶▶▶ One of the characteristic features of Poe's works is the atmosphere of fear and terror. His stories horrify and fascinate the reader at the same time. To achieve this overall effect, Poe uses literary devices such as repetition, sense imagery, metaphor, and personification. ◀◀◀***

### *First-Person Narration and Point of View*

▶1 What point of view is used to tell the story?

▶2 Does the narrator seem close to or distant from the reader? Justify your answer with proof from the story.

▶3 How does the narrator engage (involve) the reader right at the very beginning of the story?

▶4 Look carefully at the first sentence. Which points in time (past, present, and/or future) are mentioned? *(Hint: look at the verbs)*

▶5 (Circle one choice in each of the parentheses.) The narrator is telling the reader a story in the (past, present, future) that took place in the (past, present, future) and is concerned about the reader's (past, present, future) judgement.

***▶▶▶ By using a first-person narrator who speaks in the present tense, Poe triggers the reader's interest from the start and creates an immediacy to the story. ◀◀◀***

## Choice of Words

### Use of Repetition

Poe uses repetition to build up the tension. Even within sentences, he repeats adjectives, adverbs, and concrete images. For example, observe the following sentences:

"I moved it slowly — very, very slowly."
"I undid the lantern cautiously — oh, so cautiously — cautiously (for the hinges creaked) — "
"...quicker and quicker, louder and louder."
"He had the eye of a vulture — a pale blue eye, with a film over it."

▸1 Find other examples of repetition in Poe's use of adjectives, adverbs, and concrete images.

___

___

___

___

___

### Use of Imagery

▸▸▸ ***Imagery** is a literary device that allows the writer to make use of one or more of the five senses as a dominant element in descriptive writing.* ◂◂◂

▸1 Poe uses sound as a dominant element throughout this story. He creates striking contrasts between sounds that are quiet and sounds that are loud. For example:

| Quiet sounds | versus | Loud sounds |
|---|---|---|
| slight groan | | shriek |
| low-stifled sound | | ringing in my ears |
| stealthily | | heightened voice |

Find and list at least three other expressions that indicate quiet sounds and three that indicate loud sounds.

Quiet sounds:

___

___

Loud sounds:

___

___

▸2 How does the transition between quiet sound to loud sound echo the narrator's sense of guilt?

___

▸3 How does this transition from quiet to loud sound add to the atmosphere of the story?

___

### *Use of Literary Devices*

*Metaphor and Simile*

▸▸▸ ***A metaphor** is a direct comparison of two things; for example,* **the heart is a drum.** ***A simile** is a slightly less direct comparison of two things; it uses the words* **like**, *or* **as**; *for example,* **the heart is like a drum.** ◂◂◂

Find images from the text that describe the following actions. Write the exact words used and then identify them either as metaphors *(M)* or similes *(S)*. For **a)**, **b)**, and **c)**, write a phrase from the text. For **d)**, **e)**, and **f)**, fill in the missing word(s) from the text.

▸**1** **a)** The beating of the old man's heart at the beginning of the story.

______________________________

**b)** The beating of the old man's heart towards the end of the story before the sound becomes loud.

______________________________

**c)** The movement of the protagonist's hand as he opens the door the eighth night.

______________________________

**d)** "… ray fell upon the ____________ eye."

**e)** as black ____________

**f)** ____________ dead (Hint: same image appears twice)

▸▸▸ ***Vivid descriptions of what the protagonist hears, sees, and imagines (through imagery) and how he moves (through the choice of adverbs) help create mood and atmosphere.*** ◂◂◂

▸**2** Poe uses metaphors to describe an eye. It is described as "…the vulture eye…" and "the Evil Eye," meaning that it had supernatural powers and that it caused the narrator to feel a great amount of fear.

In paragraph 7 (line 42), Poe also uses a metaphor to describe death.

Find this metaphor and explain its meaning.

______________________________

______________________________

______________________________

______________________________

▸▸▸ ***Much of Poe's imagery serves to create an overall mood of fear and tension in this story. As well, he effectively creates other imagery to evoke various feelings in the reader, thus adding to the atmosphere of tension. The methods he uses include contrast of opposites and irony.*** ◂◂◂

*Contrast of Opposites*

▸1 In the first paragraph of the text, find opposites to the following expressions (some of the words are not perfect matches).

**a)** dreadfully nervous — how ____________

**b)** heard all things in heaven… — heard many things ____________

**c)** sharpened my senses — not ____________ them

**d)** The disease — how ____________

▸2 In paragraph 11 (line 68), the dreadful silence of the house is contrasted with "so strange a ____________."

▸3 Describe the contrast, at the end of the story, between the perceptions and feelings of the police officers and those of the narrator.

____________

____________

____________

____________

▸▸▸ ***By juxtaposing (placing side by side or near to each other) opposites throughout the story, Poe creates a great deal of tension in the piece.*** ◂◂◂

*Irony*

▸▸▸ **Irony** ***refers to the device of writing or saying one thing, but meaning the opposite.*** ◂◂◂

Why is the end of the story ironic?

____________

____________

____________

____________

## *Vocabulary Development: Latin and Germanic Roots, Prefixes and Suffixes*

Early in its history, the territory now known as Great Britain was invaded and occupied by several successive invaders: first, Latin-speaking Romans in the early centuries A.D., then, German-speaking tribes (Angles, Saxons, and Jutes) in the fifth and sixth centuries A.D., and finally the French-speaking Normans in 1066. Thus, the English language as we know it is a mix of words from several sources. In fact, about half the words in English come from Germanic languages and half from Latin or French. It is often very useful (and also interesting!) to see how words are put together in English. This type of exercise can definitely help to build a better vocabulary.

Linguists call the basic part of a word that carries the essential meaning the **root** (from Germanic *rot*) or **radical** (from Latin *radix*, *radic-*). We often add a **prefix** (from Latin *prae*, meaning in front of, and *fixus*, meaning fastened) before the root or a **suffix** (from Latin *sub*, meaning under) after it. Most prefixes and suffixes add particular meanings to the roots of words. Here is an example using the root *count*:

| Root | Prefix | Suffix | Both Prefix and Suffix |
|---|---|---|---|
| count | *dis*count | count*able* | *dis*count*able* |
| | *ac*count | | *ac*count*able*, *unac*count*able* |
| | *re*count | count*er* | *ac*count*ant* |
| | | count*down* | |

Using your dictionary, give the meaning of each of the following prefixes and suffixes and identify its origin as Latin or Germanic (consider Old English — that is, words that were spoken in England before 1066 — as Germanic). You will note that a good dictionary will place a hyphen after a prefix and before a suffix. This allows you to distinguish them from other words.

Then find a word from "The Tell-Tale Heart" that uses the particular prefix or suffix and identify its root. One has been done as an example. *(Please note that without a prefix or a suffix, the root may not appear to be an English word. For example, in the word "detect," "de" is the prefix and "tect" the root; "tect" does not exist on its own.)*

| Prefix | Meaning | Origin | Word from Text | Root |
|---|---|---|---|---|
| e.g.: *over-* | *too much* | *Germanic* | *over-acuteness* | *acute(ness)* |
| **a)** dis- | | | | |
| **b)** im- (in-) | | | | |
| **c)** fore- | | | | |
| **d)** de- | | | | |
| **e)** mid- | | | | |
| **f)** un- | | | | |
| **g)** con- | | | | |
| **h)** pre- | | | | |
| **i)** intro- | | | | |
| **j)** ex- | | | | |
| **Suffix** | | | | |
| **a)** –less | | | | |
| **b)** –able, -ible | | | | |

UNIT 1.1 THE TELL-TALE HEART

# DISSECTING AND CONSTRUCTING SENTENCES

**Not only is it important for people to write correct sentences when they communicate with others in a formal or official capacity — for example, in academic or workplace situations — but it is also often necessary to write with a certain amount of style. To do this, you must be able to recognise the difference between what constitutes a correct sentence and what is unacceptable. You must also work at developing style in your writing through the use of various types of sentences.**

**It is important to read the explanations that follow and to complete the accompanying exercises with care.**

## USEFUL DEFINITIONS

A **sentence** is a group of words containing a subject and a verb and expressing a complete thought.

*EXAMPLE: My brother lives in New Zealand.*

Sentences can be affirmative, negative, interrogative, imperative, or exclamatory. They also must be punctuated correctly (capitalisation and punctuation will be reviewed in a later chapter).

The following are examples of different kinds of sentences.

The sky is blue. (affirmative)
The sky is not blue. (negative)
Is the sky blue ? (interrogative)
Look at the sky. (imperative)
Look ! The sky is so blue ! (exclamatory)

Like a sentence, a **clause** is a group of words containing a subject and a verb. However, a clause does not necessarily express a complete thought. Clauses are said to be independent (or principal or main) if they express a complete thought.

*EXAMPLE: My brother lives in New Zealand. (subject = brother; verb = lives)*

Clauses are **dependent** (or **subordinate**) if they do not express a complete thought.

*EXAMPLE: which I am wearing. (subject = I; verb = am wearing)*

**N.B.** An independent clause is the same as a simple sentence. However, sentences often contain more than one clause. (Sentences are classified according to how many independent and dependent clauses they contain (see explanation below).

#### Exercise A: Identifying Different Types of Clauses

Underline the independent clauses and place parentheses around the dependent clauses.

*EXAMPLE: The man (who was driving the red car) is my father.*

▸1 Jennifer especially likes books that are written by feminist authors.

▸2 My friend Raffi, whom you met at the party last week, is leaving for Paris tomorrow.

▸3 In the early morning light, Hoa noticed flocks of parrots in the trees.

▸4 Nancy decided that she would apply for the job.

▸5 Do you know who is going to see the film with us?

### *Types of Sentences*

There are four types of sentences:

1. A **simple** sentence contains just one independent clause (i.e. one principal verb, one complete idea).

   *EXAMPLE: The children play in the park every day.*

2. A **compound** sentence comprises two independent clauses joined by a coordinate conjunction: *and, but, for, or, nor, so,* or *yet* (i.e., two principal verbs and two complete and connected ideas).

   *EXAMPLE: The children play in the park every day, and their parents go to work.*

3. A **complex** sentence comprises one independent clause and at least one dependent clause (i.e., one principal verb and complete idea, and one or more subordinate verbs and incomplete ideas).

   *EXAMPLE: The children, who are eight years old, play in the park every day.*

   (independent clause = The children play in the park every day; dependent clause = who are eight years old)

4. A **compound-complex** sentence comprises at least two independent clauses and at least one dependent clause (i.e., two principal verbs and two complete ideas; and one, or more, subordinate verbs and incomplete ideas).

   *EXAMPLE: The children, who are eight years old, play in the park every day, but their parents go to work.*

**Exercise B: Identifying Different Types of Sentences**

Identify each of the following sentences: **S** for Simple, **C** for Compound, **CX** for Complex, and **CC** for Compound-Complex.

▸1 ________ Paula, who has been studying medicine for the last three years, will work at the new clinic next summer.

▸2 ________ Next week, Ron is leaving for Haiti.

▸3 ________ Jonathan promised me that he would look after the hotel reservations and I told him that I would buy the plane tickets.

▸4 ________ Do you know which novel we will read for the course?

▸5 ________ Marilyn wants to get married next year, but Fred would like to finish his studies first.

### *Common Mistakes*

Here are three common mistakes that inexperienced writers often make: They use sentence fragments, run-on sentences, and comma splices.

A **sentence fragment** is only part of a sentence (an incomplete idea) but it has been given the punctuation of a sentence. A sentence fragment has either no main subject or no main verb and is an incomplete idea. Most sentence fragments are unacceptable in formal writing unless they are part of the dialogue.

EXAMPLE: *Because the car was fast. (This is an incomplete idea because we don't know what happened "before")*

Complete sentence: *The teenager wanted to buy the car because it was fast.*

A **run-on sentence** consists of two or more independent clauses having no punctuation or too many conjunctions between them. The two run-on sentences that follow are unacceptable.

EXAMPLE: *The students studied for their exam they all passed.*

OR

*The students studied for their exam and they all passed and two weeks later they all went out for a drink to celebrate.*

A **comma splice** results from punctuating with a comma when a period is needed between two independent clauses.

EXAMPLE: *The students studied for their exam, they all passed.*

There are four ways to correct run-on sentences and comma splices.

**1** Write separate sentences using proper terminal punctuation.

EXAMPLE: *The students studied for their exam. They all passed.*
*The students studied for their exam and they all passed.*

**2** Place a semicolon between two independent clauses that are closely connected.

EXAMPLE: *The students studied for their exam; they all passed.*

**3** Place a coordinate conjunction, preceded by a comma, between the two independent clauses.

EXAMPLE: *The students studied for their exam, and they all passed.*

**4** Make one of the independent clauses dependent.

EXAMPLE: *The students, who studied for their exam, all passed.*

**Exercise C: Correcting Sentence Errors**

Look at the following sentences. In the blanks provided, write **C** for sentences that are correct, **R** for run-on sentences or comma splices, and **F** for fragments (incomplete sentences). Then correct the errors. You may have to change the word order or add some words.

▸**1** ________ Because I had to give my little brother a present.

▸**2** ________ He travelled to Tibet, he had to get special permission from the government for his trip.

▸**3** ________ My mother comes from Brazil, people speak Portuguese there.

▸**4** ________ Can you tell me what homework we have to do for tonight I didn't hear what the teacher said.

▸**5** ________ That she was praised for her singing abilities which made her very happy.

▸**6** ________ Can you tell me where Lacombe Street is?

▸**7** ________ Who knows?

▸**8** ________ The restaurant which is Italian and very expensive and the service is slow and inefficient.

▸**9** ________ Eat.

▸**10** ________ I am very happy that we could get the hockey tickets for tonight.

#### Exercise D: Correcting Common Sentence Mistakes

Make any corrections necessary in the following paragraph in order to form complete sentences.

Scary and spooky novels have become very popular in the current culture, we know this by the sales and box office successes of books and films whose subject matter is meant to scare the reader or audience why are we so fascinated by scary subject matter, it is meant to create terror in our minds. I think that horror and terror raise our emotions to an adrenaline-driven peak. Which we find both stimulating and necessary, we like the rush that we get after a good scare: it is for this reason that people try extreme sports or choose risky professions, they like the effects of the adrenaline on their bodies, I personally avoid watching anything which scares me or causes me highly anxious moments, Scary movies keep me awake all night I am very tired the next day, I guess I will never be the one who goes diving with sharks or piranha watching in the Amazon or climbing Mount Everest, I just like to sit in my armchair reading about such adventures.

### *Paragraph Practice*

- ▸1 Write a paragraph describing your feelings when something scares you. Make sure you use several adjectives and a variety of sentence types: simple, compound, and complex.
- ▸2 Write a paragraph (about eight sentences long) that has a dominant mood. Do not state what the mood is; simply create it by using imagery and a variety of sentence types. Read your paragraph to a classmate and have him or her guess the mood you have created.

## WRAP-UP DISCUSSION OR WRITING ACTIVITIES

- ▸1 Discuss whether or not the protagonist of "The Tell-Tale Heart" is insane. Are his arguments and justifications plausible?
- ▸2 Choose one example of imagery from the story and explain why you find it effective.
- ▸3 Role-play in groups of three: Imagine that you are in a court of law at the end of the narrator's trial for first-degree murder. Two of you are lawyers and the third, the judge. The lawyer defending the narrator gives his or her final arguments; the lawyer for the prosecution then presents his or her conclusions; and the judge, after asking any questions he or she may have, makes a decision and pronounces a sentence followed by his or her reasons.

# References

## PRINT

### BIOGRAPHY

Quinn, Arthur Hobson. *Edgar Allan Poe: A Critical Biography*. New York: D. Appleton-Century, 1941, 1997.

Symons, Julian. *The Tell-Tale Heart: Life and Works of Edgar Allan Poe*. New York: Harper & Row, 1978.

Wagenknecht, Edward. *Edgar Allan Poe: The Man Behind the Legend*. New York: Oxford University Press, 1963.

### CRITICISM

Bloom, Harold, ed. *Edgar Allan Poe: Modern Critical Views*. New Haven, CT: Chelsea House Publishers, 1985

Carlson, Eric, ed., *Critical Essays on Edgar Allan Poe*. Boston: G. K. Hall, 1987.

Kesterson, David B., ed. *Critics on Poe*. Coral Gables, FL: University of Florida Press, 1973.

## INTERNET

Here are some very interesting Internet references that you may wish to check out relating to this chapter. Please note that as sites change location from time to time, some of the links may not work. We also suggest that you use a search engine to find other sites of interest on the Internet.

**LINKS:**

http://newark.rutgers.edu/~ehrlich/poesites.html
http://bau2.uibk.ac.at/sg/poe/Sites.html

**BIOGRAPHY AND SELECTED WORKS:**

http://www.pambytes.com/poe/poe.html
http://www.cais.com/webweave/poe/poe.htm

**RECORDED VERSION OF "THE TELL-TALE HEART":**

http://www.drcasey.com/radio/poe/telltale/
http://poedecoder.com/essays/ttheart/#summary

**VIRTUAL LIBRARY OF POE (interesting audio files):**

http://www.comnet.ca/~forrest/library.html

**THE EDGAR ALLAN POE MUSEUM:**

(virtual visit): http://www.poemuseum.org/

**MORE ON HORROR AND RADIO:**

http://www.drcasey.com/radio/spotlight/index.shtml

**MORE ON GOTH CULTURE:**

http://www.religioustolerance.org/goth.htm
"Rob's Gothic Pages" at: http://www.crg.cs.nott.ac.uk/~rji/Gothic/index.html
"Blackbride's Suit of Dreams" at: http://www.acc.umu.se/~yisca/yisca.htm
Directory of Goth sites at: http://www.snap.com/directory/category/0,16,-44904,00.html

UNIT 1.2

# THE STORY OF AN HOUR

**CHAPTER CONTENTS**

- **READING:** "The Story of an Hour" by Kate Chopin; the author's biography; literary trends (Romanticism, Realism)
- **WRITING:** sentences; paragraphs
- **LITERARY ELEMENTS:** narration and point of view; setting; theme; characterisation; irony; foreshadowing; imagery; use of repetition and contrast
- **GRAMMAR AND VOCABULARY:** choice of words; coordination and subordination; combining sentences; use of transitionals

## ABOUT THE AUTHOR

KATE CHOPIN (1850-1904) was born in St. Louis, Missouri, to a wealthy Irish family. Society in the southern United States at this time was oriented around male authority. Women were expected to take subordinate roles and would never question or express concern about the quality of their lives or the way things were. The possibility of a couple's divorcing was almost unthinkable.

After she graduated in 1868 from the St. Louis Academy of the Sacred Heart, a school run by Catholic nuns, Chopin was regarded as one of the belles of the city. For the next two years as she circulated on the social scene, she devoured books by contemporary writers and showed a deep interest in music. She was also a very independent young woman and was criticised for walking alone in the city and for smoking cigarettes, neither of which was "proper" decorum for a young lady of the times.

In 1870, she married Oscar Chopin, who had been abused by his cruel Creole father. The young couple set up house in New Orleans, Louisiana and had six children. The Chopin family moved to a plantation in Natchitoches Parish, and it was there that Kate became steeped in the Creole culture that would provide subject matter for many of her works. Kate and Oscar seemed to have had a happy marriage, but he died in 1882 from malaria. Kate then moved back to St. Louis with her six children to be close to her mother. In 1889, at the age of 39 after her mother died, Kate began to write poems, stories, and novels after a kindly doctor suggested that she express her disappointments with life in writing. Her early success helped her to support her six children.

Many of Chopin's stories and novels are concerned about the status of women and the quality of their lives. They portray women searching for their identity and examining their sexuality. The publication of her novel *The Awakening* in 1899 brought harsh criticism and social ostracism to Chopin. Some critics labelled the work as pornographic and immoral, and it was banned in St. Louis. Its story of a married woman, living in a rather comatose state, "awakening" to passion, discovering her selfhood, and then committing suicide would probably be considered rather tame by modern standards, but it shocked the sensibilities of the time.

After remaining forgotten for over sixty years, Kate Chopin's writings were rediscovered in the 1960s and 1970s. She is now considered to have influenced the modern feminist movement in the United States and her works are required reading in many college and university literature courses.

Two major literary movements swept through Europe and North America during the nineteenth century. The first, which began in the early 1800s, has been called *Romanticism*. The works of Edgar Allan Poe, with their emphasis on the weird, the supernatural, the dark side of humanity, and the Gothic, serve to illustrate this period very well. In the latter half of the century, many writers turned away from the exaggerated feelings of the Romantics and decided instead to turn their attention to the details of everyday life. They took a critical, truthful look at the reality of their times and portrayed it realistically, thus giving the name *Realism* to this period.

In Europe, the writers of this Realist period — Stendhal, Balzac, and Flaubert of France; Turgenev, Dostoevsky, and Tolstoy of Russia; and Dickens of England, among others — wrote about the socio-economic situations of their times. They explored various themes connected with what they perceived as common social ills of the times: child labour and working-class poverty brought on by the Industrial Revolution, the negative aspects of war, the pitfalls of the bourgeois mentality, and the social relations between the upper and lower classes, to name a few. These writers incorporated vivid imagery in their works to create realistic effects.

In the United States, people were deeply affected by the devastation of the Civil War (1861-1865). Authors such as Ambrose Bierce no longer felt the need to look towards the supernatural or unusual to find horror; it surrounded them in their mundane lives. Many of Bierce's short stories expose the almost indescribable horrors of war. The writings of Mark Twain, Henry James, and Stephen Crane also reflect the concerns of Realism.

The Civil War marked an important turning point in American life as the country rejected slavery and accepted mechanisation and industrialisation as the economic basis of society. In theory, black people were now free. However, author Kate Chopin realised that women were not. Her writings, and most especially her book *The Awakening*, shocked the literary intelligentsia of the times. Not only was she criticised harshly for questioning the current social and sexual mores — taboo subjects — but she was also ostracised. She stopped writing and was relegated into oblivion only to be rediscovered in the latter half of the twentieth century. Her works are fine examples of Realism.

### Warm-Up Discussion Topics

▸ 1 What does the word *marriage* mean to you? Write at least eight words that you associate with this word.

________________________________________

________________________________________

▸ 2 Define the word *freedom*. What importance does feeling free have for you?

________________________________________

________________________________________

**INITIAL READING** ▸ **This story was written at the end of the nineteenth century when both men and women were expected to conform to their particular social roles more fully than they do today. As you read this story the first time for personal enjoyment, try to look at life from Mrs. Mallard's point of view and to imagine the feelings and sensations that she is experiencing. Do not stop to look up each unfamiliar word in the dictionary. Just read the story straight through.**

1890

STORY

# THE STORY OF AN HOUR

KATE CHOPIN

Knowing that Mrs. Mallard was afflicted with a heart trouble, great care was taken to break to her as gently as possible the news of her husband's death.

It was her sister Josephine who told her, in broken sentences, veiled hints that revealed in half concealing. Her husband's friend Richards was there, too, near her. It was he who had been in the newspaper office when intelligence of the railroad disaster was received, with Brently Mallard's name leading the list of "killed." He had only taken to time to assure himself of its truth by a second telegram, and had hastened to forestall any less careful, less tender friend in bearing the sad message.

She did not hear the story as many women have heard the same, with a paralyzed inability to accept its significance. She wept at once, with sudden, wild abandonment, in her sister's arms. When the storm of grief had spent itself she went away to her room alone. She would have no one follow.

There stood, facing the open window, a comfortable, roomy armchair. Into this she sank, pressed down by a physical exhaustion that haunted her body and seemed to reach into her soul.

She could see in the open square before her house the tops of trees that were all aquiver with the new spring life. The delicious breath of rain was in the air. In the street below a peddler was crying his wares. The notes of a distant song which someone was singing reached her faintly, and countless sparrows were twittering in the eaves.

There were patches of blue sky showing here and there through the clouds that had met and piled one above the other in the west facing her window.

She sat with her head thrown back upon the cushion of the chair, quite motionless, except when a sob came up into her throat and shook her, as a child who has cried itself to sleep continues to sob in its dreams.

She was young, with a fair, calm face, whose lines bespoke repression and even a certain strength. But now there was a dull stare in her eyes, whose gaze was ***fixed*** away off yonder on one of those patches of blue sky. It was not a glance of reflection, but rather indicated a suspension of intelligent thought.

*FIXED*→UNMOVING

There was something coming to her and she was waiting for it, fearfully. What was it? She did not know; it was too subtle and elusive to name. But she felt it, creeping out of the sky, reaching toward her through the sounds, the scents, the color that filled the air.

Now her bosom rose and fell tumultuously. She was beginning to recognize this thing that was approaching to possess her, and she was striving to beat it back with her will — as powerless as her two white slender hands would have been.

When she abandoned herself a little whispered word escaped her slightly parted lips. She said it over and over under her breath: "free, free, free!" The vacant stare and the look of terror that had followed it went from her eyes. They stayed keen and bright. Her pulses beat fast, and the coursing blood warmed and relaxed every inch of her body.

She did not stop to ask if it were or were not a monstrous joy that held her. A clear and exalted perception enabled her to dismiss the suggestion as trivial.

She knew that she would weep again when she saw the kind, tender hands folded in death; the face that had never looked save with love upon her, fixed and gray and dead. But she saw beyond that bitter moment a long procession of years to come that would belong to her absolutely. And she opened and spread her arms out to them in welcome.

There would be no one to live for her during those coming years; she would live for herself. There would be no powerful will bending hers in that blind persistence with which men and women believe they have a right to impose a private will upon a fellow-creature. A kind intention or a cruel intention made the act seem no less a crime as she looked upon it in that brief moment of illumination.

And yet she had loved him — sometimes. Often she had not. What did it matter! What could love, the unsolved mystery, count for in face of this possession of self-assertion which she suddenly recognized as the strongest impulse of her being!

"Free! Body and soul free!" she kept whispering.

Josephine was kneeling before the closed door with her lips to the keyhole, imploring for admission. "Louise, open the door! I beg; open the door — you will make yourself ill. What are you doing, Louise? For heaven's sake open the door.

"Go away. I am not making myself ill." No; she was drinking in a very elixir of life through that open window.

*FANCY→IMAGINATION*

Her ***fancy*** was running riot along those days ahead of her. Spring days, and summer days, and all sorts of days that would be her own. She breathed a quick prayer that life might be long. It was only yesterday she had thought with a shudder that life might be long.

She arose at length and opened the door to her sister's importunities. There was a feverish triumph in her eyes, and she carried herself unwittingly like a goddess of Victory. She clasped her sister's waist, and together they descended the stairs. Richards stood waiting for them at the bottom.

Someone was opening the front door with a latchkey. It was Brently Mallard who entered, a little travel-stained, composedly carrying his grip-sack and umbrella. He had been far from the scene of accident, and did not even know that there had been one. He stood amazed at Josephine's piercing cry; at Richards' quick motion to screen himself from the view of his wife.

But Richards was too late.

When the doctors came they said she had died of heart disease — of joy that kills.

***READER'S RESPONSE***

▸ **1** Did you appreciate the ending of the story? Why or why not?

▸ **2** Did you like or dislike Louise Mallard? Why?

▸ **3** How is Louise Mallard's vision of marriage similar to or different from your own?

▸ **4** Which type of story do you prefer, a Gothic example such as "The Tell-Tale Heart," which is influenced by the imagination and the supernatural, or a more realistic one based on social concerns, such as "The Story of an Hour"?

▸ **5** What do you like about this type of story?

**CLOSE READING** ▸ **"The Story of an Hour" is filled with irony (the device of writing or saying one thing, but meaning something opposite). Sometimes the irony is quite explicit and you see it at first glance, but in other instances it is more implicit. In the latter case, you have to think about the situation and what has happened to appreciate how ironic it is in a broader context. When you read the story a second time, see if you can discover all the ironies it contains. Before we look at irony in more depth, though, answer the following questions that are designed to help you begin your exploration of the text.**

▸ **1** Why, at the beginning of the story, do Richards and Josephine try to break the bad news very gently to Mrs. Mallard?

▸ **2** According to the narrator, how would most women have reacted to such news?

▸ **3** How does Mrs. Mallard react at first?

▸ **4** Describe in your own words what Mrs. Mallard feels and realises as she continues to gaze out the window.

▸ **5** What has Brently Mallard always felt towards his wife?

▸6 Why is Louise Mallard unhappy in her marriage?

▸7 What, in effect, is the "crime" that Louise Mallard is talking about in line 47?

▸8 **a)** What does Louise Mallard recognise as "the strongest impulse of her being"?

**b)** Explain what this means in your own words.

▸9 What happens at the end of the story?

▸10 What is the significance of the title of the story?

## WRITER'S CRAFT

### *IRONY*

▸1 Explain how the following features are ironic in the context of the story:

**a)** the last sentence

**b)** Richard's actions aimed at protecting Mrs. Mallard

**c)** Mrs. Mallard's seeing her dead husband's body

**d)** Mrs. Mallard's vision of her future

**e)** Mrs. Mallard's following words: "Free! Body and soul free!"

▸2 Find at least three more examples of irony in the story.

As preparation for the following questions, read the explanations on setting, characterisation, theme, narration, and point of view found in the Literary Elements section of this book. *(Please note that the other literary elements will be presented in subsequent chapters.)*

### Third-Person Narration and Point of View

▸1 What point of view is used to tell the story? ____________

▸2 What type of narrator is used to tell the story? ____________

▸3 Does the narrator seem close to or distant from the reader in this story?

____________

▸4 Think back to "The Tell-Tale Heart" by Poe. Recall who was narrating it. Which type of narration brings the reader closer to the characters in a story?

**a)** first person **b)** third person

▸5 The story is told in the ____________ tense, which also creates a certain distance.

> ▸▸▸ ***The choice of a narrator greatly affects the tone and atmosphere of a story. A first-person narrator can speak directly to the reader and can involve him or her in a much more personal way. The reader gets a close-up view of what is happening. A third-person narrator usually keeps the reader at a greater distance from what is happening. The process is similar to watching something happen from afar.*** ◂◂◂

### Foreshadowing

> ▸▸▸ ***Foreshadowing is a literary device used by writers to hint at what will eventually happen in a story. The use of foreshadowing not only increases the enjoyment of the astute reader, who tries to predict what is going to happen, but often helps build tension and unity in the story.*** ◂◂◂

▸1 Give two examples of foreshadowing in "The Story of an Hour."

### Choice of Words

#### Use of Repetition

▸1 Like Poe, Chopin uses repetition to create effects. She especially repeats two adjectives that are full of significance to this story. What are they?

▸2 Find one other example of repetition of adjectives or concrete images.

***Use of Imagery***

▸1 "The Story of an Hour" is rich in imagery. For example, Mrs. Mallard's weeping is described as "the storm of grief" (third paragraph). This powerful image appeals to at least two senses: sight and hearing. Give four examples from the fourth and fifth paragraphs of the story and identify the sense to which they appeal. (N.B. Each example must appeal to a different sense.)

___

___

___

___

▸▸▸ ***Chopin uses a great deal of contrastive imagery (images that are opposites) connected with details about the physical setting of the story. These opposite elements in the setting serve to bring out the theme.*** ◂◂◂

*Contrast of Opposite Images*

▸2 Look at the following contrast:

| **Open** | **versus** | **Closed in/Confined** |
|---|---|---|
| open window (occurs twice) | | shut in her room |

Find three more images (spatial elements or gestures) associated with "open" and two more associated with "closed."

open: ___

___

closed: ___

___

▸3 Here is a list of words: **a)** open **b)** closed **c)** artificial, man-made **d)** natural **e)** repressed **f)** free **g)** dead **h)** alive

Which three words from the list best exemplify the kind of life existing inside the Mallard's house?

___ ___ ___

Which three could be used to describe life outside the house?

___ ___ ___

▸**4** Chopin uses the weather and the outdoors as an extended metaphor to parallel Mrs. Mallard's feelings. What do the following images represent? (Use your judgement when you're not quite sure.)

**a)** a storm of grief (line 12)

**b)** "...the tops of trees that were all aquiver with the new spring life. The delicious breath of rain..." (lines 15, 16)

**c)** "...patches of blue sky" showing through the clouds (lines 19, 26)

**d)** "...something coming to her ... creeping out of the sky, reaching toward her through the sounds, the scents, the color that filled the air" (lines 28-30)

**e)** "Spring days, and summer days..." (lines 58, 59)

▸▸▸ ***The contrasting images of "closed" and "open" and the extended metaphor of the weather add impact to the contrast between the "living death" and the repression that Mrs. Mallard experiences in her marriage and the sudden rush of aliveness and well-being she feels when she thinks she has been freed by her husband's death.*** ◂◂◂

### Theme and Characterisation

▸**1** Which of the characters in the story are round and which are flat? Justify your answer.

▸**2** What is the main theme of this story?

# Write in Style ▸ Making Transitions

**In the previous Write in Style section, you worked with various types of sentences and clauses. In this section, you will work at developing smooth transitions between sentences and paragraphs through the use of subordinate clauses and transitional expressions. Let us first discuss the meanings of coordination and subordination.**

### *Coordination and Subordination*

When you write a text, you are arranging a series of ideas that you wish to communicate to a reader. Some — but not all — of these ideas are of equal importance, so that is where the concepts of coordination and subordination come into play.

**Coordination** joins two or more ideas of equal importance.

Read the following two simple sentences:

*My sister lives in Toronto. My brother lives in New York.*

Both of these sentences contain ideas of equal importance. An appropriate **coordinating conjunction** (*and, but, for, nor, so*) can be used to transform these simple sentences into a compound sentence. A comma is usually placed before the conjunction.

***EXAMPLE OF COORDINATION:***
***My sister lives in Toronto, but my brother lives in New York.***

**Subordination** shows a relation between ideas having different degrees of importance; that is, a less important idea is subordinated to a more important one.

Now read the following two simple sentences:

*My sister lives in Toronto. She found a job there.*

Since these sentences are too short, we will transform them into a complex sentence. First we must choose the idea that we want to emphasise. For the purpose of this example, we will say it is the fact that *my sister lives in Toronto*. This idea will be expressed in the independent (or main) clause.

Now we must find a way of expressing the less important idea in a dependent or subordinate clause linked to the main clause by choosing an appropriate **subordinating conjunction** (see table below for an extensive list). For the purposes of our example, we will use the subordinate clause to show the reason my sister lives in Toronto.

***EXAMPLE OF SUBORDINATION:***
***My sister lives in Toronto because she found a job there.***

**N.B.** You must be careful that the underlying logic of your complex sentence is correct. Compare the following two sentences.

*John ate a pizza because he was hungry.*
*John was hungry because he ate a pizza.*

You can see that the second sentence contains faulty logic.

Here is a table showing common subordinating conjunctions.

***Subordinating Conjunctions***

| Usage | Subordinating Conjunctions | Example |
|---|---|---|
| To indicate time (When?) | after, before, when, since, as soon as, while | As soon as he arrives, we'll leave. |
| To indicate place (Where?) | where, wherever | I don't know where he went. |
| To show cause / purpose (Why?) | because, so, in order that, as, since | He doesn't eat dessert because he doesn't want to gain weight. |
| To show manner (How?) | as, as if, as though | Tom walks as though he's wounded. |
| To show contrast / comparison / concession | although, even if, though, than, whereas | Although she was late, she won the prize. Sarah ran faster than I thought. |
| To indicate condition | if, whether, unless | She doesn't know whether he will come. |

**Relative pronouns** *(who, whose, whom, which, that)* are also used to show subordination.

*EXAMPLE: The book that I just read was fantastic.*

(independent / main clause = The book was fantastic)
(dependent / subordinate clause = that I just read) (relative pronoun = that)

**Exercise A: Building Effective Sentences**

Transform two simple sentences into an appropriate simple, compound, or complex sentence. Sometimes you will use a coordinating or subordinating conjunction or a relative pronoun, but you may also simply delete and rearrange words.

*EXAMPLE:*

The girls rapidly ate the pizza. They were famished.

*The girls rapidly ate the pizza because they were famished.*

or

*The famished girls rapidly ate the pizza.*

▸1 Edgar Allan Poe was primarily an author of horror stories. There are also some poems that he wrote that are excellent, such as "The Raven."

▸2 Edgar Allan Poe was very interested in the mysterious and strange aspects of life. He died in a mysterious and strange way.

▸3 *The Silence of the Lambs* is one of the most macabre movies ever produced. I wonder if Poe would have written a story like it if he were alive today.

▸4 Brently Mallard arrived home in a hurry. It's as if he were dying to see his wife.

▸5 In "The Masque of the Red Death," Prince Prospero allows only his friends into his castle. This cruel prince abandons most of his subjects to an atrocious death outside the castle walls.

**Exercise B: Combining Sentences**

This exercise will give you practice in composing effective sentences; you will combine the important elements of several short sentences into a longer, better one. Sometimes you will be able to use subordinate conjunctions, but you will also have to delete repetitions, rearrange elements, and shorten phrasing to accomplish the task. Look at the example and then complete the rest of the exercise.

*EXAMPLE:*

*Menka plays the piano. She is my piano teacher and she is excellent. Menka has been playing piano for many years. She is an outstanding performer. She practises a lot.*

*Menka, my excellent piano teacher, has been playing piano for many years, and she is also an outstanding performer because she practises a lot.*

▸1 Edgar Allan Poe wrote many short stories. They always deal with death and the supernatural. His short stories are very scary. This is the reason that I really appreciate them. Poe is one of my favourite authors.

▸2 Kate Chopin lived at a time when women were oppressed. She didn't let this stop her. She expressed her views on sexuality and marriage anyway. She also demanded freedom for women.

▸3 "The Tell-Tale Heart" is a short story written by Edgar Allan Poe. It is narrated by a man who seems crazy and obsessed. This man decides to kill an old man. It's because of the old man's blue eyes. The narrator thinks that the old man's eyes have the supernatural power of the evil eye.

▸4 I read another short story by Kate Chopin. In this story, the main character is a woman who was oppressed by her marriage. This made her seem only half alive. Then she discovers passionate love outside of marriage.

▸5 Literature can be read on many different levels. Some people read it only for the story line. Others appreciate the fictional world the author has created. Others like to delve deeper. They are searching for universal truths and meanings.

### *Other Transitional Words and Expressions*

Transitional expressions make connections between sentences and paragraphs and serve to make your writing flow smoothly. In the following example, transitional expressions appear in italics.

*Indeed,* Edgar Allan Poe was truly a master of suspense, as "The Tell-Tale Heart" most certainly shows. *In this story,* Poe exploits several literary devices to their fullest in order to create tension. *For instance,* he uses imagery appealing to both hearing and sight to great effect. The striking contrasts between dark and light, *such as* the black of night in contrast to the lantern's beam of light and the reassuring light of day, create tension in the reader's mind. *Similarly,* the interplay of quiet and loud sounds, *for example,* the sound of a mouse crossing the floor in contrast to the old man's shriek or the louder and louder beating of the dead heart makes the suspense rise to an almost intolerable level. *In brief,* these few examples serve to confirm Poe's reputation as a master of suspense.

Here is a chart of common transitional expressions, arranged according to how they are used. You will notice that the coordinating and subordinating conjunctions are also included in this chart.

### Common Transitional Expressions According to Usage

| Usage | Expression |
|---|---|
| Addition / Sequence | above all, again, also, and, and then, besides, beyond that, equally important, finally, first, for one thing, further, furthermore, in addition, in fact, in the first place, last, moreover, next, second, still, then, to begin with, too |
| Cause / Effect / Reason | accordingly, and so, as a result, because, consequently, for this purpose / reason, hence, otherwise, since, so, then, therefore, thus, to this end, with this object |
| Comparison | also, as well, both (neither), equally, in the same way, likewise, similarly, too |
| Concession of a point | certainly, granted that, of course, no doubt, to be sure |
| Conclusion / Summary | all, all in all, altogether, as has been said, in brief, in any event, in conclusion, in other words, in short, in simpler terms, in summary, lastly, on the whole, that is, therefore, to summarise |
| Contrast | although, and yet, be that as it may, but, but at the same time, despite, even so, even though, for all that, however, in contrast, in one.../ in other..., in spite of, instead, nevertheless, not only... but also, notwithstanding, on the contrary, on the other hand, regardless, still, though, yet, whereas |
| Emphasis | above all, after all, especially, even, indeed, in fact, in particular, in all cases, indeed, it is true, most important, of course, surely, truly |
| Example | as an illustration of, for example, for instance, in other words, in particular, in simpler terms, namely, one such, specifically, that is, to illustrate, yet another |
| Place / Position | above, adjacent to, below, beside, beyond, elsewhere, farther on, further, here, inside, near, nearby, next to, on the other / far side, opposite to, outside, there, to the north, (east, etc.), to the right / left |
| Time | after a while, afterward, as long as, as soon as, at last, at length, at that time, at the moment, before, currently, during, earlier, eventually, firstly, formerly, gradually, immediately, in the meantime, in the past, lately, later, meanwhile, now, presently, shortly, simultaneously, since, so far, soon, subsequently, suddenly, then, thereafter, until, until now, when |

**Exercise C: Identifying Transitional Expressions**

The following paragraph contains at least eleven transitional expressions from the chart above. Identify at least ten of them and indicate their usage (i.e. Time, Addition/Sequence, Place, etc.) in the spaces provided.

Philosophy cafés are one of the most popular trends in France at the moment. Indeed, they are sprouting all over Paris. Every Sunday, many people converge on one of several cafés to discuss burning philosophical questions. In one very popular café in particular, a different philosopher leads the discussion each week. However, in other cafés, the same philosopher leads the weekly discussions and proposes the following week's topic. Then people have a week to read up and gather their thoughts on it. Moreover, in all cases, would-be participants have to arrive early to get a seat inside the café. Not only are the budding philosophers excited and enthusiastic about their weekly philosophy sessions, but café owners are also delighted because of the crowds thronging to their establishments. In fact, they are amazed that philosophy has become such a popular Sunday pastime.

(For example, "Furthermore," is a transitional expression which gives sequence.)

| TRANSITIONAL EXPRESSION | USAGE | TRANSITIONAL EXPRESSION | USAGE |
|---|---|---|---|
| ____________ | ________ | ____________ | ________ |
| ____________ | ________ | ____________ | ________ |
| ____________ | ________ | ____________ | ________ |
| ____________ | ________ | ____________ | ________ |
| ____________ | ________ | ____________ | ________ |

## PRONUNCIATION

The English language consists of words that have stressed and unstressed syllables. It is very important that a speaker place the stress or accent on the correct syllable of the word when speaking. Placing stress on the wrong syllable can either make the word sound funny or can change the meaning of the word, as in the case of pro´ duce (noun that means product or goods) and pro duce´ (verb that means manufacture or bring forward for inspection).

### Exercise D: Identifying Stressed and Unstressed Syllables in Words

Pronounce each word in the following list and accordingly indicate which syllable is stressed by placing above the stressed syllable. Then check your answers with a dictionary.

*EXAMPLE: triumph; tri´ umph, i.e. the syllable* tri *is stressed.*

| | | | |
|---|---|---|---|
| afflicted | breathed | monstrous | suspension |
| disaster | unwittingly | keyhole | fixed |
| comfortable | revealed | feverish | ahead |
| eaves | intelligence | newspaper | recognised |
| develop | assume | abandonment | |
| self-assertion | aquiver | paralysed | |

## PARAGRAPH PRACTICE

▸1 Write a paragraph about one of the stories that you have read. Be sure to include at least ten transitional expressions.

▸2 Write a paragraph about marriage from Mrs. Mallard's point of view and/or Josephine's point of view.

## WRAP-UP DISCUSSION OR WRITING ACTIVITIES

▸1 Discuss how Chopin uses irony effectively throughout the story.

▸2 Explain how Chopin can be considered a revolutionary author for her times.

▸3 Discuss Chopin's use of imagery in "The Story of an Hour."

▸4 How relevant is the main theme of "The Story of an Hour" to people today?

N.B. In your written answers, be sure to use a variety of sentence types that include transitional words and expressions.

# References

## PRINT


**BIOGRAPHY**

Seyersted, Per. *Kate Chopin. A Critical Biography.* Baton Rouge: Louisiana State University Press, 1969.
Skaggs, Peggy. *Kate Chopin*. Boston: Twayne Publishers, 1985.
Toth, Emily. *Kate Chopin*. New York: Morrow, 1990.

**CRITICISM**

Green, Suzanne Disheroon and Caudle, David J. *An Annotated Bibliography of Critical Works*. Westport, CT: Greenwood Press, 1999.
Petry, Alice Hall, ed. *Critical Essays on Kate Chopin*. New York: Hall, 1996
Toth, Emily. *Unveiling Kate Chopin*. University Press of Mississippi, 1999.


## INTERNET

You will find a great many Internet references about Kate Chopin and her work. Please note that as sites change location from time to time, some of the links may not work. You may find other excellent sites related to this topic by making your own search on the Internet.

**BIOGRAPHY AND SELECTED WORKS OF KATE CHOPIN:**

http://empirezine.com/spotlight/chopin/chopin1.htm
http://metalab.unc.edu/docsouth/chopinawake/about.html
http://www.pbs.org/katechopin/
http://www.inform.umd.edu/EdRes/ReadingRoom/Fiction/Chopin/
http://falcon.jmu.edu/~ramseyil/chopin.htm
http://www.nagasaki-gaigo.ac.jp/ishikawa/amlit/c/chopin19re.htm
http://www.vcu.edu/engweb/eng384/hourweb.htm

**HISTORICAL HOUSE AND TOWN WHERE CHOPIN LIVED WITH HER HUSBAND:**

http://www.literarytraveler.com/summer/south/clout.htm
http://www.natchitoches.net/melrose/chopin.htm

**INFORMATION ABOUT HER FAMOUS BOOK, *THE AWAKENING*:**

http://falcon.jmu.edu/~ramseyil/southchopin.htm
http://soleil.acomp.usf.edu/~smasturz/

**HISTORICAL BACKGROUND:**

http://soleil.acomp.usf.edu/~smasturz/links.html#Hist

UNIT **1.3**

# HILLS LIKE WHITE ELEPHANTS

**CHAPTER CONTENTS**

- **READING:** "Hills Like White Elephants" by Ernest Hemingway; author's biography, literary trends (Realism, twentieth-century literature, experimentation)
- **WRITING:** topic sentences; supporting details; effective paragraphs
- **LITERARY ELEMENTS:** characterisation; dialogue; symbolism
- **GRAMMAR AND VOCABULARY:** parallel construction; repetition vs. redundancy; paraphrasing; quoting

## ABOUT THE AUTHOR

ERNEST HEMINGWAY (1899-1961) was one of the most influential American writers of the twentieth century. His writing style created a stir among literary circles for its ability to cut out extraneous language, leaving only the core. That is, Hemingway used words sparingly with minimal adjectives, creating an innovative writing style that many tried to copy. For this, as well as for the astounding works he produced, Hemingway was awarded the Nobel Prize for literature in 1954.

Hemingway was born the second child in a family of six children. His father was a doctor and the family was well-off. He received a classical education in Chicago where the family lived. He started writing while at high school and some of his work was published in his school's literary magazine. Hemingway started his writing career as a journalist first in Kansas, and later in Toronto, where he wrote for the *Toronto Star*. It was as a journalist that Hemingway first started using the style that later made him famous. Journalism requires short sentences, short paragraphs, and clarity.

At the start of World War I, Hemingway volunteered for service as an ambulance driver in Italy. He soon was wounded and spent time recuperating in a military hospital. There he fell in love with an American nurse, but the romance did not last. This experience, as well as other events such as the Spanish Civil War and the Greek Civil War, which he covered as a journalist, allowed him to gain first-hand experiences of the horrors of war. He was also able to collect material for his prize-winning stories and novels. His works, such as *Men Without Women* (1927) which contains "Hills Like White Elephants"; *A Farewell to Arms* (1929), a story about a love affair between an ambulance driver and an American nurse; and *For Whom the Bell Tolls* (1940), which takes place during the Spanish Civil War, demonstrate that his wartime journalistic experiences influenced him greatly.

Hemingway had a very colourful personal life. He was a great sportsman and especially loved deep-sea fishing, the subject of his masterpiece *The Old Man and the Sea* (1952). He was married four times. He committed suicide in 1961.

## LITERARY TRENDS OF THE TIMES

During the first half of the twentieth century, realism remained a preoccupation of a great many writers, especially in North America. World War I, the Roaring Twenties, the Great Depression, and World War II influenced many writers to continue exploring human experience through a realistic perspective. Some of the more famous include Willa Cather, John Steinbeck, William Faulkner, Shirley Jackson, and Ernest Hemingway. Hemingway applied a bare, journalistic style to his short stories and novels to deal as realistically as possible with the subjects he chose to write about: war, hunting, death, masculinity, and gender relations. However, like several of his contemporaries, Hemingway began to experiment with the form of the short story by doing away with a traditionally structured plot and focusing on more subtle psychological conflicts. The story you will read in this chapter exemplifies this new approach.

### Warm-Up Discussion Topics

▸1 Have you ever been in a situation where the subject of discussion has made you feel uncomfortable? If so, how did you react to the situation?

▸2 Do you like to travel? Recount an interesting story that happened when you took a trip.

▸3 Would you rather travel than settle down in one place? Explain.

**INITIAL READING ▸ The story "Hills Like White Elephants" is very short. Read it through for the first time without worrying about unfamiliar vocabulary.**

STORY

1927

# Hills Like White Elephants

Ernest Hemingway

THE HILLS across the valley of the Ebro were long and white. On this side there was no shade and no trees and the station was between two lines of rails in the sun. Close against the side of the station there was the warm shadow of the building and a curtain, made of strings of bamboo beads, hung across the open door into the bar, to keep out flies. The American and the girl with him sat at a table in the shade, outside the building. It was very hot and the express from Barcelona would come in forty minutes. It stopped at this junction for two minutes and went on to Madrid.

"What should we drink?" the girl asked. She had taken off her hat and put it on the table.

"It's pretty hot," the man said.

"Let's drink beer."

"Dos cervezas," the man said into the curtain.

"Big ones?" a woman asked from the doorway.

"Yes. Two big ones."

The woman brought two glasses of beer and two felt pads. She put the felt pads and the beer glasses on the table and looked at the man and the girl. The girl was looking off at the line of hills. They were white in the sun and the country was brown and dry.

"They look like white elephants," she said.

"I've never seen one," the man drank his beer.

"No, you wouldn't have."

"I might have," the man said. "Just because you say I wouldn't have doesn't prove anything."

The girl looked at the bead curtain. "They've painted something on it," she said. "What does it say?"

"Anis del Toro. It's a drink."

"Could we try it?"

The man called "Listen" through the curtain. The woman came out from the bar.

"Four reales."

"We want two Anis del Toro."

"With water?"

"Do you want it with water?"

"I don't know," the girl said. "Is it good with water?"

"It's all right."

"You want them with water?" asked the woman.

"Yes, with water."

"It tastes like licorice," the girl said and put the glass down.

"That's the way with everything."

"Yes," said the girl. "Everything tastes of licorice. Especially all the things you've waited so long for, like absinthe."

"Oh, cut it out."

"You started it," the girl said. "I was being amused. I was having a fine time."

"Well, let's try and have a fine time."

"All right. I was trying. I said the mountains looked like white elephants. Wasn't that bright?"

"That was bright."

"I wanted to try this new drink. That's all we do, isn't it — look at things and try new drinks?"

"I guess so."

The girl looked across at the hills.

"They're lovely hills," she said. "They don't really look like white elephants. I just meant the coloring of their skin through the trees."

"Should we have another drink?"

"All right."

The warm wind blew the bead curtain against the table.

"The beer's nice and cool," the man said.

"It's lovely," the girl said.

"It's really an awfully simple operation, Jig," the man said. "It's not really an operation at all."

The girl looked at the ground the table legs rested on.

"I know you wouldn't mind it, Jig. It's really not anything. It's just to let the air in."

The girl did not say anything.

"I'll go with you and I'll stay with you all the time. They just let the air in and then it's all perfectly natural."

"Then what will we do afterward?"

"We'll be fine afterward. Just like we were before."

"What makes you think so?"

"That's the only thing that bothers us. It's the only thing that's made us unhappy."

The girl looked at the bead curtain, put her hand out and took hold of two of the strings of beads.

"And you think then we'll be all right and be happy."

"I know we will. You don't have to be afraid. I've known lots of people that have done it."

"So have I," said the girl. "And afterward they were all so happy."

"Well," the man said, "if you don't want to you don't have to. I wouldn't have you do it if you didn't want to. But I know it's perfectly simple."

"And you really want to?"

"I think it's the best thing to do. But I don't want you to do it if you don't really want to."

"And if I do it you'll be happy and things will be like they were and you'll love me?"

"I love you now. You know I love you."

"I know. But if I do it, then it will be nice again if I say things are like white elephants, and you'll like it?"

"I'll love it. I love it now but I just can't think about it. You know how I get when I worry."

"If I do it you won't ever worry?"

"I won't worry about that because it's perfectly simple."

"Then I'll do it. Because I don't care about me."

"What do you mean?"

"I don't care about me."

"Well, I care about you."

"Oh, yes. But I don't care about me. And I'll do it and then everything will be fine."

"I don't want you to do it if you feel that way."

The girl stood up and walked to the end of the station. Across, on the other side, were fields of grain and trees along the banks of the Ebro. Far away, beyond the river, were mountains. The shadow of a cloud moved across the field of grain and she saw the river through the trees.

"And we could have all this," she said. "And we could have everything and every day we make it more impossible."

"What did you say?"

"I said we could have everything."

"We can have everything."

"No, we can't."

"We can have the whole world."

"No, we can't."

"We can go everywhere."

"No, we can't. It isn't ours any more."

"It's ours."

"No, it isn't. And once they take it away, you never get it back."

"But they haven't taken it away."

"We'll wait and see."

"Come on back in the shade," he said. "You mustn't feel that way."

"I don't feel any way," the girl said. "I just know things."

"I don't want you to do anything that you don't want to do — "

"Nor that isn't good for me," she said. "I know. Could we have another beer?"

"All right. But you've got to realize — "

"I realize," the girl said. "Can't we maybe stop talking?"

They sat down at the table and the girl looked across at the hills on the dry side of the valley and the man looked at her and at the table.

"You've got to realize," he said, "that I don't want you to do it if you don't want to. I'm perfectly willing to go through with it if it means anything to you."

"Doesn't it mean anything to you? We could get along."

"Of course it does. But I don't want anybody but you. I don't want anyone else. And I know it's perfectly simple."

"Yes, you know it's perfectly simple."

"It's all right for you to say that, but I do know it."

"Would you do something for me now?"

"I'd do anything for you."

"Would you please please please please please please please stop talking?"

He did not say anything but looked at the bags against the wall of the station. There were labels on them from all the hotels where they had spent nights.

"But I don't want you to," he said. "I don't care anything about it."

"I'll scream," the girl said.

The woman came out through the curtains with two glasses of beer and put them down on the damp felt pads. "The train comes in five minutes," she said.

"What did she say?" asked the girl.

"That the train is coming in five minutes."

The girl smiled brightly at the woman, to thank her.

"I'd better take the bags over to the other side of the station," the man said. She smiled at him.

"All right. Then come back and we'll finish the beer."

He picked up the two heavy bags and carried them around the station to the other tracks. He looked up the tracks but could not see the train. Coming back, he walked through the barroom, where people waiting for the train were drinking. He drank an Anis at the bar and looked at the people. They were all waiting reasonably for the train. He went out through the bead curtain. She was sitting at the table and smiled at him.

"Do you feel better?" he asked.

"I feel fine," she said. "There's nothing wrong with me. I feel fine."

### *Reader's Response*

▸1 What particular characteristics did you notice about the way this story was written?

▸2 What were your impressions about the two characters in the story?

**CLOSE READING** ▸ **Reread the story, paying close attention to the subject of conversation between the two characters. You will need to read between the lines and make inferences to understand what they are talking about.**

▸1 Who are the main characters in the story?

▸2 What is their relationship and attitude toward each other?

▸3 What is the general setting of the story?

▸4 What is the specific setting of the story?

▸5 Why is the couple at this place?

▸6 **a)** What is the major topic of their conflict?

**b)** Cite one or two sentences from the text that point to this, albeit indirectly.

**WRITER'S CRAFT** ▸ **Writers reveal characters in different ways. Refer to the literary elements at the beginning of this book in order to understand the techniques writers use for character development.**

▸▸▸ ***Hemingway uses two main methods to depict the characters and unfold the central conflict:***
**Dialogue***, of course, refers to speech between two people.*
**Symbolism** ***is the practice of using something concrete to represent something else (concrete or abstract).***
**Examples:**
***Colours are often used to symbolise things: In Western cultures, black often symbolises death; white symbolises innocence and purity; green means hope or rebirth.***
***The seasons of the year can be used to symbolise different periods in a person's life.*** ◂◂◂

### DIALOGUE

▸1 This story is written in dialogue form. In your opinion, how effective is this form of writing?

▸2 What kind of conversation does the couple have openly during the course of the story? (more than one answer)

**a)** small talk **b)** casual **c)** light-hearted **d)** profound

▸3 Who starts the conversation, the man or the woman?

▸4 What is the tone of the conversation? (more than one answer)

**a)** sarcastic **b)** emotional **c)** humorous **d)** furtive **e)** tense

▸5 What observation does the woman make about the scenery?

▸6 What response does the man make to the woman's observation?

▸7 **a)** What do their respective responses reveal about the characters?

(man) ______________________________

(woman) ______________________________

**b)** What do their responses reveal about their relationship?

______________________________

▸8 The woman states,

"Everything tastes of licorice. Especially all the things you've waited so long for, like absinthe."

"That's all we do, isn't it — look at things and try new drinks?"

What do these statements suggest about the nature of their relationship? (more than one answer) That it is **a)** long term **b)** disappointing **c)** deep **d)** superficial **e)** happy

▸9 Why is the major source of their conflict only implied?

______________________________

▸10 What does their conflict indicate about the relationship of the couple? In other words, what does the continuing dialogue show about the communications in the couple?

______________________________

▸11 How does this create tension in the story?

______________________________

▸12 **a)** What is the position of the man regarding the couple's major source of conflict?

______________________________

**b)** Why does he take this position?

______________________________

▸13 What is the woman's position?

______________________________

▸14 What three strategies or arguments does the man use in order to get his own way?

______________________________

### *Action versus Dialogue*

***▸▸▸ The dialogue technique is used to reveal what is said between the couple. However, what is unsaid is also very important at revealing characters. In the case of the couple, often their inability to communicate is shown by their desire to avoid being direct about their feelings. Their feelings are communicated by gestures or actions. For example, when the man starts to talk about the operation, the woman's actions show that she avoids the conversation. Moreover, often in real situations when people are uncomfortable about a subject, they show their reluctance to speak about the topic by fiddling or doing other body movements. Here is an example from the story:***

***"The girl looked at the ground the table legs rested on."***

***"The girl looked at the bead curtain, put her hand out and took hold of two of the strings of beads." ◂◂◂***

**▸1** List two other actions by the man or the woman that indicate that each is trying to avoid discussing the subject directly.

**a)** ______

**b)** ______

**▸2** Who do you think "wins" the argument? ______

Support your answer with direct quotations from the text and explain your reasoning.

______

______

______

### *Symbolism*

**▸1** In the first paragraph of "Hills Like White Elephants," what form of writing does Hemingway use (descriptive, narrative, dialogue, monologue)?

______

**▸2** Write three different words used in the first paragraph that convey the dominant atmosphere of the setting.

______

**▸3** The woman's observations about the scenery are very symbolic when put into the perspective of the conflict of the story. The expression "hills like white elephants" is also the title of the story. The hills are compared to elephants, meaning that they are big and round. Considering the woman's condition, what else can such a symbol represent?

______

**▸4** The expression "white elephant" in English refers to something useless and unwanted. Again, considering the woman's condition, what could this expression symbolise or refer to?

______

**▸5** There are many other symbols throughout the story. Write an interpretation for the following symbols:

**a)** the general scenery (it is hot, arid, and without vegetation)

______

**b)** the train

**c)** the fact that the couple is nameless (the woman is referred to once as Jig)

**d)** the use of the definite article instead of the indefinite article in referring to the couple (the American/the girl)

**e)** where the couple is seated in comparison to the other people in the bar

**▸6** List at least two other symbols and write their interpretation.

**a)** ______

**b)** ______

## WRITE IN STYLE ▸ PARAGRAPHS

**In order to write effectively, it is important to understand how to write in a well-organised fashion.**

***Paragraphs* are the units in which a writer expresses his or her ideas. A paragraph is a group of words containing one main idea. Paragraphs have an inherent structure. They contain a *topic sentence* and *supporting details*. A topic sentence introduces the subject of the paragraph. The supporting details may either be facts, statistics, or examples, and interpretations that give further information on the main idea or topic sentence.**

There are certain points to remember when writing paragraphs.

- Paragraphs should only contain one main idea. All details should support the main idea of the paragraph.
- Paragraphs should be easy to follow. That is, information in the paragraph should be organised in such a way that the reader is very clear about the subject and the information contained in it.
- Paragraphs are generally six to ten sentences in length or between 100-150 words. (This rule is of course very general, and applies to descriptive and narrative forms rather than dialogue.) If a paragraph is too long, it will likely contain more than one main idea or be off focus, and if it is too short, it may not contain enough information on the subject.
- Paragraphs should make an impact on the reader; should be forceful and interesting.

*EXAMPLE: The discovery of scotch created such an impact on the Scots that it changed the social fabric of Scotland.*

## The Topic Sentence

- states the central idea of the paragraph and contains an opinion about the idea.
  *EXAMPLE: Driving under the influence of alcohol is extremely irresponsible.*
- should not contain "I believe" or "In my opinion…" because these expressions are considered redundant.
  *(Incorrect) EXAMPLE: I think that driving under the influence of alcohol is extremely irresponsible.*
- should not be too general or too specific.
  *EXAMPLE: Everyone who drinks should not be given a driver's license. (Too general)*
  *EXAMPLE: Ten percent of all adults drink scotch every day. (Too specific)*
- should make an impact on the reader; should be forceful and interesting.
  *EXAMPLE: The discovery of scotch created such an impact on the Scots that it changed the social fabric of Scotland.*
- usually opens the paragraph; often is the first sentence of the paragraph.
- should not contain an explanation
  *(Incorrect) EXAMPLE: Driving under the influence of alcohol is extremely irresponsible because drunk drivers can cause fatal accidents.*

**Exercise A: Building Effective Topic Sentences**

Read the following sentences and decide if they are strong or weak topic sentences. Write *W* for weak and *S* for strong in the space provided. Change the weak sentences into strong topic sentences.

▸1 All cars are very expensive.

___

▸2 Students like to travel to Europe upon graduation because they feel like exploring the world.

___

▸3 Working more than ten hours per week negatively affects student grades.

___

▸4 I prefer Hemingway's style of writing to that of Fitzgerald.

___

▸5 University education should be free.

___

**Exercise B: Identifying the Topic Sentence**

Underline the topic sentence and place a number in front of the first word of each supporting argument.

Driving over the speed limit is a sure way of becoming an accident statistic. The faster a person drives his or her car, the less control he/she has. Moreover, regular drivers are not trained to react to emergency driving situations at high speeds. Unlike professional race car drivers, most drivers do not have experience at avoiding accidents at high speeds. Furthermore, highways and city streets are not built for high-speed car racing. There are too many obstacles on roads and highways for safe high-speed driving. Therefore, drivers should slow down when driving.

**Exercise C: Writing the Topic Sentence**

Choose one sentence from Exercise A. Write a paragraph that is six–ten sentences long. Remember to make the topic sentence strong and interesting. The body of the paragraph should support the topic sentence.

______________________________

______________________________

______________________________

______________________________

**Style Tips**

Here are some tips to consider when writing good paragraphs.

- Remember to organise the ideas in your paragraph logically.
- Ideas should flow sequentially.
- Check that nouns and pronouns agree in number.

  *EXAMPLE: Incorrect: Every student should bring their book.*
  *Correct: Students should bring their books.*

  (See section on agreement in the third essay chapter for more details.)
- Avoid shifts in verb tense.

  *EXAMPLE: Incorrect: He said that he will have done that in the same situation.*
  *Correct: He said that he would have done that in the same situation.*

  (See section on shift in verb tenses in the fourth essay chapter for more details.)

## PARALLEL CONSTRUCTION

Parallel construction refers to the use of similar grammatical structures. For example, words, clauses, and phrases should be in similar grammatical form in sentences.

*EXAMPLES:*

*Incorrect: The speaker at the protest rally **waved** his arms, **jumped** up and down, and **was screaming** in a very loud voice to the audience.*

*Correct: The speaker at the protest rally **waved** his arms, **jumped** up and down, and **screamed** in a very loud voice to the audience.*

*Incorrect: My mother **was talking** on the phone, and my brother **watched** television.*

*Correct: My mother **was talking** on the phone, and my brother **was watching** television.*

*Incorrect: My friend **plays hockey**, **sails boats**, and **is swimming like a fish**.*

*Correct: My friend **plays hockey**, **sails boats**, and **swims like a fish**.*

**Exercise D: Correcting Errors in Parallel Construction**

Correct any parallel construction errors in the following sentences.

▸ 1 Successful students organise their time, study on a regular basis, and are trying to get enough sleep.

---

▸ 2 The astronauts were conducting experiments such as studying the effects of gravity, looked at behavioural problems, and examining the effects of isolation on people.

---

▸ 3 The people in the next apartment sang at the top of their voices, playing rock and roll music, and danced the night away.

---

▸ 4 My boyfriend likes looking at car magazines, going to car shows and drives very fast.

---

▸ 5 Mountains, lakes and the rivers together create a magnificent landscape.

---

### RESTATEMENTS

Restating words and ideas in a paragraph can have either a **positive** or **negative** effect.

Sometimes stating the same word or idea can be redundant and ineffective. In English, subjects and object in clauses are not repeated.

*EXAMPLE:*

*Incorrect: The **girl**, **she** is my sister. In this example, the subject* girl *is repeated with the pronoun* she.

*Correct: The **girl** is my sister.*

*Incorrect: The **basketball player**, **whom** the movie was based on **him**, played at one time for the NBA.*

*Correct: The **basketball player**, **whom** the movie was based on, played at one time for the NBA.*

Sometimes, however, repetition can be used very effectively. Restating key ideas in a paragraph can emphasise their importance. The following paragraph contains repetitions of key words.

The interest generated by the events in **World War II** has been re-exploited recently by the film industry. This **war** was one of the bloodiest, long-term **battles** of the twentieth century. During the **war**, many people died as a result of political decisions as well as in actual combat. Such events make great subjects for films such as **futility of war**, the exploitation of the weak by the strong, and the heroic efforts of many individuals. Films such as *Saving Private Ryan*, *Schindler's List*, and *The Thin Red Line* are the results of recent experimentation on an old subject, **World War II**.

#### Exercise E: Correcting Errors in Parallel Construction and Redundancy

The following paragraph contains five errors in parallel construction. It also has two examples of redundancy. Find and correct any errors.

The cat was lying in the sun and she licked her paws. She was a white Persian cat, with a lot of long, silky fur. Her eyes, they were blue-grey. Those eyes shone in the sunlight, and were gleaming as they contemplated the birds who were sitting in the apple tree. The birds suddenly became nervous, as they were becoming aware of the presence of the cat. She slowly twitched her tail, as she watches the birds. The birds flew away, shrieked in loud voices. The cat continued washing herself.

### *Paraphrasing and Quoting*

Paragraphs require supporting details. These details can be in the form of statistics, data, examples, or information from secondary sources. Whichever type of detail you use, it is very important to know how to use ideas and information from secondary sources correctly. Incorrect usage of secondary source material can be plagiarism.

**Direct Quotations**

Direct quotations are repetitions of the exact words a person has said or written. They must be placed in double quotation marks.

- Put a colon after a complete sentence when the following sentence is a direct quotation.

  *EXAMPLE: Hemingway often uses action to emphasise a character trait: "The girl looked at the bead curtain, put her hand out and took hold of two of the strings of beads."*

- Put a comma after a phrase that introduces a quotation. The first word of the quotation must be capitalised.

  *EXAMPLE: In Hemingway's story, the girl said, "They look like white elephants."*

- End the quotation with a comma if your sentence continues after the end of the quotation.

  *EXAMPLE: The female character in Hemingway's short story remarked, "Everything tastes of licorice," revealing her attitude towards life.*

- Punctuate an incomplete quotation within a sentence only with quotation marks.

  *EXAMPLE: Hemingway's short story takes place at a railway station "between two lines of rails in the sun."*

- Use ellipses marks to indicate that words are missing from a quotation.

  *EXAMPLE: The story starts in the following way: "The Hills across the valley of the Ebro…".*

### Quotations within Quotations

- Use single quotation marks to indicate a quotation within a quotation.

  *EXAMPLE: Hemingway wrote, " 'They're lovely hills,' she said. 'They don't really look like white elephants.' "*

N.B. The usage of quotations differs in English-speaking countries. The style used above is American and this style also predominates in Canada. However, the British tend to use single quotation marks around direct speech and double quotation marks for quotations within quotations (in other words, the opposite of American usage). American usage requires most end punctuation (commas, periods, etc.) to be placed inside the final quotation marks whereas British usage requires it to be placed outside the final quotation marks.

Here is how the above example would appear according to British usage.

*EXAMPLE: Hemingway wrote, ' "They're lovely hills," she said. "They don't really look like white elephants" '.*

Parallel construction refers to the use of similar grammatical structures. For example, words, clauses, and phrases should be in similar grammatical form in sentences.

### Indirect Quotations

- Quotation marks are unnecessary when the exact words of a speaker or writer are not used.

  Compare the first two examples (a statement and indirect speech) with the third (direct speech).

  *EXAMPLES:*

  *In Hemingway's work, the girl compared the hills to white elephants.*

  *I told him that in Hemingway's work, the girl compared the hills to white elephants.*

  *John answered, "In Hemingway's work, the girl compared the hills to white elephants."*

### Longer Quotations

- For quotations exceeding four lines of a text, do not use quotation marks. Indent the entire length of the quotation and use single-space.

  *EXAMPLE:*

  *The Hills across the valley of the Ebro were long and white. On this side there was no shade and no trees and the station was between two lines of rails in the sun. Close against the side of the station there was the warm shadow of the building and a curtain, made of strings of bamboo beads, hung across the open door into the bar, to keep out flies…*

### Paraphrasing

Paraphrasing refers to restating in your own words someone else's ideas or texts. A paraphrase must indicate the source of the original idea in order to avoid plagiarism. Each sentence of the original text must be paraphrased in the order it appears.

**Exercise F: Paraphrasing 1**

Write the following sentences in your own words. Remember to keep the original meaning of ideas.

▸1 The animal kingdom reflects a predominance of male–female work stereotypes.

▸2 Male birds have very colourful plumage, while female birds look more ordinary; the reason is that females need to be camouflaged in order to hatch their eggs while being safe from predators.

▸3 Male birds use their colourful looks also as a way to court females.

▸4 The Black Widow spider is aptly named because the females eat the males after mating.

▸5 Male lions are truly the lords of their domain; the females hunt for food, look after the young, as well as allow the males to eat first.

**Exercise G: Paraphrasing 2**

Here are some direct quotations from the stories that you have already read. Paraphrase these direct quotations.

▸1 "When she abandoned herself, a little whispered word escaped her slightly parted lips. She said it over and over under her breath: 'Free, free, free!' " ("The Story of an Hour")

▸2 "I've never seen one," the man drank his beer.
"No, you wouldn't have."
"I might have," the man said. "Just because you say I wouldn't have doesn't prove anything."

▸3 "When I had waited a long time, very patiently, without hearing him lie down, I resolved to open a little — a very, very little crevice in the lantern. So I opened it — you cannot imagine how stealthily, stealthily — until, at length a simple dim ray, like the thread of the spider, shot from out the crevice and fell full upon the vulture eye."

### *Paragraph Practice*

- ▸1 Write a paragraph explaining the different symbols found in "Hills Like White Elephants." What do the symbols represent?

## WRAP-UP DISCUSSION OR WRITING ACTIVITIES

- ▸1 How effective is Hemingway's writing technique, which uses dialogue, in creating the tense atmosphere between the couple?
- ▸2 The story "Hills Like White Elephants" is symbolic of the journey of life. Discuss.
- ▸3 Write a dialogue in which one person tries to convince another person to do something.

# References

## PRINT


**Biography**

Baker, Carlos. Ernest Hemingway: *A Life Story*. New York: Scribner's, 1969.

Hemingway, Leicester. *My Brother, Ernest Hemingway*. New York: Fawcett Premier Library, 1962; Sarasota, FL: Pineapple Press, Inc., 1956, 1996.

Meyers, Jeffrey. *Hemingway, A Biography*. New York: Harper & Row, 1985.

Oliver, Charles M. *Ernest Hemingway A to Z*. New York: Checkmark Books, 1999.

Ross, Lillian. *Portrait of Hemingway*. New York: Modern Library, 1999.

**Criticism**

Benson, Jackson J., ed. *New Critical Approaches to the Short Stories of Ernest Hemingway*. Durham, NC: Duke University Press, 1990.

Bloom, Harold, ed. *Modern Critical Views, Ernest Hemingway*. Broomall PA: Chelsea House, 1985.

Eby, Carl P. *Hemingway's Fetishism, Psychoanalysis and the Mirror of Manhood.* Albany, NY: SUNY Press, 1999.


## INTERNET


**List of links to Web sites about Hemingway**

http://members.atlantic.net/~gagne/hem/hemlinks.html

Keyword search: Ernest Hemingway at the following site: http://www.britannica.com/

**Biography and selected works:**

http://www.cs.umb.edu/jfklibrary/eh.htm

http://www.lostgeneration.com/hrc.htm

http://kcstar.com/aboutstar/hemingway/ernie.htm

http://www.csustan.edu/english/reuben/pal/chap7/hemingway.html

http://www.mala.bc.ca/~lanes/english/hemngway/ehlife.htm

Ernest Hemingway Foundation: http://www.hemingway.org/

*Photographs:* http://www.thomasville.com/hemingway/

*Video:* information about "biodocumentary"video: Ernest Hemingway: Famous Author Series 30 min.: http://www.americanlegends.com/Vidstore/Vidstore.htm

**Historical background**

Home: http://www.hemingwayhome.com/

Lost Generation: http://www.britannica.com/bcom/eb/article/5/0,5716,50175+1,00.html

**Hemingway's style**

http://www.usnews.com/usnews/issue/980601/1papa.htm

**UNIT 1.4**

# THE LOTTERY

## CHAPTER CONTENTS

- **READING:** "The Lottery" by Shirley Jackson; literary trends (aftermath of World War II, individual freedom vs. conformity)
- **WRITING:** paragraphs
- **LITERARY ELEMENTS:** narration and point of view; foreshadowing, irony, male / female stereotypes
- **GRAMMAR AND VOCABULARY:** mechanics: spelling, capitalisation, and punctuation

## ABOUT THE AUTHOR

SHIRLEY JACKSON (1919-1965) was born in San Francisco. Her mother, an ambitious socialite, was disappointed by her plain, intellectual daughter who showed little interest in social conventions.

Later, Jackson attended university in New York state where she met and married Stanley Edgar Hyman. Hyman became a literary critic and the couple moved to a small town in Vermont when he was offered a teaching post at Bennington College. Jackson gave birth to four daughters whom she both loved and neglected. More and more of a non-conformist and suffering from bouts of depression, she was considered a very odd and controversial figure by many of the townspeople. She often felt persecuted and some of the townspeople actually considered her to be a witch. Unfortunately, although Hyman was supportive of her radical ideas, Jackson, with her unkempt appearance and gaudy clothing, never seemed to fit in anywhere, even in her husband's liberal, academic circles.

Jackson authored spectacularly different works. She wrote funny, banal stories for popular women's magazines of the fifties while at the same time composing serious, much darker and more disturbing pieces. "The Lottery," considered as her masterpiece, stirred up more controversy than any other short story ever published in *The New Yorker* magazine.

As the years went by, Jackson became even more eccentric. She smoked, ate, and drank too much, and popped pills from dawn to dusk. She died of heart failure during an afternoon nap at the relatively young age of 46.

## LITERARY TRENDS OF THE TIMES

American prose literature since World War II is difficult to categorise. Indeed, the narrative has become multi-dimensional due to international events, the development of technology that has resulted in inventions such as television, as well as societal changes, especially in male/female relationships.

World War II greatly influenced the literature in America in the 1940s and beyond. Writers such as Norman Mailer (*The Naked and the Dead*, 1948) and Herman Wouk (*The Caine Mutiny*, 1951) wrote about the brutality of war and inhumanity towards fellow humans. War and its intrinsic evil were described in a realistic style in order to capture the grim reality of evil and violence. Writers effectively demonstrated that not only did violence negatively influence society during war, but that the effects of that violence remained and influenced civilian society as well. Furthermore, writers also explored the theme of individual freedom versus conformity in society. Beginning in the 1940s, they wrote about the conflict between individual growth and the need to belong.

**WARM-UP DISCUSSION TOPICS**

▸ **1** Would you like to win a lottery? Why or why not?

▸ **2** How important do you think it is for a society to keep its traditions?

**INITIAL READING** ▸ **Many people consider "The Lottery" to be a classic short story. Read on to discover why.**

STORY

# THE LOTTERY

1948

SHIRLEY JACKSON

The morning of June 27th was clear and sunny, with the fresh warmth of a full-summer day; the flowers were blossoming profusely and the grass was richly green. The people of the village began to gather in the square, between the post office and the bank, around ten o'clock; in some towns there were so many people that the lottery took two days and had to be started on June 26th, but in this village, where there were only about three hundred people, the whole lottery took less than two hours, so it could begin at ten o'clock in the morning and still be through in time to allow the villagers to get home for noon dinner.

The children assembled first, of course. School was recently over for the summer, and the feeling of liberty sat uneasily on most of them; they tended to gather together quietly for a while before they broke into boisterous play, and their talk was still of the classroom and the teacher, of books and reprimands. Bobby Martin had already stuffed his pockets full of stones, and the other boys soon followed his example, selecting the smoothest and roundest stones; Bobby and Harry Jones and Dickie Delacroix — the villagers pronounced this name "Dellacroy" — eventually made a great pile of stones in one corner of the square and guarded it against the raids of the other boys. The girls stood aside, talking among themselves, looking over their shoulders at the boys, and the very small children rolled in the dust or clung to the hands of their older brothers or sisters.

Soon the men began to gather, surveying their own children, speaking of planting and rain, tractors and taxes. They stood together, away from the pile of stones in the corner, and their jokes were quiet and they smiled rather than laughed. The women, wearing faded house dresses and sweaters, came shortly after their menfolk. They greeted one another and exchanged bits of gossip as they went to join their husbands. Soon the women, standing by their husbands, began to call to their children, and the children came reluctantly, having to be called four or five times. Bobby Martin ducked under his mother's grasping hand and ran, laughing, back to the pile of stones. His father spoke up sharply, and Bobby came quickly and took his place between his father and his oldest brother.

The lottery was conducted — as were the square dances, the teenage club, the Halloween program — by Mr. Summers, who had time and energy to devote to civic activities. He was a round-faced, jovial man and he ran the coal business, and people were sorry for him, because he had no children and his wife was a scold. When he arrived in the square, carrying the black wooden box, there was a murmur of conversation among the villagers, and he waved and called, "Little late today, folks." The postmaster, Mr. Graves, followed him, carrying a three-legged stool, and the stool was put in the center of the square and Mr. Summers set the black box down on it. The villagers kept their distance, leaving a space between themselves and the stool, and when Mr. Summers said, "Some of you fellows want to give me a hand?" there was a hesitation before two men, Mr. Martin and his oldest son, Baxter, came forward to hold the box steady on the stool while Mr. Summers stirred up the papers inside it.

The original paraphernalia for the lottery had been lost long ago, and the black box now resting on the stool had been put into use even before Old Man Warner, the oldest man in town, was born. Mr. Summers spoke frequently to the villagers about making a new box, but no one liked to upset even as much tradition as was represented by the black box. There was a story that the present box had been made with some pieces of the box that had preceded it, the one that had been constructed when the first people settled down to make a village here. Every year, after the lottery, Mr. Summers began talking again about a new box, but every year the subject was allowed to fade off without anything being done. The black box grew shabbier each year; by now it was no longer completely black but splintered badly along one side to show the original wood color, and in some places faded or stained.

Mr. Martin and his oldest son, Baxter, held the black box securely on the stool until Mr. Summers had stirred the papers thoroughly with his hand.

Because so much of the ritual had been forgotten or discarded, Mr. Summers had been successful in having slips of paper substituted for the chips of wood that had been used for generations. Chips of wood, Mr. Summers had argued, had been all very well when the village was tiny, but now that the population was more than three hundred and likely to keep on growing, it was necessary to use something that would fit more easily into the black box. The night before the lottery, Mr. Summers and Mr. Graves made up the slips of paper and put them in the box, and it was then taken to the safe of Mr. Summers' coal company and locked up until Mr. Summers was ready to take it to the square next morning. The rest of the year, the box was put away, sometimes one place, sometimes another; it had spent one year in Mr. Graves's barn and another year underfoot in the post office, and sometimes it was set on a shelf in the Martin grocery and left there.

There was a great deal of fussing to be done before Mr. Summers declared the lottery open. There were the lists to make up — of heads of families, heads of households in each family, members of each household in each family. There was the proper swearing-in of Mr. Summers by the postmaster, as the official of the lottery; at one time, some people remembered, there had been a recital of some sort, performed by the official of the lottery, a perfunctory, tuneless chant that had been rattled off duly each year; some people believed that the official of the lottery used to stand just so when he said or sang it, others believed that he was supposed to walk among the people, but years and years ago this part of the ritual had been allowed to lapse. There had been, also, a ritual salute, which the official of the lottery had had to use in addressing each person who came up to draw from the box, but this also had changed with time, until now it was felt necessary only for the official to speak to each person approaching. Mr. Summers was very good at all this; in his clean white shirt and blue jeans, with one hand resting carelessly on the black box, he seemed very proper and important as he talked interminably to Mr. Graves and the Martins.

Just as Mr. Summers finally left off talking and turned to the assembled villagers, Mrs. Hutchinson came hurriedly along the path to the square, her sweater thrown over her shoulders, and slid into place in the back of the crowd. "Clean forgot what day it was," she said to Mrs. Delacroix, who stood next to her, and they both laughed softly. "Thought my old man was out back stacking wood," Mrs. Hutchinson went on, "and then I looked out the window and the kids were gone, and then I remembered it was the twenty-seventh and came a-running." She dried her hands on her apron, and Mrs. Delacroix said, "You're in time, though. They're still talking away up there."

Mrs. Hutchinson craned her neck to see through the crowd and found her husband and children standing near the front. She tapped Mrs. Delacroix on the arm as a farewell and began to make her way through the crowd. The people separated good-humoredly to let her through; two or three people said, in voices just loud enough to be heard across the crowd, "Here comes your Missus, Hutchinson," and "Bill, she made it after all." Mrs. Hutchinson reached her husband, and Mr. Summers, who had been waiting, said cheerfully, "Thought we were going to have to get on without you, Tessie." Mrs. Hutchinson said, grinning, "Wouldn't have me leave m'dishes in the sink, now, would you, Joe?" and soft laughter ran through the crowd as the people stirred back into position after Mrs. Hutchinson's arrival.

"Well, now," Mr. Summers said soberly, "guess we better get started, get this over with, so's we can go back to work. Anybody ain't here?"

"Dunbar," several people said. "Dunbar, Dunbar."

Mr. Summers consulted his list. "Clyde Dunbar," he said. "That's right. He's broke his leg, hasn't he? Who's drawing for him?"

"Me, I guess," a woman said, and Mr. Summers turned to look at her. "Wife draws for her husband," Mrs. Summers said. "Don't you have a grown boy to do it for you, Janey?" Although Mr. Summers and everyone else in the village knew the answer perfectly well, it was the business of the official of the lottery to ask such questions formally. Mr. Summers waited with an expression of polite interest while Mrs. Dunbar answered.

"Horace's not but sixteen yet," Mrs. Dunbar said regretfully. "Guess I gotta fill in for the old man this year."

"Right," Mr. Summers said. He made a note on the list he was holding. Then he asked, "Watson boy drawing this year?"

A tall boy in the crowd raised his hand. "Here," he said. "I'm drawing for m'mother and me." He blinked his eyes nervously and ducked his head as several voices in the crowd said things like "Good fellow, Jack," and "Glad to see your mother's got a man to do it."

"Well," Mr. Summers said, "guess that's everyone. Old Man Warner make it?"

"Here," a voice said, and Mr. Summers nodded.

A sudden hush fell on the crowd as Mr. Summers cleared his throat and looked at the list. "All ready?" he called. "Now, I'll read the names — heads of families first — and the men come up and take a paper out of the box. Keep the paper folded in your hand without looking at it until everyone has had a turn. Everything clear?"

The people had done it so many times that they only half listened to the directions; most of them were quiet, wetting their lips, not looking around. Then Mr. Summers raised one hand high and said, "Adams." A man disengaged himself from the crowd and came forward. "Hi, Steve," Mr. Summers said, and Mr. Adams said, "Hi, Joe." They grinned at one another humorlessly and nervously. Then Mr. Adams reached into the black box and took out a folded paper. He held it firmly by one corner as he turned and went hastily back to his place in the crowd, where he stood a little apart from his family, not looking down at his hand.

"Allen," Mr. Summers said. "Anderson… Bentham."

"Seems like there's no time at all between lotteries any more," Mrs. Delacroix said to Mrs. Graves in the back row. "Seems like we got through with the last one only last week."

"Time sure goes fast," Mrs. Graves said.

"Clark… Delacroix."

"There goes my old man," Mrs. Delacroix said. She held her breath while her husband went forward.

"Dunbar," Mr. Summers said, and Mrs. Dunbar went steadily to the box while one of the women said, "Go on, Janey," and another said, "There she goes."

"We're next," Mrs. Graves said. She watched while Mr. Graves came around from the side of the box, greeted Mr. Summers gravely, and selected a slip of paper from the box. By now, all through the crowd there were men holding the small folded papers in their large hands, turning them over and over nervously. Mrs. Dunbar and her two sons stood together, Mrs. Dunbar holding the slip of paper.

"Harburt… Hutchinson."

"Get up there, Bill," Mrs. Hutchinson said, and the people near her laughed.

"Jones."

"They do say," Mr. Adams said to Old Man Warner, who stood next to him, "that over in the north village they're talking of giving up the lottery."

Old Man Warner snorted. "Pack of crazy fools," he said. "Listening to the young folks, nothing's good enough for *them*. Next thing you know, they'll be wanting to go back to living in caves, nobody work any more, live *that* way for a while. Used to be a saying about 'Lottery in June, corn be heavy soon.' First thing you know, we'd all be eating stewed chickweed and acorns. There's *always* been a lottery," he added petulantly. "Bad enough to see young Joe Summers up there joking with everybody."

"Some places have already quit lotteries," Mrs. Adams said.

"Nothing but trouble in *that*," Old Man Warner said stoutly. "Pack of young fools."

"Martin." And Bobby Martin watched his father go forward. "Overdyke... Percy."

"I wish they'd hurry," Mrs. Dunbar said to her older son. "I wish they'd hurry."

"They're almost through," her son said.

"You get ready to run tell Dad," Mrs. Dunbar said.

Mr. Summers called his own name and then stepped forward precisely and selected a slip from the box. Then he called, "Warner."

"Seventy-seventh year I been in the lottery," Old Man Warner said as he went through the crowd. "Seventy-seventh time."

"Watson." The tall boy came awkwardly through the crowd. Someone said, "Don't be nervous, Jack," and Mr. Summers said, "Take your time, son."

"Zanini."

After that, there was a long pause, a breathless pause, until Mr. Summers, holding his slip of paper in the air, said, "All right, fellows." For a minute, no one moved, and then all the slips of paper were opened. Suddenly, all the women began to speak at once, saying, "Who is it?" "Who's got it?" "Is it the Dunbars?" "Is it the Watsons?" Then the voices began to say, "It's Hutchinson. It's Bill," "Bill Hutchinson's got it."

"Go tell your father," Mrs. Dunbar said to her older son.

People began to look around to see the Hutchinsons. Bill Hutchinson was standing quiet, staring down at the paper in his hand. Suddenly, Tessie Hutchinson shouted to Mr. Summers, "You didn't give him time enough to take any paper he wanted. I saw you. It wasn't fair."

"Be a good sport, Tessie," Mrs. Delacroix called, and Mrs. Graves said, "All of us took the same chance."

"Shut up, Tessie," Bill Hutchinson said.

"Well, everyone," Mr. Summers said, "that was done pretty fast, and now we've got to be hurrying a little more to get done in time." He consulted his next list. "Bill," he said, "you draw for the Hutchinson family. You got any other households in the Hutchinsons?"

"There's Don and Eva," Mrs. Hutchinson yelled. "Make *them* take their chance!"

"Daughters draw with their husbands' families, Tessie," Mr. Summers said gently. "You know that as well as anyone else."

"It wasn't *fair*," Tessie said.

"I guess not, Joe," Bill Hutchinson said regretfully. "My daughter draws with her husband's family, that's only fair. And I've got no other family except the kids."

"Then, as far as drawing for families is concerned, it's you," Mr. Summers said in explanation, "and as far as drawing for households is concerned, that's you, too. Right?"

"Right," Bill Hutchinson said.

"How many kids, Bill?" Mr. Summers asked formally.

"Three," Bill Hutchinson said. "There's Bill, Jr., and Nancy, and little Dave. And Tessie and me."

"All right, then," Mr. Summers said. "Harry, you got their tickets back?"

Mr. Graves nodded and held up the slips of paper. "Put them in the box, then," Mr. Summers directed. "Take Bill's and put it in."

"I think we ought to start over," Mrs. Hutchinson said, as quietly as she could. "I tell you it wasn't *fair*. You didn't give him time enough to choose. *Every*body saw that."

Mr. Graves had selected the five slips and put them in the box, and he dropped all the papers but those onto the ground, where the breeze caught them and lifted them off.

"Listen, everybody," Mrs. Hutchinson was saying to the people around her.

"Ready, Bill?" Mr. Summers asked, and Bill Hutchinson, with one quick glance around at his wife and children, nodded.

"Remember," Mr. Summers said, "take the slips and keep them folded until each person has taken one. Harry, you help little Dave." Mr. Graves took the hand of the little boy, who came willingly with him up to the box. "Take a paper out of the box, Davy," Mr. Summers said. Davy put his hand into the box and laughed. "Take just *one* paper," Mr. Summers said. "Harry, you hold it for him." Mr. Graves took the child's hand and removed the folded paper from the tight fist and held it while little Dave stood next to him and looked up at him wonderingly.

"Nancy next," Mr. Summers said. Nancy was twelve, and her school friends breathed heavily as she went forward, switching her skirt, and took a slip daintily from the box. "Bill, Jr.," Mr. Summers said, and Billy, his face red and his feet over-large, nearly knocked the box over as he got a paper out. "Tessie," Mr. Summers said. She hesitated for a minute, looking around defiantly, and then set her lips and went up to the box. She snatched a paper out and held it behind her.

"Bill," Mr. Summers said, and Bill Hutchinson reached into the box and felt around, bringing his hand out at last with the slip of paper in it.

The crowd was quiet. A girl whispered, "I hope it's not Nancy," and the sound of the whisper reached the edges of the crowd.

"All right," Mr. Summers said. "Open the papers. Harry, you open little Dave's."

Mr. Graves opened the slip of paper and there was a general sigh through the crowd as he held it up and everyone could see that it was blank. Nancy and Bill, Jr., opened theirs at the same time, and both beamed and laughed, turning around to the crowd and holding their slips of paper above their heads.

"Tessie," Mr. Summers said. There was a pause, and then Mr. Summers looked at Bill Hutchinson, and Bill unfolded his paper and showed it. It was blank.

"It's Tessie," Mr. Summers said, and his voice was hushed. "Show us her paper, Bill."

Bill Hutchinson went over to his wife and forced the slip of paper out of her hand. It had a black spot on it, the black spot Mr. Summers had made the night before with the heavy pencil in the coal-company office. Bill Hutchinson held it up, and there was a stir in the crowd.

"All right, folks," Mr. Summers said. "Let's finish quickly."

Although the villagers had forgotten the ritual and lost the original black box, they still remembered to use stones. The pile of stones the boys had made earlier was ready; there were stones on the ground with the blowing scraps of paper that had come out of the box. Mrs. Delacroix selected a stone so large she had to pick it up with both hands and turned to Mrs. Dunbar. "Come on," she said. "Hurry up."

Mrs. Dunbar had small stones in both hands, and she said, gasping for breath, "I can't run at all. You'll have to go ahead and I'll catch up with you."

The children had stones already, and someone gave little Davy Hutchinson a few pebbles.

Tessie Hutchinson was in the center of a cleared space by now, and she held her hands out desperately as the villagers moved in on her. "It isn't fair," she said. A stone hit her on the side of the head.

Old Man Warner was saying, "Come on, come on, everyone." Steve Adams was in the front of the crowd of villagers, with Mrs. Graves beside him.

"It isn't fair, it isn't right," Mrs. Hutchinson screamed, and then they were upon her.

## Reader's Response

▸1 What was your first reaction to this story?

▸2 What questions come to your mind about this story?

## Close Reading

Answer the following questions.

▸1 What is the setting of the story?

▸2 Why have the villagers gathered in the square that morning?

▸3 What are the villagers' attitudes towards the lottery at the beginning of the story?

**a)** Children's attitude

**b)** Men's attitude

**c)** Women's attitude

▸4 The lottery had a history to it. What were some of rituals associated with it that were

**a)** still followed?

**b)** no longer followed?

▸5 What is Old Man Warner's opinion of some villages that have stopped having a lottery?

▸6 What is Tessie Hutchinson's initial attitude toward the lottery?

▸7 How and why does Mrs. Hutchinson's attitude toward the lottery change?

▸8 In your opinion, what is the theme of the story?

WRITER'S CRAFT

### Male / Female Stereotypes

▸1 Who is portrayed as more dominant, males or females?

▸2 List four examples from the story that support your answer to question 1.

▸3 In your opinion, how do the male/female roles reinforce the meaning of the story?

We will consider foreshadowing, irony, and narration and point of view in the following analysis.

### Foreshadowing

▸▸▸ ***Foreshadowing is a literary device that writers use to give clues to future events. Jackson uses many examples of foreshadowing in the story. One example of foreshadowing is seen in the quotation, "Bobby Martin had already stuffed his pockets full of stones, and the other boys soon followed his example, selecting the smoothest and roundest stones."*** ◂◂◂

▸1 **a)** Give three examples of foreshadowing that you discover in the story.

▸2 Explain how Tessie's change in attitude is an example of foreshadowing that helps to build tension in the plot.

### Irony

▸▸▸ ***Irony refers to the device of writing or saying one thing, but meaning the opposite.*** ◂◂◂

▸1 Why are the ordinary names of the villagers, such as Mr. Allen, Mr. Anderson, Mrs. Dunbar, the Hutchinsons, etc., ironic?

▸2 Explain how the names of the characters such as Mr. Summers and Old Man Warner are ironic.

▸3 Explain how the setting of the story is ironic.

▸4 How is the title of the story "The Lottery" ironic?

### NARRATION AND POINT OF VIEW

▸1 **a)** What type of narrator tells this story and what is the point of view?

**b)** How does the author's choice of narrator and point of view contrast with the horrific subject of the story?

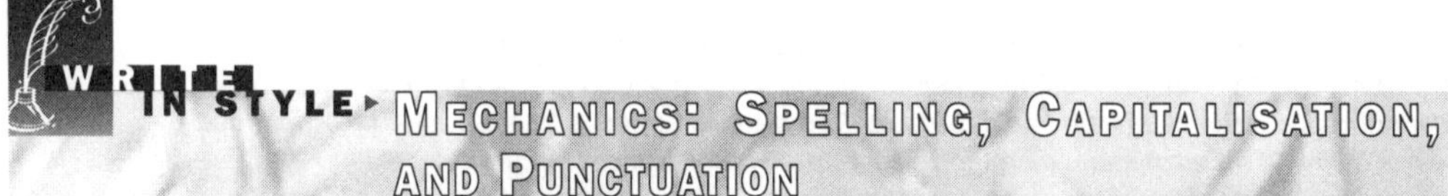


## MECHANICS: SPELLING, CAPITALISATION, AND PUNCTUATION

**It is important to pay close attention to the mechanics or technical aspects of writing. When you revise a text, you must pay close attention to spelling, capitalisation, and punctuation. Sometimes you will have a choice between certain alternatives (for example, placing a comma before *and* in a list or writing *centre* or *center*). The important idea to keep in mind is** consistency. **In other words, whatever form or format you choose, you must stick to it throughout the entire text you are writing, whether you are writing a paragraph, an essay, or a research assignment. Do not shift back and forth between two alternatives.**

### SPELLING

If you are using a word processor, you can do an automatic spell check after choosing the appropriate dictionary (See American, Canadian, and British spelling below). If you are not using a computer, you should consult a dictionary when in doubt about the spelling of a word.

Here are a few basic rules that will help you spell certain words correctly.

**1. Noun Plurals**

- Add **s** to most nouns but **es** to nouns ending in **s**, **sh**, **ch** and **x**

  *EXAMPLE: car → cars; church → churches; box → boxes, bus → buses*

- In words that end in **f** or **fe**, change the **f** to **v** and add **es**

  ***Exceptions:*** *Many words ending in* ***f*** *or* ***fe*** *take the* ***ves*** *plural ending,*

  *EXAMPLES: knife → knives; half → halves (but not belief/beliefs, roof/roofs, chief/chiefs).*

  ***Exceptions:*** *Man → men; child → children; woman → women; mouse → mice; goose → geese; foot → feet; tooth → teeth*

  ***Exceptions:*** *Words borrowed from other languages: basis → bases; hypothesis → hypotheses; criterion → criteria; medium → media*

**2. Numbers**

- Spell out any numbers that begin a sentence.

  *EXAMPLE: **Five hundred** people attended the concert.*

- In essays that are **not** scientific, spell out numbers that do not consist of more than two words.

  *EXAMPLE: The narrator of the story had robbed **twenty-five** banks before being caught.*

  (You may wish to check with your instructor, as this rule does not always apply. The field of psychology, for example, may expect you to use numerals in your essays.)

- Use numerals for time, dates, decimals, percentages, statistics, measurements and scores, exact amounts of money, addresses, chapters, pages, scenes, and line numbers.

**3. It's/its**

*It's* is the contraction for *it is*. *EXAMPLE:* **It's** Friday today.
*Its* is the possessive form. *EXAMPLE:* The cat licked **its** fur.

**4. ie/ei**

- Use **i** before **e** except after **c** or when sounded like *ay* as in *neighbour* and *weigh*.

  *EXAMPLE: bel**ie**ve, repr**ie**ve but rec**ei**ve, sl**ei**gh*

  ***Exceptions:*** *science, species, height, either, neither, leisure, foreign, seize.*

**5. Double consonants**

When adding a suffix, double the final consonants of a word when

- a vowel precedes the consonant in a one-syllable word; *EXAMPLE:* sit → si**tt**ing; hot → ho**tt**est
- the last syllable of the word is stressed; *EXAMPLE:* confer → confe**rr**ed but develop → developed (The final syllable in *confer* is stressed but the final syllable in *develop* is not.)

**6. y/i**

When adding the suffix **s** or **ed** to a word ending in a consonant followed by **y**, change **y** to **i** and add the suffix.

*EXAMPLE: carr**y** → carr**ies**, carr**ied** (but note, carrying because in this word you hear two separate* i *sounds when it is pronounced).*

- vowel followed by **y**, do not change **y**;

  *EXAMPLE: play → plays, played, playing*

  ***Exceptions:*** *pay → paid; say → said, lay → laid*

**7. Prefixes and Suffixes**

When adding a prefix or a suffix to a word, various rules apply and you may need to check a dictionary. Often, however, the original base word does not change.

*EXAMPLE: mature → premature; awful → awfully or change → changeable.*

### ***American, Canadian and British English***

Canadian English is influenced by both the language of our British forbears and that of our American neighbours. Sometimes Canadians prefer a particular spelling, but other times they can choose between two spellings. Usually a Canadian dictionary, such as the *Gage Canadian Dictionary*, will list the preferred spelling first. Vocabulary sometimes varies too; British and American meanings can be very different. As mentioned above, when you have a choice, it is important to be consistent throughout your essay.

**SPELLING VARIANTS**

| **British** | **American** | **Canadian** |
|---|---|---|
| **-yse**, **-ise**: analyse, criticise | **-yze**, -ize: analyze, criticize | either |
| **-our**: colour, flavour | **-or**: color, flavor | **-our** preferred |
| **-re**: centre, theatre | **-er**: center, theater | either |
| **-xion**: reflexion, connexion | **-ction**: reflection, connection | **-ction** |
| **-ight**: night, light | **-ite**: nite, lite **(slang)** | **-ight** |
| cheque | check | either |
| defence | defense | defence |
| dialogue | dialog or dialogue | either |
| programme | program | either |
| judgement | judgment | either |
| **double consonant -s, -l:** | **single consonant -s, -l:** | either |
| travelled, marvellous, focussed | traveled, marvelous, focused | either |

In Canada, words doubling as nouns and verbs end in **-ise, -ice: -ise** in the verb form,
*EXAMPLE: Every day, I practise piano.*

**-ice** in the noun form,
*EXAMPLE: I enjoy doing piano practice.*

**VOCABULARY VARIANTS**

| **British** | **American** | **Canadian** |
|---|---|---|
| lorry | truck | truck |
| lift | elevator | elevator |
| boot | trunk | trunk |
| flat | apartment | apartment (flat: rented, self-contained part of a house) |
| tap | faucet | tap |
| holiday | vacation | holiday, vacation |
| biscuits | cookies | biscuits, cookies |
| veranda | porch | veranda, porch |
| purse | pocketbook | purse |
| pictures | movies | movies |
| telly | T.V. | T.V. |
| pudding | dessert | dessert |

#### *Original Canadian Words*

Here are some typical Canadian words that do not come from either British or American English:

*EXAMPLES: muskeg, tuque, bush pilot, electoral riding, chinook, the Prairies, portage*

### *Canadian Pronunciation*

Very different from British pronunciation, Canadian pronunciation is similar to the pronunciation existing in certain regions of the United States. However, Canadians always give themselves away when they pronounce words ending in **-out**, such as *out* and *about*, or when they pronounce the last letter of the alphabet as "zed" (instead of the American "zee") and when they finish a sentence with **-eh**?!

**Exercise A: Correcting Misspelled Words**

Underline all the incorrectly spelled words and write them properly in the space provided. (Hint: there are three mistakes in each sentence.)

▸**1** The girl shreiked with delight at her loss in wieght of eigth pounds.

▸**2** I refered her to the manager because she sayd that she had already paied her bill.

▸**3** When he played football, he usualy carryed the ball a full 25 yards before the guards stoped him.

▸**4** Those hypothesis do not meet with the womens' approuval.

▸**5** Last nite, we purchased two boxs of special envelopes and sent the films to be developped.

**Capitalisation**

Capitalise the following:

- The first word in a sentence or direct quotation, the pronoun I, and proper nouns and adjectives
  *EXAMPLE: the Milky Way*
  *Susan asked, "What is the most interesting book that you have ever read?"*
- Certain abbreviations, especially titles
  *EXAMPLE: Dr. Guy Charpentier, Line Pritchard, M.D., Sen. Pat McDonald, 2:00 A.M. (or 2:00 a.m.), 2005 A.D.*
- Full and official titles of people, organisations, documents, literary works
  *EXAMPLE: Prime Minister Jean Chrétien;*
- Always capitalise the first and last words in the title of a literary work, film, song, or work of art. Capitalise all other words in the title except articles, conjunctions, and prepositions.
  *EXAMPLE: One Flew over the Cuckoo's Nest*
- The names of the days, months, and holidays
  *EXAMPLE: Monday, March, Easter*
- The names of historical periods, events, and eras
  *EXAMPLE: the Renaissance, the Second World War*
- The names of and pronouns referring to the Deity, religions, and religious institutions
  *EXAMPLE: God, Buddha, Islam, Jesus and His apostles*
- The points of the compass when they refer to a specific region
  *EXAMPLE: John is working in the West this summer.*
- The names of specific school courses
  *EXAMPLE: English 101*
- Personifications
  *EXAMPLE: O Love, thou wond'rous thing!*

**Exercise B: Practising Capitalisation**

Place capital letters where they are needed in the following sentences.

▶1 former british prime minister margaret thatcher and former american president ronald reagan seemed to agree on many important points.

▶2 he and i will arrive on easter monday which occurs on april 26 this year.

▶3 "what," she asked him, "is the answer to the last question on the geography 210 exam?

▶4 "hi, mom," said the boy. "what are we having for lunch?"

▶5 did you enjoy reading the catcher in the rye by j.d. salinger, or did you prefer for whom the bell tolls by ernest hemingway?

▶6 during the renaissance many christians believed that god ruled his people with an iron hand.

▶7 i'm going to the west next summer to work at chateau lake louise near banff, alberta.

## PUNCTUATION

The role of punctuation is to make writing easier to understand. Most punctuation marks serve to separate or end the writer's thoughts.

### Punctuation for Separating Parts of Sentences: Comma, Semi-colon, Colon, Dash, Parentheses, Brackets

Comma **,** Use a comma (or commas):

- To separate items in a series
- After introductory words, phrases, or clauses
- To set off words of direct address or mild interjections
- To mark off additional, but not essential, information (e.g., non-restrictive clauses, phrases, and appositives) about a noun preceding the information
- Around parenthetical expressions (words that interrupt the thought)
- Before a conjunction (and, but, for, or, nor, so, yet) linking two independent clauses in a compound sentence
- Between the day (or month) and the year and after the year if the sentence continues
- Before examples introduced by *such as* or *especially*
- After identification of the speaker and before a direct quotation

EXAMPLE: *I bought a carton of milk, a dozen eggs, and a box of cookies at the store.*
*My brother's son was born April 1, 1975.*

Semi-colon **;** Use a semi-colon or semi-colons:

- To connect two closely related thoughts (independent clauses) instead of with a conjunction
- Before conjunctive adverbs such as nevertheless, however, consequently, and others in two closely related clauses
- Between items in a series that already contain commas

EXAMPLES: *There was a tornado warning yesterday; the meteorologists had seen funnel clouds forming.*
*There was a tornado warning yesterday; however, many people were unaware of anything unusual.*

Colon **:** Use a colon:

- To introduce a list (but not after a verb or a preposition)
- To introduce a formal quotation that is a complete sentence or a block quotation
- After the salutation in a business letter

- When using numerals to express time
- In plays, biblical, and volume references
- To introduce a subtitle

EXAMPLE: *Please bring the following for the camping trip: tent, sleeping bag, warm clothes, and food for three days.*

Parentheses ( )

Use parentheses around supplementary explanations and comments:

EXAMPLE: *The supermodel (a snob) looked down her nose at the reporter asking questions during the interview.*

Dash — Use a dash:

- Before and/or after parenthetical elements, or before a sudden break in thought
- To show unfinished or interrupted dialogue
- After a statement, to explain or expand it

EXAMPLE: *Shakespeare's Hamlet — the protagonist — was a very indecisive character.*

Brackets [ ]

Use brackets to insert an editorial comment in quoted material:

EXAMPLE: *The film critic gave the movie a great review, saying that "it* [Casablanca] *was the best romance" he had seen in a long time.*

### Terminal Punctuation: Period, Question Mark, Exclamation Point

Period . Use a period:

- At the end of statements or commands
- After certain abbreviations (but not metric symbols)
- To indicate decimals

Question Mark ?

Use a question mark after a question or to indicate uncertainty.

Exclamation Point !

Use an exclamation point after a sentence that expresses strong emotion or surprise.

### Other Punctuation

Hyphen - Use a hyphen:

- In certain compound words (nouns, adjectives, phrases)
- To divide a word at the end of a line if you are not using a word processor
- In compound numbers from twenty-one to ninety-nine and with fractions used as adjectives.

EXAMPLE: *The recipe said to use one-half kilo of sugar.*

Apostrophe ' Use an apostrophe:

- To show possession (mainly for animate objects)
- For singular and plural nouns not ending in *s*
- For plural nouns ending in *s*
- In contractions

EXAMPLE: *My brother's girlfriend is an opera singer.*

*Quotation Marks* “ ” Use quotation marks:

- Around direct speech and dialogue
- Around short quotations in essays, term papers, and so on
- Around titles of short stories, poems, songs, essays, book chapters, and magazine and newspaper articles
- To emphasise specific words in a text
- Around definitions

*EXAMPLE: The prisoner said, "I am not guilty of murdering that man."*

*Ellipsis Marks* ... Use ellipsis marks:

- To indicate that something has been omitted in quoted material
- To show a pause in dialogue

*EXAMPLE: Juliet declares her love for Romeo on the balcony when she says, "O Romeo, O Romeo..."*

*Italics* ***italics*** Use italics:

- For titles of books magazines, newspapers, plays and movies, and for names of ships or planes
- To emphasise specific words in a text
- For foreign words or phrases in a text

*EXAMPLE:* My favourite play is *Man and Superman* by George Bernard Shaw.

Note: If you are writing a text by hand, use underlining instead of italics.

**Exercise C: Punctuating Correctly**

Add the necessary punctuation to the following sentences.

▸1 The flight attendant said Dont let the dog out of its cage until an American inspector has given you the OK

▸2 Twenty five students were present for the final review nevertheless six of them failed the exam

▸3 Do you know if each of us must bring the following two pens three pencils a notebook and a dictionary

▸4 The singular is child the plural is children

▸5 Wow I won the Chalmers Award Which prize did you win

▸6 She got up a 6 am and started studying the period from the second century BC to the end of first century AD

▸7 Mark Twain you know he was an amazing speaker gave lectures as far away as Australia

▸8 The boys jackets were left on the chairs and someone stole six of them

▸9 Who was it who said One small step for mankind when he first stepped onto the moons surface

▸10 One of my favourite short stories is The Lottery by Shirley Jackson and one of my favourite books is The Bone People by Keri Hulme

## Paragraph Practice

▸1 Write a paragraph about the ending of "The Lottery." Did you expect this ending?

▸2 Write a paragraph on the importance of traditions in family and society.

## WRAP-UP DISCUSSION OR WRITING ACTIVITIES

▸1 Examine the use of traditional gender roles in "The Lottery."

▸2 What aspects of human nature are explored in "The Lottery"?

▸3 Discuss how Jackson develops characterisation. Are the characters in the story fully developed or are they stereotypes?

▸4 Compare the dramatic and narrative structures of the story.

▸5 What is the most important theme of this story? Support your opinion with strong arguments.

▸6 Discuss whether or not "The Lottery" is realistic.

# References

## PRINT


**BIOGRAPHY**

Friedman, Lenemaja. *Shirley Jackson*. Boston:Twayne, 1975.

Hall, Joan Wylie. *Shirley Jackson: A Study of Short Fiction*. New York: Twayne, 1993.

Oppenheimer, Judy. *Private Demons: The Life of Shirley Jackson*. New York: G.P. Putnam, 1988.

**CRITICISM**

Carpenter, Lynette. "Domestic Comedy, Black Comedy, and Real Life: Shirley Jackson, a Woman Writer." In *Faith of a (Woman) Writer*, ed. by Alice Kessler-Harris and William McBrien. Westport, CT: Greenwood Press, 1988, p. 146.

Kosenko, Peter. "A Marxist/Feminist Reading of Shirley Jackson's 'The Lottery'." *The New Orleans Review*. Spring 1985, p. 225.

Whittier, Gayle. " 'The Lottery' as Misogynist Parable." *Women's Studies*. Jan. 1991, v. 18, n. 4, p. 353.


## INTERNET

Here are some very interesting Internet references that you may wish to check out relating to this chapter. Please note that as sites change location from time to time, some of the links may not work. We also suggest that you use a search engine to find other sites of interest on the Internet.


**LINKS:**

http://www.bhsalumni.net/sjack.htm
http://www.nt1.nagasaki-gaigo.ac.jp/ishikawa/amlit/j/jacksonshi21.htm

**BIOGRAPHY AND SELECTED WORKS OF THE WRITER:**

Jackson http://www.darkecho.com/darkecho/archives/jackson.html
http://www.kutztown.edu/~reagan/jackson.html
http://www.eng.fju.edu.tw/EnglishLiterature/Lottery/el-author-lottery.htm
http://www.salon.com/jan97/jackson970106.html
http://underthesun.cc/Classics/Jackson/shirleyjackson.htm

**CRITICISM:**

http://www.bcsd.org/BHS/english/mag97/papers/jackson.htm
http://home.rochester.rr.com/biffio/ed/eklor.html
http://www.netwood.net/~kosenko/jackson.html

UNIT 1.5

# THE VELDT

## CHAPTER CONTENTS

- **READING:** "The Veldt" by Ray Bradbury; author's biography, literary trends (science fiction)
- **WRITING:** literary essays (introduction, body, conclusion; thesis statement, supporting details, organisation)
- **LITERARY ELEMENTS:** plot (dramatic and narrative structure); setting; theme; foreshadowing symbolism; irony
- **GRAMMAR AND VOCABULARY:** revising, editing, and proofreading

## ABOUT THE AUTHOR

RAY BRADBURY (1920- ) Many consider Ray Bradbury to be one of the most influential writers in the development of science fiction as a genre. He was born in Waukegan, Illinois, in 1920, and by 1931 was already writing short stories. Throughout the 1940s, he sold an increasing number of stories to various magazines, and with the publication of the *Martian Chronicles* in 1951 and *Fahrenheit 451* in 1953, he established himself as a prominent author of science fiction. He has published more than five hundred works, including short stories, novels, plays, television and movie scripts, and poems. Over forty of his short stories were adapted for a television series (*The Ray Bradbury Television Theater*) and several of his novels were turned into movies.

Many of Bradbury's best stories deal with the effects of technology on humankind. Although the action is set in the future, they actually deal with present life and concerns. Other themes he developed include racism, nuclear war, censorship, and the importance of human values and imagination.

Throughout his life Bradbury has been awarded many prizes, including the O. Henry Memorial Award, the Benjamin Franklin Award, the World Fantasy Award for Lifetime Achievement, and the Grand Master Award from the Science Fiction Writers of America. His animated film, *Icarus Montgolfier Wright*, about the history of aviation, was nominated for an Oscar. A crater on the moon was named the Dandelion Crater by an Apollo astronaut after Bradbury's novel, *Dandelion Wine*.

Apart from writing, Bradbury actively participated in the teams that designed, among others, the United States Pavilion at the 1964 New York World's Fair, the Spaceship Earth exhibition at Epcot Center in Florida, and the Orbitron space ride at Euro-Disney in Paris.

## LITERARY TRENDS OF THE TIMES

The short story genre evolved into more complex variations during the early twentieth century as more writers began to experiment with the form. Realism continued to be explored after World War II, the Cold War, the Civil Rights movement, the hippie revolution, the sexual revolution, the Vietnam War, and the explosion of global communications. Writers of realistic stories tried to combine the best characteristics of both journalism and fiction: the detailed portrayal of real events married to the psychological truths and insights found in great fiction. This mixture often made stories more realistic in terms of setting and historical background, but it muddied the border between real and fictional people and events.

During the twentieth century, scientific and technological knowledge increased at exponential rates. Einstein's Theory of Relativity revolutionised the way many human beings viewed their place in the universe. Simple answers to the great questions of existence no longer appeared satisfactory in many cultures. Complexity and diversity increased as human populations exploded, and distances disappeared through the rise of global communications. In the 1950s, television, with its visual impact, displaced the written word as the best medium for telling stories of physical adventure and suspenseful action. Many story writers then turned inward to explore inner psychological turmoil and conflict, or worlds that do not exist. Influenced by scientific and technological developments, authors such as Ray Bradbury, Arthur C. Clarke, Frank Herbert, Robert Heinlein, Isaac Asimov, and Ursula Le Guin, to name but a few, began to compose more fanciful types of stories set in imaginary times and places. Science fiction grew into its adolescence and adulthood. Although these science fiction writers let their imaginations roam, their stories often deal with very real problems that humankind is either just beginning to face or seems likely to face in the future.

### Warm-Up Discussion Topics

▸1 Is the development of new technology synonymous with progress? Why or why not?

▸2 How does new technology affect your life and habits?

**INITIAL READING ▸ Many people have dreamed of escaping the drudgery of household chores. They would then be free to spend their time on more important things. Read on to discover what such a life could be like.**

1951

STORY

# The Veldt

Ray Bradbury

"George," I wish you'd look at the nursery."

"What's wrong with it?"

"I don't know."

"Well, then."

"I just want you to look at it, is all, or call a psychologist in to look at it."

"What would a psychologist want with a nursery?"

"You know very well what he'd want." His wife paused in the middle of the kitchen and watched the stove busy humming to itself, making supper for four.

"It's just that the nursery is different now than it was."

"All right, let's have a look."

They walked down the hall of their soundproofed, Happylife Home, which had cost them thirty thousand dollars installed, this house which clothed and fed and rocked them to sleep and played and sang and was good to them. Their approach sensitized a switch somewhere and the nursery light flicked on when they came within ten feet of it. Similarly, behind them, in the halls, lights went on and off as they left them behind, with a soft automaticity.

"Well," said George Hadley.

They stood on the thatched floor of the nursery. It was forty feet across by forty feet long and thirty feet high — it had cost half again as much as the rest of the house. "But nothing's too good for our children," George had said.

The nursery was silent. It was empty as a jungle glade at hot high noon. The walls were blank and two dimensional. Now, as George and Lydia Hadley stood in the center of the room, the walls began to purr and recede into crystalline distance, it seemed, and presently an African veldt appeared, in three dimensions; on all sides, in colors reproduced to the final pebble and bit of straw. The ceiling above them became a deep sky with a hot yellow sun.

George Hadley felt the perspiration start on his brow.

"Let's get out of the sun," he said. "This is a little too real. But I don't see anything wrong."

"Wait a moment, you'll see," said his wife.

Now the hidden odorophonics were beginning to blow a wind of odor at the two people in the middle of the baked veldtland. The hot straw smell of lion grass, the cool green smell of the hidden water hole, the great rusty smell of animals, the smell of dust like a red paprika in the hot air. And now the sounds: the thump of distant antelope feet on grassy sod, the papery rustling of vultures. A shadow passed through the sky. The shadow flickered on George Hadley's upturned, sweating face.

"Filthy creatures," he heard his wife say.

"The vultures."

"You see, there are the lions, far over, that way. Now they're on their way to the water hole. They've just been eating," said Lydia. "I don't know what."

"Some animal." George Hadley put his hand up to shield off the burning light from his squinted eyes. "A zebra or a baby giraffe, maybe."

"Are you sure?" His wife sounded peculiarly tense.

"No, it's a little late to be sure," he said, amused. "Nothing over there I can see but cleaned bone, and the vultures dropping for what's left."

"Did you hear that scream?" she asked.

"No."

"About a minute ago?"

"Sorry, no."

The lions were coming. And again George Hadley was filled with admiration for the mechanical genius who had conceived this room. A miracle of efficiency selling for an absurdly low price. Every home should have one. Oh, occasionally they frightened you with their clinical accuracy, they startled you, gave you a twinge, but most of the time what fun for everyone, not only your own son and daughter, but for yourself when you felt like a quick jaunt to a foreign land, a quick change of scenery. Well, here it was!

And here were the lions now, fifteen feet away, so real, so feverishly and startlingly real that you could feel the prickling fur on your hand, and your mouth was stuffed with the dusty upholstery smell of their heated pelts, and the yellow of them was in your eyes like the yellow of an exquisite French tapestry, the yellows of lions and summer grass, and the sound of the matted lion lungs exhaling on the silent noontide, and the smell of meat from the panting, dripping mouths.

The lions stood looking at George and Lydia Hadley with terrible green-yellow eyes.

"Watch out!" screamed Lydia.

The lions came running at them.

Lydia bolted and ran. Instinctively, George sprang after her. Outside, in the hall, with the door slammed, he was laughing and she was crying, and they both stood appalled at the other's reaction.

"George!"

"Lydia! Oh, my dear poor sweet Lydia!"

"They almost got us!"

"Walls, Lydia, remember; crystal walls, that's all they are. Oh, they look real, I must admit — Africa in your parlor — but it's all dimensional superreactionary, supersensitive color film and mental tape film behind glass screens. It's all odorophonics and sonics, Lydia. Here's my handkerchief."

"I'm afraid." She came to him and put her body against him and cried steadily. "Did you see? Did you feel? It's too real."

"Now, Lydia..."

"You've got to tell Wendy and Peter not to read any more on Africa."

"Of course — of course." He patted her.

"Promise?"

"Sure."

"And lock the nursery for a few days until I get my nerves settled."

"You know how difficult Peter is about that. When I punished him a month ago by locking the nursery for even a few hours — the tantrum he threw! And Wendy too. They live for the nursery."

"It's got to be locked, that's all there is to it."

"All right." Reluctantly he locked the huge door. "You've been working too hard. You need a rest."

"I don't know — I don't know," she said, blowing her nose, sitting down in a chair that immediately began to rock and comfort her. "Maybe I don't have enough to do. Maybe I have time to think too much. Why don't we shut the whole house off for a few days and take a vacation?"

"You mean you want to fry my eggs for me?"

"Yes." She nodded.

"And darn my socks?"

"Yes." A frantic, watery-eyed nodding.

"And sweep the house?"

"Yes, yes — oh, yes!"

"But I thought that's why we bought this house, so we wouldn't have to do anything?"

"That's just it. I feel like I don't belong here. The house is wife and mother now and nursemaid. Can I compete with an African veldt? Can I give a bath and scrub the children as efficiently or quickly as the automatic scrub bath can? I can not. And it isn't just me. It's you. You've been awfully nervous lately."

"I suppose I have been smoking too much."

"You look as if you didn't know what to do with yourself in this house, either. You smoke a little more every morning and drink a little more every afternoon and need a little more sedative every night. You're beginning to feel unnecessary too."

"Am I?" He paused and tried to feel into himself to see what was really there.

"Oh, George!" She looked beyond him, at the nursery door. "Those lions can't get out of there, can they?"

He looked at the door and saw it tremble as if something had jumped against it from the other side.

"Of course not," he said.

At dinner they ate alone, for Wendy and Peter were at a special plastic carnival across town and had televised home to say they'd be late, to go ahead eating. So George Hadley, bemused, sat watching the dining-room table produce warm dishes of food from its mechanical interior.

"We forgot the ketchup," he said.

"Sorry," said a small voice within the table, and ketchup appeared.

As for the nursery, thought George Hadley, it won't hurt for the children to be locked out of it awhile. Too much of anything isn't good for anyone. And it was clearly indicated that the children had been spending a little too much time on Africa. That sun. He could feel it on his neck, still, like a hot paw. And the lions. And the smell of blood. Remarkable how the nursery caught the telepathic emanations of the children's minds and created life to fill their every desire. The children thought lions, and there were lions. The children thought zebras, and there were zebras. Sun — sun. Giraffes — giraffes. Death and death.

That last. He chewed tastelessly on the meat that the table had cut for him. Death thoughts. They were awfully young, Wendy and Peter, for death thoughts. Or, no, you were never too young, really. Long before you knew what death was you were wishing it on someone else. When you were two years old you were shooting people with cap pistols.

But this — the long, hot African veldt — the awful death in the jaws of a lion. And repeated again and again.

"Where are you going?"

He didn't answer Lydia. Preoccupied, he let the lights glow softly on ahead of him, extinguished behind him as he padded to the nursery door. He listened against it. Far away, a lion roared.

He unlocked the door and opened it. Just before he stepped inside, he heard a faraway scream. And then another roar from the lions, which subsided quickly.

He stepped into Africa. How many times in the last year had he opened this door and found Wonderland, Alice, the Mock Turtle, or Aladdin and his Magical Lamp, or Jack Pumpkinhead of Oz, or Dr. Doolittle, or the cow jumping over a very real-appearing moon — all the delightful contraptions of a make-believe world. How often had he seen Pegasus flying in the sky ceiling, or seen fountains of red fireworks, or heard angel voices singing. But now, this yellow hot Africa, this bake oven with murder in the heat. Perhaps Lydia was right. Perhaps they needed a little vacation from the fantasy which was growing a bit too real for ten-year-old children. It was all right to exercise one's mind with gymnastic fantasies, but when the lively child mind settled on one pattern...? It seemed that, at a distance, for the past month, he had heard lions roaring, and smelled their strong odor seeping as far away as his study door. But, being busy, he had paid it no attention.

George Hadley stood on the African grassland alone. The lions looked up from their feeding, watching him. The only flaw to the illusion was the open door through which he could see his wife, far down the dark hall, like a framed picture, eating her dinner abstractedly.

"Go away," he said to the lions.

They did not go.

He knew the principle of the room exactly. You sent out your thoughts. Whatever you thought would appear.

"Let's have Aladdin and his lamp," he snapped.

The veldtland remained; the lions remained.

"Come on, room! I demand Aladdin!" he said.

Nothing happened. The lions mumbled in their baked pelts.

"Aladdin!"

He went back to dinner. "The fool room's out of order," he said. "It won't respond."

"Or."

"Or what?"

"Or it can't respond," said Lydia, "because the children have thought about Africa and lions and killing so many days that the room's in a rut."

"Could be."

"Or Peter's set it to remain that way."

"Set it?"

"He may have got into the machinery and fixed something."

"Peter doesn't know machinery."

"He's a wise one for ten. That I.Q. of his —"

"Nevertheless."

"Hello, Mom. Hello, Dad."

The Hadleys turned. Wendy and Peter were coming in the front door, cheeks like peppermint candy, eyes like bright blue agate marbles, a smell of ozone on their jumpers from their trip in the helicopter.

"You're just in time for supper," said both parents.

"We're full of strawberry ice cream and hot dogs," said the children, holding hands. "But we'll sit and watch."

"Yes, come tell us about the nursery," said George Hadley.

The brother and sister blinked at him and then at each other. "Nursery?"

"All about Africa and everything," said the father with false joviality.

"I don't understand," said Peter.

"Your mother and I were just traveling through Africa with rod and reel; Tom Swift and his Electric Lion," said George Hadley.

"There's no Africa in the nursery," said Peter simply.

"Oh, come now, Peter. We know better."

"I don't remember any Africa," said Peter to Wendy. "Do you?"

"No."

"Run see and come tell."

She obeyed.

"Wendy, come back here!" said George Hadley, but she was gone. The house lights followed her like a flock of fireflies. Too late, he realized he had forgotten to lock the nursery door after his last inspection.

"Wendy'll look and come tell us," said Peter.

"She doesn't have to tell me. I've seen it."

"I'm sure you're mistaken, Father."

"I'm not, Peter. Come along now."

But Wendy was back. "It's not Africa," she said breathlessly.

"We'll see about this," said George Hadley, and they all walked down the hall together and opened the nursery door.

There was a green, lovely forest, a lovely river, a purple mountain, high voices singing, and Rima, lovely and mysterious, lurking in the trees with colorful flights of butterflies, like animated bouquets, lingering on her long hair. The African veldtland was gone. The lions were gone. Only Rima was here now, singing a song so beautiful that it brought tears to your eyes.

George Hadley looked in at the changed scene. "Go to bed," he said to the children.

They opened their mouths.

"You heard me," he said.

They went off to the air closet, where a wind sucked them like brown leaves up the flue to their slumber rooms.

George Hadley walked through the singing glade and picked up something that lay in the corner near where the lions had been. He walked slowly back to his wife.

"What is that?" she asked.

He showed it to her. The smell of hot grass was on it and the smell of a lion. There were drops of saliva on it, it had been chewed, and there were blood smears on both sides.

He closed the nursery door and locked it, tight.

In the middle of the night he was still awake and he knew his wife was awake. "Do you think Wendy changed it?" she said at last, in the dark room.

"Of course."

"Made it from a veldt into a forest and put Rima there instead of lions?"

"Yes."

"Why?"

"I don't know. But it's staying locked until I find out."

"How did your wallet get there?"

"I don't know anything," he said, "except that I'm beginning to be sorry we bought that room for the children. If children are neurotic at all, a room like that —"

"It's supposed to help them work off their neuroses in a healthful way."

"I'm starting to wonder." He stared at the ceiling.

"We've given the children everything they ever wanted. Is this our reward — secrecy, disobedience?"

"Who was it said, 'Children are carpets, they should be stepped on occasionally?' We've never lifted a hand. They're insufferable — let's admit it. They come and go when they like; they treat us as if we were offspring. They're spoiled and we're spoiled."

"They're been acting funny ever since you forbade them to take the rocket to New York a few months ago."

"They're not old enough to do that alone, I explained."

"Nevertheless, I've noticed they've been decidedly cool toward us since."

"I think I'll have David McClean come tomorrow morning to have a look at Africa."

"But it's not Africa now, it's Green Mansions country and Rima."

"I have a feeling it'll be Africa again before then."

A moment later they heard the screams.

Two screams. Two people screaming from downstairs. And then a roar of lions.

"Wendy and Peter aren't in their rooms," said his wife.

He lay in his bed with his beating heart. "No," he said. "They've broken into the nursery."

"Those screams — they sound familiar."

"Do they?"

"Yes, awfully."

And although their beds tried very hard, the two adults couldn't be rocked to sleep for another hour. A smell of cats was in the night air.

"Father?" said Peter.

"Yes."

Peter looked at his shoes. He never looked at his father any more, nor at his mother. "You aren't going to lock up the nursery for good, are you?"

"That all depends."

"On what?" snapped Peter.

"On you and your sister. If you intersperse this Africa with a little variety — oh, Sweden perhaps, or Denmark or China —"

"I thought we were free to play as we wished."

"You are, within reasonable bounds."

"What's wrong with Africa, Father?"

"Oh, so now you admit you have been conjuring up Africa, do you?"

"I wouldn't want the nursery locked up," said Peter coldly. "Ever."

"Matter of fact, we're thinking of turning the whole house off for about a month. Live sort of a carefree one-for-all existence."

"That sounds dreadful! Would I have to tie my own shoes instead of letting the shoe tier do it? And brush my own teeth and comb my hair and give myself a bath?"

"It would be fun for a change, don't you think?"

"No, it would be horrid. I didn't like it when you took out the picture painter last month."

"That's because I wanted you to learn to paint all by yourself, son."

"I don't want to do anything but look and listen and smell; what else is there to do?"

"All right, go play in Africa."

"Will you shut off the house sometime soon?"

"We're considering it."

"I don't think you'd better consider it any more, Father."

"I won't have any threats from my son!"

"Very well." And Peter strolled off to the nursery.

"Am I on time?" said David McClean.

"Breakfast?" asked George Hadley.

"Thanks, had some. What's the trouble?"

"David, you're a psychologist."

"I should hope so."

"Well, then, have a look at our nursery. You saw it a year ago when you dropped by; did you notice anything peculiar about it then?"

"Can't say I did; the usual violences, a tendency toward a slight paranoia here or there, usual in children because they feel persecuted by parents constantly, but, oh, really nothing."

They walked down the hall. "I locked the nursery up," explained the father, "and the children broke back into it during the night. I let them stay so they could form the patterns for you to see."

There was a terrible screaming from the nursery.

"There it is," said George Hadley. "See what you make of it."

They walked in on the children without rapping.

The screams had faded. The lions were feeding.

"Run outside a moment, children," said George Hadley. "No, don't change the mental combination. Leave the walls as they are. Get!"

With the children gone, the two men stood studying the lions clustered at a distance, eating with great relish whatever it was they had caught.

"I wish I knew what it was," said George Hadley. "Sometimes I can almost see. Do you think if I brought high-powered binoculars here and —"

David McClean laughed dryly. "Hardly." He turned to study all four walls. "How long has this been going on?"

"A little over a month."

"It certainly doesn't feel good."

"I want facts, not feelings."

"My dear George, a psychologist never saw a fact in his life. He only hears about feelings; vague things. This doesn't feel good, I tell you. Trust my hunches and my instincts. I have a nose for something bad. This is very bad. My advice to you is to have the whole damn room torn down and your children brought to me every day during the next year for treatment."

"Is it that bad?"

"I'm afraid so. One of the original uses of these nurseries was so that we could study the patterns left on the walls by the child's mind, study at our leisure, and help the child. In this case, however, the room has become a channel toward — destructive thoughts, instead of a release away from them."

"Didn't you sense this before?"

"I sensed only that you had spoiled your children more than most. And now you're letting them down in some way. What way?"

"I wouldn't let them go to New York."

"What else?"

"I've taken a few machines from the house and threatened them, a month ago, with closing up the nursery unless they did their homework. I did close it for a few days to show I meant business."

"Ah, ha!"

"Does that mean anything?"

"Everything. Where before they had a Santa Claus now they have a Scrooge. Children prefer Santas. You've let this room and this house replace you and your wife in your children's affections. This room is their mother and father, far more important in their lives than their real parents. And now you come along and want to shut it off. No wonder there's hatred here. You can feel it coming out of the sky. Feel that sun. George, you'll have to change your life. Like too many others, you've built it around creature comforts. Why, you'd starve tomorrow if something went wrong in your kitchen. You wouldn't know how to tap an egg. Nevertheless, turn everything off. Start anew. It'll take time. But we'll make good children out of bad in a year, wait and see."

"But won't the shock be too much for the children, shutting the room up abruptly, for good?"

"I don't want them going any deeper into this, that's all."

The lions were finished with their red feast.

The lions were standing on the edge of the clearing watching the two men.

"Now I'm feeling persecuted," said McClean. "Let's get out of here. I never have cared for these damned rooms. Make me nervous."

"The lions look real, don't they?" said George Hadley. "I don't suppose there's any way —"

"What?"

" — that they could become real?"

"Not that I know."

"Some flaw in the machinery, a tampering or something?"

"No."

They went to the door.

"I don't imagine the room will like being turned off," said the father.

"Nothing ever likes to die — even a room."

"I wonder if it hates me for wanting to switch it off?"

"Paranoia is thick around here today," said David McClean. "You can follow it like a spoor. Hello." He bent and picked up a bloody scarf. "This yours?"

"No." George Hadley's face was rigid. "It belongs to Lydia."

They went to the fuse box together and threw the switch that killed the nursery.

The two children were in hysterics. They screamed and pranced and threw things. They yelled and sobbed and swore and jumped at the furniture.

"You can't do that to the nursery, you can't!"

"Now, children."

The children flung themselves onto a couch, weeping.

"George," said Lydia Hadley, "turn on the nursery, just for a few moments. You can't be so abrupt."

"No."

"You can't be so cruel."

"Lydia, it's off, and it stays off. And the whole damn house dies as of here and now. The more I see of the mess we've put ourselves in, the more it sickens me. We've been contemplating our mechanical, electronic navels for too long. My God, how we need a breath of honest air!"

And he marched about the house turning off the voice clocks, the stoves, the heaters, the shoe shiners, the shoe lacers, the body scrubbers and swabbers and massagers, and every other machine he could put his hand to.

The house was full of dead bodies, it seemed. It felt like a mechanical cemetery. So silent. None of the humming hidden energy of machines waiting to function at the tap of a button.

"Don't let them do it!" wailed Peter at the ceiling as if he was talking to the house, the nursery. "Don't let Father kill everything." He turned to his father. "Oh, I hate you!"

"Insults won't get you anywhere."

"I wish you were dead!"

"We were, for a long while. Now we're going to really start living. Instead of being handled and massaged, we're going to live."

Wendy was still crying and Peter joined her again. "Just a moment, just one moment, just another moment of nursery," they wailed.

"Oh, George," said the wife, "it can't hurt."

"All right — all right, if they'll only just shut up. One minute, mind you, and then off forever."

"Daddy, Daddy, Daddy!" sang the children, smiling with wet faces.

"And then we're going on a vacation. David McClean is coming back in half an hour to help us move out and get to the airport. I'm going to dress. You turn the nursery on for a minute, Lydia, just a minute, mind you."

And the three of them went babbling off while he let himself be vacuumed upstairs through the air flue and set about dressing himself. A minute later Lydia appeared.

"I'll be glad when we get away," she sighed.

"Did you leave them in the nursery?"

"I wanted to dress too. Oh, that horrid Africa. What can they see in it?"

"Well, in five minutes we'll be on our way to Iowa. Lord, how did we ever get in this house? What prompted us to buy a nightmare?"

"Pride, money, foolishness."

"I think we'd better get downstairs before those kids get engrossed with those damned beasts again."

Just then they heard the children calling, "Daddy, Mommy, come quick — quick!"

They went downstairs in the air flue and ran down the hall. The children were nowhere in sight.

"Wendy? Peter!"

They ran into the nursery. The veldtland was empty save for the lions waiting, looking at them. "Peter, Wendy?"

The door slammed.

"Wendy, Peter!"

George Hadley and his wife whirled and ran back to the door.

"Open the door!" cried George Hadley, trying the knob. "Why, they've locked it from the outside! Peter!" He beat at the door.

"Open up!"

He heard Peter's voice outside, against the door.

"Don't let them switch off the nursery and the house," he was saying.

Mr. and Mrs. George Hadley beat at the door. "Now, don't be ridiculous, children. It's time to go. Mr. McClean'll be here in a minute and..."

And then they heard the sounds.

The lions on three sides of them, in the yellow veldt grass, padding through the dry straw, rumbling and roaring in their throats.

The lions.

Mr. Hadley looked at his wife and they turned and looked back at the beasts edging slowly forward, crouching, tails stiff.

Mr. and Mrs. Hadley screamed.

And suddenly they realized why those other screams had sounded familiar.

"Well, here I am," said David McClean in the nursery doorway.

"Oh, hello." He stared at the two children seated in the center of the open glade eating a little picnic lunch. Beyond them was the water hole and the yellow veldtland; above was the hot sun. He began to perspire. "Where are your father and mother?"

The children looked up and smiled. "Oh, they'll be here directly."

"Good, we must get going." At a distance Mr. McClean saw the lions fighting and clawing and then quieting down to feed in silence under the shady trees.

He squinted at the lions with his hand up to his eyes.

Now the lions were done feeding. They moved to the water hole to drink.

A shadow flickered over Mr. McClean's hot face. Many shadows flickered. The vultures were dropping down the blazing sky.

"A cup of tea?" asked Wendy in the silence.

## READER'S RESPONSE

▸1 How does this story compare to the other stories you have read so far (in terms of genre, theme, style, etc.)?

▸2 Did you find the end of this story effective? Why do you suppose this story ends the way it does?

## CLOSE READING

Answer the following questions.

▸1 What are some of the functions that the Hadley's Happylife home performed for the family? List at least five.

▸2 Why is the home (in a general sense) a source of conflict between the parents and their children?

▸3 Why are George and Lydia worried by the nursery in particular?

▸4 What was the original purpose of the nursery, according to the psychologist?

**a)** It was an interactive, type of paint-by-numbers room.

**b)** It was a room where children could experience films in 3-D.

**c)** It was a place providing children release from destructive thoughts.

**d)** It was a place for learning geography in a realistic way.

▸5 What had the children turned the nursery into?

▸6 Why do the children prefer the Happylife home to their parents?

▸7 What does the psychologist advise concerning the room and the children?

▸8 Why don't the parents succeed in following the psychologist's advice?

**WRITER'S CRAFT ▸ Bradbury uses the elements of plot and setting in "The Veldt" to bring out the main themes of this story. Refer to the Literary Elements section in your book to read about the characteristics of plot, setting, and theme, all of which are important for the literary analysis of this piece.**

### *Dramatic Structure*

Please refer to the literary elements section in order to obtain a good understanding of the dramatic structure.

▸1 Summarise the plot of "The Veldt" in one sentence.

▸2 Is the dramatic structure traditional (using exposition, complication – refer to literary elements section for a good explanation of these terms – etc.) or experimental?

Explain:

▸3 At what point in the story does the climax occur?

▸4 Explain how Bradbury creates tension right at the outset of the story.

▸5 **a)** Give three examples of foreshadowing in the story.

**b)** Explain how the use of foreshadowing builds tension in the plot.

▸6 Give two examples of dialogue between the parents and children that are used to create tension in the story.

▸7 Here are two examples of sections from the story containing descriptive narrative.

The lions were coming. And again George Hadley was filled with admiration for the mechanical genius who had conceived this room. A miracle of efficiency selling for an absurdly low price. Every home should have one...

...How many times in the last year had he opened this door and found Wonderland, Alice, the Mock Turtle, or Aladdin and his Magical Lamp, or Jack Pumpkinhead of Oz, or Dr. Doolittle, or the cow jumping over a very real-appearing moon — all the delightful contraptions of a make-believe world...

What kind of emotional charge or aura do they have?

**a)** positive **b)** negative **c)** neutral

▸8 What purpose do the examples in question 7 serve in the context of the dramatic structure of the story?

▸9 Reread the second paragraph in question 7 above. Which literary device does it represent?

▸▸▸ ***Bradbury is a master at building tension in the dramatic structure of a story through a variety of techniques, such as through creating characters in conflict, the use of foreshadowing, flashback, and dialogue, and the juxtaposition of sections containing contrasting emotional charges.*** ◂◂◂

## *NARRATIVE STRUCTURE*

▸1 What form of writing does the majority of the story take?

▸2 From what point of view is the story narrated?

▸3 Two story lines are present in "The Veldt"; this technique is called a story within a story.

**a)** What is the story that is within the main story? (Hint: it is repeated several times and takes place on the veldt.)

**b)** What is the first part of this story (the one taking place on the veldt) that George and Lydia see? The beginning or the end? (Hint: Reread lines 28-38 of the story.)

▸▸▸ ***In the story within the story, the action almost appears to be moving backward, while in the main story, it moves forward. The two stories intertwine at the climax and the main story winds down with the children calmly serving tea to the psychologist.*** ◂◂◂

### *Setting*

▸**1** Describe the setting of the main story.

▸**2** Describe the specific setting of the story within the main story.

▸**3** How do the two settings (places) contrast?

▸**4** What literary device does the author constantly use to make the veldt and the lions seem so real to the reader? (Look at the paragraphs containing descriptions of the veldt.)

▸**5** What kind of overall atmosphere does the setting of the story-within-a-story generate?

▸▸▸ ***Using a setting within a setting, Bradbury makes a vivid contrast between the vibrant and primal atmosphere of the African veldt and the artificial and technological atmosphere of the Happyhome. This contrast leads directly into one of the major themes of the story.*** ◂◂◂

### *Theme*

▸**1** What is the main theme of the story? (Hint: it concerns technology)

▸**2** How does the plot (dramatic structure) bring out this theme?

▸**3** How does the setting enhance the theme?

▸**4** Cite at least one other theme in the story.

### Other Literary Devices

Ray Bradbury uses several other literary devices to give impact to the story. (Refer to the glossary as needed.)

#### Symbolism

▸1 What do the following things from the story symbolise?
(N.B. See glossary at the end of the book or previous chapters for definitions of symbolism and irony.)

a) the lions ____________________

b) the Happylife home and the nursery ____________________

c) George and Lydia ____________________

d) the children ____________________

#### Irony

▸2 What is ironic about the nursery?

____________________

▸3 How are the following quotations from the story ironic?

a) "The house was full of dead bodies, it seemed. It felt like a mechanical cemetery."

____________________

b) "'I wish you were dead!"

"We were, for a long while. Now we're going to really start living. Instead of being handled and massaged, we're going to live.'"

____________________

▸4 How is the last scene of the story ironic?

____________________

#### Psychological Realism

▸▸▸ ***Psychological realism means that the reasons underlying characters' behaviour are plausible.*** ◂◂◂

▸5 How do the interventions of David McClean bring psychological realism to the story?

____________________

## Write in Style ▸ Literary Essays

**Structure and Contents**

**One of the most common forms of writing you will do as a student is the thesis/support essay. This is the type of essay that you will write for the purpose of literary analysis. Normally, a short 400 to 500-word literary essay will have the following structure:**

- ***Introduction:* presentation of the thesis statement in an interesting way**
- ***Body:* three paragraphs, each built around one argument**
- ***Conclusion:* reiteration of the thesis statement from a different angle and the tying up of any loose ends.**

**Longer papers deal with more complex analyses but are essentially structured in the same fashion. The body may consist of more than three arguments, or the arguments may be presented in greater detail with more supporting facts.**

**Often, the instructor will provide you with a subject or topic that you must narrow down to fit a thesis statement.**

- **A subject is a broad category, such as "writing styles of influential twentieth-century writers."**
- **A topic is a narrower category than a subject, for example "Hemingway's writing style."**
- **A thesis statement would be "Hemingway's writing style differs radically from that of his predecessors" or "The writing styles of Ernest Hemingway and Ray Bradbury differ in many respects."**

**Next, you will be expected to think of approximately three main arguments that could be used to support your thesis. In subsequent steps, you will place your ideas in logical order and expand upon them. You will need to define your audience and choice of writing style, write an introduction and a conclusion, and revise and edit your work.**

**The facts that you have learned about writing good paragraphs apply to an essay in an extended way. For example, the topic sentence of a paragraph has a similar role to that of a thesis statement of an essay. Both state the central idea of the piece and contain an opinion about the idea. Each of the supporting details that you would find in one paragraph is expanded into an entire paragraph in an essay, and likewise, the introduction and conclusion would be longer.**

#### Exercise A: Identifying Strong Thesis Statements

Read each of the following thesis statements and decide whether it is too general (*G*), too specific (*S*) or just right (*R*) for a five-paragraph essay.

▸1 ________ "Hills Like White Elephants" is a very good short story.

▸2 ________ Kate Chopin's use of irony in "The Story of an Hour" effectively heightens the dramatic structure of the story.

▸3 ________ Ray Bradbury's "The Veldt" presents terrifying images of lions and vultures.

▸4 ________ Did you ever wonder why Edgar Allan Poe is considered to be the father of the modern short story?

▸5 ________ Louise Mallard, the protagonist of "The Story of an Hour," did not love her husband.

▸6 ________ The use of foreshadowing in "The Veldt" effectively creates a great deal of tension.

▸7 ________ Many twentieth-century writers experimented with style.

▸8 ________ "Hill's Like White Elephants" is an excellent example of Ernest Hemingway's writing style.

**Exercise B: Organising an Essay (finding a logical order)**

The paragraphs that follow come from a literary essay written by student, but they are presented here in the wrong order. Indicate their correct order by placing the number 1 beside the introduction, and so on. Paragraphs 3 and 5 have already been placed in the correct order.

Then underline the thesis statement and place parentheses around the topic sentences in each paragraph.

MODEL ESSAY: **A Comparison of "Finishing School" and "The Veldt"** by Alexandra Deschamps-Sonsino (reprinted by permission from the author)

_____ The younger Margaret has similar thoughts: "Imagine letting some white woman rename you for her convenience." We can therefore see the cultural barriers that stand between Margaret and Mrs. Cullinan. Racism is such a strong force passed on from one generation to the next, that in order to put it down and destroy the years of discrimination of blacks, Margaret symbolically breaks the family dishes, passed down from one generation to the next by Mrs. Cullinan's family. This action is a way of teaching people a lesson; to prove that if people's attitudes do not change, you have to make them change. There should be no acceptance of evil.

_____ For many writers, literature is the vehicle to expose social ills produced through human weaknesses. The fight between good and evil is one of the most fundamental themes in world literature. Evil has been portrayed through many faces. We search for evil most our lives in order to know what we must fear. However, our understanding of evil changes as we grow. In the autobiographical short story "Finishing School" by Maya Angelou, and the Ray Bradbury's famous short story "The Veldt" social evils are portrayed as a warning of what humans beings must be aware of and must overcome. If moral beings do not win this battle, there will be terrible consequences for mankind. Maya Angelou's autobiographical story "Finishing School" and Ray Bradbury's futurist story "The Veldt" both expose the latent evil in society which comes in the form of beliefs. Both stories are a strong commentary that wrong beliefs such as racism or an over-reliance on technology will lead to human destruction if not fought.

*3* The evil criticised in this story is racism of the 1930s and 40s in the southern United States towards blacks. Margaret is black and as other young, black girls, she is being prepared to go into society by a "finishing school." This finishing school is the home of a white family where Margaret learns to cook and clean and learn other duties that would be necessary for a girl of her status who would one day become a white family's maid. Mrs. Cullinan is Margaret's employer. She is middle-aged, fat, white, and bourgeois. Mrs. Cullinan's opinion of Margaret and Miss Glory is not a good one. She has absolutely no respect for these two women; she changes their names at will calling Margaret, Mary. This name change horrifies the young Margaret who in the manner of the older Margaret says:

> It was dangerous practice to call a Negro anything that could be loosely construed as insulting because of the centuries of their having been called niggers, jigs, dingos, blackbirds, crows, boots and spooks.

_____ The central focus of the story is a nursery which symbolises the children's desires and dreams and which is supposed to help them work out their neuroses in a healthy way. The nursery through its advanced technology will help the children overcome their psychological problems. The children come to depend on the nursery to meet their needs, a role which was once played by the parents. As Lydia states, "The house is wife and mother and now nursemaid." At the end of the story, when it is already too late, George and Lydia realise that their children, the usual symbol of innocence and unconditional love, have turned against them and used technology as a tool to commit acts of evil. They murder their parents.

5 Moreover, in the short story "The Veldt" Bradbury presents a futuristic view of society in which technology originally meant for good uses can be turned into evil. Lydia and George Hadley live with their two children Peter and Wendy in a modern "Happy-life Home" This house is so technically advanced that it does everything for the Hadley family, that the parents no longer are burdened with matters such as taking care of their children.

______ In conclusion, we see that both authors warn humankind to be aware of the evils existing in society. Both stories are a warning that evil takes on many different forms and must not be taken lightly. In other words, both stories remind us that we as human beings have no choice but to be aware of and continuously fight evil in all of its manifestations.

______ First of all, in "Finishing School," Maya Angelou uses point of view in a very effective way to depict attitudes by having two different people tell a story about racism. The author uses a first-person narrator to recount her autobiographical story about an encounter with social evil. Therefore, it is the author herself who is telling the tale, but at different ages of her life. The first-person narrator at the beginning of the story is the older Maya Angelou. She begins her story by writing, "Recently a white woman from Texas... asked me about my hometown. The second narrator is the protagonist of the story, Margaret, who is the author at the age of ten. Her tale is recounted from a child-like naivete which is seen, for example, when she describes her employer, Mrs. Cullinan, as "...keeping herself embalmed" in order to explain Mrs. Cullinan's reasons for drinking alcohol. Both perspectives complement each other in that they show that racism affects anyone at any age.

### *Defining your Audience and Style*

In the case of a literary essay, your audience is your instructor and other students. In an academic setting, this means using a formal style.

**Formal writing** has the following characteristics:

- serious tone
- conventional structure
- correct grammar and spelling
- clear, precise word usage

Do not use any familiar, informal language, such as "guys" or "gonna"; in other words, no slang, no jargon, no clichés, no euphemisms. Also avoid wordiness, triteness, redundancy, or any other sort of affected language. *(Please note that these stylistic traps are presented in more detail in Unit 2.2* An Unquiet Awakening, *Write in Style.)*

Check with your instructor concerning the use of the personal pronoun "I" and contractions. In some formal writing situations, it may be preferable not to use them.

**Exercise C: Transforming Informal Sentences to More Formal Ones**

Transform each of the following informal sentences into a more formal one.

▸1 At the end of the story, there's this weird guy walkin' like he was pissed or something.

---

▸2 I tell you that Hamlet ain't no wacko. He was just simulating and goofin' off so people'd leave him alone.

---

▸3 Ray's a really top-notch writer. He's got a great writing style. Ray created some really neat VR (virtual reality) effects in "The Veldt."

---

▸4 It was a real red-letter day for the hero of the story. The bad guy had croaked from a heart attack.

---

▸5 The main character is this young kook who's gonna kill this old man because he has got the evil eye.

---

▸6 In this story, a bunch of nerds face off with a bunch of jocks. It was pretty boring because all the characters were flat and you could guess what would happen.

---

### *Writing an Introduction and a Conclusion*

Both the introduction and the conclusion serve important functions in a literary essay. The introduction serves to stimulate the interest of the reader by an inviting presentation of the thesis statement. The conclusion must effectively bring the essay to completion.

When composing an introduction, it is a good idea to work from a general statement to your specific thesis statement. In other words, the last sentence of the introductory paragraph will often be the thesis statement. Consult the model essay above ("A Comparison of 'Finishing School' and 'The Veldt' ") as an example.

> Here are some ideas for adding interest to an introduction:
> - Ask a question.
> - Start with a quotation
> - Present an unusual or provocative point of view.

Do not start with the words, "The purpose of this essay…" or "In this essay, I will…" or any similar announcement of intention: these types of openings actually deaden the reader's interest.

For the conclusion, you must provide a fitting end to your argumentation. This will be a revisiting of the thesis statement but in different words. You are showing your readers where you think you have brought them; normally at this stage, you have proved your point.

A conclusion can consist of just one sentence summarising the main point you have made. If you write a longer conclusion, you will want to set it up in the opposite fashion to your introduction: from specific, a summary of your thesis, to more general. Make sure that you do not introduce any new ideas or subjects that are really different from those in your essay. Consult the model essay above ("A Comparison of 'Finishing School' and 'The Veldt'") as an example.

Here are some ideas that can add impact to your writing:

- Include a quotation.
- Use an image or symbol that synthesises your idea.
- Consider the implications of the thesis.

### Composing the Body

The body of a literary essay consists of a series of paragraphs presenting arguments that prove the thesis statement. Each paragraph contains a separate idea or argument represented by the topic sentence. Use examples from the text to support your argument or point of view. These examples should include direct and indirect quotations and summaries of the characters' thoughts and actions. They must be relevant to the point you are making and should be convincing to the reader. The arguments and examples should be linked by using transitional words and expressions, such as *firstly*, *furthermore*, *in addition*, and *for example*. For further reference, see Write in Style in 1.2, "The Story of an Hour."

### Revising, Editing, and Proofreading

It is very important to revise and edit your work once you have finished writing a first draft. Word processors have transformed this once arduous task into a far easier and more convivial one for writers. You can benefit from the advantages the computer has to offer as a writer's tool. There is no excuse to hand in a sloppily written paper that has not been carefully reread and checked over.

Revising consists of checking the content and structure of your essay to make sure that your ideas are presented in a clear and logical fashion. Editing (in the context of an essay) and proofreading refer to verifying the more superficial features of the essay, such as spelling, punctuation, grammar, and presentation format. Correct your errors. You will probably need to read over your essay twice, the first time paying attention to the content and the second to the form. Here is a checklist you can use.

**Revising and Editing Checklist**

- ☐ The content is clearly and logically organised.
- ☐ The style is suitable to the audience.
- ☐ The essay is the correct length and format.
- ☐ The essay has been proofread for spelling, punctuation, and grammatical errors.
- ☐ Direct quotations have been inserted correctly.
- ☐ The introduction contains the thesis statement.
- ☐ Each paragraph of the body contains only one main argument with pertinent, supporting examples.
- ☐ The conclusion provides an effective summary and does not introduce any new ideas.
- ☐ Transitional words and expressions are used effectively and the essay reads well as a whole.

#### Exercise D: Revising and Editing

The following paragraph is intended as the introduction to a literary essay about the importance of the setting in "The Veldt." On a separate page, revise and edit it.

**More real than real**

In the essay that follows, I will show you how the setting of "The Veldt" is very important. Even if the story of "The Veldt" took place in a futuristic house, its terrifyingly real. Ray really hit the jackpot with his descriptions! I really believe that the setting of a short story most certainly plays an important role. "The Veldt" is such a great story. By creating an image in your minds' eye, it let's you vizualise what happening. nevertheless, it create a certain mood or atmospheer and propelled you headlong into the tail. Have you ever wonder why some short story seem so realistic that you actually feel you are their?

### *Formatting the Essay*

If your instructor has not given you any guidelines concerning the presentation and formatting of your essay, here is a checklist you can use.

**Presentation and Editing Checklist**

- Use lined looseleaf (not pages torn from an exercise book) or regular size white letter paper if typing.
- Make a separate title page on which you include all the following information: the title of the essay, your name and student number, your class, your teacher's name and the date (and any other pertinent information).
- Write neatly and clearly in blue or black ink (forget the fancy colours!) with no cross outs or blotches. Better still, use a word processor and type your work.
- Leave a 2.5 cm. (1 inch) margin around all the edges, even if you are writing your essay by hand.
- Write or type on only one side of the paper.
- Number each page except the title page; then staple the pages together.

Take pride in handing in professional-looking work.

### *Paragraph Practice*

Choose one of the questions or topics from the Wrap-Up Discussions or Writing Activities and write the introduction to a 500-word essay. Compose an effective thesis statement and identify it by placing parentheses around it.

## WRAP-UP DISCUSSION OR WRITING ACTIVITIES

▸**1** Which literary devices does Bradbury use to build up suspense and tension in "The Veldt"?

▸**2** Show how Bradbury uses imagery to create very realistic and convincing scenes in "The Veldt."

▸**3** Both Ernest Hemingway and Ray Bradbury use dialogue effectively in their short stories. Describe the similarities and differences in their use of this technique in the stories "Hills Like White Elephants" and "The Veldt."

▸**4** Write a literary essay comparing the theme of good versus evil in "The Lottery" and "The Veldt."

▸**5** Write an essay comparing the use of irony in "The Lottery."

▸**6** Compare Poe's and Bradbury's use of imagery to create atmosphere and mood in "The Tell-Tale Heart" and "The Veldt."

# References

## PRINT

**Biography**

Mogen, David. *Ray Bradbury*. New York: Twayne, 1986.

Nolan, William F., ed. *The Ray Bradbury Companion*. Detroit: Gale Research Co., 1975.

Slusser, George Edgar. *The Bradbury Chronicles*. San Bernardino, CA: Borgo Press, 1977.

**Criticism**

Anderson, James and Dickison, Larry. *The Illustrated Bradbury*. Center Harbor, NH: Niekas Publications, 1990.

Reid, Robin Anne. *Ray Bradbury: A Critical Companion*. Westport, CT.: Greenwood Press, 2000.

Touponce, William F. *Ray Bradbury and the Poetics of Reverie: Fantasy, Science Fiction, and the Reader*. Ann Arbor, MI: University of Michigan Research Press, 1984.

## INTERNET

Here are some very interesting Internet references that you may wish to check out relating to this chapter. Please note that as sites change location from time to time, some of the links may not work. We also suggest that you use a search engine to find other sites of interest on the Internet.

**Links:**

http://www.brookingsbook.com/bradbury/links.htm

Keyword search: Ray Bradbury on following Web site: http://search.britannica.com/

**Biography and selected works of the writer:**

The Ray Bradbury Page: http://www.brookingsbook.com/bradbury/

http://www.fantasticfiction.co.uk/authors/RayBradbury.htm

**Interview:**

http://members.tripod.com/morecouteau/bradbury.htm

http://www.space.com/spaceimagined/bradburystroke991112.html

**Science fiction genre:**

http://www.britannica.com/bcom/eb/article/5/0,5716,68005+1,00.html

**Discussions about Bradbury's works:**

http://nantuckets.com/nantuckets/RayBradburyhall/mobydick.html

UNIT 1.6

# THE YELLOW SWEATER

## CHAPTER CONTENTS

- **READING:** "The Yellow Sweater" by Hugh Garner; author's biography; literary trends (post World War II, social, urban subjects)
- **SPEAKING:** how to do an oral presentation
- **LITERARY ELEMENTS:** characterisation; denotation and connotation; contrasting images; foreshadowing; symbols
- **VOCABULARY:** pronunciation of homographs

## ABOUT THE AUTHOR

HUGH GARNER (1913-1979) immigrated to Toronto from England with his family in 1919. Not long after, his father deserted the family, leaving his mother to raise four young children. Garner grew up in the Cabbagetown district of the city, which provided the title for a novel he published in 1950. He later described his neighbourhood as "the largest Anglo-Saxon slum in North America."

He left school at the age of sixteen and worked at unskilled jobs during the Depression. Then he fought in both the Spanish Civil War and World War II. Afterwards, he became a full-time writer, producing novels such as *Storm Below* (1949), *The Silence on the Shore* (1962), *The Intruders* (1976), as well as short stories. In 1963, he won a Governor General's award for his *Best Short Stories*. He also wrote an autobiography and three police novels during the 1970s.

Garner's anti-establishment stance led him to write about the struggles of outsiders, such as alcoholics, displaced people, and the dispossessed in Canadian society.

## LITERARY TRENDS OF THE TIMES

Literature after World War II reflected a variety of themes that touched upon social or urban subjects. Society and its values were rapidly changing and young writers had to come to terms with the loss of innocence precipitated by the war with Nazi Germany that had led to the attempted extermination of the handicapped, homosexuals, Gypsies, and that had culminated in the death of six million Jews. Even before the war, writers such as James Joyce and Virginia Woolf experimented with new forms. William Golding explored the darker side of human nature in his Nobel prize-winning work *The Lord of the Flies* (1954). Still others such as Graham Greene, Aldous Huxley, and George Orwell made social or political statements in their works of fiction.

As well as in the United States and Britain, literature in other English-speaking areas such as Australia, Canada, and India developed rapidly after the war. Canadian English post-war literature, like its British counterpart, reflected urban experiences. Post-war Canadian English authors concentrated on societal issues such as political separation, the immigrant experience, the breakdown of traditional values, racism, survival, and isolation. Contemporary Canadian English writers, such as Hugh Garner, Margaret Atwood, Robertson Davies, Mordecai Richler, Leonard Cohen, and Michael Ondaatje have gained international recognition and popularity.

### WARM-UP DISCUSSION TOPICS

▶1 Have you ever been in an uncomfortable or embarrassing situation with strangers?

▶2 Have you ever hitchhiked? What are some positive and negative aspects of hitchhiking?

STORY

# THE YELLOW SWEATER

HUGH GARNER

He stepped on the gas when he reached the edge of town. The big car took hold of the pavement and began to eat up the miles on the straight, almost level, highway. With his elbow stuck through the open window he stared ahead at the shimmering grayness of the road. He felt heavy and pleasantly satiated after his good small-town breakfast, and he shifted his bulk in the seat, at the same time brushing some cigar ash from the front of his salient vest. In another four hours he would be home — a day ahead of himself this trip, but with plenty to show the office for last week's work. He unconsciously patted the wallet resting in the inside pocket of his jacket as he thought of the orders he had taken.

Four thousand units to Slanders… his second-best line too… four thousand at twelve percent… four hundred and eighty dollars! He rolled the sum over in his mind as if tasting it, enjoying its tartness like a kid with a gumdrop.

He drove steadily for nearly an hour, ignorant of the smell of spring in the air, pushing the car ahead with his mind as well as with his foot against the pedal. The success of his trip and the feeling of power it gave him carried him along toward the triumph of his homecoming.

Outside a small village he was forced to slow down for a road repair crew. He punched twice on the horn as he passed them, basking in the stares of the yokels who looked up from their shovels, and smiling at the envy showing on their faces.

A rather down-at-heel young man carrying an army kitbag stepped out from the office of a filling station and gave him the thumb. He pretended not to see the gesture, and pressed down slightly on the gas so that the car began to purr along the free and open road.

It was easy to see that the warm weather was approaching, he thought. The roads were becoming cluttered up once more with hitchhikers. Why the government didn't clamp down on them was more than he could understand. Why should people pay taxes so that other lazy bums could fritter away their time roaming the country, getting free rides, going God knows where? They were dangerous too. It was only the week before that two of them had beaten up and robbed a man on this very same road. They stood a fat chance of *him* picking them up.

And yet they always thumbed him, or almost always. When they didn't he felt cheated, as a person does when he makes up his mind not to answer another's greeting, only to have them pass by without noticing him.

He glanced at his face in the rear-view mirror. It was a typical middle-aged businessman's face, plump and well-barbered, the shiny skin stretched taut across the cheeks. It was a face that was familiar to him not only from his possession of it, but because it was also the face of most of his friends. What was it the speaker at that service club luncheon had called it? "The physiognomy of success."

As he turned a bend in the road he saw the girl about a quarter of a mile ahead. She was not on the pavement, but was walking slowly along the shoulder of the highway, bent over with the weight of the bag she was carrying. He slowed down, expecting her to turn and thumb him, but she plodded on as though impervious to his approach. He sized her up as he drew near. She was young by the look of her back… stocking seams straight… heels muddy but not rundown. As he passed he stared at her face. She was a good-looking kid, probably eighteen or nineteen.

It was the first time in years that he had slowed down for a hiker. His reasons evaded him, and whether it was the feel of the morning, the fact of his going home, or the girl's apparent independence, he could not tell. Perhaps it was a combination of all three, plus the boredom of a long drive. It might be fun to pick her up, to cross-examine her while she was trapped in the seat beside him.

Easing the big car to a stop about fifty yards in front of her he looked back through the mirror. She kept glancing at the car, but her pace had not changed, and she came on as though she had expected him to stop. For a moment he was tempted to drive on again, angered by her indifference. She was not a regular hitchhiker or she would have waited at the edge of town instead of setting out to walk while carrying such a heavy bag. But there was something about her that compelled him to wait — something which aroused in him an almost forgotten sense of adventure, an eagerness not experienced for years.

She opened the right rear door, saying at the same time, "Thank you very much, sir," in a frightened little voice.

"Put your bag in the back. That's it, on the floor," he ordered, turning towards her with his hand along the back of the seat. "Come and sit up here."

She did as he commanded, sitting very stiff and straight against the door. She was small, almost fragile, with long dark hair that waved where it touched upon the collar of her light-colored topcoat. Despite the warmth of the morning the coat was buttoned, and she held it to her in a way that suggested modesty or fear.

"Are you going very far?" he asked, looking straight ahead through the windshield, trying not to let the question sound too friendly.

"To the city," she answered, with the politeness and eagerness of the recipient of a favor.

"For a job?"

"Well, not exactly — " she began. Then she said, "Yes, for a job."

As they passed the next group of farm buildings she stared hard at them, her head turning with her eyes until they were too far back to be seen.

Something about her reminded him of his eldest daughter, but he shrugged off the comparison. It was silly of him to compare the two, one a hitchhiking farm skivvy and the other one soon to come home from finishing school. In his mind's eye he could see the photograph of his daughter Shirley that hung on the wall of the living room. It had been taken with a color camera during the Easter vacation, and in it Shirley was wearing a bright yellow sweater.

"Do you live around here?" he asked, switching his thoughts back to the present.

"I was living about a mile down the road from where you picked me up."

"Sick of the farm?" he asked.

"No." She shook her head slowly, seriously.

"Have you anywhere to go in the city?"

"I'll get a job somewhere."

He turned then and got his first good look at her face. She was pretty, he saw, with the country girl's good complexion, her features small and even. "You're young to be leaving home like this," he said.

"That wasn't my home," she murmured. "I was living with my Aunt Bernice and her husband."

He noticed that she did not call the man her uncle.

"You sound as though you don't like the man your aunt is married to?"

"I hate him!" she whispered vehemently.

To change the subject he said, "You've chosen a nice day to leave, anyhow."

"Yes."

He felt a slight tingling along his spine. It was the same feeling he had experienced once when sitting in the darkened interior of a movie house beside a strange yet, somehow, intimate young woman. The feeling that if he wished he had only to let his hand fall along her leg…

“You’re not very talkative,” he said, more friendly now.

She turned quickly and faced him. “I’m sorry. I was thinking about — about a lot of things.”

“It’s too nice a morning to think of much,” he said. “Tell me more about your reasons for leaving home.”

“I wanted to get away, that’s all.”

He stared at her again, letting his eyes follow the contours of her body. “Don’t tell me you’re in trouble?” he asked.

She lowered her eyes to her hands. They were engaged in twisting the clasp on a cheap black handbag. “I’m not in trouble like that,” she said slowly, although the tone of her voice belied her words.

He waited for her to continue. There was a sense of power in being able to question her like this without fear of having to answer any questions himself. He said, “There can’t be much else wrong. Was it boy trouble?”

“Yes, that’s it,” she answered hastily.

“Where is the boy? Is he back there or in the city?”

“Back there,” she answered.

He was aware of her nearness, of her young body beside him on the seat. “You’re too pretty to worry about one boy,” he said, trying to bridge the gap between them with unfamiliar flattery.

She did not answer him, but smiled nervously in homage to his remark.

They drove on through the morning, and by skillful questioning he got her to tell him more about her life. She had been born near the spot where he had picked her up, she said. She was an orphan, eighteen years old, who for the past three years had been living on her aunt’s farm. On his part he told her a little about his job, but not too much. He spoke in generalities, yet let her see how important he was in his field.

They stopped for lunch at a drive-in restaurant outside a small town. While they were eating he noticed that some of the other customers were staring at them. It angered him until he realized that they probably thought she was his mistress. This flattered him and he tried to imagine that it was true. During the meal he became animated, and he laughed loudly at his *risqué* little jokes.

She ate sparingly, politely, not knowing what to do with her hands between courses. She smiled at the things he said, even at the remarks that were obviously beyond her.

After they had finished their lunch he said to her jovially, “Here, we’ve been traveling together for two hours and we don’t even know each other’s names yet.”

“Mine is Marie. Marie Edwards.”

“You can call me Tom,” he said expansively.

When he drew out his wallet to pay the check he was careful to cover the initials G.G.M. with the palm of his hand.

As they headed down the highway once again, Marie seemed to have lost some of her timidity and she talked and laughed with him as though he were an old friend. Once he stole a glance at her through the corner of his eye. She was staring ahead as if trying to unveil the future that was being overtaken by the onrushing car.

“A penny for your thoughts, Marie,” he said.

“I was just thinking how nice it would be to keep going like this forever.”

“Why?” he asked, her words revealing an unsuspected facet to her personality.

“I dunno,” she answered, rubbing the palm of her hand along the upholstery of the seat in a gesture that was wholly feminine. “It seems so — safe here, somehow.” She smiled as though apologizing for thinking such things. “It seems as if nothing bad could ever catch up to me again.”

He gave her a quick glance before staring ahead at the road once more.

The afternoon was beautiful, the warm dampness of the fields bearing aloft the smell of uncovered earth and budding plants. The sun-warmed pavement sang like muted violins beneath the spinning tires of the car. The clear air echoed the sound of life and growth and the urgency of spring.

As the miles clicked off, and they were brought closer to their inevitable parting, an idea took shape in his mind and grew with every passing minute. Why bother hurrying home, he asked himself. After all he hadn't notified his wife to expect him, and he wasn't due back until tomorrow.

He wondered how the girl would react if he should suggest postponing the rest of the trip overnight. He would make it worth her while. There was a tourist camp on the shore of a small lake about twenty miles north of the highway. No one would be the wiser, he told himself. They were both fancy free.

The idea excited him, yet he found himself too timid to suggest it. He tried to imagine how he must appear to the girl. The picture he conjured up was of a mature figure, inclined to stoutness, much older than she was in years but not in spirit. Many men his age had formed liaisons with young women. In fact it was the accepted thing among some of the other salesmen he knew.

But there remained the voicing of the question. She appeared so guileless, so — innocent of his intentions. And yet it was hard to tell; she wasn't as innocent as she let on.

She interrupted his train of thought. "On an afternoon like this I'd like to paddle my feet in a stream," she said.

"I'm afraid the water would be pretty cold."

"Yes, it would be cold, but it'd be nice too. When we were kids we used to go paddling in the creek behind the schoolhouse. The water was strong with the spring freshet, and it would tug at our ankles and send a warm ticklish feeling up to our knees. The smooth pebbles on the bottom would make us twist our feet and we'd try to grab them with our toes... I guess I must sound crazy," she finished.

No longer hesitant he said, "I'm going to turn the car into one of these side roads, Marie. On a long trip I usually like to park for a while under some trees. It makes a little break in the journey."

She nodded her head happily. "That would be nice," she said.

He turned the car off the highway and they traveled north along the road that curved gently between wide stretches of steaming fields. The speed of the car was seemingly increased by the drumming of gravel against the inside of the fenders.

It was time to bring the conversation back to a more personal footing, so he asked, "What happened between you and your boyfriend, Marie?" He had to raise his voice above the noise of the hurtling stones.

"Nothing much, she answered, hesitating as if making up the answer. "We had a fight, that's all."

"Serious?"

"I guess so."

"What happened? Did he try to get a little gay maybe?"

She had dropped her head, and he could see the color rising along her neck and into her hair behind her ears.

"Does that embarrass you?" he asked, taking his hand from the wheel and placing it along the collar of her coat.

She tensed herself at his touch and tried to draw away, but he grasped her shoulder and pulled her against him. He could feel the fragility of her beneath his hand and the trembling of her skin beneath the cloth of her coat. The odor of her hair and of some cheap scent filled his nostrils.

She cried, "Don't, please!" and broke away from the grip of his hand. She inched herself into the far corner of the seat again.

"You're a little touchy, aren't you?" he asked, trying to cover up his embarrassment at being repulsed so quickly.

"Why did you have to spoil it?"

His frustration kindled a feeling of anger against her. He knew her type all right. Pretending that butter wouldn't melt in her mouth, while all the time she was secretly laughing at him for being the sucker who picked her up, bought her a lunch, and drove her into town. She couldn't fool him; he'd met her type before.

He swung the car down a narrow lane, and they flowed along over the rutted wheel tracks beneath a flimsy ceiling of budding trees.

"Where are we going?" she asked, her voice apprehensive now.

"Along here a piece," he answered, trying to keep his anger from showing.

"Where does this road lead?"

"I don't know. Maybe there's a stream you can paddle in."

There was a note of relief in her voice as she said, "Oh! I didn't mean for us — for you to find a stream."

"You don't seem to know *what* you mean, do you?"

She became silent then and seemed to shrink farther into the corner.

The trees got thicker, and soon they found themselves in the middle of a small wood. The branches of the hardwoods were mottled green, their buds flicking like fingers in the breeze. He brought the car to a stop against the side of the road.

The girl watched him, the corners of her mouth trembling with fear. She slid her hand up the door and grabbed the handle. He tried to make his voice matter-of-fact as he said, "Well, here we are."

Her eyes ate into his face like those of a mesmerized rabbit watching a snake.

He opened a glove compartment and pulled out a package of cigarettes. He offered the package to her, but she shook her head.

"Let's get going," she pleaded.

"What, already? Maybe we should make a day of it."

She did not speak, but the question stood in her eyes. He leaned back against the seat, puffing on his cigarette. "There's a tourist camp on a lake a few miles north of here. We could stay there and go on to the city tomorrow."

She stifled a gasp. "I can't. I didn't think — I had no idea when we — "

He pressed his advantage. "Why can't you stay? Nobody'll know. I may be in a position to help you afterward. You'll need help, you know."

"No. No, I couldn't," she answered. Her eyes filled with tears.

He had not expected her to cry. Perhaps he had been wrong in his estimation of her. He felt suddenly bored with the whole business, and ashamed of the feelings she had ignited in him.

"Please take me back to the highway," she said, pulling a carefully folded handkerchief from her handbag.

"Sure. In a few minutes." He wanted time to think things out; to find some way of saving face.

"You're just like he was," she blurted out, her words distorted by her handkerchief. "You're all the same."

Her outburst frightened him. "Marie," he said, reaching over to her. He wanted to quiet her, to show her that his actions had been the result of an old man's foolish impulse.

As soon as his hand touched her shoulder she gave a short cry and twisted the door handle. "No. No, please!" she cried.

"Marie, come here!" he shouted, trying to stop her. He grabbed her by the shoulder, but she tore herself from his grasp and fell through the door.

She jumped up from the road and staggered back through the grass into the belt of trees. Her stockings and the bottom of her coat were brown with mud.

"Don't follow me!" she yelled.

"I'm not going to follow you. Come back here and I'll drive you back to the city."

"No you don't! You're the same as he was!" she cried. "I know your tricks!"

He looked about him at the deserted stretch of trees, wondering if anybody could be listening. It would place him in a terrible position to be found with her like this. Pleading with her he said, "Come on, Marie. I've got to go."

She began to laugh hysterically, her voice reverberating through the trees.

"Marie, come on," he coaxed. "I won't hurt you."

"No! Leave me alone. Please leave me alone!"

His pleas only seemed to make things worse. "I'm going," he said — hurriedly, pulling the car door shut.

"Just leave me alone!" she cried. Then she began sobbing, "Bernice! Bernice!"

What dark fears had been released by his actions of the afternoon he did not know, but they frightened and horrified him. He turned the car around in the narrow lane and let it idle for a moment as he waited, hoping she would change her mind. She pressed herself deeper into the trees, wailing at the top of her voice.

From behind him came a racking noise from down the road, and he looked back and saw a tractor coming around a bend. A man was driving it and there was another one riding behind. He put the car in gear and stepped on the gas.

Before the car reached the first turn beneath the trees he looked back. The girl was standing in the middle of the road beside the tractor and she was pointing his way and talking to the men. He wondered if they had his license number, and what sort of a story she was telling them.

He had almost reached the highway again before he remembered her suitcase standing on the floor behind the front seat. His possession of it seemed to tie him to the girl; to make him partner to her terror. He pulled the car to a quick stop, leaned over the back of the seat and picked the suitcase up from the floor. Opening the door he tossed it lightly to the side of the road with a feeling of relief. The frail clasp on the cheap bag opened as it hit the ground and its contents spilled in the ditch. There was a framed photograph, some letters and papers held together with an elastic band, a comb and brush, and some clothing, including a girl's yellow sweater.

"I'm no thief," he said, pushing the car into motion again, trying to escape from the sight of the opened bag. He wasn't to blame for the things that had happened to her. It wasn't his fault that her stupid little life was spilled there in the ditch.

"I've done nothing wrong," he said, as if pleading his case with himself. But there was a feeling of obscene guilt beating his brain like a reiteration. Something of hers seemed to attach itself to his memory. Then suddenly he knew what it was — the sweater, the damned yellow sweater. His hands trembled around the wheel as he sent the car hurtling towards the safe anonymity of the city.

He tried to recapture his feelings of the morning, but when he looked at himself in the mirror all he saw was the staring face of a fat frightened old man.

#### Reader's Response

▸1 Write down adjectives that express your feelings after you read the story.

▸2 Discuss the following statement: We must pay a price for our actions.

## CLOSE READING

▸1 In paragraphs 1-8, how is the protagonist initially presented to the readers? Fill in the chart below to understand the characteristics of the protagonist.

| Name | |
|---|---|
| Physical characteristics | |
| Attitudes | |

▸2 What are his reasons for picking up the girl hitchhiker?

▸3 In the paragraph 10 beginning at line 41, which two words indicate how the man views himself in terms of the girl?

Hint: look at the last line of the paragraph.

▸4 How is the girl described?

▸5 What reasons does the girl give for leaving home?

▸6 At the restaurant, the man is described as being "animated." Why does he behave in this manner?

▸7 Why does the man lie to the girl about his name?

▸8 What are the man's intentions towards the girl when he initially suggests that they stop for awhile by the side of the road?

▸9 How does the girl react to the man when he touches her?

▸10 How does the man rationalise the girl's reaction to his touch?

▸11 Why does the girl's hysterical reaction in the woods frighten the man?

▸12 What does the man do when he drives away?

▸13 How does the man see himself at the end of the story?

**WRITER'S CRAFT** ▸ **Hugh Garner's story "The Yellow Sweater" shows how words and their connotations (associated meanings) can depict characterisation. Garner presents the domination and subjugation of his two main characters through the use of contrasting words and images.**

### *Contrast*

▸▸▸ ***"The Yellow Sweater" is full of contrasting images. For example, the man is presented as "big and powerful," while the girl is portrayed as "fragile." In paragraph 1, Garner depicts the power of the man through word associations like "big car...," "he felt heavy... and pleasantly satiated...", "shifted his bulk...", and "patted the wallet..." In paragraph 3, for example, there is "success of his trip...," "the feeling of power..." "the triumph of his homecoming."*** ◂◂◂

▸1 Find some examples of the girl's fragility that contrast markedly with the man's power in the story.

▸2 The man's sense of power over the girl is also derived from his sexual interest in her. For example, the man's initial attitude is shown by the following statement: "But there was something about her that compelled him to wait — something which aroused in him an almost forgotten sense of adventure, an eagerness not experienced for years." Find at least four more examples of the man's powerful sexual attitude toward the girl.

▸3 Garner also uses vocabulary associated with the legal system to suggest the difference of power between the man and the girl. Look at the following sentences and explain the **denotative** (dictionary meaning) and **connotative** (associated, secondary meaning) meanings of the words in italics.

It might be fun to pick her up, *to cross-examine* her while she was trapped in the seat beside him.

denotation

connotation

They drove on through the morning, and *by skillful questioning* he got her to tell him more about her life.

denotation ________________

connotation ________________

"I've done nothing wrong," he said, as *if pleading his case* with himself.

denotation ________________

connotation ________________

▸4 At what point in the story does the man begin to lose his power over the girl?

________________

▸5 Find examples of words that show that the man loses his power over the girl.

________________

▸6 How is the man's state at the end of the story different from his state at the beginning?

________________

### Foreshadowing

▸1 Foreshadowing is also an important device in the story. Find an example of foreshadowing in the paragraph beginning with "She did as she was commanded... " Explain how your choice represents an example of what is to come.

________________

________________

▸2 Choose two other examples of foreshadowing in the story. Explain how each predicts future events.

________________

________________

________________

________________

▸3 **a)** What is the girl's real reason for leaving her aunt's house?

________________

**b)** Write a sentence or two that prove your answer for the previous question.

________________

**c)** How is this foreshadowing?

________________

### Symbolism

▸▸▸ ***Symbolism is a literary device in which one idea is represented by another concrete idea. For example, a rose may be a symbol of love.*** ◂◂◂

▸1 What is the significance of the yellow sweater?

▸2 Find at least two other symbols and explain their significance to the story.

### Theme

In your opinion, what is the theme of the story?

**ORAL PRESENTATION** ▸ **Your teacher will ask you to do a formal oral presentation of a literary analysis in front of the class. Here are some tips that will guide you to make a successful presentation.**

**Helpful Hints**

- Choose a story, poem, novel, or play that you find interesting. (In some cases your teacher may want to assign specific material.)
- Read the text carefully.
- Look up any unfamiliar words or expressions in the dictionary or ask the teacher to tell you their meanings.
- Familiarise yourself with the relevant literary terms; review the section on literary elements or check definitions in the glossary if needed.
- Analyse the story, poem, or other work, keeping in mind the basic literary elements such as theme, narrator, point of view, and so on.
- Look for figurative devices such as imagery, irony, symbolism, and so on.
- Make notes on the story.
- Define a specific thesis for the oral presentation. Your thesis should neither be too broad nor too narrow.
- Use specific examples and quotations from your text in order to prove your point of view.
- Remember to speak clearly.
- Use pertinent and accurate vocabulary in your analysis.
- Use Standard English; avoid slang.
- Do not read from your notes.
- Be prepared by reviewing the material beforehand.
- Bring visual or aural aids to add an interesting dimension to your presentation.
- Plan an interactive activity with the class. It could be a multiple-choice quiz, skit, or other type of game.
- Remember that the more actively involved the audience is in your presentation, the more interesting they will find it.

### *Pronunciation: Homographs*

In this section, as preparation for making an oral presentation, you will work with words that often cause pronunciation problems.

**Homographs** are words that are spelled the same but pronounced differently. Sometimes the same vowels in homographs are pronounced very differently.

*EXAMPLE: live It was a **live** concert. (long i as in I)*
*I **live** in Montreal. (short i as in if)*

Sometimes the syllable stressed is different (and a vowel is pronounced differently). This is often the case when one form of the word is used as a noun and the other as a verb.

*EXAMPLE: rebel John is a real rebel. (re´ bel is used as a noun; ´ indicates that* re *is the accented syllable)*
*I rebel against authority. (re bel´ is used as a verb)*

N.B. Long vowels are pronounced in the same way that they are named in the alphabet. The following words show how short vowels (*a*, *e*, *i*, *o*, and *u*)are pronounced: *bat*, *bet*, *bit*, *mop*, and *but*.

For the following sentences, rewrite the word in parentheses, placing the sign to the right of the stressed syllable. Check your answers in a dictionary if you are not sure that you have placed the sign correctly. Practise pronouncing both variants of the word.

*EXAMPLES: Take an (alternate) road home. al´ ter nate (the last syllable is pronounced "nit")*
*They agreed to (alternate) as hosts for the show. al´ ter nate´ (the last syllable is pronounced "nate", like "ate")*

▸**1** Her forgetfulness will (compound) her problems. ______________

▸**2** John sat at the (console) and began to type. ______________

▸**3** The soldier wanted to (desert). ______________

▸**4** Edgar Allan Poe has a very (elaborate) style. ______________

▸**5** My calculations were (invalid). ______________

▸**6** He broke the pill into (minute) pieces. ______________

▸**7** Jane (moped) for a week after she heard that she had lost. ______________

▸**8** What is the (object) of your visit? ______________

▸**9** Please (present) my condolences to your sister. ______________

▸**10** You will (progress) to the next step soon. ______________

▸**11** What were the results of his (research)? ______________

▸**12** My friend (Herb) was able to name every (herb) in the garden. (In which "herb" is the "h" silent? The first or the second, neither or both?) ______________

Just for fun, try to pronounce each of the following words correctly. Then fill in the blank space with an appropriate rhyming word from the box below.

| | |
|---|---|
| bough | rhymes with ________ |
| tough | rhymes with ________ |
| thorough | rhymes with ________ and ________ |
| hiccough | is pronounced hicc ________ |
| thought | rhymes with ________ |
| cough | rhymes with ________ |
| through | rhymes with ________ |
| ought | rhymes with ________ |
| though | rhymes with ________ |
| taught | rhymes with ________ |

**Rhyming Words**

| | | | |
|---|---|---|---|
| stuff | so | her | too |
| bought | off | cow | up |

After you have prepared your oral presentation, use the following self-edit list to practice your delivery.

**Oral Presentation Checklist**

- ☐ My subject is clear to the audience.
- ☐ My ideas and opinions are well organised.
- ☐ My ideas and opinions are well supported and logically argued.
- ☐ I speak in a lively way.
- ☐ The time requirement is met.
- ☐ I use a level of language and vocabulary appropriate for the type of presentation.
- ☐ I am familiar and at ease with the subject of the oral presentation.
- ☐ I use verb tenses, subject / verb agreements, word order, and the final "s" (retained for plurals or third person singular verbs — present tense) correctly.
- ☐ I have created an interactive component for my presentation.
- ☐ I have practised my presentation.

## SUGGESTIONS FOR ORAL PRESENTATIONS

Here are some suggested topics for oral presentations.

### *Short Presentation Topics* (under 5 minutes)

- ▸**1** Gender stereotyping in "The Yellow Sweater."
- ▸**2** Garner's use of legal, courtroom imagery in "The Yellow Sweater."
- ▸**3** The power struggle that occurs in "The Yellow Sweater."
- ▸**4** Symbolism in "The Yellow Sweater."
- ▸**5** Characterisation in "The Yellow Sweater."
- ▸**6** How the power abuse presented in "The Yellow Sweater" represents various sorts of power abuse in society in general.

### LONGER PRESENTATION TOPICS

- ▸1 The influence of an idea, person, philosophy, political situation, or artistic movement on a specific work or author that you have covered during the term.
- ▸2 The origins of a particular work (choose a piece that you read this term).
- ▸3 The origins and history of the English novel or short story.
- ▸4 Experimentation with the novel or short story form in the twentieth century.
- ▸5 Film techniques such as use of colour, camera angle, or acting techniques of a film seen during the course, or connected with one of the short stories studied.
- ▸6 Comparison of one of the short stories with its film version.
- ▸7 One or two literary devices and their significance to the overall meaning of a text.
- ▸8 One or two figurative devices and their significance to the overall meaning of a text (from the term).
- ▸9 The characteristics of a fairytale. What values are reflected in fairytales? Any literary element that you have studied in terms of a work you read in class.
- ▸10 The characteristics of different literary genres such as poetry, short story, essay, novel, biography, diary, and so on.
- ▸11 Compare and contrast an element from two texts.
- ▸12 Does modern literature reflect classical myths or Jung's archetypes?

# References

## PRINT


**BIOGRAPHY**

Marsh, James H., ed. *The Canadian Encyclopedia: Year 2000 Edition*. Toronto: McClelland & Stewart, 1999, p. 951.

Stuewe, Paul. *The Storms Below: The Turbulent Life and Times of Hugh Garner*. Toronto: James Lorimer, 1988.

Vinson, James, ed. *Contemporary Novelists*. New York: St. Martin's Press, 1972.

**CRITICISM**

Kennedy, Michael P.J. *The Short Stories of Hugh Garner* (Ph.D. Dissertation). Ottawa: University of Ottawa, 1989.


## INTERNET


**HISTORICAL BACKGROUND OF HUGH GARNER'S CABBAGETOWN:**

http://www.tgmag.ca/magic/mt37.html
http://www.geocities.com/Hollywood/Club/7400/
http://www.cabbagetown-toronto.com/cabbagetownhistory.html

UNIT 1.7

# SHORT SHORT STORIES

**CHAPTER CONTENTS**

- **READING:** "The New Food" by Stephen Leacock; "Bread" by Margaret Atwood; "Old Habits Die Hard" by Makeda Silvera
- **LITERARY ELEMENTS:** style; literary devices including denotation and connotation; simile; metaphor; personification; imagery; alliteration; assonance; consonance; repetition; syntax; level of language; tone
- **WRITING:** book report versus literary essay

In this chapter, we will approach the short story and literary analysis from a new angle. To complete our study of the various elements comprising traditional analysis of a short story, we will compare and contrast the styles used to write three rather unique and very short short stories called "The New Food" by Stephen Leacock, "Bread" by Margaret Atwood, and "Old Habits Die Hard" by Makeda Silvera. Then we will examine how a literary analysis differs from a traditional book report.

## ABOUT THE AUTHORS

STEPHEN LEACOCK (1869-1944) was considered to be the best-known humorist in the English-speaking world between 1915 and 1925. Leacock was a professor of economics and political science at McGill University in Montreal, but is best remembered for his witty, satirical short stories. He also wrote literary essays and articles on social issues. Many of his works were first published in magazines and later collected to make up more than sixty books. *Sunshine Sketches of a Little Town* (1912) and *Arcadian Adventures with the Idle Rich* (1914) are two of Leacock's most famous works.

MARGARET ATWOOD, born in Ottawa in 1939, is one of Canada's most widely read authors. A prolific author of more than twenty-five books, she has received international recognition for her novels and poetry, and has also written several children's books and television scripts. Atwood has received many prestigious awards and honours including the Governor General's Award, the Centennial Medal from Harvard University, The Sunday Times Award for Literary Excellence in the United Kingdom, and Le Chevalier dans l'Ordre des Arts et des Lettres in France as well as many honorary doctorates. Her recent work includes *Alias Grace* (1998), a highly acclaimed historical novel, *Morning in the Burned House* (1995), a collection of poems as well as her latest book *The Blind Assassin* (2000), which won her the Booker Prize.

MAKEDA SILVERA was born in Jamaica in 1955 and came to Canada in 1967 where she is very active in developing and promoting the writing of women of colour. She has edited and written for many anthologies. Silvera has published two collections of her own short stories, *Remembering G* (1991) and *Her Head a Village* (1994). Much of Silvera's work deals with the issues of being "other": Black, lesbian, immigrant, working class, or old.

Short stories vary widely in length. Many twentieth-century writers experimented with extremely short versions of the genre. In spite of their brevity, these stories can be quite complex and often have a powerful impact on the reader. Many, although experimental, follow in the realist and romantic traditions. Some deal succinctly with important social issues while others take a more fanciful or poetic approach to the universal in human experience.

### Warm-Up Discussion Topics

▸ 1 Could new techniques for faster food preparation, involving "instant" foods, be of major benefit for people today?

▸ 2 What does the word *bread* bring to mind? Brainstorm five associations.

▸ 3 How do you imagine your life as an elderly person? What kind of conditions do you hope for?

**INITIAL READING ▸ Each of the following three stories deals with a social issue that is relevant today. However, each story has a unique style and approach. Read and savour each one before continuing on to the next. Pay particular attention to the writing style that the author has chosen to use.**

STORY

1910

# The New Food

Stephen Leacock

I see from the current columns of the daily press that "Professor Plumb, of the University of Chicago, has just invented a highly concentrated form of food. All the essential nutritive elements are put together in the form of pellets, each of which contains from one to two hundred times as much nourishment as an ounce of an ordinary article of diet. These pellets, diluted with water, will form all that is necessary to support life. The professor looks forward confidently to revolutionizing the present food system."

Now this kind of thing may be all very well in its way, but it is going to have its drawbacks as well. In the bright future anticipated by Professor Plumb, we can easily imagine such incidents as the following: —

The smiling family were gathered round the hospitable board. The table was plenteously laid with a soup plate in front of each beaming child, a bucket of hot water before the radiant mother, and at the head of the board the Christmas dinner of the happy home, warmly covered by a thimble and resting on a poker chip. The expectant whispers of the little ones were hushed as the father, rising from his chair, lifted the thimble and disclosed a small pill of concentrated nourishment on the chip before him. Christmas turkey, cranberry sauce, plum pudding, mince pie, it was all there, all jammed into that little pill and only waiting to expand. Then the father with deep reverence, and a devout eye alternating between the pill and heaven, lifted his voice in a benediction.

At this moment there was an agonized cry from the mother.

"Oh, Henry, quick! Baby has snatched the pill!" It was too true. Dear little Gustavus Adolphus, the golden-haired baby boy, had grabbed the whole Christmas dinner off the poker chip and bolted it. Three hundred and fifty pounds of concentrated nourishment passed down the oesophagus of the unthinking child.

"Clap him on the back!" cried the distracted mother. "Give him water!"

The idea was fatal. The water striking the pill caused it to expand. There was a dull rumbling sound and then, with an awful bang, Gustavus Adolphus exploded into fragments!

And when they gathered the little corpse together, the baby lips were parted in a lingering smile that could only be worn by a child who had eaten thirteen Christmas dinners.

1983

STORY

# BREAD

MARGARET ATWOOD

Imagine a piece of bread. You don't have to imagine it, it's right here in the kitchen, on the bread board, in its plastic bag, lying beside the bread knife. The bread knife is an old one you picked up at an auction; it has the word BREAD carved into the wooden handle. You open the bag, pull back the wrapper, cut yourself a slice. You put butter on it, then peanut butter, then honey, and you fold it over. Some of the honey runs out onto your fingers and you lick it off. It takes you about a minute to eat the bread. This bread happens to be brown, but there is also white bread, in the refrigerator, and a heel of rye you got last week, round as a full stomach then, now going mouldy. Occasionally you make bread. You think of it as something relaxing to do with your hands.

Imagine a famine. Now imagine a piece of bread. Both of these things are real but you happen to be in the same room with only one of them. Put yourself into a different room, that's what the mind is for. You are now lying on a thin mattress in a hot room. The walls are made of dried earth and your sister, who is younger than you are, is in the room with you. She is starving, her belly is bloated, flies land on her eyes; you brush them off with your hand. You have a cloth too, filthy but damp, and you press it to her lips and forehead. The piece of bread is the bread you've been saving, for days it seems. You are as hungry as she is, but not yet as weak. How long does this take? When will someone come with more bread? You think of going out to see if you might find something that could be eaten, but outside the streets are infested with scavengers and the stink of corpses is everywhere.

Should you share the bread or give the whole piece to your sister? Should you eat the piece of bread yourself? After all, you have a better chance of living, you're stronger. How long does it take to decide?

Imagine a prison. There is something you know that you have not yet told. Those in control of the prison know that you know. So do those not in control. If you tell, thirty or forty or a hundred of your friends, your comrades, will be caught and will die. If you refuse to tell, tonight will be like last night. They always choose the night. You don't think about the night however, but about the piece of bread they offered you. How long does it take? The piece of bread was brown and fresh and reminded you of sunlight falling across a wooden floor. It reminded you of a bowl, a yellow bowl that was once in your home. It held apples and pears; it stood on a table you can also remember. It's not the hunger or the pain that is killing you but the absence of the yellow bowl. If you could only hold the bowl in your hands, right here, you could withstand anything, you tell yourself. The bread they offered you is subversive, it's treacherous, it does not mean life.

There were once two sisters. One was rich and had no children, the other had five children and was a widow, so poor that she no longer had any food left. She went to her sister and asked her for a mouthful of bread. "My children are dying," she said. The rich sister said, "I do not have enough for myself," and drove her away from the door. Then the husband of the rich sister came home and wanted to cut himself a piece of bread; but when he made the first cut, out flowed red blood.

Everyone knew what that meant.

This is a traditional German fairy-tale.

The loaf of bread I have conjured for you floats about a foot above your kitchen table. The table is normal, there are no trap doors in it. A blue towel floats beneath the bread, and there are no strings attaching the cloth to the bread or the bread to the ceiling or the table to the cloth, you've proved it by passing your hand above and below. You didn't touch the bread though. What stopped you?

You don't want to know whether the bread is real or whether it's just a hallucination I've somehow duped you into seeing. There's no doubt that you can see the bread, you can even smell it, it smells like yeast, and it looks solid enough, solid as your own arm. But can you trust it? Can you eat it? You don't want to know, imagine that.

1994

STORY

# Old Habits Die Hard

MAKEDA SILVERA

Old man, skin scaly tree bark to touch. Rust eyes, water hazy. The iron is gone. Legs, arms, ready kindling. Bedbug. Bedridden. Bedlam. Bedpan. Bedraggled. Bedfast.

Faeces don't give ear to him any more. Old man in diapers. Old man in white gown. Mashed potatoes with milk is all he can eat. Old man needs steady hand to feed him. Out of habit, old woman folds clean, neatly ironed pyjamas. Clean towel. Wash rag. Enamel carrier filled with mashed potatoes.

Disordered eyes. Looks past visitors. Old man recollects just one, old woman. The others bear no memory. Disappointed, you can see it on their faces, the tight turn of the lips, the begging in the eyes. Talk to us. Touch us. Remember us. He only sits, no teeth to his grin. Old man looks and looks. Memory escapes. No longer father, husband, grandfather, uncle, brother, friend.

Old man pulls towards old woman. Grab him, he'll shit, piss on the floors, run around like a madman, a bedlamite. The visitors approve of the restraint. We love him, they say. Old man wants to run, old man wants to go home. The visitors go. Room too depressing: some stringy flowers in a mug, a plastic balloon the only grace, a heavy curtain shuts out the light.

Old woman stays behind. She feeds him potatoes, eggs, milk through a straw. She talks to him. He cannot answer. She tells him things, answers for him. His hands are cool. She pulls the blankets closer to his body. His face sweet like dark plums. Time to leave. Keepers in white come to lead her out. She kisses old man. Water in his eyes. He stares. He stares. Night is a black sheet. Old man pass away, old man dead, old man gone. She had felt it. Hands cool, getting cold, heat leaving the face, purple turning black, eyes turning.

The mourners come, eat, sing, cry, drink, help to bury him. They go home. Old woman must bury him a second time: clothes to give away — Salvation Army, Goodwill; mattress to turn over; bank account to settle; pension to straighten out. One pot to cook, one mouth to feed. Out of habit, old woman does the wash, folds her nightgown. She always irons it. Washes towels, washes rags, folds them. Those go into the suitcase. Changes her bed sheets. Best pillowcase; lovely lace, that. Lies down. Pulls up the black sheet of night.

### *Reader's Response*

▸1 Which story of the three did you prefer? Why?

---

## Close Reading

Answer the following questions.

▸1 Identify the type of narration (first person, third person, etc. Refer to the section on literary elements for definitions of narration and point of view) used in each story. *(Hint: Two stories contain two types of narration because in each there is a story [or stories!] within a story.)*

**a)** "The New Food": ______

**b)** "Bread": ______

**c)** "Old Habits Die Hard": ______

▸2 (Circle the correct answers.) In which stories does the narrator ask the reader directly to imagine a scene or scenes?

**a)** "The New Food" **b)** "Bread" **c)** "Old Habits Die Hard"

▸3 (Circle the correct answer.) In which story is the narrator the most distant from the reader?

**a)** "The New Food" **b)** "Bread" **c)** "Old Habits Die Hard"

Explain your answer.

---

---

---

---

▸4 (Circle the correct answer.) Which story needs to assume that the reader comes from a privileged society, such as middle-class North America, in order to have the greatest impact?

**a)** "The New Food" **b)** "Bread" **c)** "Old Habits Die Hard"

Give details from the story to prove your answer.

---

---

---

▸5 Match the story with one of its main themes.

a) "The New Food"

b) "Bread"

c) "Old Habits Die Hard"

i) Nothing is left in the lives of old couples as they await death.

ii) People can use their imaginations to imagine anything.

iii) Technological advances are not necessarily positive.

iv) Love and compassion are very much alive in banal daily actions.

v) New technology can transform people's lives in many ways.

vi) Materially well-off people take important aspects of their lives for granted.

**WRITER'S CRAFT ▸ The essence of literature is in its distinct use of language for a specific purpose. Each writer has his or her unique *style* of writing and it is this style that creates the overall effect of the literary work on the reader. Writers often craft short short stories with a very particular attention to style. In such stories, style is intrinsically connected with theme.**

**The three short stories in this section have very different styles. Each serves to illustrate the importance of style in enhancing meaning and aesthetic enjoyment. Refer to the literary elements at the beginning of this book (and the glossary) in order to understand the various aspects of style that appear as headings in the following section.**

## *Style*

When analysing the style of a work, two aspects are usually taken into consideration: **diction** (choice of words) and **syntax** (arrangement of words, phrases, and sentences). The questions that follow in this section are designed to help you learn to analyse these aspects in order to write convincingly about them. Moreover, you may wish to apply some of the concepts to your own writing.

**Exercise A: Three Short Short Stories: Aspects of Style**

### *Diction*

#### *Denotation and Connotation*

▸▸▸ **Denotation** *refers to the dictionary meaning of a term.* **Connotation** *refers to additional implications of the meaning of a word.* ◂◂◂

*(N.B. For specific exercises on connotation, see Writer's Craft in Unit 1.6, Write in Style in Unit 2.2, "An Unquiet Awakening" in the Essay section, as well as "The Yellow Sweater" in the short story section.)*

▸1 (Circle the best answer.) What is the predominant connotation of "scientific progress" in most people's minds?

a) positive b) negative c) neutral

▸2 (Circle the best answer.) Which story was written to refute the connotation in question 1?

a) "The New Food" b) "Bread" c) "Old Habits Die Hard"

▸3 What word in the second paragraph (of the story chosen in answer to question 2) indicates that the narrator is planning to refute this? ______________________

▸**4** What are the connotations concerning "bread" that are developed at the middle and end of the story? Complete each phrase with qualitative adjectives. Then state whether the connotations are positive, negative, or a mix of the two. (See the example for the beginning of the story.)

*EXAMPLE:*

Beginning: in a middle class kitchen — connotations concerning bread: *Something common, everyday, abundant, taken for granted, something we can waste; baking bread is a pleasurable activity and not a necessity;* ***neutral or positive connotations.***

Middle: famine situation — connotations concerning bread:

prison situation — connotations concerning bread:

German fairytale — connotations concerning bread:

End: connotations concerning bread:

▸**5** What possible effects do these contrasting connotations have on the reader by the end of the story?

## Figurative Devices (similes, metaphor, personification, imagery)

***All three stories use very powerful imagery and metaphors to create meaning. (Refer to the glossary for a definition of these terms.) "Bread" and "Old Habits Die Hard" literally abound in figurative devices. Note how these aspects of style draw readers into the story, engaging both their imagination and interest, thus adding impact to the theme(s) of each work.***

▸**6** How might "the new food" be seen as a metaphor for technological development?

▸**7** **a)** Briefly explain why imagery is a very important aspect of the short story "Bread."

**b)** Give one example of an image that you found particularly effective in "Bread."

▸**8** How might the short story "Bread" be seen as a metaphor for fiction or a work of art?

▸**9** **a)** Quote the metaphor concerning night that appears twice (with slightly different syntax) in "Old Habits Die Hard."

**b)** What does this metaphor signal the first time it appears?

**c)** What then could it signify at the end of the story?

### Rhythm, Alliteration, Assonance, Consonance, Repetition

(refer to the glossary for definitions of these terms)

▸**10** Which two stories use very rhythmical language?

**a)** "The New Food" **b)** "Bread" **c)** "Old Habits Die Hard"

▸**11** Quote six words from the first paragraph of one of the stories to exemplify how one of the authors exploits several different rhythmical devices both cleverly and effectively.

***Note how the author cleverly depicts the essence of the person's situation in just two lines at the very beginning of story "Old Habits Die Hard." Although these lines are presented as prose, they have a very poetic feel to them. This poetic quality characterises the whole piece.***

***Level of Language***

▸**12** Which story is written in a journalistic, factual style at the beginning?

**a)** "The New Food" **b)** "Bread" **c)** "Old Habits Die Hard"

▸**13** Which story is written as a conversation (i.e., using fairly informal language)?

**a)** "The New Food" **b)** "Bread" **c)** "Old Habits Die Hard"

▸**14** Which story contrasts formal and informal levels of language and includes dialogue to add both humour and realism to the piece?

**a)** "The New Food" **b)** "Bread" **c)** "Old Habits Die Hard"

***Syntax***

▸**15** Which story has much shorter sentences and more sentence fragments (sentences that lack a main verb and are not a complete idea) than the others?

**a)** "The New Food" **b)** "Bread" **c)** "Old Habits Die Hard"

▸**16** Explain how this bared-to-the-bone writing style fits the

**a)** characters in the story: ______________________________

**b)** situations described: ______________________________

▸**17** What can the reader conclude about the essence of the relationship between the two main characters?

______________________________

▸**18** Read the last paragraph of "Bread."

**a)** What do you notice about the length and the grammatical construction of the second sentence?

______________________________

**b)** Comment on the length and kinds of sentences that follow the second sentence of the last paragraph.

______________________________

______________________________

***▸▸▸ In "Old Habits Die Hard," Makeda Silvera consistently uses short sentences and sentence fragments. This syntax fits the characterisations and essence of the story.***

***In "Bread," Margaret Atwood uses long sentences, which transport the reader to another world, with short, troubling questions that bring the reader back to earth, creating an uneasiness that permeates the story. ◂◂◂***

***Tone***

▸**19** The three stories all describe awful situations. Which story does this using exaggeration and irony?

**a)** "The New Food" **b)** "Bread" **c)** "Old Habits Die Hard"

What effect does this have on the tone of this story?

___

▸**20** Which story has a general tone of

**a)** sadness? ___

**b)** uneasiness? ___

***Attitude***

▸**21** In which story does the attitude of the author seem clear and unambiguous?

**a)** "The New Food" **b)** "Bread" **c)** "Old Habits Die Hard"

How does this attitude fit the overall style of the piece?

___

___

___

**Exercise B: Different Literary Styles**

Read the following paragraphs taken from three different stories.

**a)** An excerpt from Hemingway's "Hills Like White Elephants"

"What did you say?"
"I said we could have everything."
"We can have everything."
"No, we can't."
"We can have the whole world."
"No, we can't."
"We can go everywhere."
"No, we can't. It isn't ours any more."
"It's ours."
"No, it isn't. And once they take it away, you never get it back."
"But they haven't taken it away."
"We'll wait and see."

**b)** An excerpt from Oscar Wilde's "The Nightingale and the Rose" (See the *Style and Substance* website for this story.)

She said that she would dance with me if I brought her red roses," cried the young Student; "but in all my garden there is no red rose."

From her nest in the holm-oak tree the Nightingale heard him, and she looked out through the leaves, and wondered.

"No red rose in all my garden!" he cried, and his beautiful eyes filled with tears. "Ah, on what little things does happiness depend! I have read all that the wise men have written, and all the secrets of philosophy are mine, yet for want of a red rose is my life made wretched."

**c)** An excerpt from Kate Chopin's "The Story of an Hour"

She could see in the open square before her house the tops of trees that were all aquiver with the new spring life. The delicious breath of rain was in the air. In the street below a peddler was crying his wares. The notes of a distant song which some one was singing reached her faintly, and countless sparrows were twittering in the eaves.

▸**1** Which excerpt has the most poetic quality?

**a)** **b)** **c)**

▸**2** What characteristics makes it the most poetic? (You can choose more than one answer.)

**a)** longer sentences

**b)** rhythmic quality to the words

**c)** alliteration

**d)** repetition

▸**3** Which excerpt contains the most concrete imagery? Give examples.

___

▸**4** Which excerpt contains the most usage of everyday language? Explain your answer.

___

▸**5** Describe the dominant mood found in each of the excerpts. (Use adjectives)

___

___

▸**6** Give concrete examples from each excerpt to illustrate the mood you have chosen above.

___

___

___

___

**Sometimes when asked to do a literary analysis, students write a descriptive text instead of an analytical one. A very effective way to understand the essence of a literary analysis is to contrast this type of essay with a book report. Read the two essays below, written by college students, and then answer the questions about them. (You do not have to read the literary works referred to in the essays in order to answer the questions following the essays.)**

ESSAY 1 **by Josée Bissonnette (Reprinted by permission of the author.)**

*The Outsiders* is a story written by S.E. Hinton. Recipient of the American Library Association award, she wrote this first novel when she was sixteen. S.E. Hinton now lives with her husband and son in Tulsa, Oklahoma.

Ponyboy Michael Curtis is a fourteen-year old orphan living with his two older brothers in a very tough neighbourhood. One day, his best friend, Johnny, kills Bob, a member of the rival gang. They must run away in order not to get caught. With Dallas Winston's help, they end up hiding in a Windrixville church. In that week, the friendship between Pony and Johnny becomes stronger. When Dally comes to take them home, the whole gang's life is about to be changed forever.

Ponyboy: He is the main character of the story. Ponyboy is a dreamer. He is often told that he doesn't use his head. He excels in school and is an excellent runner. He is the narrator of the story.

Johnny: Under his tough crust, Johnny is scared to death since he was beat up badly by the Socs (rival gang). He killed Bob to save Ponyboy's life and to keep the Socs from beating him up again.

Dallas: Dally is the most bitter member of the gang. In New York, he blew off steam in gang fights. He became hard and cold at an early age. The only thing he loves is Johnny.

Soda: He is the middle child of the Curtis family. He is Ponyboy's favourite brother. Soda dropped out of school and works at a gas station.

Darry: He is Ponyboy and Soda's older brother. Darry didn't go to college to give Ponyboy that chance. Instead he roofs houses to pay the bills.

Two bit: Two bit is the oldest member of the gang. He barely ever takes anything seriously but he is a good friend to have.

Steve: Steve Randle knows everything there is to know about cars. He is Soda's best friend and they work at the same gas station.

The very first time I read *The Outsiders*, I decided that I had never read a better book. It is truly an extraordinary novel. It makes you experience about a thousand different emotions. The author really lets you see the world with the characters' eyes. *The Outsiders* is filled with thrilling action from the beginning to the end.

ESSAY 2 **by Alexandra Deschamps-Sonsino (Reprinted by permission of the author.)**

Because of the different times they lived in, Katherine Mansfield and John Steinbeck have very different ways of seeing the world that surrounds them. In "Miss Brill," Katherine Mansfield deals with issues such as aging and loneliness, whereas John Steinbeck is able to capture feelings of sadness and weakness of the human soul in his short story, "The Chrysanthemums." By using imagery, characterisation and various styles of narration, both these authors have been able to portray two different women's reactions to their individual situation, and allow their distressed emotions to come forward.

First of all, the use of imagery and the vocabulary in both stories help us to understand the world in which both Miss Brill and Elisa Allen live in. In "Miss Brill," the use of imagery is particularly obvious. Miss Brill is an elderly woman who is in the habit of going to the "Jardins Publiques" every Sunday. The park is described as being "like white wine splashed over the Jardins Publiques" and the air "like a chill from a glass of iced water before you sip it," the people around "still as statues." All these comparisons and metaphors put the reader in an atmosphere of delighted perplexity, as the characters seem superficial, as if they were playing a part.

In "The Chrysanthemums," however, the Salinas Valley where Elisa Allen lives is described by the author with the use of very unusual vocabulary: "sharp and positive yellow leaves," "the air was cold and tender," "high grey-flannel fog," "like a lid on the mountains and made of the valley a closed pot." These descriptions, metaphors, and oxymorons give the reader a very clear and yet childlike image of the setting in this story. As we have seen, in their own unique way, both authors communicate the setting of their story so as to give us a first impression of the events.

Furthermore, each character has his own personality which is projected onto the reader in various ways. In "Miss Brill," there is no actual description of the main character, apart from the fact that she is wearing a wrap made of a fox fur and a red eiderdown. This allows the reader to imagine her appearance based on the way she thinks and sees herself. In this story, the narrator has the ability to allow us to read Miss Brill's thoughts as she sits in the park.

This is quite the opposite in John Steinbeck's story for Elisa is described as being "thirty-five... Her face was lean and strong and her eyes were as clear as water. Her figure looked blocked and heavy." All the adjectives used to describe her can also be used to describe a man; this indicates to the reader that she is a very powerful woman whose feminine side is hidden. However, these conclusions can only be made by the reader for there is no follow-up on Elisa's thoughts or feelings as there is for Miss Brill. Therefore, in both stories, the author does not reveal all so as not to make the characters seem too easy to figure out. The reader's imagination is required so as to make the characters seem more real.

Thirdly, in both stories, the character's personality clashes with the way the world views them. In "Miss Brill," for example, the main character is convinced that the world she evolves in resembles a play in which everyone, including herself, plays an essential part. However, as soon as the young couple came to sit beside her, her view of the world is torn apart for she is brought back to reality: she is a lonely old woman with nothing to look forward to but a life of detail and habits. Just as she had thought the others had come from "dark little rooms or even... cupboards" she goes back to "her room like a cupboard." An object which plays an important part in the story is her wrap which is personified and is given the repressed feelings Miss Brill is having. Just as she "had taken it out of its box that afternoon, then shaken out the moth powder... and rubbed the life back into the dim little eyes," it is actually her who is getting ready to go out, old and rusty that she is.

In "The Chrysanthemums," Elisa's feelings about herself are present everywhere in the story as she is "over-eager, overpowerful... her eyes hardened with resistance... irritably." However, as soon as the man from the wagon talks to her about her flowers, her fear and anger disappear and this is expressed by "the gloves were forgotten now" meaning that she is now naked in front of him, her true nature and vulnerability showing.

In conclusion, various styles and methods of writing allow us to understand the characters that the author puts forward. Katherine Mansfield and John Steinbeck both allow us to dig deep inside their characters' emotions and, at the same time, into the human spirit.

**Questions**

▸1 Does Essay 1 have a thesis statement? If yes, what is it?

▸2 Does Essay 2 have a thesis statement? If yes, what is it?

▸3 a) How are the characters presented in Essay 1?

b) In a sentence or two, explain how this differs from the way they are presented in Essay 2.

▸4 a) How does the Essay 1 conclude?

b) How is this type of conclusion very different from the one in Essay 2?

▸5 Which essay is a literary analysis?

▸6 What are the major differences between the book report and the literary analysis presented here?

▸7 Indicate whether each of the following statements is true or false.

| | TRUE | FALSE |
|---|---|---|
| a) A book report has a thesis statement. | | |
| b) A literary essay always contains short biographical information about the author. | | |
| c) A book report gives in-depth analysis of a character. | | |
| d) A literary essay includes analysis of elements and devices. | | |
| e) A book report contains the writer's personal opinion of the book. | | |
| f) A literary analysis contains the writer's personal opinion of the book. | | |
| g) A literary analysis gives a synopsis of the story. | | |
| h) A book report examines the theme of a story in detail. | | |

## WRAP-UP: DISCUSSION ACTIVITIES

▸1 Using the Leacock story as a basis, discuss how it differs in style from one of the two other stories.

▸2 Explore various interpretations and layers of meaning for the story "Bread."

▸3 Discuss whether each of the stories is part of the realist tradition.

▸4 Read and discuss another story by one of the authors.

## WRITING ACTIVITIES

▸1 Choose one of the short stories and write an essay that shows how the author's style infuses meaning and aesthetic enjoyment into the story.

▸2 Analyse how the narrator in "Bread" manipulates the reader.

▸3 Discuss the importance and role of the reader's imagination in "Bread."

▸4 Explain the techniques Silvera uses to breathe life into the two main characters of "Old Habits Die Hard."

▸5 Compare the writing styles of two authors as illustrated by the short stories in this chapter.

▸6 Write about the relevance of the theme of one of the short stories in this chapter.

▸7 Write a short story in which you experiment with some of the aspects of style.

# References

## PRINT


**STEPHEN LEACOCK**

Anderson, Allan. *Remembering Leacock: An Oral History*. Ottawa: Deneau, 1983.

Bowker, Alan. *The Social Criticism of Stephen Leacock*. Toronto: University of Toronto Press, 1973.

Lynch, Gerald. *Stephen Leacock: Humour and Humanity*. Montreal-Kingston: McGill-Queen's University Press, 1988.

Staines, David, ed. *Stephen Leacock : A Reappraisal.* Ottawa: University of Ottawa Press, 1986.

**MARGARET ATWOOD**

McCombs, Judith, ed. *Critical Essays on Margaret Atwood.* Boston: G.K. Hall & Co., 1988.

Rosenberg, Jerome H. *Margaret Atwood.* Boston: Twayne, 1984.

York, Lorraine M., ed. *Various Atwoods: Essays on the Later Poems, Short Fiction, and Novels.* Toronto: House of Anansi Press, 1995.

**MAKEDA SILVERA**

Bucknor, Michael A. "Postcolonial Crosses: Body-Memory and Inter-nationalism in Caribbean/Canadian Writing." Diss. London, ON: University of Western Ontario, 1998.

Milz, Sabine. "Hybridity in Culture, Literature and Language: A Comparative Study of Contemporary Caribbean Canadian and Turkish German Women Writing Exemplified by the Writers M.N. Philip and E.S. Özdamar." Thesis. Hamilton, ON: McMaster University, 1999.


## INTERNET

**BIOGRAPHY AND SELECTED WORKS OF THE WRITERS**

**Stephen Leacock**

schwinger.harvard.edu/~terning/bios/Leacock.html
National Library of Canada: http://www.nlc-bnc.ca/leacock/leaw.htm

**Margaret Atwood**

Site of Margaret Atwood Society: http://www.cariboo.bc.ca/atwood/
Atwood's own site: http://www.web.net/owtoad/

**Makeda Silvera**

http://www.scream.interlog.com/97/silvera.html
http://www.yorku.ca/research/aconline/silvera.html
National Library of Canada: http://www.nlc-bnc.ca/digiproj/women/women98/evision.htm

UNIT 1.8

# OTHER APPROACHES: NEWTON

## CHAPTER CONTENTS

- **READING:** "Newton" by Jeannette Winterson; author's biography; literary trends (twentieth-century scientific and technological discoveries: quantum mechanics, Einstein's theory of relativity, Freud's psychoanalytical theories; artistic experimentation: surrealism; major historical events);
- **WRITING:** paragraphs; literary essays
- **LITERARY ELEMENTS:** style (breaking traditional rules); dialogue and interior monologue; Biblical references; imagery; symbols; black humour and irony; repetition
- **GRAMMAR AND VOCABULARY:** connotations, levels of language, clear and concise language

## ABOUT THE AUTHOR

JEANNETTE WINTERSON was born in Manchester, England in 1959. She was adopted into a deeply religious family, and religion was a dominant factor in her childhood. As a result of this strong religious environment, Jeanette Winterson started her writing career as a preacher and sermon writer. Her novel, *Oranges Are Not the Only Fruit* (1985), is somewhat autobiographical, dealing with her time as a preacher. Soon after joining, she left the Church due to a difference in values about personal lifestyle choices such as homosexuality. She then obtained a Bachelor of Arts degree from Oxford University in 1981 and started to write fiction, essays, and articles. She has received many awards for works, including the Whitbread Prize in 1985 for the best fiction of a first-time writer for her novel *Oranges Are Not the Only Fruit*, and the John Llewelyn Rhys Memorial Prize for her novel *The Passion* (1987). She also won the American Academy of Arts and Letters' E.M. Forster Award for her book *Sexing the Cherry*. She has gained immense popularity in recent years.

## TWENTIETH-CENTURY TRENDS

Before the twentieth century, the scientific and Judeo-Christian thinking patterns prevalent in Western societies led people to think about reality in terms of absolutes. Classical physics explained the behaviour of many natural phenomena in terms of laws affecting the two basic elements of the universe: energy (emitted in continuous waves) and matter (concerning solid particles, the smallest of which was the atom). Many scientists were confident that they were close to unlocking the basic secrets of a mechanical universe. Judeo-Christian religions, which had dominated Western societies for centuries, required individuals to conform to precepts presented as laws handed down to humankind by the Creator. In the Judeo-Christian view of creation, a caring God had placed human beings at the centre of a meaningful universe that they were destined to control. Such concepts as "right and wrong," "evil and good" and "true and false" were considered absolutes; time was seen as a constant that would never be subject to change.

The twentieth century witnessed spectacular discoveries and inventions in science and technology that would shake the foundations of beliefs about the universe and ourselves. In 1900, the German physicist Max Planck hypothesised that energy was emitted in discrete bundles or quanta; in other words, it behaved like matter (particles) in some instances and like waves in others. Quantum mechanics, which focused on the study of minute particles, developed over the next thirty years and carved itself an important place next to classical physics (which continued to explain large-scale events). In 1905, Albert Einstein formulated his famous theory of relativity that states how the space/time continuum becomes curved as something approaches the speed of light. No longer was time an absolute. As scientists made new discoveries, they realised that the universe was far more complex than they had thought. Gradually many people began to see everything around them in relative rather than absolute terms.

Sigmund Freud's psychoanalytical theories, which divided the human psyche into the ego (the conscious) and the id (the subconscious), began to take hold early on in the century. Previously, most influential thinkers had held to a strictly rationalist view of human behaviour, saying that a person's reason was very much in control of everything that the person did. Freud's theories placed the rationalist view in doubt. He theorised that people are not aware of many subconscious elements that influence their behaviour. Later thinkers postulated that the imagination and artistic creation both issue from the subconscious.

At the same time that the scientific world was undergoing a revolution, so, too, was the universe of the arts.

A vast amount of experimentation took place that transcended traditional artistic boundaries. Art changed radically and rapidly with the advent of many new movements. Visual art became less representational and more abstract. Surrealism was an artistic movement that flourished in Europe between the world wars, affecting both painting and literature. Its adherents included painters Salvador Dali and René Magritte and authors Gertrude Stein and James Joyce. Surrealists fought against the rationalist view of reality and tried to express the role of the subconscious. They juxtaposed fantastic and realistic imagery in incongruous combinations that gave a dreamlike quality to much of their work. This combination of the conscious and unconscious realms was termed *surreality* by the poet André Breton.

Politically, the twentieth century witnessed major events and clashes in ideologies that sent shockwaves through most strata of human endeavour: World War I (1914-1918) — supposedly the war that would end all wars — the Roaring Twenties, the Great Depression (1929-1939), the rise of Nazism, World War II (1939-1945) and the hydrogen bomb, the Cold War of the 1950s, the wars in southeast Asia in the latter half of the century, the rise of Communism early in the century and its fall in the 1990s, the break-up of the great empires, and genocide attempts throughout the century. These and other historical events served to shake the foundations of Western humankind's faith in rationalism and to disturb our understanding and vision of ourselves, our role, and our planet.

This brief overview of the twentieth century is very incomplete because it concentrates only on the aspects important to the study of the short story in this section. We encourage you to consult other sources of information on the Internet and in a library should you wish to pursue your study of this fascinating century.

### Warm-Up Discussion Topics

▸1 People use both the arts and the sciences and technology to explore and interpret reality. What basic differences can you see between the approaches these fields use in their exploration and interpretations?

---

▸2 Are you more attracted to the sciences and technology or to the arts? Why?

---

**INITIAL READING** ▸ **The story you are about to read exemplifies some of the experimentation that has emerged in the short story genre over recent years. Its surrealistic approach and its challenge to tradition and old ways of doing things are an excellent example of the spirit that reigned during much of the twentieth century. Moreover, it points out some very common but rather serious human failings in a humorous light-hearted manner.**

**Before continuing, make sure that you read the section above entitled Twentieth-Century Trends, as it will add to your understanding and enjoyment of the piece. Here is further information to prepare you for this challenging story.**

**Exercise: Glossary**

Match the word or expression in the left-hand column with its definition/explanation on the right.

| | |
|---|---|
| ▸1 knickers | a) Hypothetical tendency for all matter and energy in the universe to evolve to a state of inert uniformity |
| ▸2 Grim Reaper | b) Weird, eccentric person *(Slang)* |
| ▸3 Newton | c) Underwear, panties *(British English)* |
| ▸4 entropy | d) Home-improvement centre |
| ▸5 screwball | e) 17th-century English mathematician and scientist who invented differential calculus and who formulated "laws" concerning the physical universe |
| ▸6 Camus | f) Personification of Death dressed in a black hooded cloak and holding a scythe |
| ▸7 DIY | g) 20th-century French writer and philosopher whose book *L'Étranger* deals with the absurdity of the human condition. |

As you read the story, try to **visualise** the scenes and enjoy them as surreal art. Many are full of **black humour** (see definition in the Writer's Craft section after the story) or **irony**. Also, note the **repetitions**, recurring **imagery**, and **contrasts** between opposites, as these will hint at the theme(s). Try to appreciate the **connotations** associated with words, phrases, images and so on, because these, too, will lead you to the underlying meanings in the work. Lastly, please note that this story uses British punctuation style.

STORY

# NEWTON

JEANNETTE WINTERSON

1 This is the story of Tom.
This is the story of Tom and his neighbours.
This is the story of Tom and his neighbours and his neighbour's garden.
This is the story of Tom.

2 'All of my neighbours are Classical Physicists,' said Tom. 'Their laws of motion are determined. They rise at 7 a.m. and leave for work at 8 a.m. The women take coffee at 10 a.m. If you see a body on the street between 1 and 2 p.m. lunchtime, it can only be the doctor, it can only be the undertaker, it can only be the stranger.

'I am the stranger,' said Tom.

3 'What is the First Law of Thermodynamics?' said Tom.

'You can't transfer heat from a colder to a hotter. I've never known any warmth from my neighbours so I would reckon this is true. Here in Newton we don't talk much. That is, my neighbours talk all the time, they swap gossip, but I never have any, although sometimes I am some.'

• • •

4 'What is the Second Law of Thermodynamics?' said Tom.

'Everything tends towards the condition of entropy. That is, the energy is still there somewhere but for all useful purposes it is lost. Take a look at my neighbours here in Newton and you'll see what it means.'

My neighbour has a garden full of plastic flowers. 'It's easy,' she says, 'and so nice.' When her husband died she had him laminated, and he stands outside now, hands on his hips, carefully watching the sky.

'What's the matter Tom?' she says, her head bobbing along the fence like a duck in a shooting parlour.

'Why don't you get married? In my day nobody had any trouble finding someone. We just did it and made the best of it. There were no screwballs then.'

5 'What none?'

6 She bobbed faster and faster, gathering a bosom-load of underwear from the washing line. I knew she wanted me to stare at it, she wants to prove that I am a screwball. After all, if it's me, it's not her, it's not the others. You can't have more than one per block.

She wheeled round, ready to bob back up the other way, knickers popping from every pore.

'Tom, we were glad to be normal. In those days it was something good, something to be proud of.'

• • •

7 Tom the screwball. Here I am with my paperback foreign editions and my corduroy trousers ('You got something against Levi's?' he asked me, before he was laminated). All the men round here wear Levi's, denims or chinos. The only stylistic difference is whether they pack their stomach inside or outside the waistband.

They suspect me of being a homosexual. I wouldn't care. I wouldn't care what I was if only I were something.

8 'What do you want to be when you grow up?' said my mother, a long time ago, many times a long time ago.

'A fireman, an astronaut, a spy, a train driver, a hard hat, an inventor, a deep sea diver, a doctor and a nurse.'

'What do you want to be when you grow up?' I ask myself in the mirror most days.

'Myself. I want to be myself.'

And who is that, Tom?

9 Into the clockwork universe the quantum child. Why doesn't every mother believe her child can change the world? The child can. This is the joke. Here we are still looking for a saviour and hundreds are being born every second. Look at it, this tiny capsule of new life, indifferent to your prejudices, your miseries, unmindful of the world already made. Make it again? They could if we let them, but we make sure they grow up just like us, fearful like us. Don't let them know the potential that they are. Don't let them hear the grass singing. Let them live and die in Newton, tick-tock, the last breath.

10 There was a knock at my door, I hid my Camus in the fridge and peered through the frosted glass. Of course I can't see anything. They never remind you of that when you fit frosted glass.

'Tom? Tom?' RAP RAP.

It's my neighbour. I shuffled to the door, feet bare, shirt loose. There she is, her hair coiled on her head like a wreath on a war memorial. She was dressed solely in pink.

'I'm not interrupting am I Tom?' she said, her eyes shoving past me into the kitchen.

'I was reading.'

'That's what I thought. I said to myself, poor Tom will be reading. He won't be busy. I'll ask him to help me out. You know how difficult it is for a woman to manage alone. Since my husband was laminated, I haven't had it easy, Tom.'

11 She smelled of woman; warm, perfumed, slightly threatening. I had to be careful not to act like a screwball. I offered her coffee. She seemed pleased, although she kept glancing at my bare feet and loose shirt. Never mind, she needs me to help her with something in the house. That's normal, that's nice, I want to be normal and nice.

12 'My mother's here. Will you help me get her into the house.'

'Now? Shall we go now?'

'She's had a long journey. She can rest in the truck a while. Shall we have that coffee you offered me first?'

13 I don't love my neighbour but still my hand trembled over the sugar spoon. They've made me feel odd and outside for so long, that now even the simplest things feel strange.

How does a normal person make coffee? What is it about me that worries them so much? I'm clean. I have a job.

14 'Tom, tell me, is it the modern thing to keep books in the refrigerator?'

In cheap crime novels, you often read the line, 'He spun round.' It makes me laugh to imagine a human being so animated, but when she asked me that question, I spun. One second I was facing the sink, the next second I was facing her, and she was facing me, holding my copy of Camus.

'I was just fetching out the milk Tom. Who is Albert K Mew?' She pronounced it like an enraged cat.

'He's a Frenchman. A French writer. I don't know how he came to be in the fridge.'

She repeated my words slowly as though I had just offered her a universal truth.

'You don't know how he came to be in the fridge?' I shrugged and smiled and tried to disarm her.

'It's a big fridge. Don't you ever find things in the fridge you had forgotten about?'

'No Tom. Never. I store cheese at the top, and then beer and bacon underneath, and underneath those I keep my weekend chicken, and at the bottom I have salad things and eggs. Those are the rules. It was the same when my husband was alive and it is the same now.'

I was beginning to regard her with a new respect. The Grim Reaper came to call. He took her husband from the bed but left the weekend chicken on the shelf.

O Death, where is thy sting?

15 My neighbour, still holding my Camus, leaned forward confidentially, her arms resting on the table. She looked intimate, soft, I could see the beginning of her breasts.

'Tom, have you ever wondered whether you need help?' She said HELP with four capital letters, like a doorstep evangelist.

'If you mean the fridge, anyone can make a mistake.' She leaned forward a little further. More breast.

'Tom, I'm going to be tough with you. You know what your problem is? You read too many geniuses. I don't know if Mr K Mew is a genius but the other day you were seen in the main square reading Picasso's notebooks. Children were coming out of school and you were reading Picasso. Miss Fin at the library tells me that all you ever borrow are works of genius. She has no record of you ever ordering a sea story. Now that's unhealthy. Why is it unhealthy? You yourself are not a genius, if you were we would have found out by now. You are ordinary like the rest of us and ordinary people should lead ordinary lives. Like the rest of us, here in Tranquil Gardens.'

She leaned back, her bosom with her.

'Shall we go and help your mother?' I said.

Outside, my neighbour walked towards a closed van parked in front of her house. I'd seen her mother a couple of years previously but I couldn't see her now.

'She's in the back Tom. Go round the back.'

My neighbour flung open the back doors of the hired van and certainly there was her mother, sitting upright in the wheel-chair that had been her home and her car. She was smiling a fearful plasticy smile, her teeth as perfect as a cheetah's.

'Haven't they done a wonderful job Tom? She's even better than Doug, and he was pretty advanced at the time. I wish she could see herself. She never guessed I'd laminate her. She'd be so proud.'

'Are those her own teeth?'

'They are now Tom.'

'Where will you put her?'

'In the garden with the flowers. She loved flowers.'

• • •

16 Slowly, slowly, we heaved down mother. We wheeled her over the swept pavement to the white-washed house. It was afternoon coffee time and a lot of neighbours had been invited to pay their respects. They were so respectful that we were outside talking plastic until the men came home. My neighbour gets an incentive voucher for every successful lamination she introduces. She reckons that if Newton will only do it her way, she'll have 75 percent of her own lamination costs paid by the time she dies.

'I've seen you hanging around the cemetery Tom. It's not hygienic.'

What does she think I am? A ghoul? I've told her before that my mother is buried there but she just shakes her head and tells me that young couples need the land.

'Until we learn to stop dying Tom, we have to live with the consequences. There's no room for the dead unless you treat them as ornamental.'

I have tried to tell her that if we stop dying, all the cemeteries in the world can never release enough land for the bulging, ageing population. She doesn't listen, she just looks dreamy and thinks about the married couples.

Newton is jammed with married couples. We need one-way streets to let the singles through. I hate going shopping in Newton. I hate clubbing my way through the crocodile files, two by two in Main street, as though the ark has landed. Complacent shoulder blades, battered baby buggys. DIY stores crammed with HIM and shopping malls heaving with HER. Don't they know that too much role playing is bad for the health? Imagine being a wife and saying 'Honey, have you got time to fix the toilet?' Imagine being a husband and figuring out how to clean the toilet when she's left you.

Why are they married? It's normal, it's nice. They do it the way they do everything else in Newton. Tick-tock says the clock.

17 'Tom, thank you Tom,' she cooed at me when her mother was safely settled beside the duck pond. The ducks are bathtime yellow with chirpy red beaks and their pond has real water with a bit of chlorine in it just in case. I had never been in my neighbour's garden before. It was quiet. No rustling in the undergrowth. No undergrowth to rustle in. No birds yammering. She tells me that peace is what the countryside is all about.

'If you were a genius Tom you could work here. The silence. The air. I have a unit you know, filters the air as it enters the garden.'

It was autumn and there were a few plastic leaves scattered about on the AstroTurf. At the bottom of the garden, my neighbour has a shed, made of imitation wood, where she keeps her stocks for the changing of the seasons. She has told me many times that a garden must have variety and in her ventilated Aladdin's cave are the reassuring copies of nature. Tulips, red and white, hang meekly upside down by their stems. Daffodils in bright bunches are jumbled with loose camellia blooms, waiting to be slotted into the everlasting tree. She even has a row of squirrels clutching identical nuts.

'Those are going out soon, along with the autumn creeper.' She has Virginia Creeper cascading down the house. It's still green. This is the burnt and blazing version.

'Mine's turning already,' I said.

'Too early,' she said. 'You can't depend on nature. I don't like leaves falling. They don't fall where they should. If you don't regulate nature, why, she'll just go ahead and do what she likes. We have to regulate her. If we don't, it's volcanoes and forest fires and floods and death and bodies scattered everywhere, just like leaves.'

Like leaves. Just like leaves. Don't you like them just a little where they fall? Don't you turn them over to see what is written on the other side? I like that. I like the simple text that can be read or not, that lies beneath your feet and mine, read or not. That falls, rain and wind, though nobody scoops it up to take it home. Life fell at your feet and you kicked her away and she bled on your shoes and when you came home, your mother said, 'Look at you, covered in leaves.'

You were covered in leaves. You peeled them off one by one, exposing the raw skin beneath. All those leavings. And when what had to fall was fallen, you picked it up and read what was written on the other side. It made no sense to you. You screwed it up in your pocket where it burned like a live coal. Tell me why they left you, one by one, the ones you loved? Didn't they like you? Didn't they, like you, need a heart that was a book with no last page? Turn the leaves.

'The leaves are turning,' said Tom.

18 She asked me back to supper as a thank you, and I thought I should go because that's what normal people do; eat with their neighbours, even though it is boring and the food is horrible. I searched for a tie and wore it.

19 'Tom, come in, what a lovely surprise!'

She must mean what a lovely surprise for me. It can hardly be a surprise for her, she's been cooking all afternoon.

Once inside the dining room, I know she means me. I know that because the entire population of Newton is already seated at the dinner table, a table that begins crammed up against the display cabinet of Capodimonte and extends… and extends… through a jagged hole blown in the side of the house, out and on towards the bus station.

'I think you know everyone Tom,' says my neighbour. 'Sit here, by me, in Doug's place. You're about his height.' Do I know everyone? It's hard to say, since beyond the hole, all is lost.

'Tom, take a plate. We're having chicken cooked in bacon strips and stuffed with hard-boiled eggs. There's a salad I made and plenty of cheese and beer in the fridge if you want it.'

She drifted away from me, her dress clinging to her like a drowned man. Nobody looked up from their plates. They were eating chicken, denims and chinos all, eating the three or four hundred fowl laid on the table, half a dozen eggs per ass. I was still trying to work out the roasting details, the oven size, when BAM, one of the chickens exploded, pelting my neighbour with eggs like hand-grenades. One of her arms flew off but luckily for her, not the one she needed for her fork. Nobody noticed. I wanted to speak, I wanted to act, I began to speak, to act, just as my neighbour herself returned carrying a covered silver dish.

'It's for you Tom,' she says, as the table falls silent. Already on my feet I was able to lift the huge lid with some dignity. Underneath was a chicken.

'It's your chicken Tom.'

She's telling the truth. Poking out of the ass of the chicken, I can see my copy of *L'Étranger* by Albert Camus. It hasn't been shredded, so I can take it out. When I open it I see that there are no words left on any of the pages. The pages are blank.

'We wanted to help you Tom.' Her eyes are full of tears. 'Not just me. All of us. A helping hand for Tom.'

Slowly the table starts to clap, faster and louder. The table shakes, the dishes roll from side to side like the drunken tableware in a sea story. This is a sea story. The captain and the crew have gone mad and I am the only passenger. Reeling, I ran from the dining room into the kitchen and slammed the door behind me. Here was peace. Hygienic enamelled peace.

Tom slid to the floor and cried.

Time passed. In Newton it always does and everyone knows how long it takes for time to pass and so nobody gets confused. Tom didn't know how much time had passed. He woke from an aching sleep and put his fist through the frosted glass kitchen door. He went home and took his big coat and filled the pockets with books and the books seemed like live coals to him. He walked away from Newton, but he did look back once, and what he saw was a table stretching out past the bend in the road and on through the streets and houses joining them together in an orgy of matching cutlery. World without end.

'But now,' says Tom, 'the hills are ripe and the water leaps at my throat when I shave.'

Tick-tock says the clock in Newton.

## Reader's Response

▸1 What was your first reaction to this story? List some adjectives to indicate what you were thinking and feeling.

▸2 In your opinion, are the attitudes of the townspeople of Newton similar or different from the attitudes of others in contemporary society? Explain your answer.

## Close Reading

▸1 When does the story take place? **a)** In the future (realistic) **b)** In contemporary times **c)** In the past **d)** In a time beyond time (surrealistic)

Justify your answer.

▸2 Why does Tom think that his neighbours can be compared to classical physics? Give one direct example from the text to prove your answer.

▸3 Describe how Tom applies the first and second Law of Thermodynamics in order to portray his neighbours' characteristics.

▸4 In your opinion, is Tom's opinion of his neighbours positive or negative? Justify your answer.

▸5 During her conversation with Tom, it is obvious that the neighbour's attitude toward life is different from Tom's. Find three things that Tom's neighbour says or does that shows this difference.

▸6 Find three different characteristics about Tom that reveal how he is different from his neighbours.

▸7 What does Tom say he wants to be when he grows up? How is this significant to the story?

▸8 Write the statement made by the neighbour that reveals the purpose behind the neighbour's dinner invitation to Tom.

▸9 What has the neighbour done to Tom's book by Camus?

▸10 Why has she done what she did to Tom's book?

▸11 What is Tom's reaction to events during the dinner? What does he think and feel when he sees his book?

▸12 Why does Tom leave Newton?

## WRITER'S CRAFT

### Connotations

▸▸▸ **Connotations** *are meanings or ideas suggested by or associated with words.* ◂◂◂

Match the following words, phrases or sentences from the story with their connotations.

| | |
|---|---|
| ▸1 Newton | **a)** Judeo-Christian religions, help from outside |
| ▸2 plastic | **b)** mechanical, predictable, unthinking repetition |
| ▸3 nature | **c)** hiding reality from view, obscuring clear vision |
| ▸4 normal | **d)** accepted norm, everyday, what ordinary people eat |
| ▸5 Tick-tock says the clock. | **e)** uncontrolled, unregulated, unpredictable, alive |
| ▸6 leaves | **f)** conformist, society's expectations |
| ▸7 a saviour | **g)** dead, artificial, imitation |
| ▸8 frosted glass | **h)** scientific laws, rules |
| ▸9 chicken | **i)** trees (nature), pages (book, story, art), quits (change) |
| ▸10 quantum child | **j)** new direction, possibility for change, potential |

▸▸▸ ***Jeanette Winterson uses connotations extensively in this story to add layers of meaning to the work.*** ◂◂◂

### Biblical References

▸1 Paragraph 14 ends with the question "O Death, where is thy sting?" This celebrated phrase comes from the Bible: I Corinthians 15-55 and is used ironically here to imply that Tom's neighbour seems more upset about someone breaking "refrigerator rules" than about her husband's death. There are several other biblical references in the text in the paragraphs indicated. Quote the references (the wording can be a little different from that of the original).

**a)** para. 9: ______________________

**b)** para. 13: ______________________

**c)** para. 15: ______________________

**d)** para. 20: ______________________

▸2 The garden of Tom's neighbour evokes a famous biblical garden (although very ironically). Which one?

______________________

▸3 The scene of the banquet also evokes a famous biblical image. Which one?

______________________

▸▸▸ ***Winterson, like a great many artists in the Occident, uses biblical imagery to add depth and meaning to her work. For example, a reference to the Garden of Eden often indicates humankind's relentless search for a paradise, an ideal existence.*** ◂◂◂

### *Imagery*

▸1 Which sense is solicited the most often by Winterson's imagery? ______

▸2 Describe one image that you find to be particularly surreal.

______

▸▸▸ *"Newton" abounds in surrealistic imagery designed to breathe life into the story and to stimulate the reader's imagination and thoughts. The use of surreal elements is characteristic of many of Winterson's short stories.* ◂◂◂

### *Symbols*

▸▸▸ *Many writers use symbols as clues to help you understand the overall meaning of the story. Many symbols in this story will help to show the principal theme of the story.* ◂◂◂

▸1 Write your interpretation of the following symbols:

**a)** Tom's neighbour's garden (Find something different from the ironical religious evocation)

______

______

**b)** *L'Étranger* by Albert Camus

______

**c)** The name of the town, Newton

______

▸2 Find two other symbols that show that Tom does not fit into Newton.

**a)** ______

**b)** ______

### *Black Humour and Irony*

▸▸▸ **Black humour** *can be defined as the deliberate placing of the morbid or absurd side by side with the comical. This is often meant to shock or disturb the intended audience.* ◂◂◂

▸1 Explain how the idea of laminating the dead can be seen as black humour and surreal at the same time.

______

▸2 Describe another example of Winterson's use of black humour in the story.

______

▸3 How is the situation where Tom's neighbour finds his book in the fridge ironic?

______

______

***▸▸▸ Winterson uses many instances of black humour and irony in this story to underline meaning and to add to the overall surreal quality of the piece. This also adds an element of surprise and unpredictability to the story — the reader can't guess what aspect of traditional Western society she will attack next! This gives impact to the style. ◂◂◂***

### BREAKING TRADITIONAL RULES

▸1 In this story, Winterson deliberately breaks many traditional rules for stylistic reasons. (This is called artistic license and is not something a student should imitate in the context of academic writing!)

Explain how she goes beyond traditional rules and usage with regard to the following:

**a)** paragraph format and content:

**b)** narration and point of view:

**c)** flow of the main story line:

**d)** sequence of tenses:

**e)** characterisation:

▸2 Read the following excerpt. Note three words that the author repeats with a different meaning each time and one punctuation mark that when added (twice) changes the meaning.

Tell me why they left you, one by one, the ones you loved? Didn't they like you?
Didn't they, like you, need a heart that was a book with no last page? Turn the leaves.
'The leaves are turning,' said Tom.

**a)** Three words:

**b)** Punctuation mark:

***▸▸▸ Winterson has used repetition in this story. There is repetition of words and sentences, images and ideas. Repetition is used as a means of enhancing the theme. ◂◂◂***

## REPETITION

▸▸▸ ***Winterson plays with the multiple meanings of words and grammatical structure to evoke meaningful associations and connections in the mind of the reader.*** ◂◂◂

▸ **1** The first four sentences of the story are repetitions. What do you notice about their structure or patterns?

▸ **2** Which clause is repeated most often in the first four sentences? What is its significance?

▸ **3** The second paragraph also indicates repetition. What is being repeated in this paragraph?

▸ **4** What quality (adjective) would you ascribe to the type of repetition of the townspeople's lifestyle as described by Tom?

▸ **5** Tom's neighbour is characterised through repetition. List two things referring to the neighbour that show repetition.

▸ **6** When talking to Tom in his house, the neighbour tells him what she keeps in her refrigerator. What is significant about how she keeps her fridge?

▸ **7** The story is full of repeated references to the classical physicist Newton and his scientific laws. Read the last sentence of the story. What can you imply from it concerning the author's vision of traditional society as exemplified by the town?

### DIALOGUE AND INTERIOR MONOLOGUE

▸▸▸ **Interior monologue** *consists of the direct written presentation of the ongoing thoughts and emotions (often disjointed and unorganised) a character experiences in his or her head. The theme is also revealed through* **dialogue** *and* **interior monologue** *or what Tom is thinking.* ◂◂◂

▸**1** Reread the conversation between Tom and his neighbour beginning with the line "'Tom? Tom?' RAP RAP," which ends with the sentence, "She leaned back, her bosom with her."

In your opinion, what is the central conflict between Tom and his neighbour as indicated during their conversation?

▸**2** Write one sentence from this dialogue to prove your answer to the preceding question.

▸**3** Tom reveals his own philosophy on life when he reflects on the neighbours' words and actions.

Write an interpretation of the following quotations (which are Tom's thoughts).

Into the clockwork universe the quantum child. Why doesn't every mother believe her child can change the world? The child can. This is the joke. Here we are still looking for a saviour and hundreds are being born every second. Look at it, this tiny capsule of new life, indifferent to your prejudices, your miseries, unmindful of the world already made. Make it again? They could if we let them, but we make sure they grow up just like us, fearful like us. Don't let them know the potential that they are. Don't let them hear the grass singing. Let them live and die in Newton, tick-tock, the last breath.

Like leaves. Just like leaves. Don't you like them just a little where they fall? Don't you turn them over to see what is written on the other side? I like that. I like the simple text that can be read or not, that lies beneath your feet and mine, read or not. That falls, rain and wind, though nobody scoops it up to take it home. Life fell at your feet and you kicked her away and she bled on your shoes and when you came home, your mother said, 'Look at you, covered in leaves.'

▸**4** Find one other example of interior monologue that reveals Tom's opinions and attitudes.

▸**5** What is the central conflict of the story?

▸**6** In your opinion, what is the principal theme of the story?

▸7 What images does the author use to describe the following items in the last paragraph of the story?

**a)** books

**b)** hills

**c)** shaving

What characteristic do all these images share?

▸8 If we consider that Tom symbolises "the artist," what statement could Winterson be making about the effects of science and technology on human civilisation?

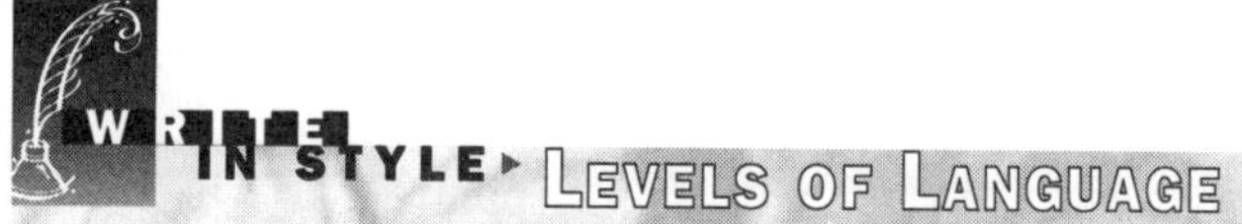


**Good writers are aware of the appropriateness of the language they are using for their particular situation. For example, language choice differs between a formal, academic report and a letter to a friend or between a business report and creative writing. It is important to understand what is being written and the intended audience. Language usage revolves around diction. Diction refers to the choice of words used by the speaker or writer. The following is a list of different types of usage.**

- **Standard English**

  In general, it is the accepted form of usage in English-speaking countries. Although Standard English can vary from one English-speaking country to another, it is the common language of the country and is taught in schools. It is considered to be formal language.

  *EXAMPLE: Hello. I am very pleased to meet you.*

- **Colloquial English** is common language or informal language.

  *EXAMPLE: That boy keeps* hanging around *my girlfriend.*

- **Slang** is language that uses "words and phrases either peculiar to or used in special senses by some class or profession." That is, it is language common to a group.

  *EXAMPLE: My friends and I* pigged out *on pizza last night.*

- **Dialect** is a variety of English found in a particular geographic region, spoken by a particular group.

  *EXAMPLE: I told you not to do that,* eh? *(This particular use of "eh" is found in the English-speaking parts of Canada.)*

- **Jargon** is language filled with unfamiliar terms, most of which are specific to a profession.

  *EXAMPLE: The* psychometric analysis *of the* standardised formative *test was used to determine the* intelligence quotient *of the* study group.

- **Euphemism** is vague or inoffensive language that is substituted for harsher words.

  *EXAMPLE: He works as a* sanitary engineer. *(a garbage man in Standard English)*

**Exercise A: Levels of Language**

Replace the word in italics with a word (or words) conforming to Standard English.

▸ 1 My neighbour is such a *jerk*. He blocks my driveway with his car.

▸ 2 The boy's *ego was battling with the forces of his id in order to gain hegemony of the conscious.*

▸ 3 The new English teacher is *really with it*.

▸ 4 That child *ain't never* going to listen to his babysitter.

▸ 5 My mother *freaked out* when I told her I *flunked* my math test.

**Exercise B: Using Clear and Concise Language**

On looseleaf or in a notebook, rewrite the following paragraph, making any necessary changes in order to have a clear and concise text.

Food has become the hot topic of conversation of late. Everyone seems to be getting into the food and cooking frenzy. And everyone seems to be writing recipe books. I went to the book store the other day and in the section on food, there were tons of books on how to cook food, how to eat food, how to lose weight, how to gain weight, how to get more nutritious food, how to avoid bad fat, how to get good fat, how to barbecue, how to be a vegetarian, etc. etc. etc. It seems that everybody has become an expert on food and nutrition and everybody wants to tell everyone what they know. This is called imparting knowledge or certainly implied knowledge, with a vengeance. I see this happening in many other areas as well, like medicine and psychology. Everybody is an expert. Except me. I will remain in my den of ignorance living, breathing, eating, and enjoying my neuroses.

**Style Tips**

Here are some tips to consider when writing for academic purposes.

- Use Standard English.
- Check a dictionary in order to know the precise meaning of words and to make informed word choices.
- Avoid slang, jargon, or vague language.

### Paragraph Practice

- ▸1 Compare the different values of the two main characters in the story "Newton."
- ▸2 How is nature portrayed in the story "Newton" and what is its significance?

## WRAP-UP: DISCUSSION ACTIVITIES

- ▸1 Discuss the appropriateness of the title of the story.
- ▸2 Explain Winterson's vision of the artist as exemplified by Tom.
- ▸3 What is Winterson's view of science and technology as shown by the short story?
- ▸4 What are the similarities and the differences between Louise Mallard in "The Story of an Hour" and Tom in "Newton"?

## WRITING ACTIVITIES

Write a literary essay of between 750 and 1000 words.

- ▸1 The story "Newton" is a warning of what contemporary society is and will become. Discuss.
- ▸2 The story "Newton" is all about conflict. Explain the different conflicts found in the story and their significance in terms of the theme.
- ▸3 Analyse the style of one of the other writers that you have studied during the term.
- ▸4 Analyse Jeannette Winterson's writing style.
- ▸5 How does Winterson's use of imagery enhance the theme of "Newton"?
- ▸6 Compare the settings of "The Veldt" and "Newton" and discuss their importance in terms of tone and atmosphere as well as theme.

# References

## PRINT


**BIOGRAPHY**

Anshaw, Carol. "Into the Mystic: Jeanette Winterson's Fable Manner." *Village Voice Literary Supplement 86*, 1990. pp. 16-17.

Barr, Helen. "Face to Face: A Conversation between Jeanette Winterson and Helen Barr." *The English Review*, 2, 1991, pp. 30-33.

d'Adesky, Anne-Christine. "Still Life With Winterson" OUT, Feb/March, 1993, pp. 33-39.

Rich, Ruby B. "In Profile: Jeanette Winterson." *The Advocate*, June 24, 1997. p. 105.

**CRITICISM**

Bengtson, Helene, Borch, Marianne / Maagaard, Cindie (eds.) *Sponsored by Demons: The Art of Jeanette Winterson*. Scholar's Press, 1999.

Burns, Christy L. "Fantastic Language: Jeanette Winterson's recovery of the postmodern word." *Contemporary Literature* 37 (1996): 274-306.

Cambell, Bea. "The Naked Novelist." Diva. Dec./Jan. 1996/97: 17-18.

Grice, Helena, and Tim Woods, eds. *'I'm Telling You Stories': Jeanette Winterson and the Politics of Reading*. Amsterdam: Rodopi, 1998.

Palmer, Paulina. "Postmodern Trends in Contemporary Fiction: Margaret Atwood, Angela Carter, Jeanette Winterson." In *Postmodern Subjects/Postmodern Texts*. ed. Jane Dowson and Steven Earnshaw. Amsterdam: Rodopi, 1995, pp. 181-199.


## INTERNET


**BIOGRAPHY:**

http://home8.swipnet.se/~w-83331/
http://www.adlbooks.com/wntrsn.html
http://www.uni-koeln.de

**INTERVIEW**

http://www.salonmagazine.com/april97/winterson970428.html

**CRITICISM**

http://home.swipnet.se/~w-83331/reviews.html


WWW

UNIT 2

# Essays

UNIT 2

# Essays

**The essay section comprises an introduction and five chapters containing essays that range in theme, style, and type. This section presents the basic techniques needed to write different types of essays.**

WHAT IS AN ESSAY? All writing in English is usually classified as **prose** or **poetry** (although some modern writing does not fit neatly into either category!). What is the basic difference between prose and poetry? Many people would answer that prose is not made up of lines having a specific meter (poetic feet) or a rhyming scheme (see glossary for meaning), but many modern poems do not exhibit these two characteristics, either. A poem, with its special rhythms and vivid imagery, generally seems akin to a musical composition or a painting. Prose is more like the ordinary language we use in our daily affairs.

Prose falls into two categories: fiction and nonfiction. Fiction consists of works created largely by the imagination, including novels and short stories. Nonfiction is everything that is not fiction, including biographies, historical accounts, newspaper articles, diaries, research reports, reference books and manuals, and essays. It is this last type of prose that we will explore in this section of the book.

> ***"A good essay must have this permanent quality about it; it must draw its curtain round us, but it must be a curtain that shuts us in not out."***
>
> — Virginia Woolf (1882–1941), British novelist. *The Common Reader*

The essay is a short written composition on a single subject. It usually represents the personal experience and view of the author. Essays range from accounts of special events such as a jazz festival, to descriptions of life in New York, to an argument about genetic manipulation. The early Greeks and Romans used oral essays or rhetoric to argue particular subjects. Rhetoric, like the modern essay or speech, was applicable to the context of the subject matter and its audience. The ancient Greeks and Romans used rhetoric to persuade audiences on political and philosophical issues such as democracy, truth, and morality.

When you write an essay, you usually have a purpose; you are trying to achieve something. Perhaps it is to analyse a poem or to persuade someone to do something. Or perhaps it is to explain a process or to complain about a product that doesn't work. The list is endless.

Here are some basic types of essays:

- Narrative
- Descriptive
- Expository
- Analytic
- Argumentative

## BRIEF HISTORY OF THE ESSAY

The sixteenth-century French writer, Michel de Montaigne, first used the word *essai* to describe his attempts to express his thoughts and feelings in short written pieces. His *Essais*, published in 1588, still exemplify excellence in style. Montaigne wrote essays and personal reflections on Catholicism and humanity's relationship to God and nature.

The first great English essayist was Francis Bacon, whose *Essayes* were published in 1597. Written in rather heavy-sounding language, Bacon's essays dealt with serious and weighty topics such as truth, death, and revenge. They were very different from Montaigne's more personal thoughts on himself and his travels.

During the seventeenth and eighteenth centuries, and into the early nineteenth century, the English essay form developed and became a very popular form under the pen of such writers as Abraham Cowley, Joseph Addison and Richard Steele, Samuel Johnson, Oliver Goldsmith, and, especially, Charles Lamb and Thomas De Quincey. Alexander Pope wrote his *Essay on Man*, which is an argument in poetic form. Poets considered it a true art to place their arguments in strict rhyme and rhythm.

In the last half of the nineteenth century, Robert Louis Stevenson in Britain, and Henry David Thoreau and Ralph Waldo Emerson in the United States, also produced essays on spirituality, transcendentalism, religion, and political philosophy. At the dawn of the twentieth century, Samuel Clemens, using the pen name of Mark Twain, brought a delightful touch of humour to the form, which was developed further by Stephen Leacock, James Thurber, and Dorothy Parker, to name but a few. Essays still remain a very popular form of expression today. In modern form, they are found in editorials and opinion articles in newspapers, as well as in the traditional forms of expository, descriptive, and narrative essays. (Please note that details about the different types of essays will be presented in the chapters of this section.)

### WARM-UP

Read the following excerpts and answer the questions that follow.

EXCERPT A: FROM

## DOVER BEACH

MATTHEW ARNOLD (1822-1888)

...Ah, love, let us be true
To one another! for the world, which seems
To lie before us like a land of dreams,
So various, so beautiful, so new,
Hath really neither joy, nor love, nor light,
Nor certitude, nor peace, nor help for pain;
And we are here as on a darkling plain
Swept with confused alarms of struggle and flight,
Where ignorant armies clash by night.

EXCERPT B: FROM

## PORNOGRAPHY

D.H. LAWRENCE (1930)

What is pornography to one man is the laughter of genius to another...

One essay on pornography, I remember, comes to the conclusion that pornography in art is that which is calculated to arouse sexual desire, or sexual excitement. And stress is laid on the fact, whether the author or artist intended to arouse sexual feelings. It is the old vexed question of intention, become so dull today, when we know how strong and influential our unconscious intentions are. And why a man should be held guilty of his conscious intentions, and innocent of his unconscious intentions, I don't know, since every man is more made up of unconscious intentions than of conscious ones. I am what I am, not merely what I think I am...

EXCERPT C: FROM

## MARRAKECH

GEORGE ORWELL (1945)

As the corpse went past the flies left the restaurant table in a cloud and rushed after it, but they came back a few minutes later.

The little crowd of mourners — all men and boys, no women — threaded their way across the marketplace between the piles of pomegranates and the taxis and the camels, wailing a short chant over and over again. What really appeals to the flies is that the corpses here are never put into coffins, they are merely wrapped in a piece of rag and carried on a rough wooden bier on the shoulders of four friends. When the friends get to the burying-ground they hack an oblong hole a foot or two deep, dump the body in it and fling over it a little of the dried-up, lumpy earth, which is like broken brick. No gravestone, no name, no identifying mark of any kind. The burying-ground is merely a huge waste of hummocky earth, like a derelict building-lot. After a month or two no one can even be certain where his own relatives are buried...

EXCERPT D: FROM

## A DILL PICKLE

KATHERINE MANSFIELD

And then, after six years, she saw him again. He was seated at one of those little bamboo tables decorated with a Japanese vase of paper daffodils. There was a tall plate of fruit in front of him, and very carefully, in a way she recognized immediately as his "special" way, he was peeling an orange.

He must have felt that shock of recognition in her for he looked up and met her eyes. Incredible! He didn't know her! She smiled; he frowned. She came towards him. He closed his eyes an instant, but opening them his face lit up as though he had struck a match in a dark room. He laid down the orange and pushed back his chair, and she took her little warm hand out of her muff and gave it to him…

▸**1** What is the major difference between Excerpt A and the other three texts?

---

▸**2** First indicate if each excerpt is a poem (*P*), an essay (*E*) or a short story (*SS*) in the blank to the left of each title.

Then match each title with its most appropriate descriptor by drawing a line between the two.

| | | |
|---|---|---|
| ______ | **A.** "Dover Beach" | **a)** narration |
| ______ | **B.** "Pornography" | **b)** lyric |
| ______ | **C.** "Marrakech" | **c)** argument |
| ______ | **D.** "A Dill Pickle" | **d)** description |

▸**3** How is each excerpt narrated (first-person singular, second-person singular, etc.)?

**A.** "Dover Beach" ______ **C.** "Marrakech" ______

**B.** "Pornography" ______ **D.** "A Dill Pickle" ______

▸**4** In which two excerpts does the narrator seem more informal with and less distant from the reader?

---

UNIT 2.1

# Old Times on the Mississippi

**CHAPTER CONTENTS**

- **READING:** "Old Times on the Mississippi; The Continued Perplexities of 'Cub' Piloting" by Mark Twain; a brief biography
- **STYLISTIC ELEMENTS:** metaphor and comparison; contrast; description
- **WRITING:** descriptive essay; the essay writing process (prewriting, writing, revising)
- **GRAMMAR AND VOCABULARY:** revising practice (capitalisation and punctuation, homonyms)

The first essay that we will analyse is a descriptive essay by Mark Twain. Note how he uses comparison to bring home his point.

**ABOUT THE AUTHOR**

SAMUEL LANGHORNE CLEMENS (1835-1910), better known as Mark Twain, is one of America's most beloved authors. Not only did he write such classics as *Tom Sawyer*, *Life on the Mississippi*, *The Prince and the Pauper*, *Huckleberry Finn*, and *A Connecticut Yankee in King Arthur's Court*, but he was recognised as one of the world's greatest humourists and as one of the foremost American philosophers of his day. Underlying all his works is a concern for honesty and sincerity, and a disdain for sham. His stories are told in a realistic style; the characters, their dialects, their attitudes, and their homes, are described so astutely that his readers had no trouble transporting themselves into such settings like the Mississippi River region. Twain toured the world as a lecturer who kept his audiences laughing heartily. He was awarded honorary doctorates from Yale, Columbia, and Oxford for his outstanding contribution to literature.

**INITIAL READING** ▸ **Read the essay a first time to discover the main point (thesis) that the author wishes to make. Write a sentence stating the thesis of the essay in your own words.**

___

___

*FROM* OLD TIMES ON THE MISSISSIPPI:

## "The Continued Perplexities of 'Cub' Piloting"

MARK TWAIN

1875

The face of the water, in time, became a wonderful book — a book that was a dead language to the uneducated passenger, but which told its mind to me without reserve, delivering its most cherished secrets as clearly as if it uttered them with a voice. And it was not a book to be read once and thrown aside, for it had a new story to tell every day. Throughout the long twelve hundred miles there was never a page that was void of interest, never one that you could leave unread without loss, never one that you would want to skip, thinking you could find higher enjoyment in some other thing. There never was so wonderful a book written by man; never one whose interest was so absorbing, so unflagging, so sparklingly renewed with every re-perusal. The passenger who could not read it was charmed with a peculiar sort of faint dimple on its surface (on the rare occasions when he did not overlook it altogether); but to the pilot that was an *italicized* passage; indeed, it was more than that, it was a legend of the largest capitals with a string of shouting exclamation points at the end of it; for it meant that a wreck or a rock was buried there that could tear the life out of the strongest vessel that ever floated. It is the faintest and simplest expression the water ever makes, and the most hideous to a pilot's eye. In truth, the passenger who could not read this book saw nothing but all manner of pretty pictures in it, painted by the sun and shaded by the clouds, whereas to the trained eye these were not pictures at all, but the grimmest and most dead-earnest of reading-matter.

Now when I had mastered the language of this water and had come to know every trifling feature that bordered the great river as familiarly as I knew the letters of the alphabet, I had made a valuable acquisition. But I had lost something, too. I had lost something which could never be restored to me while I lived. All the grace, the beauty, the poetry had gone out of the majestic river! I still keep in mind a certain wonderful sunset which I witnessed when steamboating was new to me. A broad expanse of the river was turned to blood; in the middle distance the red hue brightened into gold, through which a solitary log came floating, black and conspicuous; in one place a long, slanting mark lay sparkling upon the water; in another the surface was broken by boiling, tumbling rings, that were as many-tinted as an opal; where the ruddy flush was faintest, was a smooth spot that was covered with graceful circles and radiating lines, ever so delicately traced; the shore on our left was densely wooded, and the sombre shadow that fell from this forest was broken in one place by a long, ruffled trail that shone like silver; and high above the forest wall a clean-stemmed dead tree waved a single leafy bough that glowed like a flame in the unobstructed splendor that was flowing from the sun. There were graceful curves, reflected images, woody heights, soft distances; and over the whole scene, far and near, the dissolving lights drifted steadily, enriching it, every passing moment, with new marvels of coloring.

I stood like one bewitched. I drank it in, in a speechless rapture. The world was new to me, and I had never seen anything like this at home. But as I have said, a day came when I began to cease noting the glories and the charms which the moon and the sun and the twilight wrought upon the river's face; another day came when I ceased altogether to note them. Then, if that sunset scene had been repeated, I would have looked upon it without rapture, and would have commented upon it, inwardly, after this fashion: This sun means that we are going to have wind to-morrow: that floating log means that the river is rising, small thanks to it; that slanting mark on the water refers to a bluff reef which is going to kill somebody's steamboat one of these nights, if it keeps on stretching out like that; those tumbling "boils" show a dissolving bar and a changing channel there; the lines and circles in the slick water over yonder are a warning that that execrable place is shoaling up dangerously; that silver streak in the shadow of the forest is the "break" from a new snag, and he has located himself in the very best place he could have found to fish for steamboats; that tall, dead tree, with a single living branch, is not going to last long, and then how is a body ever going to get through this blind place at night without the friendly old landmark?

No, the romance and the beauty were all gone from the river. All the value any feature of it had for me now was the amount of usefulness it could furnish toward compassing the safe piloting of a steamboat. Since those days, I have pitied doctors from my heart. What does the lovely flush in a beauty's cheek mean to a doctor but a "break" that ripples above some deadly disease? Are not all her visible charms sown thick with what are to him the signs and symbols of hidden decay? Does he ever see her beauty at all, or doesn't he simply view her professionally, and comment upon her unwholesome condition all to himself? And doesn't he sometimes wonder whether he has gained most or lost most by learning his trade?

## CLOSE READING ▸ Answer the following questions.

▸1 What does the narrator mean by "the language of this water" (line 18)?

▸2 What was the difference between the pilot's view and a passenger's view of the Mississippi?

▸3 What had the narrator lost when he became a river boat pilot?

▸4 Why does the narrator pity doctors?

## WRITER'S CRAFT

### Use of Metaphor and Comparison

(REFER TO THE GLOSSARY FOR DEFINITION OF TERMS)

▸1 **a)** What is the extended metaphor that Twain uses to describe the surface of the river?

**b)** List at least six words or expressions from the first paragraph that Twain uses to extend the metaphor (i.e., to make it more comprehensive). For example, he uses the phrase "dead language."

▸2 **a)** What second metaphor concerning the river does Twain use in the very first sentence of the piece (line 1) that connects up with the fourth and last paragraph?

**b)** Which two things are connected by this metaphor?

**c)** How are they similar?

**d)** How is a doctor similar to a river pilot?

---

▸▸▸ ***The use of the second metaphor gives unity to this essay by connecting its beginning with its end. The example concerning the doctor serves to emphasise and prove the thesis that Twain is making.*** ◂◂◂

### USE OF CONTRAST

▸**3** **a)** Summarise in a sentence how Twain views the sunset scene in the second paragraph.

---

**b)** Summarise how he views the same sunset scene in the third paragraph.

---

**c)** What purpose does this contrast serve?

---

### USE OF DESCRIPTION

Reread the description of the sunset in the second paragraph.

▸**4** **a)** To which sense does the description of the sunset appeal? ________

**b)** What kinds of words (parts of speech such as nouns, verbs, adjectives, etc.) does the author use in particular to replicate the scene in the reader's mind? ________

▸**5** Which two similes does the author use to convey both beauty and wealth? (Reminder: similes are comparisons using the words "like" or "as".)

---

▸▸▸ ***Note how the author creates an overall feeling of softness by his frequent use of the "s" sound throughout the paragraph. He uses many other soft consonant sounds.*** ◂◂◂

▸**6** **a)** What feeling does Twain's vivid description in paragraph 2 convey to the reader?

---

**b)** Why didn't he just tell the reader what he felt in one sentence?

---

### CONCLUSION

▸**7** On what kind of note does the piece end? (See last sentence.) Circle the most appropriate answer:

**a)** conversational **b)** analytic **c)** philosophical **d)** religious **e)** affirmative

What possible effect does asking a question at the end have on the reader?

---

## ESSAY WRITING PROCESS

In the short story chapters, you learned how to write a literary essay. Since all the essays you will write in an academic setting will be structured in a similar fashion, review the Write in Style in Unit 1.5, "The Veldt," before continuing. In the sections that follow, we will deal with other important aspects of essay writing.

There are three steps in writing an essay: prewriting, writing, and revising. You will find it much easier to follow these steps, and more efficient and pleasant, too, if you use a word processor on a computer. (This will take the chore out of rearranging, revising and editing!) However, you may not always be able to have access to a word processor, especially when writing exams. Therefore, it is advisable to make an essay plan containing the thesis, main arguments, and examples, when you are pressed for time. The plan will help you to better organise your ideas.

### Prewriting

Identify the purpose.

- Purposes can include the following: to analyse, to compare/contrast, to convince, to criticise, to defend, to describe, to entertain, to explain, to illustrate, to inform, to support, to tell a story. Some questions to ask yourself: What is the goal of the essay? What is the subject of the essay? Who is the intended audience?
- Make sure you know exactly what you are expected to do. Understand the question, if there is one.
- Determine how you want to approach the subject; then write a thesis statement.

Identify the audience.

- Determine the style you would like to use, taking into account the tone and the level of language.
- Collect information and research the question; take notes; conduct interviews if necessary.

Make a list of general points, details, supporting facts, and opinions.

### Writing

Organise the information.

- Decide how you want to present the information in general (through description, narration, illustration, comparison, etc.).
- Choose an arrangement (chronological order, order of importance, etc.) and create an outline.

Write a rough draft.

### Revising

Check the content of the rough draft for any inaccuracies and illogical sequencing of ideas.

- The introductory paragraph should contain the thesis statement.
- Each paragraph of the body should contain only one main argument with pertinent support.

Verify the style of the piece, checking for consistency, correct register or level of language (formal, informal, academic, etc.), tone, suitability for the chosen audience, variety of sentence types,* inclusion of transitional words and expressions,** clarity of language.

Check the mechanics: spelling, capitalisation, punctuation.***

Write the final draft, making sure to follow the conventions and any special instructions for formatting and presentation.

** See Write in Style: Dissecting and Constructing Sentences, in 1.1 "The Tale-Tale Heart."*
*** See Write in Style: Making Transitions, in 1.2 "The Story of an Hour."*
**** See Write in Style: Mechanics, in 1.4 "The Lottery."*

**Exercise A: Revising Practice: Capitalisation and Punctuation**

Here is an exercise for you to practise revising a text. Place capital letters and punctuation where they are needed in the following text. (To make your task easier, some periods have already been added.)

mark twain born samuel l clemens led a very interesting and varied life his father judge john clemens brought the family up first in a town called florida. in 1839 the family moved to hannibal near the mississippi river a river which was to influence clemens enormously young samuel left school at the age of twelve where he learned the printers trade and a few years later worked at setting the type of a newspaper called the hannibal journal. it was here that samuel first began to write at the age of eighteen he left for new york philadelphia cincinnati and finally new orleans where he completed studies to become a river pilot the american civil war broke out and clemens served for two weeks as a confederate soldier before leaving for california where he tried his hand at gold mining. soon he was to pick up the pen again his articles and stories now signed mark twain a term used by river pilots to indicate the depth of the water became increasingly popular but he still didn't make much money. since he was an excellent story teller a friend suggested that he become a lecturer his lectures were so popular that he ended up touring the world

**Exercise B: Revising Practice: Tricky Pairs: Homonyms**

English has many pairs of words that are pronounced the same, but are not spelled the same way and mean different things.

The following paragraph contains spelling mistakes and errors in meanings of words. Underline all the errors and list them below the paragraph. Then write the correct word beside each error. Write the grammatical explanation of both the error and the correct word in your list. The first one has been done for you.

My to friends and I decided to go on vacation. We where really excited about the idea, but could not agree with the destination. Should it bee near the see, or should it be in the mountains? We just could not decide. After much debate, we finally agreed too go two the beach on a tropical island. I thought that this was a great idea, and my friends taught so to. Hour suitcases packed, we met one our before our plane was to take of. Their was so much noise and excitement at the airport. It was filled with travellers going on wonderful vacations, and leaving there worries behind them. At the check in counter, we all put our bags on the belt and their was some confusion about who's bag was whose. We finally arrived at our destination and we our looking forward to a hole weak of rest and relaxation.

- ▸1 to — preposition; two — number
- ▸2 ________
- ▸3 ________
- ▸4 ________
- ▸5 ________
- ▸6 ________
- ▸7 ________
- ▸8 ________
- ▸9 ________
- ▸10 ________
- ▸11 ________
- ▸12 ________
- ▸13 ________
- ▸14 ________
- ▸15 ________
- ▸16 ________

### *Paragraph Practice*

- ▸1 Write a paragraph describing an outdoor scene.
- ▸2 Describe your favourite room.
- ▸3 Describe an outstanding person you know.

## WRAP-UP: DISCUSSION TOPICS

▸1 Are Mark Twain's works worth reading today?

▸2 Role-play a journalist interviewing Mark Twain.

▸3 Discuss Samuel Clemens' achievements.

## ESSAY TOPICS

▸1 Write a three-paragraph essay in which you use comparison and contrast to prove your point.

▸2 Write a three-paragraph descriptive essay about a place or person that had an influence on your life.

▸3 Write an essay about Samuel Clemens that shows that he was an exceptional person and author.

▸4 Write an essay about another work by Mark Twain.

▸5 Describe Mark Twain's writing style.

# References

## PRINT


**Biography**

Emerson, Everett. *Mark Twain: A Literary Life*. Philadelphia: University of Pennsylvania Press, 1999.

Hoffman, Andrew. *Inventing Mark Twain: The Lives of Samuel Langhorne Clemens*. New York: William Morrow, 1997.

Kaplan, Justin. *Mr. Clemens and Mark Twain: A Biography*. New York: Touchstone, 1991.

**Criticism**

*American Literary Scholarship* (Durham, NC: Duke Univ. Press) and the *Mark Twain Circular* are two excellent sources.

Fishkin, Shelley Fisher. *Lighting Out for the Territory: Reflections on Mark Twain and American Culture*. New York: Oxford University Press, 1998.

Rasmussen, R. Kent. *Mark Twain A to Z: The Essential Reference to His Life and Writings*. Rev. ed. New York: Oxford University Press, 1996.

Tenney, Thomas A. *Mark Twain: A Reference Guide*. Boston: G. K. Hall, 1977.


## INTERNET


**Biography and other links about the author**

http://marktwain.about.com/arts/marktwain/mbody.htm
http://etext.lib.virginia.edu/railton/index2.html
http://www.twainquotes.com/

**Tips on essay writing**

http://www.essaypunch.com/
http://members.tripod.com/~lklivingston/essay/links.html
http://www.studyweb.com/links/1120.html
http://www.livhope.ac.uk/gnu/stuhelp/essay4.htm#Ten 'Dos'

UNIT 2.2

# AN UNQUIET AWAKENING

## CHAPTER CONTENTS

- **READING:** "An Unquiet Awakening" by Mordecai Richler; brief biography
- **STYLISTIC ELEMENTS:** narration; imagery; humour (satire, contrasting levels of language); repetition
- **WRITING:** choosing your style (own voice, concise, compelling);
- **GRAMMAR AND VOCABULARY:** concise language; euphemisms and clichés; concrete words and precise language; connotations.

In the first essay, Samuel Clemens/Mark Twain chooses the metaphor of a book to describe the surface of the Mississippi River and how it could be read. In the second essay, Mordecai Richler narrates how a real book revealed a world that would prove very important to his life and career.

## ABOUT THE AUTHOR

MORDECAI RICHLER was born in Montreal in 1931. He is well known for his satirical and often controversial newspaper articles as well as his novels, which include *The Apprenticeship of Duddy Kravitz* (1959), *St. Urbain's Horseman* (1971), and *Joshua Then and Now* (1980). Richler has also written two popular books for children: *Jacob Two-Two Meets the Hooded Fang* (1975) and *Jacob Two-Two and the Dinosaur* (1987). Among his awards are two Canadian Governor General Awards, a Screenwriters Guild of America Award, and a Ruth Schwartz Children's Book Award. His works are humorous and often satirise the political situation in his native Quebec or in other parts of the world. Although he often makes himself the centre of the controversies he writes about, he at the same time shows sensitivity for his characters and their situations. His works enjoy a universal appeal.

## INITIAL READING

▶ 1 Write the first three words of the sentence in the text that expresses the author's thesis *(Hint: it is found between lines 12-15 or 19-32.*

___

___

▶ 2 In your own words, state the main idea of the essay in one sentence.

___

___

___

ESSAY

# AN UNQUIET AWAKENING

MORDECAI RICHLER

Reading was not one of my boyhood passions. Girls, or rather the absence of girls, drove me to it. When I was 13 years old, short for my age, more than somewhat pimply, I was terrified of girls. They made me feel sadly inadequate.

Retreating into high seriousness, I acquired a pipe, which I chewed on ostentatiously, and made it my business to be seen everywhere, even at school basketball games, absorbed by books of daunting significance. The two women who ran the lending library, possibly amused by my pretensions, tried to interest me in fiction.

"I want fact. I can't be bothered with stories," I protested, waving my pipe at them affronted, "I just haven't got the time for such nonsense."

Novels, I knew, were mere romantic make-believe, not as bad as poetry, to be fair, but bad enough.

I fell ill with a childhood disease, I no longer remember which, but obviously I meant it as a rebuke to those girls in tight sweaters who continued to ignore me. Never mind, they would mourn at my funeral, burying me with my pipe. Too late, they would say, "Boy, was he ever an intellectual."

The women from the lending library, concerned, dropped off books for me at our house. The real stuff. Fact-filled. Providing me with the inside dope on Theodore Herzl's [founder of Zionism] childhood and *Brazil Yesterday, Today, and Tomorrow.*

One day they brought me a novel: *All Quiet on the Western Front* by Erich Maria Remarque. The painting on the jacket that was taped to the book showed a soldier wearing what was unmistakably a German Army helmet. What was this, I wondered, some sort of bad joke? Nineteen forty-four that was, and I devoutly wished every German left on the face of the earth an excruciating death. The Allied invasion of France had not yet begun, but I cheered every Russian counter-attack, each German city bombed, and — with the help of a map tacked to my bedroom wall — followed the progress of the Canadian troops fighting their way up the Italian boot. Boys from our street had already been among the fallen. Izzy Draper's uncle. Harvey Kegelmass' older brother. The boy who was supposed to marry Gita Holtzman.

*All Quiet on the Western Front* lay unopened on my bed for two days. Finally, I was driven to picking it up out of boredom. I never expected that a mere novel, a stranger's tale, could actually be dangerous, creating such turbulence in my life, obliging me to question so many received ideas. About Germans. About my own monumental ignorance of the world. About what novels were.

At the age of 13 in 1944, happily as yet untainted by English 104, I couldn't tell you whether Remarque's novel was

a. a slice of life
b. symbolic
c. psychological
d. seminal.

I couldn't even say if it was well or badly written. In fact, as I recall, it didn't seem to be "written" at all. Instead, it just flowed. Now, of course, I understand that writing that doesn't advertise itself is art of a very high order. It doesn't come easily. But at the time I wasn't capable of making such distinctions. I also had no notion of how *All Quiet on the Western Front* rated critically as a war novel. I hadn't read Stendhal or Tolstoy or Crane or Hemingway. I hadn't even heard of them. I didn't know that Thomas Mann, whoever he was, had praised the novel highly. Neither did I know that in 1929 the judges at some outfit called the Book-of-the-Month Club had made it their May selection.

But what I did know is that, hating Germans with a passion, I had read only 20, maybe 30, pages before the author had seduced me into identifying with my enemy, 19-year-old Paul Baumer, thrust into the bloody trenches of the First World War with his schoolmates: Muller, Kemmerich and the reluctant Joseph Behm, one of the first to fall. As if that weren't sufficiently unsettling in itself, the author, having won my love for Paul, my enormous concern for his survival, then betrayed me in the last dreadful paragraphs of his book:

"He fell in October 1918, on a day that was so quiet and still on the whole front, that the army report confined itself to the single sentence: All Quiet on the Western Front."

"He had fallen forward and lay on the earth as though sleeping. Turning him over one saw that he could not have suffered long; his face had an expression of calm, as though almost glad the end had come."

The movies, I knew from experience, never risked letting you down like that. No matter how bloody the battle, how long the odds, Errol Flynn, Robert Taylor, even Humphrey Bogart could be counted on to survive and come home to Ann Sheridan, Lana Turner or — if they were sensitive types — Loretta Young. Only character actors, usually Brooklyn Dodger fans, say George Tobias or William Bendix, were expendable.

Obviously, having waded into the pool of serious fiction by accident, I was not sure I liked or trusted the water. It was too deep. Anything could happen.

There was something else, a minor incident in *All Quiet on the Western Front* that would not have troubled an adult reader but, I'm embarrassed to say, certainly distressed that 13-year-old boy colliding with his first serious novel:

Sent out to guard a village that has been abandoned because it is being shelled too heavily, Katczinsky, the incomparable scrounger, surfaces with suckling pigs and potatoes and carrots for his comrades, a group of eight altogether:

"The suckling pigs are slaughtered, Kat sees to them. We want to make potato cakes to go with the roast. But we cannot find a grater for the potatoes. However, that difficulty is soon over. With a nail we punch a lot of holes in a pot lid and there we have a grater. Three fellows put on thick gloves to protect their fingers against the grater, two others peel the potatoes, and business gets going."

The business, I realized, alarmed — not affronted — was the making of potato latkes, a favorite of mine as well as Paul Baumer's, a dish I had always taken to be Jewish, certainly not a German concoction.

What did I know? Nothing. Or, looked at another way, my real education, my life-long addiction to fiction, began with the trifling discovery that the potato latke was not of Jewish origin, but something borrowed from the German and now a taste that Jew and German shared in spite of everything.

I felt easier about my affection for the German soldier Paul Baumer once I was told by the women from the lending library that when Hitler came to power in 1933 he had burned all of Erich Maria Remarque's books and in 1938 he took away his German citizenship. Obviously Hitler had grasped that novels could be dangerous, something I learned when I was only 13 years old. He burned them; I began to devour them. I started to read at the breakfast table and on streetcars, often missing my stop, and in bed with benefit of a flashlight. It got me into trouble.

I grasped, for the first time, that I didn't live in the centre of the world but had been born into a working-class family in an unimportant country far from the cities of light: London, Paris, New York. Of course this wasn't my fault, it was my inconsiderate parents who were to blame. But there was, I now realized, a larger world out there beyond St. Urbain Street in Montreal.

Preparing myself for the Rive Gauche, I bought a blue beret, but I didn't wear it outside, or even in the house if anybody else was at home. I looked at but lacked the courage to buy a cigarette holder.

As my parents bickered at the supper table, trapped in concerns now far too mundane for the likes of me — what to do if Dworkin raised the rent again, how to manage my brother's college fees — I sat with but actually apart from them in the kitchen, enthralled, reading for he first time, "All happy families are alike but an unhappy family is unhappy after its own fashion."

Erich Maria Remarque, born in Westphalia in 1897, went off to war, directly from school, at the age of 18. He was wounded five times. He lost all his friends. After the war he worked briefly as a schoolteacher, a stonecutter, a test driver for a tire company and an editor of Sportbild magazine. His first novel, *Im Westen Nichts Neues*, was turned down by several publishers before it was brought out by the Ullstein Press in Berlin in 1928. *All Quiet on the Western Front* sold 1.2 million copies in Germany and was translated in 29 languages, selling some four million copies throughout the world. The novel has been filmed three times; the first time, memorably by Lewis Milestone in 1930. The Milestone version, with Lew Ayres playing Paul Baumer, won Academy Awards for best picture and best direction.

Since *All Quiet on the Western Front* once meant so much to me, I picked it up again with a certain anxiety. After all this time, I find it difficult to be objective about the novel. Its pages still evoke for me a back bedroom with a cracked ceiling and a sizzling radiator on St. Urbain Street: mice scrabbling in the walls, and a window looking out on the sheets frozen stiff on the laundry line.

Over the years the novel has lost something in shock value. The original jacket copy of the 1929 Little, Brown & Company edition of *All Quiet on the Western Front* warns the reader that it is "at times crude" and "will shock the supersensitive by its outspokenness." Contemporary readers, far from being shocked, will be amused by the novel's discretion, the absence of explicit sex scenes, the unbelievably polite dialogue of the men in the trenches.

The novel also has its poignant moments, both in the trenches and when Paul Baumer goes home on leave, an old man of 19, only to find insufferably pompous schoolmasters still recruiting the young with mindless prattle about the fatherland and the glory of battle. Strong characters are deftly sketched. Himmelstoss, the postman who becomes a crazed drillmaster. Tjaden, the peasant soldier. Kantorek, the schoolmaster.

On the front line the enemy is never the Frogs or the Limeys, but the insanity of the war itself. It is the war, in fact, and not even Paul Baumer, that is the novel's true protagonist. In a brief introduction to the novel Remarque wrote: "This book is to be neither an accusation nor a confession, and least of all an adventure, for death is not an adventure to those who stand face to face with it. It will try simply to tell of a generation of men who, even though they may have escaped its shells, were destroyed by the war."

Since the First World War we have become altogether too familiar with larger horrors. The Holocaust, Hiroshima, the threat of a nuclear winter. Death by numbers, cities obliterated by decree. At peace, as it were, we live the daily dread of the missiles in their silos, ours pointed at them, theirs pointed at us. None of this, however, diminishes the power of *All Quiet on the Western Front*, a novel that will endure because of its humanity, its honor and its refusal to lapse into sentimentality or strike a false note.

## CLOSE READING ▸ Answer the following questions.

▸1 Why didn't Richler like either stories or novels when he was young?

▸2 What image does the thirteen-year-old Richler try to project to his peers?

▸3 What causes Richler to change his mind about novels?

▸4 What contrast does Richler make between novels and movies that causes the former to be far more disturbing?

▸5 a) What important thing does Richler learn from identifying with Paul Baumer?

b) What second incident serves to bring this point home?

▸6 What does Richler realise about

a) the importance of his own world?

b) his knowledge of the world in general?

▸7 What characteristics of the novel *All Quiet on the Western Front* make Richler conclude that the book's impact is tremendous?

▸8 In what ways is the title of the essay very appropriate?

## WRITER'S CRAFT

### USE OF NARRATION

▸1 Richler uses narration to construct his essay. Three story lines about the lives of three people are interwoven throughout the essay (i.e., references to them occur more than once). Name and identify the three people.

### USE OF IMAGERY

▸2 **a)** What metaphor does Richler use to describe serious fiction (see paragraph starting at line 63)? ______________

**b)** Find four words in the paragraph that refer directly to the metaphor.

______________________________________________

▸▸▸ ***Note how this metaphor is almost a mirror image of the one Mark Twain uses to describe the surface of the Mississippi. "The face of the water, in time, became a wonderful book — a book that was a dead language to the uneducated passenger, but which told its mind to me without reserve, delivering its most cherished secrets as clearly as if it uttered them with a voice."*** ◂◂◂

### USE OF HUMOUR

#### Satire

▸▸▸ ***A satire is a literary work that uses irony, derision (poking malicious fun at someone), or wit (clever humour) to attack human vice or folly. Richler's works are often very satirical, and this essay, too, contains several elements of satire.*** ◂◂◂

▸3 Who is satirised repeatedly in the essay and why? (To satirise can mean to poke fun at people or ideas in order to show how foolish or wicked they are.)

______________________________________________

▸4 What is satirised in paragraph 9 (lines 33-38)?

______________________________________________

#### Contrasting Levels of Language

▸▸▸ ***Richler also uses contrasting levels of language (slang versus formal) to add touches of humour to the essay and to single out pretention. For example, "...the judges at some outfit (slang) called the Book-of-the-Month Club..." and "...creating such turbulence (formal) in my life..." demonstrate his use of slang and formal language.*** ◂◂◂

▸5 Complete the three word pairs referring to nonfiction that illustrate the contrast between formal and informal language used by Richler to add a touch of humour in the following paragraphs:

Paragraph 2: "books of ______________" (formal language)

Paragraph 6: "the real ______________"; "the inside ______________" (slang)

#### Other Humour

▸6 Find one other element of humour in the text and say whether it represents a humorous image, a situation, or a use of language.

______________________________________________

### USE OF REPETITION

▸▸▸ ***Another stylistic device that Richler uses to advantage is repetition. This gives rhythm to the writing and links paragraphs stylistically. For example, the word "writer" and its many relatives such as "written" and "wrote" are repeated throughout the essay.*** ◂◂◂

▸7 a) Look closely at how the sixth, seventh, and eighth paragraphs end. What is similar about the endings? (Hint: look at the grammatical structure.)

---

b) Find another paragraph where this same stylistic device is used. Write the first three words of the paragraph.

---

▸▸▸ ***Please note that this essay comes from the introduction Richler wrote for a new edition of*** **All Quiet on the Western Front.** ***Thus the essay's structure, content, and style reflect its particular purpose and audience.*** ◂◂◂

## WRITE IN STYLE ▸ CHOOSING YOUR STYLE

**You can improve your style by choosing specific and accurate words rather than general ones and by reading extensively to improve your vocabulary. Moreover, the more you write, the better you will get at it. However, there are certain basic principles that you can follow.**

**Style Tips**

Be yourself (and true to yourself!).

- Choose a voice (or persona) for the essay that is suitable for the purpose and audience in terms of tone and register.
- Write about subjects that interest you (as much as possible). If you are bored by the topic, your reader will be, too!

Be concise.

- Use specific examples and details, not generalities.
- Write clear sentences, using the fewest words possible to express your ideas.
- Choose direct, easily understood words. For example, *beauty* is a better choice than *pulchritude*; *love* is sometimes better than *amorousness* or *sentimental attachment*.
- Use concrete nouns, verbs and modifiers such as *novel*, to *describe*, blue, etc.
- Use active verbs except for special effects. Here is an example: Yesterday someone stole my watch. (*Active:* emphasises the doer of the action, i.e., someone) Yesterday my watch was stolen. (*Passive:* emphasises the receiver of the action, i.e., my watch).
- Avoid clichés, euphemisms, slang, and jargon. (See Exercise B on the next page.)
- Be sensitive to gender and ethnic differences; avoid stereotypes.

Be compelling.

- Choose strong, vivid words. (See Exercise E on page 174.)
- Hook the reader's interest by presenting a fresh perspective and strong arguments.
- Avoid a weak stance or a wishy-washy presentation of your ideas.

In the exercises that follow, you will practise making choices that will help improve your writing style.

**Exercise A: Using Concise Language**

Rewrite each sentence to make it more concise. Replace the words in italics by a single word or by a shorter, more concise phrase, or remove them altogether. Change the word order if necessary.

*EXAMPLE: It is necessary that you study. → You must study.*

▶1 *At this point in time* it is *in our own best interests* to stop the investigation *owing to the fact that* no new evidence has been found.

▶2 *Regardless of the fact that* Samuel Clemens did not have a university education, *it did happen that* his work was highly regarded by *people from all walks of life*.

▶3 *Due to the fact that* Mark Twain was an entertaining story teller, *it came about that* he was invited *to many different spots and locations* around the world where *he was in the habit of giving lectures along the lines of* his short stories.

▶4 *The point I am trying to make is about the reason why* Twain was so appreciated worldwide; *it was because* of the universal appeal of his humour.

▶5 *I am going to write an essay concerning the matter of* Mark Twain's vision of the truth.

**Exercise B: Avoiding Euphemisms and Clichés**

▸▸▸ ***The term euphemism means to substitute a vague term for one that is harsher and more direct. The term cliché means an overused expression or idea.*** ◂◂◂

Replace the euphemisms and clichés (in italics) by more direct and suitable language.

*EXAMPLE: After John's beloved wife* passed away *she was* laid to rest *in Notre Dame cemetery.*
*died* *buried*

▶1 You mustn't drive *under the influence*. Otherwise, you will soon find yourself in the custody of a *law enforcement officer*.

▶2 Mark Twain *came into the world* in the town of Florida, Missouri on November 30, 1835. It was *a red-letter day* for readers.

▸3 *Last but not least,* do not forget to mention Twain's experience as a river pilot.

___

▸4 *Taking stock of the situation,* the hero realised that *the writing was on the wall.*

___

▸5 The villain, however, *making the best of a bad situation,* decided to *turn over a new leaf.*

___

▸6 Several participants in the ride were *physically challenged.* Some suffered from *hearing impairments* while others had *visual impairments.*

___

**Exercise C: Using Concrete Words**

It is always preferable to use specific words rather than vague ones. In the following sentences, replace the vague word (in italics) by a better, more concrete term chosen from the box below.

*EXAMPLE: I am* really hungry.
*famished*

▸1 She could do many *things* ____________, such as make simple electrical or plumbing repairs and fix a flat tire.

▸2 He is a *nice* ____________ person. He always listens to people's problems.

▸3 The book was really *good* ____________.

▸4 She *said* ____________ to him in a very quiet voice that she had to leave early.

▸5 The child *was* ____________ very frightened because he was in a *bad* ____________ situation.

▸6 I *was* ____________ so *mad* ____________ that I *started walking* ____________ around the room very angrily.

▸7 The sun *was out* ____________ and the breeze *was making little waves on* ____________ the surface of the lake. It was a *nice* ____________ day for a picnic.

▸8 The grapefruit tasted ____________ *bad* .

▸9 She *was looking closely at* ____________ the rip in his shirt.

| perfect | stomped | dangerous | shone | enraged |
|---|---|---|---|---|
| well-written | rippled | examined | understanding | repairs |
| whispered | rotten | felt (2) | | |

**Exercise D: Determining Connotation**

The **denotation** of a word refers to its meaning. The **connotation** is the emotional association accompanying a word. The connotation can be positive, negative, or neutral. For example, we can refer to an intelligent person as brilliant or as nerdy. *Brilliant* has a very positive connotation whereas *nerdy* has a negative one. Thus, it is very important to pay close attention to word choice since synonyms can have the same denotation but very different connotations. When you are writing to convince, you will want to use language that makes a greater impact on the reader.

Indicate whether each word in the following groups of synonyms (N.B., some are not perfect synonyms) has a positive (+), negative (−) or neutral (0) connotation. If you aren't sure, check your dictionary. (Choose the most common connotation.)

▸1 ______ thin ______ lean ______ wiry ______ skinny
______ cadaverous ______ slender

▸2 ______ guru ______ pro ______ expert ______ teacher
______ authority ______ mentor ______ shark ______ savant
______ cunning person

▸3 ______ house ______ home ______ shack ______ cottage
______ dump ______ slum

▸4 ______ smart ______ foxy ______ brilliant ______ clever
______ intelligent ______ gifted ______ wily ______ cagey
______ shrewd ______ learned

▸5 ______ strong ______ violent ______ powerful ______ warlike
______ influential ______ great

Indicate with a (+) sign which of the two words has a more positive connotation and emotional impact.

▸1 ______ buyers ______ clients

▸2 ______ educational ______ pedantic

▸3 ______ famous ______ notorious

▸4 ______ adds to ______ complements

▸5 ______ genuine ______ real

▸6 ______ yellow ______ gold

#### Exercise E: Determining Intensity

Synonyms often have a different intensity. Keeping this in mind when you write will help you choose more concrete and precise words.

Underline the more intense word.

| | | | | | |
|---|---|---|---|---|---|
| ▸1 | cold | freezing | ▸7 | tired | exhausted |
| ▸2 | hilarious | funny | ▸8 | terror | fear |
| ▸3 | wet | soaking | ▸9 | respect | veneration |
| ▸4 | plummet | fall | ▸10 | rage | anger |
| ▸5 | happy | ecstatic | ▸11 | interest | fascinate |
| ▸6 | sadness | grief | ▸12 | shout | say |

### *Paragraph Practice*

▸1 Recount your happiest (saddest, most exciting, most terrifying) moment.

▸2 Write about something that happened to you when you were a child.

▸3 Describe a funny incident.

## WRAP-UP: DISCUSSION TOPICS

▸1 Discuss the advantages and disadvantages of looking at yourself and your life in a humorous way.

▸2 Tell how a television program, movie, or book has influenced your life.

▸3 Recount a humorous episode from your life.

▸4 What role does humour play in your life?

## ESSAY TOPICS

Write a narrative essay of at least five paragraphs. Here are some suggestions.

▸1 Recount an incident that had an important influence on your life.

▸2 Write about a book that has influenced you.

▸3 Compare the humour of Mark Twain and Mordecai Richler.

▸4 Research information about either Mark Twain or Mordecai Richler and write a narrative essay about the author you have chosen.

▸5 Write an essay using narrative techniques to tell about a fictional meeting between Mordecai Richler and his former classmates.

▸6 Write an autobiographical essay.

▸7 Create a fictional character and write his or her autobiography.

▸8 Write an essay about an important historical event and its influence.

# References

## PRINT


**Biography**

Davidson, Arnold E. *Mordecai Richler*. New York: Ungar, 1983.

Lecker, Robert. *The Annotated Bibliography of Canada's Major Authors*. Downsview, ON: ECW Press, 1985.

Ramraj, Victor J. "Richler, Mordecai," in *The Canadian Encyclopedia: Year 2000*. Toronto: McClelland & Stewart, 1999.

*Who's Who in Canadian Literature*. Toronto: Reference Press, 1983.

**Criticism**

Groening, Laura. "The Jew in History: A Comparative Study of Mordecai Richler and Bernard Malamud." Ed. by Michael Darling. Toronto: ECW Press, 53-74.

McSweeney, Kerry. "Mordecai Richler," in *Canadian Writers and Their Works*, ed. Robert Lecker, Jack David, and Ellen Quigley. Downsview, ON: ECW Press, 1985.


## INTERNET


**Biography of the Author**

http://www.tceplus.com/richler.htm
http://schwinger.harvard.edu/~terning/bios/Richler.html
http://quarles.unbc.ca/donne/open430/richler.html

**Interview with Mordecai Richler: February 11, 2000**

http://209.52.189.2/article.cfm/canadianliterature/33056

UNIT 2.3

# Marilyn Monroe: The Woman Who Died Too Soon

## CHAPTER CONTENTS

- **READING:** "Marilyn Monroe: The Woman Who Died Too Soon" by Gloria Steinem; a brief biography; feminism; about Marilyn Monroe
- **STYLISTIC ELEMENTS:** supporting arguments with evidence (facts, statistics, personal anecdotes, quotations from expert sources)
- **WRITING:** persuasive or opinion essay (goal, structure, structural models)
- **GRAMMAR AND VOCABULARY:** subject / verb agreement, pronoun / antecedent and pronoun / case agreement

The persuasive essay in this chapter examines the life of a famous movie star.

## ABOUT THE AUTHOR

GLORIA STEINEM was born in 1934 in Toledo, Ohio and is considered to be a leading figure in the feminist movement. She completed her university studies in the United States and India, and soon after graduating started working as a journalist for *Help*, a political satire magazine published in New York City. She became a successful journalist after getting recognition for an article titled "I Was a Playboy Bunny," based on her experience as an "undercover" hostess at the Playboy Club in Manhattan. By 1968, Steinem was actively involved in the feminist movement. She founded the National Women's Political Caucus in 1971 along with fellow feminist author Betty Friedan and politicians Bella Abzug and Shirley Chisholm. Steinem also helped to establish *Ms.* Magazine, which functioned to debate feminist issues. She has published many newspaper and magazine articles and essays as well as a biography on Marilyn Monroe. She has been a role model for both men and women who seek the equalisation of the genders in our society.

## TRENDS OF THE TIMES: FEMINISM

The feminist movement advocates women's equality in all areas of life, including the political, professional, educational, and social. It has at its roots the writings of Mary Wollstonecraft, who lived in England in the early 1800s and was the mother of Mary Shelley, the author of *Frankenstein.* Wollstonecraft is most famous for her essays on the status of women. In the United States, the status of nineteenth-century women was enhanced by Susan B. Anthony and others, who fought for the rights of women in a male-dominated political system. In Canada, women's suffrage movements were led by Dr. Emily Howard Stowe, Canada's first woman doctor, and her daughter Dr. Augusta Stowe-Gullan (in Ontario), Nellie McClung (in the Prairies), and Thérèse Casgrain (in Quebec), among others. By the mid 1920s, through pressure from early feminists, women acquired the right to own property, to be considered full citizens in law, and of course, the right to vote in the United States, Great Britain, and most of Canada.

The second wave of feminists became active in the 1960s. Advocates such as Betty Friedan pressured government and society to ensure equal pay for equal work, the creation of day care centres, and the right to have an abortion. The writings of feminists expressed concerns about sexual stereotyping and sexual harassment. Today, many women benefit in their home and work life because of the efforts of the earlier feminists. Feminism is still an influential movement today and the works of writers such as Naomi Wolfe, Margaret Atwood, Makeda Silvera, Jeanette Winterson, and others continue to examine the role of women in society.

**INITIAL READING ▸ Here is a little background information to prepare you for this essay. Marilyn Monroe, born Norma Jean Mortenson on June 1, 1926 in Los Angeles, was a legendary 1950s sex goddess and American actress who, for many people, personified the glamour of Hollywood. She made thirty films and was married three times, the first time to an aircraft factory worker, the second, to famous baseball player Joe DiMaggio, and the third to the well-known playwright Arthur Miller. It is also said that she had an alleged affair with former U.S. president, John F. Kennedy. Named the "World's Most Popular Star" by Golden Globe in 1962, she died of an overdose of sleeping pills later that year at the age of 36. The myths and legends surrounding Marilyn Monroe and her life have continued to grow through the years.**

Now read the essay for the first time and answer the following question: What was particularly sad about Marilyn Monroe's short life

ESSAY

1972

# Marilyn Monroe: The Woman Who Died Too Soon

GLORIA STEINEM

Saturday afternoon movies — no matter how poorly made or incredible the plot, they were a refuge from my neighborhood and all my teenage miseries. Serials that never ended, Doris Day, who never capitulated, cheap travelogues, sci-fi features with zippers in the monster suits: I loved them all, believed them all, and never dreamed of leaving until the screen went sickeningly blank.

But I walked out on Marilyn Monroe. I remember her on the screen, huge as a colossus doll, mincing and whispering and simply hoping her way into total vulnerability. Watching her, I felt angry, even humiliated, but I didn't understand why.

After all, Jane Russell was in the movie, too (a very bad-taste version of *Gentlemen Prefer Blondes*), so it wasn't just the vulnerability that all big-breasted women seem to share. (If women viewers prefer actresses who are smaller, neater — the Audrey Hepburns of the world — it is not because we're jealous of the *zoftig* ones as men suppose. It's just that we would rather identify with a woman we don't have to worry about, someone who doesn't seem in constant danger.) Compared to Marilyn, Jane Russell seemed in control of her body and even of the absurd situations in this movie.

Perhaps it was the uncertainty in the eyes of this big, blond child-woman; the terrible desire for approval that made her different from Jane Russell. How dare she express the neediness that so many women feel, but try so hard to hide? How dare she, a movie star, be just as unconfident as I was?

So I disliked her and avoided her movies, as we avoid that which reflects our fears about ourselves. If there were jokes made on her name and image when I was around, I joined in. I contributed to the laughing, the ridicule, the put-downs, thus proving that I was nothing like her. Nothing at all.

I, too, got out of my neighborhood in later years, just as she had escaped from a much worse life of lovelessness, child abuse, and foster homes. I didn't do it, as she did, through nude calendar photographs and starlet bits. (Even had there been such opportunities for mildly pretty girls in Toledo, Ohio, I would never have had the courage to make myself so vulnerable.) Yes, I was American enough to have show-business dreams. The boys in my neighborhood hoped to get out of a lifetime in the factories through sports; the girls, if we imagined anything other than marrying a few steps up in the world, always dreamed of show business careers. But after high-school years as a dancer on the Toledo show-business circuit, or what passed for show business there, it seemed hopeless even to me. In the end, it was luck and an encouraging mother and a facility with words that got me out; a facility that helped me fake my way through the college entrance exams for which I was totally unprepared.

But there's not much more confidence in girls who scrape past college boards than there is in those who, like Marilyn, parade past beauty contest judges. By the time I saw her again, I was a respectful student watching the celebrated members of the Actors Studio do scenes from what seemed to me very impressive and highbrow plays (Arthur Miller and Eugene O'Neill were to be served up that day). She was a student too, a pupil of Lee Strasberg, leader of the Actors Studio and American guru of the Stanislavski method, but her status as a movie star and sex symbol seemed to keep her from being taken seriously even there. She was allowed to observe, but not to do scenes with her colleagues.

So the two of us sat there, mutually awed, I think, in the presence of such theater people as Ben Gazzara and Rip Torn, mutually insecure in the masculine world of High Culture, mutually trying to fade into the woodwork.

I remember thinking that Strasberg and his actors seemed to take positive pleasure in their power to ignore this great and powerful movie star who had come to learn. Their greetings to her were a little too studiously casual, their whispers to each other about her being there a little too self-conscious and condescending. Though she stayed in the back of the room, her blond head swathed in a black scarf and her body hidden in a shapeless black sweater and slacks, she gradually became a presence, if only because the group was trying so hard not to look, to remain oblivious and cool.

As we filed slowly out of the shabby room after the session was over, Marilyn listened eagerly to the professional postmortem being carried on by Ben Gazzara and others who walked ahead of us, her fingers nervously tracing a face that was luminous and without makeup, as if she were trying to hide herself, to apologize for being there. I was suddenly glad she hadn't participated and hadn't been subjected to the criticisms of this rather vulturous group. (Perhaps it was an unschooled reaction, but I hadn't enjoyed watching Strasberg encourage an intimate love scene between an actor and actress, and then pick them apart with humiliating authority.) Summoning my nerve, I did ask the shy, blond woman in front of me if she could imagine playing a scene for this group.

"Oh, no," Marilyn said, her voice childish, but much less whispery than on the screen, "I admire all these people so much. I'm just not good enough." Then, after a few beats of silence: "Lee Strasberg is a genius, you know. I plan to do what he says."

Her marriage to Arthur Miller seemed quite understandable to me and to other women, even those who were threatened by Miller's casting off of a middle-aged wife to take a younger, far more glamorous one. If you can't be taken seriously in your work, if you have an emotional and intellectual insecurity complex, then marry a man who has the seriousness you've been denied. It's a traditional female option — far more acceptable than trying to achieve that identity on one's own.

Of course, Marilyn's image didn't really gain seriousness and intellectuality. Women don't gain serious status by sexual association any more easily than they do by hard work. (At least, not unless the serious man dies and we confine ourselves to being keepers of the flame. As Margaret Mead has pointed out, widows are almost the only women this country honors in authority.) Even Marilyn's brave refusal to be intimidated by threats that she would never work in films again if she married Miller, who was then a "subversive" called to testify before the House UnAmerican Activities Committee, was considered less brave than Miller's refusal to testify. Indeed, it was barely reported at all.

Perhaps she didn't take her own bravery seriously either. She might be giving up her livelihood, the work that meant so much to her, but she was about to give that up for marriage anyway. As Mrs. Arthur Miller, she retired to a Connecticut farm and tried to limit her life to his solitary work habits, his friends, and his two children. Only when they badly needed money did she come out of retirement again, and that was to act in *The Misfits*, a film written by her husband.

On the other hand, the public interpretation was very different. She was an egocentric actress forcing one of America's most important playwrights to tailor a screenplay to her inferior talents: that was the gossip-column story here and in Europe. But her own pattern argues the case for her. In two previous marriages, to an aircraft factory worker at the age of sixteen and later to Joe Di Maggio, she had cut herself off from the world and put all her energies into being a housewife. When it didn't work out, she blamed herself, not the role, and added one more failure to her list of insecurities. "I have too many fantasies to be a housewife," she told a woman friend sadly. And finally, to an interviewer: "I guess I am a fantasy."

*The Misfits* seemed to convey some facets of the real Marilyn: honesty, an innocence and belief that survived all experience to the contrary, kindness toward other women, a respect for the life of plants and animals. Because for the first time she wasn't only a sex object and victim, I also was unembarrassed enough to notice her acting ability. I began to see her earlier movies — those in which, unlike *Gentlemen Prefer Blondes*, she wasn't called upon to act the female impersonator.

For me as for so many people, she was a presence in the world, a life force.

Over the years, I heard other clues to her character. When Ella Fitzgerald, a black artist and perhaps the greatest singer of popular songs, hadn't been able to get a booking at an important Los Angeles nightclub in the fifties, it was Marilyn who called the owner and promised to sit at a front table every night while she sang. The owner hired Ella, Marilyn was faithful to her promise each night, the press went wild, and, as Ella remembers with gratitude, "After that, I never had to play a small jazz club again."

Even more movingly, there was her last interview. She pleaded with the reporter to end with "What I really want to say: That what the world really needs is a real feeling of kinship. Everybody: stars, laborers, Negroes, Jews, Arabs. We are all brothers... Please don't make me a joke. End the interview with what I believe."

And then she was gone. I remember being told, in the middle of a chaotic student meeting in Europe, that she was dead. I remember that precise moment on August 5, 1962 — the people around me, what the room looked like — and I've discovered that many other people remember that moment of hearing the news, too. It's a phenomenon usually reserved for the death of family and presidents.

She was an actress, a person on whom no one's fate depended, and yet her energy and terrible openness to life had made a connection to strangers. Within days after her body was discovered, eight young and beautiful women took their lives in individual incidents clearly patterned after Marilyn Monroe's death. Some of them left notes to make that connection clear.

Two years later, Arthur Miller's autobiographical play, *After the Fall*, brought Marilyn back to life in the character of Maggie. But somehow that Maggie didn't seem the same. She had Marilyn's pathetic insecurity, the same need to use her sexual self as her only way of getting recognition and feeling alive. But, perhaps naturally, the play was about Miller's suffering, not Marilyn's. He seemed honestly to include some of his own destructive acts. (He had kept a writer's diary of his moviestar wife, for instance, and Marilyn's discovery of it was an emotional blow, the beginning of the end for that marriage. It made her wonder: Was her husband exploiting her, as most men had done, but in a more intellectual way?) Nonetheless, the message of the play was mostly Miller's view of his attempts to shore up a creature of almost endless insecurities; someone doomed beyond his helping by a mysterious lack of confidence.

To women, that lack was less mysterious. Writer Diana Trilling, who had never met Marilyn, wrote an essay just after her death that some of Marilyn's friends praised as a more accurate portrayal than Miller's. She described the public's "mockery of [Marilyn's] wish to be educated"; the sexual awareness that came only from outside, from men's reactions, "leaving a great emptiness where a true sexuality would have supplied her with a sense of herself as a person with connection and content." She questioned whether Marilyn had really wanted to die, or only to be asleep, not to be conscious through the loneliness of that particular Saturday night.

Trilling also recorded that feeling of connection to Marilyn's loneliness felt by so many strangers ("especially women to whose protectiveness her extreme vulnerability spoke so directly"), so much so that we fantasized our ability to save her, if only we had been there. "But we were the friends," as Trilling wrote sadly, "of whom she knew nothing."

"She was an unusual woman — a little ahead of her times," said Ella Fitzgerald. "And she didn't know it."

Now that women's self-vision is changing, we are thinking again about the life of Marilyn Monroe. Might our new confidence in women's existence with or without the approval of men have helped a thirty-six year-old woman of talent to stand on her own? To resist the insecurity and ridicule? To stop depending on sexual attractiveness as the only proof that she was alive — and therefore to face aging with confidence? Because the ability to bear a child was denied to her, could these new ideas have helped her to know that being a woman included much more? Could she have challenged the Freudian analysts to whom she turned in her suffering?

Most of all, we wonder if the support and friendship of other women could have helped. Her early experiences of men were not good. She was the illegitimate daughter of a man who would not even contribute for her baby clothes; her mother's earliest memory of her own father, Marilyn's grandfather, was his smashing a pet kitten against the fireplace in a fit of anger; Marilyn herself said she was sexually attacked by a foster father while still a child; and she was married off at sixteen because another foster family could not take care of her. Yet she was forced always to depend for her security on the goodwill and recognition of men; even to be interpreted by them in writing because she feared that sexual competition made women dislike her. Even if they had wanted to, the women in her life did not have the power to protect her. In films, photographs, and books, even after her death as well as before, she has been mainly seen through men's eyes.

We are too late. We cannot know whether we could have helped Norma Jean Baker or the Marilyn Monroe she became. But we are not too late to do as she asked. At last, we can take her seriously.

## CLOSE READING

▸1 a) How does Steinem feel about Marilyn Monroe at the beginning of the essay?

b) What are the reasons the author gives in paragraphs 3-6 for feeling this way?

▸2 In line 35, the author mentions that she ran into Marilyn Monroe at the Actors Studio. What was the author's opinion of Monroe during this encounter?

▸3 At what moment does the author start to admire Monroe? Find a direct quotation from the text to prove this.

▸4 Find evidence in the text to show that the author respects Monroe.

▸5 What opinions does the author have about the men in Monroe's life?

▸6 In paragraphs 16 (starting at line 89), 17, and 18, what is the author's attitude towards Monroe?

▸7 Find a statement in paragraph 16 (lines 89-93) that shows a change in the author's actions that clearly reflects her changing attitude towards Monroe.

▸8 What questions does the author eventually ask herself about the possible effects of social changes on the outcome of Marilyn Monroe's life?

▸9 How does Steinem feel about Marilyn Monroe at the end of the essay?

▸10 What is the main thesis of the essay? (Hint: remember that the thesis includes a point of view whereas the subject is more general and neutral.)

**WRITER'S CRAFT ▸** **The essay about Marilyn Monroe is** a persuasive **or** opinion essay. **This type of essay usually deals with a** controversial subject **or** issue. **The author's** goal **in writing it is** to convince the reader to agree with the main opinion **of the essay.**

▸1 Who is this essay written for? In other words, who is the audience?

▸2 State in your own words what the initial issue is for the author at the outset of this essay.

▸3 **a)** Later in the essay, what does the author wish to convince the reader about Marilyn Monroe? (Hint: infer this from her change in attitude.)

**b)** Give three of the arguments that the author uses to support her opinion and prove her point.

▸4 In your opinion, does the author present her arguments in a convincing fashion? Explain.

## STRUCTURE OF THE PERSUASIVE ESSAY

Persuasive essays, like other essays, have an intrinsic structure consisting of an **introduction**, a **thesis statement**, **convincing arguments** in the **body** of the text, and a **summary** in the **conclusion**.

In fairly complex essays, the thesis statement is sometimes **implicit** rather than **explicit**; that is, the reader must infer what the author's thesis is from the context and arguments because the text does not give an explicit thesis statement.

Convincing arguments are built using **facts, statistics, personal anecdotes**, and **quotations from expert sources**.

▸**5** (Circle the appropriate letter.) The introduction in this essay consists of the first two paragraphs. What does the first paragraph include?

**a)** personal anecdote

**b)** a quotation

**c)** definition

▸**6** The second paragraph grabs the reader's attention. Which sentence keeps the audience's interest and makes them want to continue reading?

---

▸**7** What types of arguments does the author use in order to convince the reader of her position? (More than one answer.)

**a)** statistics

**b)** personal anecdotes

**c)** facts

**d)** quotations from expert sources

▸**8** Is the thesis statement in this essay implicit or explicit? ______

▸**9** At what point in the essay does the reader realise what the author's thesis is?

**a)** at the end of the introductory paragraph

**b)** in the middle of the supporting evidence

**c)** in the conclusion

Sometimes in persuasive essays, authors will **acknowledge** and then **refute the objections** of people who disagree with their opinions. Here is an example of an "objection" argument: "*Although many people say that smokers should be free to choose, they forget that non-smokers have the right to clean air.*" (See Exercise A below.)

Moreover, writers of persuasive essays usually place the points in their **arguments from weaker to stronger**, in order to save the greatest impact for the end of the essay when they hope to have convinced the reader.

▸**10** How is the body of the essay about Monroe structured? The author

**a)** only gives arguments in support of the thesis.

**b)** starts by showing objections to the thesis and then supports it.

▸▸▸ ***Sometimes in persuasive essays, the order in which the various elements (introduction, thesis, arguments, etc.) are presented varies. (Look at the structure models below.)*** ◂◂◂

▸**11** Choose one of the following. The actual structure of the essay about Marilyn Monroe is

**a)** introduction, objection arguments, thesis, supporting arguments, conclusion

**b)** objection arguments, introduction, thesis, supporting arguments, conclusion

**c)** introduction, thesis, objection arguments, supporting arguments, conclusion

**There are many different ways to structure a persuasive or opinion essay. Many instructors ask students to write essays according to the first model below (A); however, as you become a more proficient writer, you will probably wish to experiment with other models, such as B and C. Moreover, it is important to remember that models are provided in order to help novice writers learn how to write more effectively. The writing features of experienced essayists usually go far beyond any particular model, yet their essays still must be structurally sound and remain coherent to inner logic. A consistent level is usually easier to achieve if you have learned the basics first.**

Here are some examples of models suitable for persuasive essays:

**A.**

Introduction
- Thesis statement

Body Paragraphs
- Supporting Arguments
  Facts, examples, personal anecdotes, quotations from experts

Conclusion
- Summary of main points

**B.**

Thesis Statement

Introduction

Body Paragraphs
- Refuting arguments
- Supporting Arguments
  Facts, examples, personal anecdotes, quotations from experts

Conclusion
- Summary of main points

C.

Introduction
Body Paragraphs
- Refuting arguments
- Supporting Arguments
  Facts, examples, personal anecdotes, quotations from experts

Conclusion
- Thesis Statement

**Exercise A: Structural Elements in a Persuasive Essay**

Each of the following phrases or sentences is a structural element in a persuasive essay except for one example that indicates just a general subject. From the list of structural elements below, indicate which one pertains to the example by writing the appropriate letter in the blank space beside each phrase or sentence. Please note that there are several supporting arguments, objection arguments, and supporting pieces of evidence. Indicate them all.

**List of Structural Elements**

- Subject (S)
- Introduction (I)
- Thesis Statement (T)
- Supporting Argument (SA)
- Supporting Evidence (SE)
- Objection Argument (OA)
- Objection Evidence (OE)
- Conclusion (C)

The first example has been done for you.

**a)** Business owners interviewed during our investigation said that they were in business to make money, not to look after non-smokers' health. They were worried that they would lose customers if smoking was not allowed. __OE__

**b)** Smoking causes cancer. ______

**c)** There should be a law prohibiting smoking in all restaurants and bars. ______

**d)** Tobacco smoke contains more than 2,000 chemicals; more than 40 of these chemicals are carcinogenic and 8 are Class A carcinogens; in other words, no level of exposure is safe. ______

**e)** Smoking in public places ______

**f)** Many people die from smoking. ______

**g)** Although cigarette companies would have you believe otherwise, it has been proven that smoking is addictive. ______

**h)** Have you ever had a lovely meal in a restaurant spoiled by the stale smell of cigarette smoke? ______

**i)** In developed countries, in the late '90s a total of three million deaths per year resulted from tobacco-related causes. ______

**j)** Even second hand smoke is dangerous. ______

**k)** For all these reasons, I fully support legislation that prohibits smoking in all restaurants and bars. Just think of that lovely meal in a smoke-free restaurant. Now you can eat without an offensive smell ruining your enjoyment and without worrying about all that passive smoke! ______

l) Experts say that second hand cigarette smoke causes many different respiratory diseases in people exposed to it and it is also the third leading preventable cause of death (30,000 to 50,000 deaths per year in the U.S.) ______

m) Some people argue that business owners should be allowed to set their own rules, but restaurant and bar owners would not restrict smoking of their own accord. ______

n) Furthermore, recent studies have shown that tobacco companies actually tried to increase addiction in smokers by adding certain chemicals to cigarettes. ______

**Exercise B: Ordering Structural Elements in a Persuasive Essay**

Place the phrases and sentences in *Exercise A* in an order appropriate for a persuasive essay (just list the corresponding letters; there is no need to write out whole sentences). Start with the subject followed by the introduction, and end with the conclusion. The supporting and objection arguments do not have to be placed in a particular order but must be followed by their corresponding supporting evidence.

---

The most important thing to remember about writing a persuasive essay is that it should convince the reader to accept the writer's opinion about an issue.

**Style Tips**

In the previous chapter you received many tips on writing effective essays. Here are more tips to consider when writing a persuasive essay.

- Choose the issue of the essay and know your position on it.
- Decide who your audience is. Are they supporters of your position or do they oppose it?
- Find out as much as possible about the issue.
- Define a thesis statement that will clearly show your position on the issue.
- Decide what structure the essay will follow (for beginning writers, the traditional essay structure will be easiest).
- Think of supporting arguments that may consist of facts, personal anecdotes, quotations from expert sources, and examples.
- Choose an introduction that will grab the attention of the reader.
- Create a conclusion that will summarise the main points of the essay.

### Subject/Verb Agreement

When you are revising your essay, it is important to verify that your subjects and verbs agree in person and number. Problems concerning subject/verb agreement are among the most common ones found in student writing. Make sure that you know the following rules:

- Nouns and Verbs must agree in number.
  Third-person singular verbs end in **-s** or **–es.**

  *EXAMPLE: The boy sings in the choir.*

  Plural nouns end in **-s** or **–es.**

  *EXAMPLE: The boys sing in the choir.*

N.B. In sentences that start with the constructions "One of the workers..." or "Each of the girls...," you must pay close attention to the word that is actually the subject of the sentence. Otherwise, you might not choose the correct verb form.

EXAMPLE: *One of the workers was hurt yesterday at the construction site.*

One *is the subject; because it is singular, the verb is singular* (was *not* were).

*Each of the girls and boys excels at a different sport.*

Each *is the subject so the verb* excels *is singular.*

- Compound Subjects with **and** use plural verbs.

  EXAMPLE: *My sister and her friend* ***play*** *on a soccer team.*

  **Exceptions:**

  1. If a compound subject with **and** expresses a singular idea, use a singular verb.

     EXAMPLE: *The waning and waxing of the tide* ***is*** *one of nature's basic natural rhythms.*

  2. If a compound subject is preceded by the adjective *each* or *every*, use a singular verb.

     EXAMPLE: *Every man and woman* ***has*** *many similar experiences.*

- Verbs, after compound subjects with **or, nor, either...or, neither...nor, not...but**, agree with the subject closest to it.

  EXAMPLE: *Neither you nor your* brothers ***play*** *hockey.*

  *Neither his brothers nor* he ***plays*** *hockey.*

- Collective nouns, such as *family*, *jury*, *salt*, and *furniture*, take singular verbs.

  EXAMPLE: *The furniture in the house* ***is*** *new.*

- Nouns that are singular in meaning but plural in form — such as politics, economics, or news — take a singular verb.

  EXAMPLE: *Mathematics* ***is*** *a difficult subject.*

- Words such as *some*, *all*, *part*, *half*, and *fractions* take either a singular or plural verb, depending on the noun that follows.

  EXAMPLE: *All of the bananas* ***are*** *ripe.*

  *All the rice* ***has*** *been eaten.*

- In sentences containing *there* or *here* and a verb, the verb is either singular or plural, depending on the noun that follows.

  EXAMPLE: *There* ***is*** one window *in the kitchen.*

  *There* ***are*** two windows *in the kitchen.*

- A title takes a singular verb.

  EXAMPLE: The Boats of the Oceans ***is*** *a funny book.*

- *Who*, *which*, and *that* take verbs that agree with their antecedents (the word, phrase, or clause to which they refer).

  EXAMPLES: *My father was not the person who was late.*

  *The antecedent of* who *is* person *(singular antecedent, singular verb)*

  *My father was among the people who were late.*

  *The antecedent of* who *is* people *(plural antecedent, plural verb)*

  *My sister is one of the people who rescue stranded animals.*

  *The antecedent of* who *is* people *(plural antecedent, plural verb)*

  *My sister is the only one of them who is qualified to do the job.*

  *The antecedent of* who *is* one *(singular antecedent, singular verb)*

These last two examples are very tricky because you must stop to consider which word is actually the antecedent.

**Exercise C: Subject / Verb Agreement**

Underline the correct answer.

▸1 There (was, were) lots of people at the concert last night.

▸2 Each of the girls (want, wants) to buy a new car.

▸3 How many of the students (was, were) absent?

▸4 News of the accident (was, were) broadcast on all TV channels.

▸5 My homework (is, are) not complicated this week.

▸6 A pile of garbage (is, are) sitting outside the boss's office.

▸7 Mathematics (is, are) my favourite subject.

▸8 Everyone (is, are) happy that he got the job.

▸9 There (is, are) cake, pie, or ice cream for dessert.

▸10 Neither of them (want, wants) to go to court next week.

▸11 One of the girls (has, have) forgotten her books.

▸12 Many a musician (has, have) to work long hours to make a decent salary.

▸13 Both the cat and the dog (has, have) a special place to sleep.

▸14 If you want to make lunch, there (is, are) cheese, ham, lettuce, mustard, and fresh bread.

▸15 The TV and radio (was, were) playing at the same time.

▸16 (Has, Have) anybody remembered to bring the tablecloth?

▸17 The information (was, were) very important.

▸18 (Don't, doesn't) either of you remember his phone number?

▸19 Some members of the baseball team (was, were) late for the game.

▸20 Five dollars (is, are) the price of the ticket to the game.

▸21 On the desk (is, are) several letters from his friend.

▸22 Either he or I (is, are, am) going on the trip.

▸23 A period of two weeks (is, are) not long enough to appreciate that country.

▸24 The winner of the race, surrounded by his fans, (was, were) trying to catch the attention of his family.

▸25 (Do, Does) James and Jennifer want to go to the movies this afternoon?

▸26 *The Lies of Silence* (is, are) a good book to read.

### Pronoun/Antecedent and Pronoun/Case Agreement

- Pronouns should agree in person, number, and gender with their antecedents.

  *EXAMPLES: At that college, **every student** must bring **his or her** own portable computer to class.*
  *At that college, **students** must bring **their** own portable computers to class.*

**Incorrect usage**: Constructions such as *Every student* must bring *their…*

- Pronouns must also agree in case. This refers to whether they function as a subject or an object.

  *EXAMPLES: Both **you** and **I** are excited about the award.*
  *You and I function as a subject.*
  *He gave a copy of the document to both **you** and **me**.*

**Case of Pronouns**

| Number | Singular | | Plural | |
|---|---|---|---|---|
| **Case** | **Subject** | **Object** | **Subject** | **Object** |
| **Person:** first (1st) | I | me | we | us |
| second (2nd) | you | you | you | you |
| third (3rd) | he | him | they | them |
| she | her | they | them | |
| it | it | they | them | |

*Examples*

| | | | | |
|---|---|---|---|---|
| *She* (subj.) and | *I* (subj.) | gave | *them* (obj.) | all the maps. |
| *Each* (subj.) | of | | *them* (obj.) | was pleased with the results. |

**Exercise D: Pronoun / Antecedent / Case Agreement**

Underline the correct answer.

▸1 Between you and (me, I), I think that he should have won the debate.

▸2 (We, Us) people are all in agreement on that question.

▸3 Each person must prepare (his or her, their) own itinerary.

▸4 (He, Him) and John make a great duo.

▸5 Letitia and (me, I) are planning to leave early on (their, our) trip.

▸6 I think it was (she, her) who started the fight.

▸7 May Carlos and (I, me) borrow your typewriter tomorrow?

▸8 Janice is a better writer than (she, her).

▸9 I wonder if (him, he) and Hoa are going to the convocation ceremony.

▸10 I do not think of you and (I, me) as rivals.

▸ **11** Did you ask (he, him) to arrive early.

▸ **12** To (we, us) teachers, the remarks were very interesting.

▸ **13** It must have been (they, them) who sent the message.

▸ **14** The house had a huge dent in (her, his, its) aluminum siding after the accident.

**Exercise E: Error Analysis**

Correct any errors that you find in the following items. Cross out the incorrect words and write correct replacements above them.

▸ **1** My father and mother is going to the cinema tonight.

▸ **2** The boy told her own mother that he preferred the pies that she baked for him to the ones at school.

▸ **3** Each one will bring their own car.

▸ **4** Economics are my favourite course but I like math, too.

▸ **5** Neither Jurgen nor William want to go to Carla's party.

▸ **6** All of the pie were eaten it was so delicious.

▸ **7** Much people prefer rock to classical music but I prefer classical.

▸ **8** None of them are going to the dance.

▸ **9** Five dollars are a lot for a nine-year old.

▸ **10** Anyone would know their own address!

▸ **11** The news were terrible last night. What a bad accidents!

▸ **12** My dad love his new car but he lent her to my mum for this evening.

▸ **13** I like much sugar in my tea but none in my coffee.

▸ **14** One of them are lying. Which one do you think its could be?

▸ **15** Yao and Jacob are lending his books to Rhonda before the exam.

▸ **16** Everyone are shouting at me that mathematics are the best.

▸ **17** Have anyone called while I was out?

▸ **18** Neither Genevieve nor Youssef have completed the homeworks.

▸ **19** Do he has any informations about the trip to Europe next summer?

▸ **20** The women was walking while her children was running.

### Paragraph Practice

- ▸1 Write an opinion paragraph on one of your favourite movie or sports idols. What do you find positive or negative about your idol? How is the idol portrayed in the media?
- ▸2 In your opinion, what did Marilyn Monroe symbolise for American popular culture?

## WRAP-UP: DISCUSSION TOPICS

- ▸1 Debate a controversial topic with a partner or in groups.
- ▸2 What is the role of movie stars in our society?
- ▸3 Discuss the oppression of minority groups today.
- ▸4 Do blondes really have more fun?
- ▸5 Equality of the sexes.
- ▸6 Gender roles.

## ESSAY TOPICS

- ▸1 Compare the status of women and men in contemporary society.
- ▸2 What is the role of the feminist movement in establishing equal status for women?
- ▸3 Advertising exploits sexual stereotypes to sell products.
- ▸4 How to be taken seriously (this could be a humorous topic!).
- ▸5 The differences between men and women.
- ▸6 Write a persuasive essay about a person who has never received due credit for his or her achievements.
- ▸7 Do research on someone who has had great influence on society through his or her involvement in human rights.

# References

## PRINT

**Biography and Criticism**

Daffron, Carolyn. *Gloria Steinem*. New York: Chelsea House, 1988.

Gilbert, Lynn, and Gaylen Moore. *Particular Passions*. New York: Clarkson N. Potter, 1981.

Heilburn, Carolyn G. *The Education of a Woman: The Life of Gloria Steinem*. New York: Random House, 1996.

Henry, Sondra, and Emily Taitz. *One Woman's Power*. Minneapolis: Dillon Press, 1987.

Hoff, Mark. *Gloria Steinem: The Women's Movement*. Brookfield, CT: Millbrook Press, 1991.

Lazo, Caroline. *Gloria Steinem*. Minneapolis: Lerner Publishing Group, 1998.

## INTERNET

**Biography and selected works of the author**

http://www.britannica.com/bcom/eb/article

http://www.feminist.com/gloria.htm

http://www.greatwomen.org/stnem.htm

http://www.lifetimetv.com/onair/intimate/frameset.shtml/port9847.html

http://www.theglassceiling.com/biographies/bio32.htm

**About Marilyn Monroe**

http://www.marilynmonroe.com/

**Historical background of the feminist movement**

http://www.blythe.org/peru-pcp/doc_en/feminist.html

http://www.jeremiahproject.com/prophecy/feminist.html

http://val.looksmart.com/eus1/eus317828/eus317850/eus53829/eus655

http://www.pbs.org/onewoman/suffrage.html

(in Canada) http://www.niagara.com/~merrwill/

UNIT 2.4

# PRETTY LIKE A WHITE BOY: THE ADVENTURES OF A BLUE-EYED OJIBWAY

## CHAPTER CONTENTS

- **READING:** "Pretty Like a White Boy" by Drew Hayden Taylor; Native literature
- **STYLISTIC ELEMENTS:** tone; connotations; humour
- **WRITING:** persuasive essay
- **GRAMMAR AND VOCABULARY:** homonyms; shift in verb tense; error analysis

The persuasive essay in this chapter takes a humorous look at stereotypes in society.

## ABOUT THE AUTHOR

DREW HAYDEN TAYLOR was born in 1962 and is a member of the Ojibway people. He comes from Curve Lake First Nation near Peterborough, Ontario, and is well known for his sense of humour and for his writing of plays. His play, *Toronto at Dreamer's Rock*, won the Chalmer's Playwriting Award for Best Play for Young Audiences in 1992. *The Bootlegger Blues* won the CAA Literary Award for Best Drama in 1992. His other plays include *Someday* and *The Girl Who Loved Horses.* He has also written scripts for television and articles for magazines and newspapers such as *Maclean's*, *The Toronto Star*, and *The Globe and Mail.* He is currently the Artistic Director of Native Earth Performing Arts, a Native theatre company based in Toronto.

## TRENDS OF THE TIMES: NATIVE LITERATURE

Written Native literature has developed only in recent times, even though it has roots in a very ancient oral tradition. Songs and stories, told from one generation to the next, enabled literature and culture to be passed on over time. A great body of Native literature, including legends, stories, and songs, used to be studied within the framework of white literature. However, it is generally thought that in the past the image of Natives in literature was stereotyped. Furthermore, it is important to remember that older specimens of Native literature were translated and probably reflected more of white literary traditions than Native ones. Some older Native writers did, however, write in English. Among them were Joseph Brant (1742-1807, a Mohawk), George Copway (1818-1869, an Ojibway), and E. Pauline Johnson (1861-1913, a Mohawk). Christian missionaries whose vocation was to convert the so-called savages, taught English to early Native writers. Some of the first works in English of these and other earlier Native writers explore the influence of missionaries on traditional Native life.

Contemporary Native written literature varies greatly in form, content, and opinion. Writers show a concern for the past and the present. Young writers such as Jeannette C. Armstrong (b. 1948), who is Okanagan; Alootook Ipellie (b. 1951), who is Inuit; Jordan Wheeler (b. 1964), who is Cree, and many others, explore themes on environmental factors such as pollution, social issues such racism or biculturalism, and political concerns such as Native land claims.

## INITIAL READING ▸ Do the glossary exercise to prepare yourself for the initial reading.

**Exercise: Glossary**

Many words in the following essay relate to Native Indian culture. Find the definitions of the following in your dictionary.

▸1 Ojibway

___

▸2 bulrush

___

▸3 Reserve (the American word *reservation* has the same meaning as this Canadian term.)

___

▸4 Mohawk

___

▸5 warriors

___

▸6 longhouse

___

▸7 Métis

___

▸8 Status card: a card that Canadian Indians carry in order to prove their identity as a native person. In Canada, a status Indian is a registered member of an Indian band who has certain rights and privileges (living on a reserve and exemptions from taxes) as well as certain restrictions (restricted ability to pass on Indian status to children in certain situations).

There are also some specific political, cultural, and historical references in this essay.

- Brian Mulroney was the prime minister of Canada between 1984 and1993.
- The Oka crisis occurred in 1990. Oka is a small village in Quebec. The local golf club wanted to build a golf links on an old Native Indian burial ground. The Mohawk nation, who lived in the area, protested. Eventually there was a stand-off between the army and Native protestors.
- One of the Mohawk leaders during the Oka crisis was a man nicknamed Lasagna.
- The Queen Charlotte Islands are a group of islands off the main coast of British Columbia.
- Manitoulin Island is an island in Lake Huron.

Please note that this essay uses British punctuation.

ESSAY

# Pretty Like a White Boy: The Adventures of a Blue-Eyed Ojibway

Drew Hayden Taylor

1992

In this big, huge world, with all its billions and billions of people, it's safe to say that everybody will eventually come across personalities and individuals that will touch them in some peculiar yet poignant way. Individuals that in some way represent and help define who you are. I'm no different, mine was Kermit the Frog. Not just because Natives have a long tradition of savouring Frogs' legs, but because of his music. If you all may remember, Kermit is quite famous for his rendition of 'It's Not Easy Being Green'. I can relate. If I could sing, my song would be 'It's Not Easy Having Blue Eyes in a Brown Eyed Village'.

Yes, I'm afraid it's true. The author happens to be a card-carrying Indian. Once you get past the aforementioned eyes, the fair skin, light brown hair, and noticeable lack of cheekbones, there lies the heart and spirit of an Ojibway storyteller. Honest Injun, or as the more politically correct term may be, honest aboriginal.

You see, I'm the product of a white father I never knew, and an Ojibway woman who evidently couldn't run fast enough. As a kid I knew I looked a bit different. But, then again, all kids are paranoid when it comes to their peers. I had a fairly happy childhood, frolicking through the bulrushes. But there were certain things that, even then, made me notice my unusual appearance. Whenever we played cowboys and Indians, guess who had to be the bad guy, the cowboy.

It wasn't until I left the Reserve for the big bad city, that I became more aware of the role people expected me to play, and the fact that physically I didn't fit in. Everybody seemed to have this preconceived idea of how every Indian looked and acted. One guy, on my first day of college, asked me what kind of horse I preferred. I didn't have the heart to tell him 'hobby'.

I've often tried to be philosophical about the whole thing. I have both white and red blood in me, I guess that makes me pink. I am a 'Pink' man. Try to imagine this, I'm walking around on any typical Reserve in Canada, my head held high, proudly announcing to everyone 'I am a Pink Man'. It's a good thing I ran track in school.

My pinkness is constantly being pointed out to me over and over and over again. 'You don't look Indian?' 'You're not Indian, are you?' 'Really?!?' I got questions like that from both white and Native people, for a while I debated having my status card tattooed on my forehead.

And like most insecure people and specially a blue-eyed Native writer, I went through a particularly severe identity crisis at one point. In fact, I admit it, one depressing spring evening, I died my hair black. Pitch black.

The reason for such a dramatic act, you may ask? Show Business. You see for the last eight years or so, I've worked in various capacities in the performing arts, and as a result I'd always get calls to be an extra or even try out for an important role in some Native oriented movie. This anonymous voice would phone, having been given my number, and ask if I would be interested in trying out for a movie. Being a naturally ambitious, curious, and greedy young man I would always readily agree, stardom flashing in my eyes and hunger pains from my wallet.

A few days later I would show up for the audition, and that was always an experience. What kind of experience you may ask? Picture this, the picture calls for the casting of seventeenth-century Mohawk warriors living in a traditional longhouse. The casting director calls the name 'Drew Hayden Taylor, and I enter.

The casting director, the producer, and the film's director look up from the table and see my face, blue eyes flashing in anticipation. I once was described as a slightly chubby beachboy. But even beachboys have tans Anyway, there would be a quick flush of confusion, a recheck of the papers, and a hesitant Mr Taylor? Then they would ask if I was at the right audition. It was always the same. By the way, I never got any of the parts I tried for, except for a few anonymous crowd shots. Politics tells me it's because of the way I look, reality tells me it's probably because I can't act. I'm not sure which is better.

It's not just film people either. Recently I've become quite involved in Theatre, Native theatre to be exact. And one cold October day I was happily attending the Toronto leg of a province-wide tour of my first play, *Toronto at Dreamer's Rock*. The place was sold out, the audience very receptive and the performance was wonderful. Ironically one of the actors was also half-white.

The director later told me he had been talking with the actor's father, an older Non-Native type chap. Evidently he had asked a few questions about me, and how I did my research. This made the director curious and asked about his interest. He replied 'He's got an amazing grasp of the Native situation for a white person.'

Not all these incidents are work related either. One time a friend and I were coming out of a rather upscale bar (we were out YUPPIE watching) and managed to catch a cab. We thanked the cab driver for being so comfortably close on such a cold night, he shrugged and nonchalantly talked about knowing what bars to drive around. 'If you're not careful, all you'll get is drunk Indians.' I hiccuped.

Another time this cab driver droned on and on about the government. He started out by criticizing Mulroney, and eventually to his handling of the Oka crisis. This perked up my ears, until he said 'If it were me, I'd have tear-gassed the place by the second day. No more problem.' He got a dime tip. A few incidents like this and I'm convinced I'd make a great undercover agent for one of the Native political organizations.

But then again, even Native people have been known to look at me with a fair amount of suspicion. Many years ago when I was a young man, I was working on a documentary on Native culture up in the wilds of Northern Ontario. We were at an isolated cabin filming a trapper woman and her kids. This one particular nine-year-old girl seemed to take a shine to me. She followed me around for two days both annoying me and endearing herself to me. But she absolutely refused to believe that I was Indian. The whole film crew tried to tell her but to no avail. She was certain I was white.

Then one day as I was loading up the car with film equipment, she asked me if I wanted some tea. Being in a hurry I declined the tea. She immediately smiled with victory crying out 'See, you're not Indian, all Indians drink tea!'

Frustrated and a little hurt I whipped out my Status card and thrust it at her. Now there I was, standing in a Northern Ontario winter, showing my Status card to a nine-year-old non-status Indian girl who had no idea what one was. Looking back, this may not have been one of my brighter moves.

But I must admit, it was a Native woman that boiled everything down in one simple sentence. You may know that woman, Marianne Jones from 'The Beachcombers' television series. We were working on a film together out west and we got to gossiping. Eventually we got around to talking about our respective villages. Hers on the Queen Charlotte Islands, or Haida Gwaii as the Haida call them, and mine in central Ontario.

Eventually childhood on the Reserve was being discussed and I made a comment about the way I look. She studied me for a moment, smiled, and said 'Do you know what the old women in my village would call you?' Hesitant but curious, I shook my head. 'They'd say you were pretty like a white boy.' To this day I'm still not sure if I like that.

Now some may argue that I am simply a Métis with a Status card. I disagree, I failed French in grade 11. And the Métis as everyone knows have their own separate and honourable culture, particularly in western Canada. And of course I am well aware that I am not the only person with my physical characteristics.

I remember once looking at a video tape of a drum group, shot on a Reserve up near Manitoulin Island. I noticed one of the drummers seemed quite fair-haired, almost blond. I mentioned this to my girlfriend of the time and she shrugged saying 'Well, that's to be expected. The highway runs right through the Reserve.'

Perhaps I'm being too critical. There's a lot to be said for both cultures. For example, on the left hand, you have the Native respect for Elders. They understand the concept of wisdom and insight coming with age.

On the white hand, there's Italian food. I mean I really love my mother and family but seriously, does anything really beat good Veal Scallopini? Most of my aboriginal friends share my fondness for this particular brand of food. Wasn't there a warrior at Oka named Lasagna? I found it ironic, though curiously logical, that Columbus was Italian. A connection I wonder?

Also Native people have this wonderful respect and love for the land. They believe they are part of it, as mere chain in the cycle of existence. Now as many of you know, this conflicts with the accepted Judeo-Christian i.e. western view of land management. I even believe somewhere in the first chapters of the Bible it says something about God giving man dominion over Nature. Check it out, Genesis 4:?, 'Thou shalt clear cut.' So I grew up understanding that everything around me is important and alive. My Native heritage gave me that.

And again, on the white hand, there's breast implants. Darn clever them white people. That's something Indians would never have invented, seriously. We're not ambitious enough. We just take what the Creator decides to give us, but no, not the white man. Just imagine it, some serious looking white man, and let's face it people, we know it was a man who invented them, don't we? So just imagine some serious looking white doctor sitting around in his laboratory muttering to himself, 'Big tits, big tits, hmm, how do I make big tits?' If it was an Indian, it would be 'Big tits, big tits, white women sure got big tits' and leave it at that.

So where does that leave me on the big philosophical scoreboard, what exactly are my choices again; Indians — respect for elders, love of the land. White people — food and big tits. In order to live in both cultures I guess I'd have to find an Indian woman with big tits who lives with her grandmother in a cabin out in the woods and can make Fettuccini Alfredo on a wood stove.

Now let me make this clear, I'm not writing this for sympathy, or out of anger, or even some need for self-glorification. I am just setting the facts straight. For as you read this, a new Nation is born. This is a declaration of independence, my declaration of independence.

I've spent too many years explaining who and what I am repeatedly, so as of this moment, I officially secede from both races. I plan to start my own separate nation. Because I am half Ojibway, and half Caucasian, we will be called the Occasions. And I of course, since I'm founding the new nation, will be a Special Occasion.

## CLOSE READING

▸1 What are the author's two cultures?

---

▸2 With which culture does the author mainly identify?

---

▸3 What is the thesis statement of the essay?

---

▸4 What types of arguments does the author present in order to prove his thesis?

**a)** examples **b)** facts **c)** personal experiences **d)** quotes from informed sources

---

▸5 At which point does the author state that he became aware of the problem concerning his looks?

---

▸6 List at least three arguments the author makes in order to convince the reader of his thesis.

▸7 What reasons does the author give for writing this essay?

▸8 In your opinion, are those reasons credible?

▸9 What conclusion(s) does the author reach in this essay?

## WRITER'S CRAFT

### Tone and Connotations

#### *Tone*

▸▸▸ ***Tone refers to the quality of sentiments exhibited in an essay. The language used to express ideas demonstrates the writer's attitude towards the reader. This attitude may be formal, informal, hostile, etc.***

***In a persuasive or opinion essay, the arguments may be very strong or weak. Arguments may appeal to the reader's emotions or his or her ability to reason. In all cases, the goal of the opinion essay is to convince the reader of the validity of a thesis. Words such as* must *and* should *have very strong connotations and are used for absolute commands. Other words such as* might *or* may *are less absolute and more along the lines of suggestions in their tone. Therefore, the language a writer uses conveys the tone and is fundamental for the arguments of an opinion essay.*** ◂◂◂

**Exercise A: Identifying Tone**

The five excerpts that follow have each been taken from an essay in this section. From the words to describe tone listed below, identify the predominant tone of each excerpt. Support your answer with proof from the text in the form of cited words or phrases. State whether the excerpt appeals more to the emotions, to reason, or to both fairly equally.

**Words to describe tone**: formal, hostile, satirical, ironic, witty, visually descriptive, narrative, sarcastic, cynical, informative

**A.** I still keep in mind a certain wonderful sunset which I witnessed when steamboating was new to me. A broad expanse of the river was turned to blood; in the middle distance the red hue brightened into gold, through which a solitary log came floating, black and conspicuous; in one place a long, slanting mark lay sparkling upon the water; in another the surface was broken by boiling, tumbling rings, that were as many-tinted as an opal; where the ruddy flush was faintest, was a smooth spot that was covered with graceful circles and radiating lines, ever so delicately traced; the shore on our left was densely wooded, and the sombre shadow that fell from this forest was broken in one place by a long, ruffled trail that shone like silver; and high above the forest wall a clean-stemmed dead tree waved a single leafy bough that glowed like a flame in the unobstructed splendor that was flowing from the sun. There were graceful curves, reflected images, woody heights, soft distances; and over the whole scene, far and near, the dissolving lights drifted steadily, enriching it, every passing moment, with new marvels of coloring.

Tone: ______________ Proof: ______________________________

Appeals to **a)** emotion **b)** reason **c)** both

**B.** Reading was not one of my boyhood passions. Girls, or rather the absence of girls, drove me to it. When I was 13 years old, short for my age, more than somewhat pimply, I was terrified of girls. They made me feel sadly inadequate.

Retreating into high seriousness, I acquired a pipe, which I chewed on ostentatiously, and made it my business to be seen everywhere, even at school basketball games, absorbed by books of daunting significance. The two women who ran the lending library, possibly amused by my pretensions, tried to interest me in fiction.

Tone: ______________ Proof: ______________________________

Appeals to **a)** emotion **b)** reason **c)** both

**C.** Of course, Marilyn's image didn't really gain seriousness and intellectuality. Women don't gain serious status by sexual association any more easily than they do by hard work. (At least, not unless the serious man dies and we confine ourselves to being keepers of the flame. As Margaret Mead has pointed out, widows are almost the only women this country honors in authority.) Even Marilyn's brave refusal to be intimidated by threats that she would never work in films again if she married Miller, who was then a "subversive" called to testify before the House UnAmerican Activities Committee, was considered less brave than Miller's refusal to testify. Indeed, it was barely reported at all.

Tone: ______________ Proof: ______________________________

Appeals to **a)** emotion **b)** reason **c)** both

**D.** Perhaps I'm being too critical. There's a lot to be said for both cultures. For example, on the left hand, you have the Native respect for Elders. They understand the concept of wisdom and insight coming with age...

And again, on the white hand, there's breast implants. Darn clever them white people. That's something Indians would never have invented, seriously. We're not ambitious enough. We just take what the Creator decides to give us, but no, not the white man. Just imagine it, some serious looking white man, and let's face it people, we know it was a man who invented them, don't we? So just imagine some serious looking white doctor sitting around in his laboratory muttering to himself, 'Big tits, big tits, hmm, how do I make big tits?' If it was an Indian, it would be 'Big tits, big tits, white women sure got big tits' and leave it at that.

Tone: ______________ Proof: ______________________________

Appeals to **a)** emotion **b)** reason **c)** both

**E.** So what is an honest charlatan? We better start by defining what a charlatan is. Simply put, a charlatan pretends to have some power, skill, or knowledge that he actually does not possess. Claims can range from the "ability" to remove tumors without making an incision to causing spoons to bend by psychic means. An "honest" charlatan can produce the same effects but freely admits that it is all done by trickery.

Tone: ______________ Proof: ______________________________

Appeals to **a)** emotion **b)** reason **c)** both

**Exercise B: Detailed Study of Tone: Pretty Like a White Boy**

▸1 What is the attitude of the writer towards the reader? There may be more than one answer.

**a)** distant **b)** formal **c)** hostile **d)** friendly **e)** informal

▸2 Read the following paragraph.

"Yes, I'm afraid it's true. The author happens to be a card-carrying Indian. Once you get past the aforementioned eyes, the fair skin, light brown hair, and noticeable lack of cheekbones, there lies the heart and spirit of an Ojibway storyteller. Honest Injun, or as the more politically correct term may be, honest aboriginal."

The sentences (more than one answer)

**a)** are short and simple

**b)** are very elaborate with many unfamiliar words

**c)** use colloquial language

**d)** use academic, formal language

▸3 Cite one sentence from the paragraph in question 2 to support your answers for both questions one and two.

___

___

▸4 Find two other sentences in the essay that are examples of informal language.

___

___

▸5 The tone of this essay is also humorous. Give three examples from the author's personal experience that prove this statement.

___

___

___

▸6 The author uses a funny and popular character, Kermit the Frog, in the introduction. This sets the mood or atmosphere for the rest of the essay. How is Kermit used to create a humorous mood in the introduction?

___

▸7 Why does the author describe himself physically?

___

▸8 How do his physical characteristics add to the humorous situations he finds himself in?

___

▸9 The author makes fun or light of certain situations. Explain how the following situations are funny:

a) "One guy, on my first day of college, asked me what kind of horse I preferred. I didn't have the heart to tell him 'hobby'."

b) "I have both white and red blood in me, I guess that makes me pink. I am a 'Pink' man. Try to imagine this, I'm walking around on any typical Reserve in Canada, my head held high, proudly announcing to everyone 'I am a Pink Man'. It's a good thing I ran track in school."

▸10 Write down the statement in which the author acknowledges an opposing point of view.

▸11 What humorous contrasts does the author show when he compares his two backgrounds? Cite three examples.

▸12 What is the purpose of this form of humour?

## CONNOTATIONS

▸▸▸ ***The author uses many words and expressions with connotations that on one level have a light, humorous meaning, but on another level have a more serious meaning. For example, the phrase "Honest Injun" is humorous because the word* Injun*, which was the slang pronunciation of the word* Indian*, by the early white settlers, is used by the author to poke fun at white people's way of regarding natives. On the other hand,* Injun *also has racist connotations, as the word was used in a pejorative way to denigrate Native peoples. Therefore, in this essay the word* Injun *is both funny and serious.*** ◂◂◂

▸1 Explain the funny and serious level of connotation for the following.

a) "card-carrying Indian" (see definition of Status card in Initial Reading)

funny

serious

b) "an Ojibway woman who evidently couldn't run fast enough"

funny

serious

**c)** "Whenever we played cowboys and Indians, guess who had to be the bad guy, the cowboy."

funny ______

serious ______

**d)** "I noticed one of the drummers seemed quite fairhaired, almost blond. I mentioned this to my girlfriend of the time and she shrugged, saying 'Well, that's to be expected. The highway runs right through the Reserve'."

funny ______

serious ______

▸**2** In your opinion, what is the author's purpose in writing this essay?

______

▸**3** Would a serious or formal style have been more appropriate to get the point across to the audience? Explain your answer.

______

______

**In this section, you will work on exercises designed to help you hone your writing and revising skills.**

### *More Tricky Pairs*

#### Exercise A: More Homonyms

The following words are homonyms, words that are pronounced the same, but are spelled differently and are different in meaning.

Find the definition for the following words in your dictionary. Then write a sentence, using each word correctly.

▸**1** ascent ______

______

assent ______

______

▸**2** accept ______

______

except ______

______

▸**3** affect ______

______

effect ______

______

▸**4** altar ______________________________

______________________________

alter ______________________________

______________________________

▸**5** cite ______________________________

______________________________

site ______________________________

______________________________

sight ______________________________

______________________________

▸**6** complement ______________________________

______________________________

compliment ______________________________

______________________________

▸**7** council ______________________________

______________________________

counsel ______________________________

______________________________

▸**8** principle ______________________________

______________________________

principal ______________________________

______________________________

## SHIFT IN VERB TENSE

If there is an incorrect shift in tense, then the point of view of the text becomes illogical and it is often hard to follow the author's train of thought. There are two main problem areas in shift in point of view:

- Past to Present Tense
  Avoid shifting verb tenses. It is important to be consistent in the use of verb tenses. A shift from present to past or past to present should be avoided unless there is a concrete change in time in the event being described.

  *EXAMPLE: The night **was** dark. There **is** no moon. (Incorrect)*
  *The night **was** dark. There **was** no moon. (Correct)*

- Passive to Active Voice
  Avoid shifting from passive voice to active voice, or vice versa.

  *EXAMPLE: The tree was cut by the man and he chopped the branches. (Incorrect)*
  *The man cut the tree and chopped the branches. (Correct)*

**Exercise B: Correcting Errors in Tense Shift**

Correct the errors in the sentences below.

▸1 Yesterday I went to an outdoor concert, but it was so crowded that it is impossible to hear the music.

---

▸2 The car was inspected by the mechanic because somebody buys it.

---

▸3 I swim everyday in the morning. This morning, I do not go swimming because I have a bad cold.

---

▸4 Do you see the accident when you went to work yesterday?

---

▸5 At present, the boy was sick and is being examined by the nurse on duty.

---

**Exercise C: Error Analysis**

Underline the errors and correct them in the following paragraph.

The girl was about ten years old. She and her family lived in a cottage by the lake. Every day the girl and her younger brother, a boy of eight or so are being taught fishing by the neighbour, a teenager who is around 16. The teenager's name was Lisa and she seems to be a pretty proficient fisher. Yesterday morning, the three fishers went out on the lake in a canoe. It was very early in the morning. I can barely see them through the steam rising from the warm water of the lake. The canoe was stopped in the middle of the lake and the three had their lines in the water. They fished all morning, but I don't think they are successful. I couldn't see any fish when they came back to shore.

**Style Tips**

Here are more tips to consider when writing an essay:

- Chose a tone and writing style that is appropriate for the subject and goal of your essay.
- Verify that each argument is logical and that it supports your thesis.
- Proofread your essay.

### *Paragraph Practice*

▸1 *Pretty Like a White Boy* is a prime example of a serious subject (stereotyping, racism) being explored with a sense of humour. Write a paragraph stating your opinion about the effectiveness of such a style.

▸2 Write a humorous paragraph on a topic that interests you. Possible topics could be food, beauty, education, love, or money.

## WRAP-UP: DISCUSSION TOPICS

▸1 What kind of a personality do you think the author of *Pretty Like a White Boy* has?

▸2 Are you familiar with Native political, social, and economic issues? Discuss your knowledge of Native culture.

▸3 Discuss the stereotypes that exist towards different groups in society.

▸4 What are some reasons for the stereotyping of groups? Is there any merit or demerit to stereotyping?

▸5 Are the humorous stereotypes in jokes examples of racism?

## ESSAY TOPICS

▸1 Compare the structure and style of the two essays "Marilyn Monroe: The Woman Who Died Too Soon" and "Pretty Like a White Boy: The Adventures of a Blue-Eyed Ojibway." Are they both structured in a traditional opinion essay format? If not, then how are they different? Which essay contains more convincing arguments?

▸2 Write an opinion essay on racism in contemporary society.

▸3 Write an opinion essay on a controversial topic relevant to contemporary society.

▸4 Belonging to a minority culture is difficult in many societies.

▸5 Designating Native people as Status Indians with special privileges helps keep prejudice alive.

▸6 It is impossible to eradicate stereotypes from human thought.

▸7 Write an essay about discrimination that you have experienced.

▸8 Compare Drew Hayden Taylor's use of humour with Mordecai Richler's use of humour.

# References

## PRINT

### BIOGRAPHY

Glaap, Albert-Reiner. "Margo Kane, Daniel David Moses, Yvette Nolan, Drew Hayden Taylor: Four Native Playwrights from Canada: An Interview." In *Anglistik: Mitteilungen des Verbandes Deutscher Anglisten* 7.1: 5-25, 1996.

Miska, John P. *Ethnic and Native Canadian Literature: A Bibliography*. Toronto: University of Toronto Press, 1990.

### CRITICISM

Comer, Shelley. "Theatre: Playing Around with Prejudice." *The Peak*, 11, vol. 103. Burnaby, B.C.: Simon Fraser University, November 15, 1999.

D'Aeth, Eve. "Taking Soundings." *Canadian Literature*, 165, Summer 2000.

Zivanovic, Judith. "Books in Review: *New Canadian Drama 6*, ed. Rita Much and *Someday* by Drew Hayden Taylor," in *Canadian Literature*, 144, Spring, 1995.

## INTERNET

### BIOGRAPHY OF THE AUTHOR

http://www.canadiantheatre.com/t/taylord.html
http://www.puc.ca/cgi-bin/puc/catalogue.cgi?function=detail&Authors_vid=324
http://www.unipissing.ca/department/publicrelations/030497.htm
http://www.nativebooks.com/

### HISTORICAL BACKGROUND

http://www.tedigna.com/history/index.htm
http://www.indigenouspeople.org/natlit/chippewa.htm

UNIT 2.5

# Bending Spoons and Bending Minds

## CHAPTER CONTENTS

- **READING:** "Bending Spoons and Bending Minds" by Joe Schwarcz; brief biography of the author; brief history of the newspaper
- **STYLISTIC ELEMENTS:** journalistic form (hook, lead, details, main argument, resolution); plays on words and popular images
- **WRITING:** journalistic essay
- **GRAMMAR AND VOCABULARY:** word origins (Greek and Latin, prefixes and suffixes); dangling and misused modifiers; general error analysis

Magic has fascinated humankind for centuries. In this chapter, a popular scientist, amateur magician, and media personality looks at the truth underlying a famous psychic's claims.

## ABOUT THE AUTHOR

DR. JOE SCHWARCZ was born in Hungary in 1947. Presently the director of the McGill Office for Chemistry and Society and a senior adjunct professor at McGill University in Montreal, he is perhaps best known for his fascinating explanations, in lay people's terms, of the mysteries of chemistry. This versatile communicator often expounds his favourite subject in a weekly "phone-in" radio program (on station CJAD in Montreal) and in a regular television show called "Joe's Chemistry Set" on the Canadian Discovery Channel. He also writes a very instructive and entertaining weekly column called "The Right Chemistry" in the *Montreal Gazette* newspaper. Dr. Schwarcz has received many prizes and is the first non-American to have been awarded the James T. Grady-James H. Stack prize from the American Chemistry Society for his efforts to bring chemistry to the lay person.

## TRENDS OF THE TIMES: A BRIEF HISTORY OF THE NEWSPAPER

The *Acta Diurna*, possibly the earliest example of journalism, was a daily publication of important social and political events in Rome that began in 59 B.C. Centuries later in 1609 (about one hundred and fifty years after the invention of the printing press), the first actual newspaper was published in Strasbourg by Johann Carolus. Between these dates, a variety of newsletters, published sporadically, brought political, social, and commercial "news" to those Europeans who could read.

In the early seventeenth century, newspapers began to appear throughout Europe, but it was not until the eighteenth century that journalism reached a certain maturity in England. Providing informed comments about current political events in a leading article, Daniel Defoe introduced the editorial to his readers in his triweekly *Review*, published from 1704 to 1713. About the same time, improvements to the postal system made daily newspapers possible. In *The Tatler* (published triweekly from 1709 to 1711) and *The Spectator* (published daily in 1711 and 1712), Sir Richard Steele and Joseph Addison incorporated social and artistic news as well as commentary. *The Spectator's* readership of 3,000 was great enough to attract advertising. However, politicians decided to tax both advertising and the newspapers themselves, and this caused the demise of *The Spectator* and several other newspapers. But the seeds had been sown and nothing could prevent the subsequent explosion of this popular medium.

The late eighteenth century and early nineteenth century witnessed rapid technological changes in printing techniques and in transportation and communication. Many different newspapers appeared on both sides of the Atlantic. *The Times* of London was now able to meet the demand for more newspapers by increasing its output to 5,000 copies per hour. Its circulation rose from 5,000 to

50,000 by mid-century. *The New York Tribune* (1886) and *The Newcastle Chronicle* (1889) began to use the revolutionary Linotype machine, greatly increasing typesetters' efficiency. Electricity, the telephone, the telegraph, and railway networks made rapid communication of news events possible and helped increase newspaper production and circulation.

Not only did these technological developments increase newspaper production and circulation, but they also redefined the journalist's task. Seventeenth-century European journalists were generalists: they wrote and edited articles, and then printed the newspapers themselves. Exploiting their own particular writing styles, these journalists often tried to influence public opinion. As newspapers became increasingly diversified and comprehensive, the nature of a journalist's task became more and more specialised. Occasional correspondents were replaced by full-time reporters who covered specific types of events. Press agencies were set up to provide international coverage.

By the end of the nineteenth century, in both England and the United States, several newspapers clearly separated two distinct types of journalism: factual reporting and editorial opinion. Many had developed very particular styles that sometimes changed quite radically when a new owner or editor took over. Several popular newspapers approached a circulation of 1,000,000 at this time. In the United States, syndicates began to provide ready-to-use articles and columns on specialised topics such as medicine, astrology, book reviews and, later, movie reviews as well as comic strips. This practice of syndication continues today.

Western journalism is distinguished by the fact that it is not under government control. During the nineteenth century, the idea of a politically independent press, free from censorship (except in wartime or other emergencies), was fostered both in Britain and, more especially, in the United States. During the twentieth century, this freedom has allowed the press to criticise governments, institutions, corporations, and individuals. Lack of censorship has proved to be one of the cornerstones of democracy in many countries, in spite of the fact that true journalistic freedom may only exist as an ideal. A newspaper expresses its opinion on a topic in its editorials (in a collective opinion, usually agreed upon by the editors of the newspaper). Moreover, on the opposite page from the editorials, columnists and freelance journalists often express their personal opinions on current or controversial issues. These articles are called op-eds (*opposite* the *editorial* page).

In current times, although television (with the Internet close on its heels!) has become the main provider of news in many countries, serious newspapers still offer in-depth coverage of events as well as pertinent analysis and informed opinion about current affairs and other subjects of interest to the public. Readers want to have accurate information and guided insight to help them make sense of complex issues and the world around them. Furthermore, leading contemporary journalists are not only appreciated for the articles they write but also for their finely honed styles. Dr. Joe Schwarcz of Montreal is one example of a journalist whose essays exemplify many of the finest characteristics found in contemporary journalism.

### Warm-up Discussion Topics

▸ 1 According to you, do the following psychic phenomena really exist: telepathy (sending and receiving messages); telekinesis (moving objects) or bending spoons?

Yes ________ or no ________ ? Why do you think this?

___

▸ 2 What differences do you see among science, psychic phenomena, and magic?

___

## INITIAL READING

In your own words, state the main idea of the essay in one sentence.

---

---

1999

ESSAY

# BENDING SPOONS AND BENDING MINDS

JOE SCHWARCZ

Everyone should go to a magic convention at least once in their lives. You'll be fooled and entertained as coins vanish, selected cards rise out of decks and ten dollar bills float in mid-air in front of your eyes. But most important, you'll never look at the world the same way again. Frankly, I can't think of a better way to foster critical thinking than to be fooled by the honest charlatans at a magic convention.

So what is an honest charlatan? We better start by defining what a charlatan is. Simply put, a charlatan pretends to have some power, skill, or knowledge that he actually does not possess. Claims can range from the "ability" to remove tumors without making an incision to causing spoons to bend by psychic means. An "honest" charlatan can produce the same effects but freely admits that it is all done by trickery.

The Dean of honest charlatans is The Amazing Randi, one of my idols. He is a world famous magician, but more significantly, he is the superman of rational thought, fighting for truth, justice and the scientific way.

What a delight it was for me to finally meet the Amazing One at Montreal's annual magic convention! For two hours we chatted about the current widespread belief in various types of silliness and the importance of exposing fraud wherever it exists.

Randi has built a formidable career on such exposures. And he has put his money, currently $1.1 million, where his mouth is. Anyone can claim the money, providing they can produce a paranormal phenomenon under controlled conditions. Let them telepathically determine the contents of a sealed envelope, move an object by "psychokinesis" or bend a spoon by mental power.

While many challengers have been tested, no one so far has walked away with the money. Uri Geller hasn't even applied for it. Oh yes, Uri Geller. It is virtually impossible to discuss Randi without talking about Geller, the psychic superstar who for nearly three decades has been bending spoons, and bending minds for a living.

Geller, a seemingly charming, former Israeli magician claims to have abilities that he himself doesn't understand. He gently rubs keys and they bend, he runs his hands above sealed canisters and determines which ones contain water. Strangely though, he cannot do these things with Randi around.

When Geller first came to the U.S., he guested on the Tonight Show. The appearance was anticipated eagerly because Geller had already captivated huge live audiences with his psychic feats and now millions of TV viewers would finally get a chance to see the phenomena that science could not explain.

The appearance was a total fiasco. Geller was unable to produce anything. He didn't feel right, he said, the energy just wasn't there that night. But it was quite apparent that the psychic powers had actually failed Geller earlier. Otherwise he would have known that Johnny Carson [a very popular late-night T.V. talk-show host from 1962 to 1992, now retired] was an amateur magician and that the show's producers had consulted Randi about how "psychic" feats could be carried out using magicians' tricks.

Geller couldn't bend the spoons supplied by the show, he couldn't determine which sealed film canister contained water because on Randi's advice the canisters were firmly attached to the table. Geller's usual trick of imperceptibly shaking the table to see which canister moved did not work. Only Geller was visibly shaken.

Strangely, the psychic flop did not destroy Geller's career. His next appearance was on the Donahue Show, and everything worked! Proof, Geller said, that he was not a magician, he was for real. If he was just doing tricks, they would work all the time!

Eventually numerous articles and books appeared explaining how Geller performed his stunts and North American interest in the spoon bender declined. He moved to England where he now claims to help companies find gold and oil by psychic map reading and markets Uri Geller's Mind Power Kit with crystal quartz for psychic healing.

Belief in psychic spoon bending may seem harmless enough. But it is not. If you can believe that metal can be bent by thought processes, you can also believe that tumors can be removed from the body without any trace of an incision being left. Such "psychic surgery" is performed by standard sleight of hand tricks and looks very impressive. But what about actual cancer patients who are taken in by the ruse? Might they be foregoing some effective therapy?

Randi's purpose is not to uncritically debunk. It is to fairly evaluate claims. He, like any scientist, would be thrilled if our scientific sphere could be expanded. How exciting it would be if we could send messages to each other telepathically, if we really were being visited by aliens, if we could treat disease by therapeutic touch!

Therapeutic touch is the supposed ability to affect body processes by moving hands over the body at a distance of roughly 8-10 inches. The explanation offered is that the body is surrounded by an energy field which can be altered by the therapist's energy field. Practitioners, nurses in many cases, claim to actually feel the presence of this field and describe it like "spongy rubber." There are numerous accounts of patients being helped. But is the energy field or the placebo effect at play?

Randi described how he had recently advertised in nursing magazines for anyone who could detect the human energy field, offering the standard reward. A sleeve would be constructed in such a way that an arm could be placed in it without the therapist seeing whether the sleeve was "armed" or not. The goal was to determine, in a statistically significant fashion, when the arm was in the sleeve by feeling for the energy field.

In spite of the heavy advertising and offer of the reward, only one lady showed up at the Philadelphia hospital where the experiment was to be performed. She got the arm placement right half the time. After, she blamed jet lag for the failure, despite having signed a form previously that everything was to her satisfaction. Randi told me that his offer of course still stands.

Two hours had flown by and I couldn't monopolize the Amazing One any more. Anyway, I had to go and check out the magic dealers. My psychic key bender had worn out and I needed a new one. I also found a new spoon effect. "Spoon Spinner" allows the magician to charge an ordinary tea spoon with his "aura" and use it to pick up another spoon. Of course no one else can repeat this. I had to have it.

I could hardly wait to get home and demonstrate my acquisition. But when I took the spoons out of my pocket, one of them was bent! Could it be that I have some unrecognized psychic power? Maybe. Or maybe I just sat on the spoon.

## CLOSE READING ▸ Answer the following questions.

▸**1** According to the author, what benefit can attending a magic convention bring to a person?

___

▸**2** **a)** In your own words, what is the difference between a charlatan and an "honest" charlatan?

___

▸**3** Joe Schwarcz most admires The Amazing Randi because he

**a)** is a world famous magician

**b)** believes in exposing trickery

**c)** is a magician who is also a scientist

▸**4** What is the major difference between The Amazing Randi and Uri Geller in

**a)** how they present themselves to the public?

___

**b)** their purpose in performing in public?

___

▸**5** **a)** What well-paying offer has The Amazing Randi made to psychics?

___

**b)** Why is he offering this?

___

**c)** Up to the time of publication of this article, has anyone claimed the money?

Yes ______ No ______

▸**6** What can you conclude from Randi's experiment about the nurse's ability to use therapeutic touch?

___

▸**7** Why does Joe Schwarcz believe that belief in psychic spoon bending is not harmless?

___

___

▸**8** To whom does the title of the essay refer?

___

## WRITER'S CRAFT

### *Journalistic Form*

The essay in this chapter comes from a weekly column that Dr. Schwarcz writes for a major Montreal newspaper.

Here are the basic elements constituting the form of a journalistic essay:

- **Hook:** thought-provoking phrase or statement to grab the reader's interest; often found in headlines; can also be found in introduction.

  *EXAMPLE (headline): Miss Alma Carlson Heroine in Great 1888 Blizzard*

- **Lead:** tells what article is about and why readers should care; presents author's thesis; found in introductory paragraph(s)

  *EXAMPLE: Miss Alma Carlson, the teacher near Colon, who was out in the blizzard for nine hours, is now recovering from the partial freezing of her feet and hands… After all, who has been braver than she?*

- **Details and background:** interesting details support thesis and build up to main point or argument.

  *EXAMPLE: She kept her little flock together in the school house until dark… and as she fell into the door, said, "my hands and feet are frozen," and then fainted.*

- **Main point or argument:** author reveals the importance of his or her thesis.

  *EXAMPLE: In spite of all this, Miss Carlson has continued her school every day… she has gone on with her work to the present time.*

- **Resolution:** author's comment on or insight about the situation.

  *EXAMPLE: At 17 years of age, who can give a better record? When you count heroines, count Alma Carlson one. (from article in the* Wahoo Newspaper, *Nebraska, February 10, 1888)*

**N.B.** To make reading easier and quicker, paragraphs in journalistic writing are usually limited to one, two, or three sentences at the most.

▸**1** What is the "hook" in the headline (title) of Joe Schwarcz's essay?

▸**2** What is the "lead" in the introductory paragraphs?

▸**3** Underline the five words in the text that provide the essence of Schwarcz's thesis. *(Hint: It's at a strategic point in the first four paragraphs.)*

▸**4** About whom are details and background given at first?

▸5 Based on your answer in question 2, explain briefly how Schwarcz uses the following techniques to support his thesis in subsequent paragraphs:

a) comparison and contrast

b) narration

▸6 Write the first three words of the paragraph in which the author focuses on his main point (i.e., where he gives the principle argument that underlies his thesis).

▸7 In the example about therapeutic touch, which technique (given in question 4 above) does Schwarz use to support his thesis and principal argument?

▸8 a) Describe the tone the author uses for the resolution of the essay in the last two paragraphs.

b) How does the author create this tone? Once again, what technique does he use?

### Plays on Words and Popular Images

In order to catch the audience's attention, many writers use popular movie stars, cultural items, and current usages of expression in their works.

▸▸▸ ***An oxymoron** is a stylistic device in which incongruous or contradictory terms are combined for impact. Examples include* **"The Sounds of Silence", burning cold.** ◂◂◂

▸1 Is the term "honest" charlatan an oxymoron? Why or why not?

▸2 Which popular comic strip hero does the author use as a metaphor for The Amazing Randi in the third paragraph?

---

N.B. This comic strip-, TV- and movie hero was said to be "fighting for truth, justice and the *American* way." Note the word play in the phrase that Schwarcz uses instead.

▸3 Next, the author refers to Randi as "the Amazing One." Which highly respected sports figure has a similar nickname and what is it? *(Hint: he retired from professional sport in 1999.)*

---

▸4 Explain the play on the word "armed" in the following sentence (lines 66-68):

"A sleeve would be constructed in such a way that an arm could be placed in it without the therapist seeing whether the sleeve was 'armed' or not."

---

---

▸5 Find at least two examples of words being repeated in a humorous or playful manner in different contexts or phrases.

---

---

▸6 In paragraph 5 (lines 17-20), Schwarcz uses a popular phrase to lighten the rest of the scientific and rather formal language of the paragraph. What is it?

---

---

▸7 Check off the following sentence types that are used in this essay:

| | | | |
|---|---|---|---|
| **a)** statements | ______ | **b)** questions | ______ |
| **c)** exclamations | ______ | **d)** simple | ______ |
| **e)** compound | ______ | **f)** complex | ______ |
| **g)** compound-complex | ______ | **h)** fragments | ______ |
| **i)** comma splice | ______ | | |

***▸▸▸ Plays on words and popular images as well as a wide variety of sentence types characterise Schwarcz's style in this essay. These characteristics add a playful touch to an otherwise serious topic and lighten the effect of the formal scientific vocabulary present in the essay, thus making it an enjoyable and informative text for a busy newspaper reader. ◂◂◂***

### *Word Origins: Greek and Latin—Prefixes and Suffixes*

Many scientific words have Latin or Greek origins. The essay you have just read contains words that have the following prefixes and suffixes. Take note of each prefix and suffix and its corresponding meaning. The examples given are not from the essay.

| Prefixes | Meaning | Origin | Example |
|---|---|---|---|
| **1.** con- (com-) | -together, with | Old Latin *com* | condescend |
| **2.** de- | -from, out of | Latin *de*, from, of | define |
| **3.** en- (em-) | -in, into, within | Greek *en*, in, at | entropy |
| **4.** in-, im- | -in, into | Latin *in*, in, within | instruct |
| **5.** para- | -beyond | Greek *para*, beside | paragraph |
| **6.** pheno- | -showing, displaying | Greek *phaino*, from *phainein*, to show | phenotype |
| **7.** psych- | -mind, mental | Greek *psukho*, soul, life | psychology |
| **Suffixes** | **Meaning** | **Origin** | **Example** |
| **8.** -fic | -causing, making | Latin *-ficus*, from *facere*, to do | terrific |
| **9.** -ion | -action, process | Latin *-ion*, (noun suffix) | decision |
| **10.** -ist | -one that performs a specific action | Greek *-istes*, agent | journalist |
| **11.** -ive | -performing or tending towards a specific action | Latin *-ìvus*, (adj. suffix) | massive |

In the lines from the essay indicated in parentheses, find a word that contains each of the above prefixes and suffixes. For example, ▸**1** requires a word with the prefix *con-*, and so on down the list on page 193. Write an original sentence to illustrate its meaning. Include the word in your sentence. The first one has been completed for you.

▸**1** lines 1-5 convention

The teacher went to many workshops and presentations at the annual convention

▸**2** lines 79-81 ______________

______________________________________________

▸**3** lines 33-38 ______________

______________________________________________

▸**4** lines 50-54 ______________

______________________________________________

▸**5** lines 17-20 ______________

______________________________________________

▸6 lines 21-24 ____________

▸7 lines 17-20 ____________

▸8 lines 11-13 ____________

▸9 lines 50-54 ____________

▸10 lines 59-64 ____________

▸11 lines 50-54 ____________

## WRITE IN STYLE ▸ JOURNALISTIC ESSAY

**Although the basic form of a journalistic essay may appear to be a little different from that of the other essays presented in this book, many of the writing skills and techniques that you have already learned also apply to writing this type of essay.**

**Style Tips**

Here is a brief overview of the points that are essential to good journalism.

- Create a title with a hook.
- Write an attention-catching introduction with a strong lead and clear thesis.
- Conclude the essay with a fitting resolution.
- Use specific and concrete details; report facts accurately.
- Keep paragraphs short.
- Respect the form required by the style guidelines of the particular newspaper or magazine.
- Use active verbs. Write clearly, avoiding sexist language and misused modifiers (see Exercise B, below).
- Choose an appropriate tone.

## *Dangling and Misused Modifiers*

Many people do not use modifiers correctly when they write an essay. **Modifiers** are words, phrases, or clauses that describe or qualify another element in the sentence, usually a noun, pronoun, or verb. They are often left dangling (with no word to modify) if placed too far from the word they describe.

Here are some examples of modifiers and two important rules to follow.

*EXAMPLES: The young boy lives next door.* Young *modifies boy and* next *modifies door.*

*The girl wearing the red dress is my niece.* Wearing the red dress *modifies girl and* red *modifies dress.*

*She is walking quickly.* Quickly *modifies walking.*

**Rules: 1)** A modifier must always have a word to modify.

*Correct:* Coming home late, he rushed into the dining room where dinner had been served.

*Coming home late* modifies he; i.e., it is he who has come home late.

*Incorrect:* Coming home late, dinner had already been served in the dining room.

*Coming home late* does not modify any other word in the sentence; i.e., it is not dinner who has come home late but some unmentioned person. *Coming home late* has been left dangling with nothing to modify and is termed a "dangling modifier."

**2)** It is usually very important to place modifiers close to the word they are modifying.

In the next example, we want to indicate that a plane that is on fire is landing on a tarmac.

*Correct:* The plane, now on fire, finally landed on the tarmac.

*or*

Now on fire, the plane finally landed on the tarmac.

*Incorrect:* The plane finally landed on the tarmac, now on fire.

This sentence is incorrect because *now on fire* modifies tarmac when in this particular context, we want to say that the plane is on fire.

#### Exercise A: Identifying Dangling and Other Misused Modifiers

Write a *C* beside each sentence in the pair that has a correctly used modifier.

▸1 ______ **a)** Inventing a new recipe, the meal was truly a success.

______ **b)** Inventing a new recipe, the chef made a truly successful meal.

▸2 ______ **a)** After failing to brake, John had an accident when his car swerved out of control.

______ **b)** After failing to brake, the car swerved out of control and John had an accident.

▸3 ______ a) Stuck outside the house, the phone rang and rang and I couldn't answer it.

______ b) Stuck outside the house, I couldn't answer the phone and it rang and rang.

▸4 ______ a) Mother talked on the phone while I was trying to study in a very animated way.

______ b) Mother talked on the phone in a very animated way while I was trying to study.

▸5 ______ a) When writing the book, Frederick often used to gaze at the river for inspiration.

______ b) When writing the book, the river provided plenty of inspiration for Frederick.

**Exercise B: Correcting Dangling or Misplaced Modifier**

Rewrite each of the following sentences in order to correct any dangling modifiers.

*Incorrect:* Going to the gym regularly, John's weight loss was substantial.

*Correct:* Going to the gym regularly, John lost a substantial amount of weight.

▸1 After turning out the lights, the book was very hard to read in the dark room.

______

▸2 When on a hunting safari, the animals were lucky to escape Hemingway's sharp aim.

______

▸3 An "honest charlatan," Joe Schwarcz has a very high opinion of the Amazing Randi.

______

▸4 When finished college, my parents took me out for a huge celebration.

______

▸5 Screaming loudly and recognising their own screams, the hungry lions savagely ate the children's parents.

______

▸6 The ending of the "The Veldt" was shocking for me, while reading this popular short story by Ray Bradbury.

______

▸7 Thinking himself very different from the others, the banquet seemed very boring to Tom.

______

**Exercise C: General Error Analysis I**

The following items were taken from compositions by college students. The purpose of the assignment was to have the students introduce themselves. Each phrase or sentence has at least one error. Correct the error(s).

▸1 Their's ways to see life that is generally not told are talk about.

▸2 ...but i know i can make a real good presentation...

▸3 In my last course, I learn all king of way to rite texts.

▸4 Sometime little detail is importants like...

▸5 In 1998, I've taken a course in... but I've never read or wrote much in english.

▸6 Reading worths a lot... but I did'nt read a lot in english before this course.

▸7 I'm reading a lot of English books at home but I'm not writing that much.

▸8 Each person as is own personnality.

▸9 I live in St. Jerome since august, before, I lived in St. Agathe where is my family.

▸10 Does it worth it to do a job wich you do'nt appreciate?

**Exercise D: General Error Analysis II**

The following items were taken from paragraphs written by students. Each phrase or sentence has at least one error. Correct the error(s).

▸1 The General Zaroff is a man who have hunted every kind of animals. He dosen't have...

▸2 Equality shouln't be base on materials possesions.

▸3 That what show us that the sentense is…

▸4 Everybody have a life and do what he want's with it.

▸5 …its true than in those days society there is not much place for the weaks…

▸6 Divorce wasn't existing at this time.

▸7 These storys often have ironics element witch brings an unexpected ending to them.

▸8 She feel free because she have learn…

▸9 Its about human beings taking advantage of it's supremacy toward's other animal's.

▸10 The author present the same theme in this second storie.

### *Paragraph Practice*

▸1 Write a journalistic paragraph on a famous scientist for a science magazine.

▸2 Write the introductory paragraph to a newspaper article describing a new scientific procedure or discovery.

▸3 Write a "Famous Date in History" paragraph concerning a scientific discovery.

▸4 Write a paragraph (or two) intended to convince a young person that science is important.

## WRAP-UP: DISCUSSION TOPICS

▸1 Most news "papers" will soon be replaced by news coverage on the Internet.

▸2 Less emphasis should be given to the theoretical aspects of science at the high school level. More emphasis should be placed on explaining to students the practical applications of science.

▸3 People will always continue to believe in UFOs, horoscope predictions, and the like, in spite of lack of scientific evidence. Why?

## ESSAY TOPICS

Write a journalistic essay from 750 to 1000 words long. Try to use some of the stylistic elements and devices you have studied in this section of the book. Here are some suggestions for topics:

- ▸1 Write an essay about a contemporary issue using journalistic form and style.
- ▸2 Write a journalistic essay about an imagined meeting between the Amazing Randi and Uri Geller.
- ▸3 Learn more about the Amazing Randi or Uri Geller and write a journalistic essay about him.
- ▸4 Interview two students about their perceptions of psychic phenomena and write a journalistic essay about your findings.
- ▸5 In a journalistic essay, report on a situation that affects students at your college.
- ▸6 Compare "Bending Spoons and Bending Minds" to one of the other essays in this section.
- ▸7 The sciences are more worthy of serious attention than the arts.
- ▸8 Science should be fun and informative at the same time.
- ▸9 The uses and abuses of science.

# References

## PRINT


### Biography and Criticism

Kerr, Ellyn. "Casting Spells for Scientific Literacy" in *McGill Reporter*, 31, No. 5, November 5, 1998.

Labinger, Jay A. "Book and Media Reviews: Radar, Hula Hoops, and Playful Pigs: 67 Digestible Commentaries on the Fascinating Chemistry of Everyday Life (by Joe Schwarcz)" in *Journal of Chemical Education*, July 2000, p. 834.

Polak, Monique. "High-School Students Get a Taste of Science." "Education 2000" in the *Montreal Gazette*, August 12, 2000.

## INTERNET

### Biography of the Author

http://www.mcgill.ca/uro/Rep/r3105/schwarcz.html
http://blizzard.cc.mcgill.ca/chempublic/joecv.htm

### Interview January 20, 1997

http://www.plant.uoguelph.ca/riskcomm/archives/fsnet/1997/1-1997/fs-01-21-97-01.txt

### Questions and Answers from Radio Show

http://blizzard.cc.mcgill.ca/chempublic/media.htm

### Articles

http://www.chirowatch.com/Chiro-news/mg-000326schwarcz.html
http://www.gene.ch/info4action/1999/Jul/msg00037.html

### History of Journalism (in particular, newspapers)

http://metalab.unc.edu/journalism/jhistory/
http://www.britannica.com/bcom/eb/article/6/0,5716,45046+1+44030,00.html
http://www.britannica.com/bcom/eb/article/0/0,5716,117360+8+109461,00.html
http://cyberschool.4j.lane.edu/~barr/journalism1/lessons/lessonhomepage.html

### Journalistic Style

http://www.homeworkhelp.com/homeworkhelp/freemember/text/english/high/lessons/jr001/02/main.htm
http://www.masscomm.eku.edu/Fraas/NEWS/style.htm
http://www.smcccd.net/accounts/sevas/esl/classnotes/thehook.html

# UNIT 3
# POETRY

UNIT 3

# POETRY

**THE POETRY SECTION COMPRISES AN INTRODUCTION AND TWO CHAPTERS. THE INTRODUCTION CONSISTS OF WARM-UP ACTIVITIES, BRIEF PRESENTATIONS OF HISTORICAL INFORMATION, AND DEFINITIONS OF TERMS NEEDED FOR POETIC ANALYSIS AND INTERPRETATION. UNIT 3.1 FEATURES TRADITIONAL APPROACHES TO POETIC ANALYSIS AND UNIT 3.2 INTRODUCES MORE CONTEMPORARY APPROACHES.**

## CONTENTS

- **LISTENING:** When I Was One-and-Twenty
- **READING:** what is poetry? Brief history of poetry, poetics
- **SPEAKING:** warm-up discussions
- **WRITING:** interpretative exercises

WHAT IS POETRY? The words *poet* and *poetry* have a long history that dates back to ancient Greece: the Greek word *poietes* means *maker* or *composer* and comes from the verb *poiein*, to create. We can thus say that poetry is word art designed to express elevated thought and emotion in a striking and imaginative way through the musicality of language. Poetry has often been intimately connected with song, for the two have many things in common, such as rhythmic patterns and the use of evocative words and images.

> ***"When power narrows the areas of man's concerns, poetry reminds him of the richness and diversity of his existence. When power corrupts, poetry cleanses."***
>
> —John F. Kennedy, speech, October 26, 1963

Literature is first introduced to children in the form of poetry. For example, songs, lullabies, and nursery rhymes are all a part of our earliest childhood recollections. Literature at its earliest period in the history of civilisation took the form of poetry — stories that were told in the earliest times of recorded history had a certain musicality to them. It is believed that the structure of a repetitive rhythmic pattern made it easier for storytellers to remember their tales. The oral tradition was strong before the invention of the printing press and before literacy was common.

N.B. All the poems in this section have been recorded so that you can listen to them before doing the activities. Hearing them recited should both increase your enjoyment and help you in your interpretations.

## *Warm-Up*

Here are some activities to get you started on this new section.

**Activity 1: Discussion**

▸1 **a)** "Poetry is hard to understand." Do you agree or disagree with this statement?

**b)** If you answered yes, list three characteristics of poetry that make it hard to understand.

▸2 List some of your favourite songs. Are the meanings of the songs difficult to understand? Explain your answer.

**Activity 2: When I Was One-and-Twenty**

Poetry, like music, must be listened to for full enjoyment. In the next activity, you will first listen to the poem which follows and then discuss your reactions with a small group of classmates.

### About the Author

ALFRED EDWARD HOUSMAN was born in 1859 in Worcestershire, England. He studied classics and philosophy at Oxford University, but failed his final exams in 1881 and started working as a civil servant. He continued his studies in classics and eventually acquired a reputation as a great critic of Latin literature. He eventually became Chair of Latin at University College in London, a position he held until his death in 1936. He wrote two small volumes of poetry, *A Shropshire Lad* (1896) and *Last Poems* (1922). His poetry was influenced by Greek and Latin lyric poetry, as well as by traditional ballads, and his thematic topics included youth, nature, love, life, and death.

Listen to the recording of the poem "When I Was One-and-Twenty."

# When I Was One-and-Twenty

A.E. Housman

When I was one-and-twenty
I heard a wise man say,
"Give crowns and pounds and guineas
But not your heart away;
Give pearls away and rubies
But keep your fancy free."
But I was one-and-twenty,
No use to talk to me.

When I was one-and-twenty
I heard him say again,
"The heart out of the bosom
Was never given in vain;
'Tis paid with sighs a plenty
And sold for endless rue."
And I am two-and-twenty,
And oh, 'tis true, 'tis true.

*RUE*→SORROW, REMORSE

1896

### *Reader's Response*

In your small group, choose one person to read the poem out loud again. Then, discuss the following questions:

▸1 What did you like about the poem? Give specific examples from the poem itself.

▸2 What didn't you understand about the poem? Be specific. Discuss possible interpretations with your group. Ask your teacher for help if there are still some aspects like vocabulary or theme that you don't understand.

▸3 What kind of advice does the speaker in the poem give the reader?

▸4 Does the speaker take his own advice? How do you know?

▸5 Is the advice relevant to today's youth?

**Activity 3: Discussion**

Discuss the following quotations with your group. In your opinion, are the ideas they express valid?

▸1 "Poetry lifts the veil from the hidden beauty of the world and makes familiar objects be as if they were not familiar…" — Percy Bysshe Shelley, "The Utility of Poetry"

▸2 "Poetry begins in delight and ends in wisdom…" — Robert Frost

▸3 "Poetry is the art of uniting pleasure with truth, by calling imagination to the help of reason." — Samuel Johnson

▸4 "Poetry, that is to say the poetic, is a primal necessity." — Marianne Moore

# Brief History of Poetry

The following section contains a short historical approach to the development of poetry. That is, poetry is examined within the context of history. This is not to suggest that poetry or any other form of literature develops within neat categories of socio-historical trends. Rather, the creation and development of literature is fluid. It can be argued that such categories of literary trends are artificial. However, the socio-historical approach to studying literature can give a general overview of the spirit of the times and help the reader to understand the meaning and purpose of the writings of a particular era.

Early English poetry originated in the oral tradition. Pre-fifteenth-century poetry was usually sung by court minstrels and was about the great deeds of chieftains or lords. These records of heroic deeds were called epics or romances. Some records and texts of English poetry before the fifteenth century have been lost because records and texts of literary works, which were written on parchment and kept in monasteries, have disappeared. However, some poetry did survive, and we can actually categorise it by form. Much of it was religious poetry that adapted warrior imagery from a Germanic tradition. It didn't rhyme until it adopted the French and Latin traditions, after the Norman Conquest of 1066. It did, however, have strong rhythm and alliteration. It is important to remember that the language of this period was not English as we know it. With the Norman Conquest of England in 1066, Old French became the language of the English court and the aristocracy. Thus, the poetry of that time would not be very understandable to the modern reader.

It might be argued that English poetry started with Geoffrey Chaucer (1340/43-1400). Before his era, much of the existing poetry in Britain was written with short lines that had a break in the middle, alliteration, and no end rhyme. Medieval poetry was concerned with the themes of courtly love and religion. Chaucer wrote in English, which by his time had become the official language of the land. He changed the usual metric form to the iambic pentameter, a pattern that has remained popular in English poetry. Chaucer's most famous work is called *The Canterbury Tales.* This masterpiece consists of a series of poetic tales or stories about common themes; the stories are usually written in rhyming couplets, and contain elements of comedy, irony, satire, and love.

The fifteenth century was not a particularly innovative period for English poetry. However, a corpus of anonymous poetry shows that two trends in poetry can be identified: popular poems such as ballads and folk songs (which had their origins in traditional songs and tales); and historical or religious poems that were usually written by clerics.

By contrast to the fifteenth century, the sixteenth century marked the Golden Age of English poetry. It was the century of Queen Elizabeth I and William Shakespeare (1564–1616). Life in England during this period was greatly influenced by the Italian Renaissance ("rebirth"). The Renaissance brought new heights to the arts, and artists were elevated to the status of creator or master. The beauty of man, nature, and God was exalted. Elizabeth I was a grand patron of the arts, and under her support, Renaissance poetry and drama became formidable vehicles of literature. Themes of idealised love, passion, beauty, and virtue were popular topics in literature. The artist also looked back to the ancients in Greek and Roman mythology for inspiration. Shakespeare, though known mainly for his plays, excelled in writing sonnets.

In the seventeenth century (the late Renaissance), two streams in poetry predominated. In one, poets attempted to write with smooth, rhythmic versification, using colourful imagery, pastoral scenes, and portrayals of nature. Poetry of this school also showed a more reflective mood.

The second popular stream of poetry was called Metaphysical. It reflected a desire on the part of poets to experiment with verse, form, and rhyme. Imagery was bizarre and powerful. Poets of this school wrote satires, epigrams, elegies, and sonnets. Their topics emphasised the new scientific discoveries and knowledge of their era. John Donne (1572-1631) was the most famous of these metaphysical poets. His sonnets reflected passionate love, not the idealised love that the earlier Renaissance poets wrote about, but the realistic love and passion between a man and a woman.

It was also at this time that poetry, which had always been concerned with humanity's relationship with God, started to reflect more rational themes about human beings and their world. Poets wrote about man's ability to reason about himself and his place in the universe. For example, even though Donne wrote many poems and sermons with religious themes, he also questioned humanity's role in terms of its existence. Another great poet of this age was John Milton (1607-1674), whose epic poem *Paradise Lost* was about the fall of Adam and Eve from Grace and their removal from the Garden of Eden. In his work, Milton tried to rationalise God's divine plan for mankind.

By the eighteenth century, the rationalistic approach was very much the norm. This period is often called The Age of Reason or the Enlightenment because faith in science and great scientific discoveries dominated. It was believed that man's greatest virtue was his ability to reason, and literary themes reflected this new sensibility. Indeed, good sense and non-extravagance were the ideals. The eighteenth century was also the age of great prose writing. The novel and the essay became a very popular form of literature during this period, and consequently, poetry had competition in conveying the newly popular themes of rationality. Indeed, Jonathan Swift (1667-1745), best known for his novel *Gulliver's Travels*, wrote poetry as well. Another famous poet of this period was Alexander Pope (1688-1744). The underlying theme of his works reflects philosophical musings and self-analysis and satire. Thomas Gray (1716-1771) elevated the elegy, a poem characterised by five or six feet to a line, depicting melancholic pondering.

The first part of the nineteenth century was called the age of Romanticism (c. 1798-1832). Romanticism turned away from cold, dispassionate ways of looking at humanity and society, stressing, instead, passionate attempts at creativity. This philosophy was nowhere better seen than within the genre of poetry. The Romantic period began with William Wordsworth's publication of *Lyrical Ballads* in 1798. Poets such as William Blake (1757-1827), Wordsworth (1770-1850), and Samuel Taylor Coleridge (1772-1834) were also influenced by political events. The French Revolution stirred in these men a belief that a great new political and social change was going to happen. The spirit of the times focused on human rights and social justice.

Poetry in the Romantic Age reflected the belief that inspiration came from the inside of the individual and not from the outside world. Wordsworth and others thought that poems should reflect inner feelings and emotions. Accordingly, the lyrical poem, which uses the first-person narrator, became the most popular type of poem. Romantic poets also believed in inspiration, and relied on spontaneous composition. They gained their inspiration from nature and the surrounding landscape. The Romantics were fascinated with the supernatural. For example, Coleridge wrote *Christabel* and *Kubla Khan*, dealing with magic and the supernatural. Lord Byron (1788-1824) was very much interested in the occult; some of his poems had satanic figures for their major characters.

The Romantic poets lauded the artistic quest to experience all the human senses profoundly. Two other important poets — Percy Bysshe Shelley (1792-1822) and John Keats (1795-1821) — along with Byron, were considered to be Romantic poets of the second generation. Shelley's poetry expressed a rejection of political tyranny and extolled the inherent goodness in human nature. Keats's poetry speculated on the nature of beauty and experiences in human emotions.

The Victorian Age (1832-1901) — the years of Queen Victoria's reign in Great Britain — was characterised by great social and economic change. First, industrialisation shifted the structure of English society from one based on an agrarian model to one based on commerce. There was a tremendous shift in the population as people migrated from farms to cities, where most worked in factories or mines under very poor conditions. Second, science and technology experienced a great growth spurt, especially in the areas of engineering, architecture, and experimental science. Charles Darwin's treatises on *The Origins of the Species* (1859) and *The Descent of Man* (1871) caused great controversy and led to an ongoing debate on the existence of God.

The Victorian poets reacted to these social changes. Alfred, Lord Tennyson (1809-1892), wrote poems concerned with social and economic ills, as well as on the nature of humanity and our relationship with God. Other Victorian poets such as Robert Browning (1812-1889) and Matthew Arnold (1822-1888) reflected on the nature of human relationships and the social ills confronting English society due to changing economic structures. Elizabeth Barrett Browning (1806-1861), Robert Browning's wife, also wrote on the nature of love, as well as on the condition of women and children.

In the United States, the publication of *Leaves of Grass* in 1855 by Walt Whitman (1819-1892) marked the emergence of American poetry. In this lengthy poem written in unconventional meter and rhyme, the poet celebrates his self and his country. During the latter half of the nineteenth century, a shy recluse named Emily Dickinson (1830-1886) wrote over one thousand poems. The first were printed in 1890 and only then did people begin to discover the richness and intensity of her poetry. Her very individual techniques influenced many of the poets that followed her.

The twentieth century was characterised by great changes in social attitudes, norms, and political and economic relations. The century saw two world wars and rapid advances in science and technology. Poetry reflected the nature of these changes. Poets at the beginning of this century, influenced by the French Symbolist writers Charles Baudelaire (1821-1867), Stéphane Mallarmé (1842-1898), and Arthur Rimbaud (1854-1891) experimented with images, focusing on the object in its concrete form, and avoiding anything that confused the image. Language came under great scrutiny as poetry turned away from past verse forms in order to reflect a more conversational style. Ezra Pound (1885-1972) and T.S. Eliot (1888-1965), two American expatriates, exemplified the new modernist spirit. Eliot experimented with concrete images and symbols, adding ironic elements when discussing social disillusion. His poem *The Waste Land* is considered by many to be the most famous poem of the twentieth century. William Butler Yeats (1865-1939) wrote poetry based on Irish mythology as well as metaphysical speculations.

Across the Atlantic in the United States, Wallace Stevens (1879-1955) exalted the imagination and Marianne Moore (1887-1972) experimented with the use of quotations in her brilliant verse. The poetry of many American poets of this period shows a preoccupation with realism and common speech. William Carlos Williams (1883-1963) wrote about the everyday in a very spare but vivid style and e. e. cummings (1894-1962) presented his lyrical poems using very unusual typographical forms. In the British Isles, poetry by Siegfried Sassoon (1886-1967) and Robert Graves (1895-1985) reflected concerns about the violence of war, death, and life, and questioned traditional religious beliefs. Dylan Thomas (1914-1953), C.D. Lewis (1904-1972), and W.H. Auden (1907-1973) wrote about death, tyranny, and man's inhumanity.

After World War II, the new generation of British poets such as Philip Larkin (1922-1985) and Ted Hughes (1930-1999) continued to write themes reflecting the social concerns of modern times. Unlike many of the modernists, Robert Frost (1874-1963), perhaps the best loved of the twentieth-century American poets, wrote poems using traditional devices, although he, too, wrote in the vernacular. Poets such as Sylvia Plath (1933-1963) wrote about love and death.

In the 1950s and 1960s, many American poets such as Allan Ginsberg (1926-1997) and his collaborator, poet/publisher Lawrence Ferlinghetti (1919-), both of whom exemplified the Beat generation and its concerns, experimented with poetic form and meaning. Ginsberg's live reading of his poem "Howl" electrified audiences. Since the late 1960s, postmodernist John Ashbery (1927-) has been the dominant figure in Amercian poetry. Many contemporary poets seem to fall into two distinct schools: the traditionalists who build on past conventions and the innovators, often part of the L=A=N=G=U=A=G=E writing movement, who reject past conventions and who are preoccupied with the act of writing itself and with work consisting of nonsense and unmeaning.

English poetry also flourished outside of Britain and the United States during the twentieth century. Poets from Canada, Australia, New Zealand, the Caribbean, and India continue to experiment with the creation of poetry that is both unique and deeply universal. In Canada, Earle Birney (1904-1995), Margaret Avison (1918-), and Irving Layton (1912-) wrote poetry that was concerned with social themes.

## POETICS

Poetry, like prose, may be enjoyed in many different ways. Some people like to listen to poems as triggers for their own ideas or writing. Others enjoy the imaginative way the poet plays with words and creates images that evoke meaning. Still others enjoy reading poems for the special musicality in the language, the particular words the poet has chosen, and the special rhythms they create together. With the activities in this section, you will be invited to communicate your thoughts and feelings about particular poems, both orally and in writing. Sometimes you will be asked to give a personal response to a poem, and sometimes you will be expected to use a more traditional analytic approach, looking at such aspects as the poet's use of imagery, meter, and rhyme.

You may well ask yourself at this point what the purpose is behind analysing a work of art such as a poem. There are, in fact, several purposes. Poets are highly skilled craftspeople. Their imaginative insight and honed language skills enable them to communicate important ideas and feelings in striking ways. Very often, poems not only illustrate the most beautiful elements in a language, but they also make us look at things in new ways. Examining how a poet uses words heightens our own awareness of language and its possibilities, and we become better communicators and writers in the process.

Every well-written poem is like a beautiful, skilfully cut diamond; every facet is polished and perfect, and stands at just the right angle. There is nothing extra, nothing out of place. A well-crafted poem, like a diamond, is unique and complete unto itself. One of your tasks in the analysis of poetry is to reveal the artistry and craft that underlie a particular poem. To do this effectively, you will need to look at how the poet uses language and imagery; you will then describe this particular usage in appropriate language. Certain terms that describe poetry date back to the ancient Greeks. These terms, and others that have been added over the years, will be presented and explained in the following paragraphs.

Traditionally, we use certain language to talk about poetry. A **poem** consists of a series of **lines** (sometimes referred to as verses) presented visually on a page. It usually has both a visual and rhythmical pattern, but not always. A poem is often divided into sections called **stanzas** composed of two or more lines; these sections often have similar patterns. A **refrain** is a line, phrase, or stanza that is repeated at intervals throughout a poem or song. The word **verse** refers to the fact that a line of poetry usually has a particular rhythm and, often, a certain rhyme. (Please note that it is preferable to use the word *stanza* to refer to the different divisions of a poem, but in a song, this is not the case.) Finally, a poem often has a **persona**, which refers to the voice or speaker in the poem itself. Sometimes the persona represents the voice of the poet him- or herself, but not necessarily. Often the persona is a fictional character.

Poetry can be analysed from a number of different approaches: traditional, formalist, reader response, historical, sociological, structuralist, feminist, minority, Marxist, and so on. In all of these approaches, the analyst pays attention to two basic elements: 1) **theme**, or the significant or overall meaning found in the poem; and 2) **mood**, which is the overall feeling or atmosphere of the poem that the poet creates and the reader experiences. Many **poetic devices** are used to help to create the theme and mood of poetry. We will now look at some of these devices, and then examine how poets use them in special ways to add depth to a work of art.

## POETIC DEVICES

### *FIGURES OF SPEECH*

Figures of speech are found in prose writing as well. They aid in the creation of tone and theme in a poem. In order to analyse poetry, you should have a grasp of the following figures of speech:

- **Imagery:** descriptive word pictures usually related to one or more of the five senses.
  *EXAMPLE: The sand on the beach shone yellow and gold.*
- **Suggestion:** the choice of evocative words to enhance meaning. Words are chosen for their **connotations**, for the feelings and emotions associated with their literal meaning.
  *EXAMPLE: the difference between house and home.*
- **Simile**: a comparison of two objects using "like" or "as."
  *EXAMPLE: The boat is as big as a whale.*
- **Metaphor**: an implied comparison of two objects, *not* using "like" or "as."
  *EXAMPLE: My love is the universe.*
- **Personification**: giving human qualities to inanimate or abstract objects.
  *EXAMPLE: The boat smiled into the wind.*
- **Apostrophe**: often seen in poetry, this device is used to address a dead person as if he or she were still alive.
  *EXAMPLE: Shakespeare, you rare poet.*
- **Hyperbole**: an exaggeration.
  *EXAMPLE: I am as hungry as a horse.*
- **Antithesis**: a linking of two contrasting ideas in order to make each more vivid.
  *EXAMPLE: "Believing nothing or believing all" (Dryden)*
- **Oxymoron**: a juxtaposition of two ideas that reflect opposite concepts.
  *EXAMPLE: "cruel kindness."*
- **Irony**: the opposite to what is intended or expressed.
  *EXAMPLE: Experience is something you don't get until just after you need it.*

#### Exercise A: Use of Figures of Speech

Let us return to the poem "When I Was One-and-Twenty" to see which figures of speech the poet uses and to what effect.

▸1 **a)** What metaphors does the poet use regarding the heart?

---

**b)** What kind of value do these metaphors bestow upon the heart?

---

▸2 Cite two words in the second stanza that connect to the imagery used in the third and fifth lines of the first stanza.

---

▸▸▸ ***Note how this choice of vocabulary extends the metaphor and how the poet places this metaphor in contrast with the idea of "giving away one's heart." This enhances the theme of the poem and adds to its unity.*** ◂◂◂

▶3 What is ironic about the last two lines of the second stanza?

▸▸▸ ***Housman uses irony to point to a basic "truth" about life.*** ◂◂◂

### *Structure, Sound, and Rhythm*

Next, let us look at other aspects of the poetry that bring out the meaning and theme by creating the atmosphere and mood in a poem. The actual **form** of a poem — in other words, how it looks on the page — influences our perception of it and the mood it creates. For example, the form may be a traditional, four-line verse with lines of equal length, or it may have a very special shape on the page. Some common traditional forms are the **couplet,** consisting of two consecutive lines of verse that rhyme and are approximately the same length, and the **quatrain** or four-line stanza. Others include **tercets** (three-line stanzas), **sestets** (six-line stanzas), and **octaves** (eight-line stanzas). Some poets also experiment with capitalisation (or the lack of it) and punctuation; these visual factors influence how the reader experiences the poem.

Of course, among the most important aspects of poetry are the actual **sound** of the words and the underlying **rhythms** the poet creates. The sound and rhythm of the words, phrases, and sentences often resemble musical patterns. Both serve to create a general mood in the poem. Here are some basic sound devices:

- **Soft and hard consonant sounds:** sounds produced by letters **b, p, t, k, g** can be harsh; for example, think of the words *bucket* and *puck*. The letters **l, m, n,** and **v** are soft sounds; for example, think of the words *love*, *longing*, and *mother*. Harsh and soft sounds influence the **tone** of the poem (the attitude of the poet towards the subject). The sounds chosen can reflect different degrees of unpleasantness and pleasantness.
- **Alliteration**: the repetition of the initial letter or sound in words, which can emphasise the musicality of the series of words and the last word in the series. Example: big, brown bicycle.
- **Onomatopoeia**: sound imitates meaning of words. Example: buzzing bee.
- **Rhyme**: repetition of identical sounds in words, usually at the end of a poetic line. Example: The rain in Spain stays mainly on the plain. The **rhyme scheme** refers to the pattern of rhyme in a poem, as, for example, *abba cddc* (each letter refers to a different rhyme and the letters are grouped according to the stanzas).
- **Assonance**: repetition of identical vowel sounds. Example: The wind is whispering its intentions. In this example the short "*i*" sound is repeated.
- **Consonance**: repetition of identical consonant sounds. Example: Sally saw serpents slithering slowly.
- **Repetition**: the repetition of certain words, phrases, or elements to create a special effect.

When we speak about the **rhythms** in English, we are referring to the patterns of **stressed** and **unstressed** syllables in the spoken language. That is to say, stressed syllables are emphasised or accented in natural speech, whereas unstressed syllables are not emphasised or are unaccented. For example, the word *table* has two syllables. The first syllable, "*ta*," is stressed and this is shown by the following accent mark: ´ The second syllable, "*ble*," is unstressed; this is shown by this accent mark: ˘ (or a dot). The accent marks are placed above the appropriate syllables; thus, táblĕ. (Please note that dictionaries indicate stressed syllables in slightly different ways.)

Poetry uses **meter** (the way in which rhythm is measured) as an intrinsic form of its structure. English poetry measures rhythm or meter in terms of groups of stressed and unstressed syllables called **poetic feet**. Meter is established by the dominant poetic foot — in other words, the stress that is repeated the most often in a line of poetry. English poetry has five main types of stressed and unstressed syllables or poetic feet.

**Poetic Feet**

| Name | Syllables | Stress Pattern | Example |
|---|---|---|---|
| iambic foot* | 2 | unstressed, stressed | prĕ páre, rĕ páir |
| trochaic foot | 2 | stressed, unstressed | ím ăge, pó ĕt |
| anapestic foot | 3 | unstressed, unstressed, stressed | ĭn hŭ máne, ŭn dĕr stánd |
| dactylic foot | 3 | stressed, unstressed, unstressed | é lĕ phănt, cró cŏ dĭle |
| spondaic foot | 2 | stressed, stressed | shórt cút, híde óut |

The **iambic foot** is considered by many to be the basic rhythmic element in English, so it is not unusual for many English poems use this form. An iambic foot or **iamb** consists of an unstressed syllable followed by a stressed syllable; for example, prĕ páre, and dĕ féat. It is found in most of Shakespeare's works. The number of feet per line is counted and this determines the metrical pattern. The feet are separated by a slash. The number of poetic feet found in a verse line is referred to by a Greek name. There are a number of different lengths (see table below).

**Meter**

**Monometer** means one foot, but this form is rare in poetry.

*EXAMPLE: The sun.*

**Dimeter** consists of two feet and is also very rare.

*EXAMPLE: The sun/shone down.*

**Trimeter** is three feet.

*EXAMPLE: The sun/shone warm/and bright.*

**Tetrameter** is four feet.

*EXAMPLE: The sun/shone warm/and bright/on the town.*

**Pentameter*** is five feet.

*EXAMPLE: The sun/shone warm/and bright/on the town/today.*

**Hexameter** is six feet (sometimes also referred to as an Alexandrian)

*EXAMPLE: The gold/en sun/shone warm/and bright/on the town/today.*

**Heptameter** is seven feet and is very rare.

*EXAMPLE: Again/the gold/en sun/shone warm/and bright/on the town/today.*

*The most common type of foot in English poetry is the iambic pentameter. That is, there are five repetitions of unstressed, stressed syllables per line. A good example is Shakespeare's sonnet XLVI, whose first line is "Mine eye and heart are at a mortal war,..."

Prior to the twentieth century, most poems in English were written in metrical verse (in other words, the poetry employed rhyme and meter). However, early in the twentieth century many poets, like other artists, started to experiment with both the form and content of their works. Many began to write in **free verse** that does not conform to any fixed pattern (in either rhyme or rhythm) but that often has its own subtle rhythms.

N.B. Shakespeare wrote his plays in **blank verse**, which has meter but no rhyme scheme. Here is an example from *Richard III*, Act 5, Sc. 5, in iambic pentameter.

My conscience hath a thousand several tongues,
And every tongue brings in a several tale,
And every tale condemns me for a villain.

**Exercise B: Use of Form, Sound, and Rhythm**

Once again, let us return to the poem "When I Was One-and-Twenty" to see how the author uses form, sound, and rhythm to advantage in the poem.

▸**1** Describe the form, rhythm (meter), and rhyme scheme of this poem.

___

▸▸▸ ***Note how the poet uses the words "one-and-twenty" and "two-and-twenty" (and not "twenty-one" and "twenty-two") in order to keep the rhythm more regular and poetic.*** ◂◂◂

▸**2** What do you notice about the rhyme scheme of the stanzas in terms of similarities and differences?

___

▸**3** Quote a line where the normal grammatical structure (for example, the word order) has been varied to fit the poetic meter chosen by the poet.

___

▸**4** Give one example of each of the following:

**a)** assonance: ___ **b)** consonance: ___

**c)** alliteration: ___ **d)** repetition: ___

▸**5** How would you qualify the tone of this poem?

**a)** deadly serious **b)** light-hearted **c)** happy **d)** depressed **e)** comical

Justify your answer.

___

▸**6** Is this poem written using a) a traditional or b) an experimental approach and structure?

▸▸▸ ***The regular rhythms and use of rhyme and various poetic devices give this poem a lyrical, song-like quality that is in keeping with the poem's theme and mood.*** ◂◂◂

In the two chapters that follow, you will read and interpret poems according to the notions presented in this Introduction. In Unit 3.1, traditional approaches are featured for analysing several older works. Unit 3.2, by contrast, uses other types of approaches to explore more contemporary poems.

UNIT 3.1

# TRADITIONS

**CHAPTER CONTENTS**

- **LISTENING:** "A Divine Image"; "The Eagle: A Fragment"; Sonnet XVIII, "My Love is Like to Ice"; "Death Be Not Proud"; "To the Ladies"
- **READING:** biographical information on poets; background information on the sonnet
- **WRITING:** using traditional approaches for interpreting poetry
- **SPEAKING:** group discussions about poems

## POEM 1: A DIVINE IMAGE

**ABOUT THE AUTHOR**

WILLIAM BLAKE was born in 1757 and died in 1827. By the age of 14 he started to draw and to write poetry. He married at 24 years of age. His wife was illiterate, but he taught her to read and write. He was also said to have been an emotional and jealous husband. His temper led him to have words with a soldier who accused him of sedition. Blake was acquitted of this crime, but the experience greatly affected him. He published his first book of poetry, *Poetical Sketches*, at the age of 26. These poems were lyrical and in his works he experimented with rhyme and rhythm. His most famous poems were published under the title *Songs of Innocence* (1789); later, these were combined with others to comprise *Songs of Innocence and of Experience* (1794). These poems demonstrate Blake's philosophy that the state of human existence is divided into two contrary groups roughly equivalent to the qualities of reason and passion. Blake was also an engraver who illustrated his writings. During his lifetime, he remained almost unknown, becoming popular only in the mid-nineteenth century. By the twentieth century, he was recognised as one of the great poets of English literature.

Listen to the following poem.

# A DIVINE IMAGE

WILLIAM BLAKE

Cruelty has a Human Heart
And Jealousy a Human Face,
Terror, the Human Form Divine,
And Secrecy, the Human Dress.

The Human Dress is forged Iron,
The Human Form, a fiery Forge,
The Human Face, a Furnace seal'd,
The Human Heart, its hungry Gorge.

1790-1791

**WRITER'S CRAFT** ▸ **Discuss the following questions, using the preceding explanations on poetics to guide you.**

▸**1** What type of form does the poem have?

**a)** couplet **b)** tercet **c)** free verse **d)** quatrain

▸**2** What type of poetic foot and meter does the poem have?

▸**3** Is there any use of repetition found in the poem? If yes, give examples.

▸**4** Explain the rhyming pattern of the poem.

▸**5** Find examples of the following from the poem.

| | **ALLITERATION** | **ASSONANCE** | **CONSONANCE** |
|---|---|---|---|
| Stanza 1 | | | |
| Stanza 2 | | | |

▸**6** What kind of image does the poet paint of humankind? (more than one answer)

**a)** positive **b)** negative **c)** neutral **d)** gentle **e)** fierce **f)** loving

Cite two examples from the text to justify your answer.

▸▸▸ ***Note how the poet's use of repeated short sentences and alliteration, assonance, and consonance highlight his view of humankind.*** ◂◂◂

▸**7** What is the significance of the title? Do you think it is meant to be ironic?

## POEM 2: THE EAGLE: A FRAGMENT

**ABOUT THE AUTHOR**

ALFRED, LORD TENNYSON (1809-1892) is considered to be one of the greatest and most popular of the Victorian poets. Tennyson was the fourth in a family of twelve children. He had a difficult childhood; his father was an alcoholic and very temperamental. Tennyson went to Cambridge, but had to leave before he graduated because of his family's financial difficulties. He had started to write poetry at a young age, and became renowned for his elegiac poem *In Memoriam*, which he wrote in 1850. He became Poet Laureate in 1850 and in that same year married his sweetheart of twenty years, Emily Sellwood. In 1884, he was given a peerage that granted him the title of Lord. Tennyson's poetry was concerned with the themes of progress, an important phenomenon of the Industrial Revolution. He is also known for his philosophical renderings on life and death.

Listen to the following poem.

# THE EAGLE: A FRAGMENT

ALFRED, LORD TENNYSON

He clasps the crag with crooked hands;
Close to the sun in lonely lands,
Ringed with the azure world, he stands.

The wrinkled sea beneath him crawls;
He watches from his mountain walls,
And like a thunderbolt he falls.

ca. 1850

**WRITER'S CRAFT ▸ Discuss the questions with a partner or group. Use the explanations on poetics on the previous pages to guide you.**

▸1 What is the relationship between the title of the poem and the poem itself?

---

▸2 What type of form (couplet, tercet, quatrain, etc.) and rhyming scheme does the poem have?

---

▸3 What is the rhythm or meter (number of poetic feet)?

___

▸4 What are the sound patterns in this poem? Fill in the table below.

| | ALLITERATION | ASSONANCE | CONSONANCE |
|---|---|---|---|
| Stanza 1 | | | |
| Stanza 2 | | | |

▸5 Find examples of poetic devices such as:

a) simile ___

b) metaphor ___

c) personification ___

d) imagery ___

e) symbols ___

▸6 Which three of the following adjectives best describe the eagle as depicted in the poem?

a) strong b) tyrannical c) independent d) magnificent e) powerful f) man-like

___

▸7 How do the formal elements of the poem (length, structure, poetic and sound devices, etc.) and the subject of the poem complement and reinforce each other?

___

## THE SONNET

The sonnet has been one of the most popular forms of poetry since the Renaissance. It reached its height of popularity in sixteenth-century England when William Shakespeare perfected the form.

The sonnet was first developed by the Italian poet Francesco Petrarch (1304-1374), but was only popularised in England in the early sixteenth century under the influence of the Italian Renaissance. The sonnet follows strict rules of versification. Each sonnet consists of fourteen lines in iambic pentameter (five poetic feet of unstressed, stressed syllables).

Two types of sonnet forms exist. The Petrarchan, named after the Italian poet, has eight lines (called an octave) with a rhyming pattern usually of *abbaabba* and 6 lines (called a sestet) with the rhyming pattern *xyzxyz*. The English or Shakespearean sonnet is formed of three quatrains whose rhyming pattern is *abab cdcd efef*, and a couplet at the end whose rhyming pattern is *gg*. The strict form of the sonnet is very relevant to the meaning of the sonnet itself. For example, the Petrarchan sonnet form usually develops the subject or conflict in the first eight lines and changes direction in order to release the tension in the next six lines. The Shakespearean sonnet usually introduces the subject in the first quatrain, adds a complication in the second quatrain, and furthers the complication in the third quatrain, finally resolving it in the couplet.

### POEM 3: SONNET XVIII

**ABOUT THE AUTHOR**

Much has been written about the life and works of William Shakespeare, who is considered to be the greatest writer in the English language. He was born in 1564 during the period of the Renaissance when English drama and poetry flourished under the patronage of Elizabeth I. Much about his life remains a mystery. We know that he was married to Anne Hathaway and that they had three children. By 1592, he had moved to London from Stratford-upon-Avon, where he established himself as a playwright and sometime actor. Shakespeare wrote 18 comedies, 10 historical dramas, and 10 tragedies, as well as 154 sonnets and 6 other poems. His works gained him recognition and wealth during his lifetime and have also stood the test of time; they continue to be interpreted into modern drama, musicals, and films. Shakespeare died in 1616 at the age of 52 of unknown causes. Listen to the following poem.

Listen to and read the following sonnet to get a feeling for the poem. Pay particular attention to its rhythm. You might want to read it out loud to appreciate its rhythm. Then refer to the list of unfamiliar words in order to help you get a better understanding of the poem. Don't be worried if you do not immediately understand its meaning.

## SONNET XVIII

WILLIAM SHAKESPEARE

Shall I compare *thee* to a summer's day?
Thou art more lovely and more temperate:
Rough winds do shake the darling buds of May,
And summer's lease hath all too short a date:
Sometimes too hot the eye of heaven shines,
And often is his gold complexion *dimm'd*:
And every fair from fair sometime declines,
By chance, or nature's changing course *untrimm'd*;
But thy eternal summer shall not fade,
Nor lose possession of that fair thou *ow'st*,
Nor shall death brag thou *wander'st* in his shade,
When in eternal lines to time thou *grow'st*;
So long as men can breathe, or eyes can see,
So long lives this, and this gives life to thee.

*THOU/THEE/THY*→YOU/YOUR
*DIMM'D*→DIM OR FADED
*UNTRIMM'D*→UNTRIMMED, CUT SHORT
*OW'ST*→OWN
*WANDER'ST*→WANDER, WALK
*GROW'ST*→GROW

1609

### READER'S RESPONSE

▸1 What were your first impressions of the poem?

▸2 Was the language difficult to understand? Explain.

▸3 What feelings or emotions did the poem evoke in you?

Reread the sonnet now, paying particular attention to the words and sounds. Look for images and expressions that make a strong impression on you. To help you understand the sonnet better, answer the following questions.

## WRITER'S CRAFT

### FORM

▸1 What type of poetic feet does this sonnet contain? Measure the number of stressed and unstressed syllables.

▸2 What is the rhyming scheme of this sonnet?

▸3 Based on the rhyming scheme, is it a Petrarchan or English sonnet?

▸4 Find examples of repetitions of words, phrases, or ideas in the poem.

▸5 a) Look at the sound created by letters of the words and phrases. Are they mainly harsh sounds or soft sounds? Give examples.

b) What is the general tone of this sonnet?

c) Does the sound quality affect the subject of the poem?

▸6 **a)** Are there any examples of alliteration, assonance, or consonance? ____________

**b)** If yes, write them.

______________________________________________

**c)** How do they influence the subject of the poem?

______________________________________________

______________________________________________

### *MEANING*

▸7 The poet is making a comparison in the first line. What is he comparing?

______________________________________________

▸8 Based on the text of the second line, what realisation does the poet come to?

______________________________________________

▸9 In the next two lines, the poet makes reference to two seasons. Which seasons does he mean? What do they symbolise? Think of the seasons in terms of the cycle of life.

Seasons: ____________ ____________

Symbolisation: ______________________________

▸10 What does the poet feel will happen to these two seasons?

______________________________________________

▸11 What two images does he create in order to show the effect on the seasons?

______________________________________________

▸12 The main idea of the first quatrain is expressed through a metaphor. Compare the ideas of the first two lines with those of the second two lines in the first quatrain.

**a)** What is the main idea? ______________________

**b)** What is the metaphor? ______________________

▸13 In the second quatrain, the poet makes an allusion to the passing of time. What words or expressions does he use to pursue this idea?

______________________________________________

______________________________________________

▸14 What fear does he express in the second quatrain?

______________________________________________

▸ **15** Find a word or expression in each line of the second quatrain that produces a negative connotation.

▸ **16** What is the main idea of the second quatrain?

▸ **17** In the third quatrain, the poet uses the words "eternal summer." What does this expression mean?

▸ **18** In the third quatrain, how does the poet refute the fear he expressed in the second quatrain?

▸ **19** What figure of speech does the poet use when he refers to death?

▸ **20** How is death viewed in this quatrain?

▸ **21** What is the main idea of the third quatrain?

▸ **22** What ideas are repeated in the three quatrains?

▸ **23** How are the three main ideas of the three quatrains linked to each other?

▸ **24** How does the poet develop the element of time in this sonnet?

▸ **25** What does the poet conclude in the last two lines of the poem?

▸ **26** What is the function of the last two couplets of this sonnet?

▸ **27** What is the theme of this sonnet?

## DISCUSSION AND WRITING TOPICS

▸1 What is the interrelation between the form of Sonnet 18 and its theme? In other words, how does the form help to develop the theme?

▸2 Explain how different figures of speech — such as metaphor, personification, symbolism — are used for developing the theme of this sonnet.

## OTHER POEMS

The following three poems were written before the nineteenth century. Each reflects a different subject matter, and each is still relevant.

Listen to and read each one. Then, answer the questions that your instructor assigns from the section entitled Discussion and Writing Topics II, after Poem 6.

### POEM 4: MY LOVE IS LIKE TO ICE

**ABOUT THE AUTHOR**

EDMUND SPENSER was born in 1552 to a wealthy family. He studied at Cambridge University and by 1576 he had received a Master's degree. After graduating, he formed a literary group called Areopagus whose purpose was to support political and religious causes through their writings. Spenser's most famous work is *The Faerie Queene*, published in 1589. He died in 1599.

# MY LOVE IS LIKE TO ICE

EDMUND SPENSER

My love is like to ice, and I to fire:
How comes it then that this her cold so great
Is not dissolved through my so hot desire,
But harder grows the more I her entreat?
Or how comes it that My exceeding heat
Is not allayed by her heart-frozen cold,
But that I burn much more in boiling sweat,
And feel my flames augmented manifold?
What more miraculous thing may be told,
That fire, which all things melts, should harden ice,
And ice, that is congealed with senseless cold,
Should kindle fire by wonderful device?
Such is the power in gentle mind,
That it can alter all the course of kind.

1594

## POEM 5: DEATH BE NOT PROUD

**ABOUT THE AUTHOR**

JOHN DONNE was born in 1572 into a Catholic family at a time when England was becoming increasingly Protestant. He attended Cambridge and Oxford universities, but could not complete his studies because his family objected to swearing an oath of allegiance to a Protestant king. Donne started to work soon after he left university, but he had to leave his job because he eloped with the underage niece of his employer who had him jailed for marrying a minor. He broke definitively with the Catholic Church in 1610 and even urged Catholics to take the oath of allegiance to King James, a Protestant. After many years of raising a family in poverty, under pressure from the king, Donne became an ordained minister in 1615. Donne wrote many sonnets, poems, and essays. His works showed a concern for the spiritual and real worlds. He died in 1631.

# DEATH BE NOT PROUD

JOHN DONNE

Death be not proud, though some have called thee
Mighty and dreadful, for thou art not so;
For those whom thou think'st thou dost overthrow
Die not, poor Death; nor yet canst thou kill me.
From rest and sleep, which but thy pictures be,
Much pleasure, then from thee much more must flow;
And soonest our best men with thee do go,
Rest of their bones and soul's delivery.
Thou'rt slave to fate, chance, kings, and desperate men,
And dost with poison, war, and sickness dwell;
And poppy or charms can make us sleep as well
And better than thy stroke. Why swell'st thou then?
One short sleep past, we wake eternally,
And Death shall be no more; Death, thou shalt die.

1618

## POEM 6: TO THE LADIES

**ABOUT THE AUTHOR**

LADY MARY CHUDLEIGH (1656-1710) was a self-educated woman who wrote and published three feminist works, although it is not known if her own marriage served as a model. She achieved fame for the "The Ladies Defence," her controversial answer to a sermon on conjugal duty. In her writing, Lady Chudleigh deplored the inequality between men and women, the lack of educational possibilities for women, and the oppression of married women. Her poems have appeared in anthologies since the eighteenth century.

# TO THE LADIES

LADY MARY CHUDLEIGH

Wife and servant are the same,
But only differ in the name:
For when that fatal knot is tied,
Which nothing, nothing can divide:
When she the word *obey* has said,
And man by law supreme has made,
Then all that's *kind* is laid aside, *KIND*→NATURAL
And nothing left but *state* and pride, *STATE*→POMP
Fierce as an Eastern prince he grows,
And all his innate rigour shows,:
Then but to look, to laugh, or speak,
Will the nuptial contract break.
Like mutes she signs alone must make,
And never any freedom take:
But still be governed by a nod,
And fear her husband as her God:
Him still must serve, him still obey,
And nothing act, and nothing say,
But what her haughty lord thinks fit,
Who with the power, has all the wit.
Then shun, oh! shun that wretched state,
And all the fawning flatt'rers hate:
Value you selves, and men despise,
You must be proud, if you'll be wise.

1703

## DISCUSSION AND WRITING TOPICS

▸1 Explain how the author of "My Love is Like to Ice" uses contrasting imagery to express the theme.

▸2 Discuss how the poet presents death in "Death Be Not Proud."

▸3 Compare the poems "Fire and Ice" and "To the Ladies." Write an analysis comparing their forms and themes.

▸4 Discuss the relevance of the theme of "To the Ladies." Explain whether its ideas still apply to modern relationships.

▸5 Alone or with a partner, choose a period of time and choose some poets from that era. Study their backgrounds and read their key works. Prepare a short report for the class. Your teacher may want you to present it in a group or in front of the class, or he or she may want it in written form.

Here is a list of poets to consider:

Margaret Atwood
William Blake
Gwendolyn Brooks
Elizabeth Barrett Browning
Robert Browning
Lord Byron
Geoffrey Chaucer
Leonard Cohen
Emily Dickinson
Walter de la Mare
John Donne
Louis Dudek
T.S. Eliot
Phyllis Gottlieb
Ted Hughes
John Keats
Irving Layton
Dorothy Livesay
John Milton
Marianne Moore
P.K. Page
Sylvia Plath
Alexander Pope
Al Purdy
Robyn Sarah
William Shakespeare
Edna St. Vincent Millay
Percy Bysshe Shelley
Gertrude Stein
Alfred, Lord Tennyson
Dylan Thomas
Miriam Waddington
Anne Wilkinson
William Carlos Williams
William Wordsworth

▸6 Do a more in-depth analysis about a literary period. Research the social, political, and economic trends of the time, and take note of their influence on poetry. Prepare a short report for the class. Your teacher may want you to present it in a group or in front of the class, or may want it in written form.

UNIT 3.2

# OTHER APPROACHES

**CHAPTER CONTENTS**

- **LISTENING:** "I Wandered Lonely as a Cloud"; "In Flanders Fields"; "Stopping by Woods on a Snowy Evening"; "Treblinka Gas Chamber"; "Calamity"; "Meditations on the Declension of Beauty"
- **READING:** approaches: formalist; reader response; historical; sociological; structuralist; feminist; minority; Marxist
- **WRITING:** using other approaches to interpret poetry
- **SPEAKING:** group discussions about poems

Of the next two examples, the first poem is Romantic and the second comes from the early twentieth century (the time of the first World War). They were written as a response to deeply moving personal experiences, albeit very different. We will consider them through two different but complementary approaches to analysing poetry: formalist and reader response.

The **formalist** approach to literary criticism developed in the early twentieth century. Formalists examine the form of the language and study how it is used in order to gain insight into the meaning of the work. Formalists look at the varied structural and linguistic parts to understand how the writer created a work. Such type of criticism will only consider the work itself and will not give too much importance to external factors such as historical context or the author's personal experiences. Thus, formalism concentrates on rhetoric and linguistics when analysing a poem. Formalist critics created a concrete methodology akin to that of the sciences to study poetry.

The **reader response** approach believes that the reader plays a central role in the literary work. The feelings of the reader must be considered and valued when analysing a work of literature. With this approach, the reader brings his or her own personal knowledge to the literary work in order to develop a connection and to understand his or her response. When analysing a poem from a reader response perspective, the reader might want to compare his or her own personal experience with that of the poet. This could be done through telling an anecdote as well as through discussing the emotional responses the poem has evoked in a reader.

## POEM 1: I WANDERED LONELY AS A CLOUD

### ABOUT THE AUTHOR

ROMANTIC POET WILLIAM WORDSWORTH was born in 1770 in West Cumberland, England. He went to Cambridge University and graduated in 1791. While at university, Wordsworth vacationed in France and became a supporter of the French Revolution. At the same time he fell in love with a Frenchwoman, Annette Vallon, with whom he had a daughter out of wedlock. They planned to marry, but the French Revolution prevented them from joining each other and the marriage never took place. He began writing poetry while at Cambridge. Wordsworth published a volume of poetry in 1798 entitled *Lyrical Ballads, with a Few Other Poems.* This volume was a joint effort with another great poet, Samuel Taylor Coleridge, and is considered to be the first major statement of Romanticism in England. In 1805, Wordsworth married Mary Hutchinson, a friend from childhood. In 1807 his *Poems in Two Volumes* was published, bringing him great recognition. Three of his most famous works include"Tintern Abbey," "Ode: Intimations of Immortality," and *The Prelude.* His themes reflected his reminiscences of his past, of moments in time that were meaningful to him. He became the Poet Laureate in 1843 and died in 1850.

Listen to the following poem.

# I Wandered Lonely as a Cloud

William Wordsworth

I wandered lonely as a cloud
That floats on high o'er vales and hills,
When all at once I saw a crowd,
A host, of golden daffodils;
Beside the lake, beneath the trees,
Fluttering and dancing in the breeze.

Continuous as the stars that shine
And twinkle on the milky way,
They stretched in never-ending line
Along the margin of a bay:
Ten thousand saw I at a glance,
Tossing their heads in sprightly dance.

The waves beside them danced; but they
Out-did the sparkling waves in glee:
A poet could not but be gay,
In such a jocund company:
I gazed — and gazed — but little thought
What wealth the show to me had brought:

For oft, when on my couch I lie
In vacant or in pensive mood,
They flash upon that inward eye
Which is the bliss of solitude;
And then my heart with pleasure fills,
And dances with the daffodils.

1804

**Writer's Craft**
**Formalist Approach**

▸1 What does the poet see on his walk?

▸2 What feelings do the flowers invoke in the poet? Write two or three lines to prove your answer.

▸3 How do the feelings or emotions of the persona (narrator) change through the poem? Give examples.

▸4 What is the structure (note the number of lines and verses) and the rhyming scheme?

▸5 What is the rhythm or meter? (If you can't remember, refer to page 232.)

▸6 Use the chart below to indicate the sound patterns of this poem.

| | ALLITERATION | ASSONANCE | CONSONANCE |
|---|---|---|---|
| Stanza 1 | | | |
| Stanza 2 | | | |
| Stanza 3 | | | |
| Stanza 4 | | | |

▸7 Find examples of poetic devices such as:

a) simile

b) metaphor

c) personification

d) imagery

e) symbols

▶8 What is the theme of the poem?

______________________________________________

______________________________________________

▶9 What is the mood of the poem?

______________________________________________

▶10 How does the form of the poem reinforce the mood of the poem? Look at the imagery, as well as the diction and sound in the poem.

______________________________________________

______________________________________________

**POEM 2: IN FLANDERS FIELDS**

**ABOUT THE AUTHOR**

POET JOHN MCCRAE was born in 1872 in Ontario, Canada. He was a respected university teacher and doctor in Montreal before joining the army and fighting in World War I on the western front in 1914. He was eventually sent to France with a medical unit. It was during his service that he experienced firsthand the horrible nature of war. He died in 1918 of pneumonia in France while still on active duty. His book of poetry *In Flanders Fields and Other Poems* was published in 1919.

Listen to the following poem.

# IN FLANDERS FIELDS

JOHN MCCRAE

In Flanders fields the poppies blow
Between the crosses, row on row,
That mark our place; and in the sky
The larks, still bravely singing, fly
Scarce heard amid the guns below.

We are the Dead. Short days ago
We lived, felt dawn, saw sunset glow,
Loved, and were loved, and now we lie
In Flanders fields.

Take up our quarrel with the foe:
To you from failing hands we throw
The torch; be yours to hold it high.
If ye break faith with us who die
We shall not sleep, though poppies grow
In Flanders fields.

1915

## WRITER'S CRAFT
### Formalist Approach

▸1 What is the setting of the poem?

▸2 What type of narrator is found in the poem?

▸3 What is the subject of the poem?

▸4 What is the rhyming scheme?

▸5 How would you define the rhythm or meter?

▸6 Use the chart below to indicate the sound patterns of this poem.

| | ALLITERATION | ASSONANCE | CONSONANCE |
|---|---|---|---|
| Verse 1: | | | |
| Verse 2: | | | |
| Verse 3: | | | |

▸7 Find examples of poetic devices such as:

a) simile

b) metaphor

c) personification

d) imagery

e) symbols

▸8 What is the theme of the poem?

▸9 What is the mood of the poem?

▸10 How does the form of the poem reinforce the mood of the poem? Consider the use of imagery and symbolism (especially Christian symbolism).

**Reader Response Approach**

▸1 Reread both poems. What feelings or reactions did you have when you first read the poems? Write a list of adjectives that describe your feelings about each poem.

Poem 1:

Poem 2:

▸2 Wordsworth and McCrae wrote their respective poems in response to something that each saw and that moved each poet deeply. In your experience, has an image or an event ever moved you profoundly? If so, what were your reactions to the image or event?

▸3 Read the two poems again. Make a list of meaningful words that relate to the subject of the poems.

| "I WANDERED LONELY AS A CLOUD" | "IN FLANDERS FIELDS" |
|---|---|
| | |

▸4 From your list in question 3, state some general conclusions about how those words illustrate the meaning or theme of the poem. Then compare your answers with those of other students.

### *PARAGRAPH PRACTICE*

▸1 Write two descriptive paragraphs on the image/picture that each poem ("I Wandered…" and "In Flanders Fields") created in your mind. Describe the scene and the subject matter, paying close attention to how each is described in the poems.

## OTHER APPROACHES, OTHER POEMS

There are different approaches to analysing a poem. Sometimes an analysis will combine more than one approach.

The **historical** approach studies literature within the context of history. For example, the historical events and the spirit of the times are considered to be very important as background to the literary works. Critics who use this approach feel that a writer cannot be divorced from the events that he or she writes about. Therefore, a writer will necessarily be influenced by the ideas of the times. For example, the poem "In Flanders Fields" was written by a Canadian doctor serving in the First World War in Flanders, Belgium. The subject matter of the poem grew out of the poet's experience as a result of the events of war.

The **sociological** approach is similar to the historical approach in that it, too, considers the spirit of the times but from a sociological perspective. This approach includes the following types of factors: economic status, education, male/female roles, adult versus child, group versus individual, urban versus rural, as well as social groups such as family, tribe, community, country, and nationality.

The **structuralist** approach attempts to discover the unifying elements of a work by looking at its different parts. It is similar in this sense to the formalist approach; however, it diverges by trying to understand the deeper structures of the work itself. For example, an important concern of a structuralist is to look at the relationship between *langue* or language as a whole and *parole* or utterance, a particular use of individual components of language. Structuralist scholars look at language as a sign system. They also consider literary works in two ways: in terms of language and in terms of the system used to create a literary text, such as its genre. Such an approach uses the Jungian idea of archetypes to understand the deeper, universal elements to literature. Karl Jung was a German philosopher who theorised that all literary works may be categorised into universal archetypes or primary models.

The **feminist** approach presumes that literature favours a masculine perspective and disfavours the importance of feminine characters and their concerns. This approach attempts to reverse the male-dominant perspective in order to study literature through the perspective of women and their role in the creation of literature.

The **minority** approach uses the perspective of issues facing minorities to analyse literature. This includes such factors as marginalisation, racism, discrimination, intolerance of other cultural perspectives and value systems, majority versus minority, and so on.

The **Marxist** approach to literary analysis seeks to analyse literature in terms of class struggle. Characters are evaluated through an analysis of their class status. A Marxist approach observes whether characters are poor or rich, and looks at the effects of political and economic trends on the work itself.

The following are a sampling of poetry written in the latter half of the twentieth century. As you respond to and analyse these works, you will integrate what you have learned from the writing and discussion activities of the previous sections of this unit. In the activities proposed, you will be asked to incorporate both reader response and elements from other types of analysis. Your instructor may choose to have you first listen to, and then read and discuss each poem in small groups before you actually write about it.

## POEM 3: STOPPING BY WOODS ON A SNOWY EVENING

**ABOUT THE AUTHOR**

The first poem was published in 1923 and appears in *The Poetry of Robert Frost*. Frost often set his poems in the New England countryside and he followed in the steps of the Romantic poets. His very individualistic and lyrical poetry, simple on the surface but often infused with darker meaning, is still popular today.

Listen to the following poem.

# STOPPING BY WOODS ON A SNOWY EVENING

ROBERT FROST

Whose woods these are I think I know.
His house is in the village though;
He will not see me stopping here
To watch his woods fill up with snow.

My little horse must think it queer
To stop without a farmhouse near
Between the woods and frozen lake
The darkest evening of the year.

UNIT 3.2 OTHER APPROACHES

He gives his harness bells a shake
To ask if there is some mistake.
The only other sound's the sweep
Of easy wind and downy flake.

The woods are lovely, dark and deep,
But I have promises to keep,
And miles to go before I sleep,
And miles to go before I sleep.

1923

## WRITING ACTIVITY

Write an essay that interprets this poem. Incorporate the reader response and structuralist approaches.

Here are some suggestions to help you begin your analysis of "Stopping by Woods on a Snowy Evening." They are intended to help you articulate your written response.

▸1 To start responding to this poem:

- Think about the images connected with the setting; consider how they affect the mood and theme.
- Look for contrasts and hidden meanings (metaphors, symbolism).
- Support your interpretation with "proof" from the text.

▸2 Reflect on the significance of the following points:

- *the image of the woods*
  How are the woods portrayed?
  What kind of mood or feeling is connected with them?
  Whom could they belong to?
  What could they represent or symbolise?
- *the time of year and season*
  Which words are associated with the season?
  Why this time of year? (significance to the theme)
  What feelings are engendered by the seasonal imagery?
  What could the season symbolise?
- *the significance of the setting for the theme*
- *the little horse*
  How is he portrayed and what does he do?
  What does he add to the poem?
  What is his role in the poem?
  What does he represent?
- *the promises*
  What they could be?
  What could they signify?
- *the poem's narrator and the feelings he is experiencing*

▸3 Examine the formal elements of the poem (rhythm, rhyming scheme, etc.).

**POEM 4: TREBLINKA GAS CHAMBER**

**ABOUT THE AUTHOR**

This poem was originally published in 1982 in a book called *The Vision Tree: Selected Poems.* The book won a Governor General's Award for author Phyllis Webb. Born in British Columbia, Webb is known for her poems about philosophical and social concerns.

Listen to the following poem.

# TREBLINKA GAS CHAMBER

PHYLLIS WEBB

Klostermayer ordered another count of the children. Then their stars were snipped off and thrown into the center of the courtyard. It looked like a field of buttercups. — JOSEPH HYAMS. *A Field of Buttercups*

fallingstars
'a field of
buttercups'
yellow stars
of David
falling

the prisoners
the children
falling
in heaps
on one another
they go down

Thanatos
showers
his dirty breath
they must breathe
him in
they see stars
behind their
eyes

David's
'a field of
buttercups'
a metaphor
where all that's
left lies down

1982

## WRITING ACTIVITY

Write an interpretation of this poem that incorporates elements from the reader response, historical, and formalist approaches.

You will have noticed that this poem is arranged into a special shape. It is an example of a poem issuing from an international, post-World War II movement known as **concrete** poetry. Concrete poets rejected conventional forms and structure, and experimented with unusual grammatical structures, spelling, sounds, and the actual shape of the written poem on a page.

Here are some aspects to examine in your approach to this piece.

▸1 **Historical context**

- If you don't already know, find out what the historical context of Treblinka was.
- Whom does "David" refer to?
- Who is Thanatos?

▸2 **Shape of the poem**

- What is the significance of the special shape of this poem?
- What do you notice about grammatical conventions such as sentence structure?
- What could this signify?

▸3 **Imagery**

- metaphors and comparisons
- different uses and meanings of the word "stars"
- links between the images
- repetition of certain words
- predominant colour
- feeling of movement; predominant movement

▸4 **Tone**

- Reread the poem several times, paying attention to the images and form. How does this poem make you feel? Why?

Here are questions to ask yourself.

▸1 Why do you think the author chose this particular form for the poem?

▸2 Is the form of the poem effective? Why or why not?

▸3 What effect does the recurrent use of the image of a field of buttercups have on the unity of the poem?

▸4 What do you perceive as the poet's reaction to the events she describes? What makes you think this?

### POEM 5: CALAMITY

**ABOUT THE AUTHOR**

F. R. SCOTT, a social philosopher and law professor, often wrote about social concerns. His poem "Calamity" was part of *The Collected Poems of F. R. Scott* (1981) which won a Governor General's Award for that year.

Listen to the following poem.

# CALAMITY

F.R. SCOTT

A laundry truck
Rolled down the hill
And crashed into my maple tree.
It was a truly North American calamity.
Three cans of beer fell out
(Which in itself was revealing)
And a jumble of skirts and shirts
Spilled onto the ploughed grass.
Dogs barked, and the children
Sprouted like dandelions on my lawn.
Normally we do not speak to one another on this avenue,
But the excitement made us suddenly neighbours.
People exchanged remarks
Who had never been introduced
And for a while we were quite human.
Then the policeman came —
Sedately, for this was Westmount —
And carefully took down all names and numbers.
The towing truck soon followed,
Order was restored.
The starch came raining down.

1981

UNIT 3.2 OTHER APPROACHES

## WRITING ACTIVITY

Write an interpretation of this poem that incorporates elements from the reader response, sociological, and formalist approaches.

**Suggestions:**

Examine the following:

- ironic elements: title, situation, last line of poem
- images — types, significance, way they are placed and used
- story line

  How does the author use narrative techniques (a story with a dramatic structure) to make his point?
- humorous and journalistic elements

Ask yourself the following questions:

▶1 What can you deduce about Westmount (an autonomous municipality within the urban community of Montreal, Quebec)?

___

___

▶2 How does the narrator feel about Westmount?

___

___

▶3 How do you know? (choose a line from the poem)

___

___

▶4 What kind of sociological judgements does this poem make?

___

___

**POEM 6: MEDITATIONS ON THE DECLENSION OF BEAUTY BY THE GIRL WITH THE FLYING CHEEK-BONES**

**ABOUT THE AUTHOR**

M. NOURBESE PHILIP'S poetry and other writings have been published widely in Canada, the United States, and Great Britain. The award-winning Toronto author was named a Guggenheim Fellow in poetry in 1990.

Listen to the following poem.

# MEDITATIONS ON THE DECLENSION OF BEAUTY BY THE GIRL WITH THE FLYING CHEEK-BONES

M. NORUBESE PHILIP

If not If not If<br>
Not<br>
If not in yours<br>
In whose<br>
In whose language<br>
Am I<br>
If not in yours<br>
In whose<br>
In whose language<br>
Am I I am<br>
If not in yours<br>
In whose<br>
Am I<br>
(if not in yours)<br>
I am yours<br>
In whose language<br>
Am I not<br>
Am I not I am yours<br>
If not in yours<br>
If not in yours<br>
In whose<br>
In whose language<br>
Am I...

Girl with the flying cheek-bones:
She is
I am
Woman with the behind that drives men mad
And if not in yours
Where is the woman with a nose broad
As her strength
If not in yours
In whose language
Is the man with the full-moon lips
Carrying the midnight of colour
Split by the stars — a smile
If not in yours
In whose
In whose language
Am I
Am I not
Am I I am yours
Am I not I am yours
Am I I am
If not in yours
In whose
In whose language
Am I
If not in yours
Beautiful

## WRITING ACTIVITY

Write an interpretation of this poem that incorporates elements from reader response, formalist, feminist, and minority approaches.

**Suggestions:**

Examine the following:

- the use of repetition and other rhythmic elements
- word play and its importance to the meaning and form
  *EXAMPLE: Am I, Am I not* and *Am I, I am*
- overall form of the poem
- central section and its purpose
- images and their effects

Ask yourself the following questions:

- ▸1 Why does the narrator of the poem repetitively ask questions? How are these questions similar and different?
- ▸2 What does the author mean by the word "language"?
- ▸3 What is the underlying question that the poem asks?
- ▸4 How effective are the form and wordplay in this poem?
- ▸5 What is the significance of the final word of the poem?

## LIGHT VERSE AND HUMOROUS POEMS

Some poetry is not meant to be taken too seriously; it is written mainly for fun and entertainment. These types of poetry include nonsense verse, satire, parody, limericks, acrostic poems, jingles, riddles, and punning verses, among others. We will end our brief study of poetry with a look at the lighter side of verse.

### POEM 7: WISHES OF AN ELDERLY MAN AT A GARDEN PARTY

**ABOUT THE AUTHOR**

SIR WALTER ALEXANDER RALEIGH (1861-1922) was a distinguished university professor of English in Britain.

I wish I loved the Human Race;
I wish I loved its silly face;
I wish I liked the way it walks;
I wish I liked the way it talks;
And when I'm introduced to one
I wish I thought *What Jolly fun!*

### POEM 8: BIRDS, BAGS, BEARS, AND BUNS

ANONYMOUS

The common cormorant or shag
Lays eggs inside a paper bag.
The reason you will see, no doubt
It is to keep the lightning out,
But what these unobservant birds
Have never noticed is that herds
Of wandering bears may come with buns
And steal the bags to hold the crumbs.

## POEMS 9, 10, AND 11: LIMERICKS

Here are a few famous limericks written by anonymous authors (the last selection is known as a macaronic because it combines two languages). Limericks often contain puns and can be nonsensical or ribald.

A flea and a fly in a *flue*
Were imprisoned, so what could they do?
Said the fly: "Let us flee"
Said the flea: "Let us fly"
So they flew through a flaw in the flue.

*FLUE*→A PIPE THAT CONDUCTS HOT AIR, GASES, SMOKE ETC. TO A CHIMNEY FROM A STOVE OR FIREPLACE.

*Titian* was mixing rose *madder.*
His model posed nude on a ladder.
Her position to Titian
Suggestion coition.
So he nipped up the ladder and 'ad 'er.

*TITIAN*→FAMOUS VENETIAN PAINTER (EARLY 1500S)

*MADDER*→A RED OR PURPLISH COLOUR (DYE FROM A PLANT).

There was a young lady of Nantes
*Très jolie, et très élégante,*
But her **** was so small
It was no good at all,
Except for *la plume de ma tante.*

## WRITING ACTIVITIES

▸1 Write about one of the poems above, paying particular attention to the use of poetic devices and humour.

▸2 Try your hand at writing a limerick or other form of light verse.

## WRAP-UP ESSAY TOPICS

▸1 Compare an example of the music (for example, a song) of a period to a poem of the same era.

▸2 Compare a short story and a poem from the Romantic Age. Illustrate how they reflect the preoccupations of artists of the period.

▸3 Compare a contemporary poem in which the poet experiments with form to a short story in which the author experiments with short story conventions.

▸4 There are many other types of poems in English poetry, including the narrative, lyric, ode, elegy, epic, and ballad. Research the form and development of one of these other types of poems.

▸5 Research in detail the life and works of a particular poet.

▸6 Choose a poem that you particularly like. Read it aloud and present an oral analysis to the class.

▸7 Write about Canada's involvement in World War I or II. Relate it either to "In Flander's Fields" or "Treblinka."

# References

## PRINT


Ciardi, J. *How Does a Poem Mean?* Boston: Houghton Mifflin Co., 1959.

Drucker, Johanna. "The Visible Word: Experimental Typography and Modern Art, 1909-1923." Chicago: University of Chicago Press, 1994.

Koch, K. and Farrell, K. *Sleeping on the Wing: An Anthology of Modern Poetry with Essays on Reading and Writing*. New York: Random House, 1981.

McGann, Jerome J. *Social Values and Poetic Acts: A Historical Judgment of Lliterary Work*. Cambridge, MA: Harvard University Press, 1988.

*The Norton Anthology of Modern Poetry*, eds. Ellmann, Richard and Robert O'Clair. New York: W. W. Norton, 1973.

Purves, A. and Rippere, V. *Elements of Writing about a Literary Work: A Study of Response to Literature*. Urbana, IL: NCTE, 1986.


## INTERNET


**BRITISH POETRY 1780-1910: A HYPERTEXT ARCHIVE OF SCHOLARLY EDITIONS**
http://etext.lib.virginia.edu/britpo.html

**MODERN AND CONTEMPORARY AMERICAN POETRY:**
http://www.english.upenn.edu/~afilreis/88/home.html

**THE MODERN ENGLISH COLLECTION:**
http://etext.lib.virginia.edu/modeng/modeng0.browse.html

**ELECTRONIC POETRY TEXT ARCHIVES:**
http://wings.buffalo.edu/epc/connects/etextsites.html~

**GLOSSARY OF POETIC TERMS:**
http://www.library.utoronto.ca/utel/rp/poetterm.html
http://shoga.wwa.com/~rgs/glossary.html

**INTRODUCTION TO REPRESENTATIVE POETRY ON-LINE:**
http://www.library.utoronto.ca/utel/rp/intro.html

**POETRY ARCHIVE:**
http://www.everypoet.com/archive/index.htm

**SOUNDS LIKE POETRY- POETIC DEVICES:**
http://kidswriting.about.com/teens/kidswriting/library/weekly/aa092099.htm

**LIST OF LINKS:**
http://www.dmoz.org/Arts/Literature/Poetry/
Interactive quiz on metre: http://www.wmich.edu/english/tchg/quiz/meter/q2/quiz.html

**STEP-BY-STEP METHOD OF EXPLICATING A POEM (VERY ORIGINAL):**
http://www.sjsu.edu/faculty/patten/vendler.html

**CRITICISM:**
http://www.library.utoronto.ca/utel/rp/indexcriticism.html
http://www.gradnet.de/pomo2.archives/pomo99.papers/Milz99.htm

# UNIT 4
# DRAMA

UNIT 4

# DRAMA

**THE DRAMA SECTION COMPRISES AN INTRODUCTION WITH A WARM-UP ACTIVITY AND A BRIEF HISTORY OF DRAMA FOLLOWED BY TWO CHAPTERS. UNIT 4.1 FEATURES A ONE-ACT PLAY WRITTEN IN THE EARLY 1900S AND UNIT 4.2, A RADIO PLAY PRODUCED IN THE LATE 1990S.**

BRIEF HISTORY OF DRAMA. Drama as a literary form has existed since the earliest civilisations. The ancient Greeks and Romans developed highly sophisticated forms of the genre, writing both tragedies and comedies. Tragedy originated in Greece in the fifth century B.C., and stressed the relationships of human beings and the gods, who gave insightful advice on problems. For example, the great playwright Sophocles (496 B.C.-406 or 405 B.C.) showed man to be both weak and heroic, as is evident in his *Oedipus Rex*. In this tragedy, Oedipus becomes king by unknowingly slaying his father and marrying his mother, thereby fulfilling his destiny. The tragedies of Euripides (480 B.C.-406 B.C.) questioned the traditional role of the gods. In plays such as *Electra* (date unknown), *Helen* (412 B.C.) and *Iphigenia in Aulis* (405 B.C.), he showed great psychological insights into his characters.

Ancient Roman theatre was influenced by Greek tragedy and comedy. The early Roman dramas were performed at festivals and sporting contests. The first theatre in Rome was built of stone in the first century B.C. Comedies, farces, and slapstick were favourites of the public. Among some ancient Roman comedy playwrights were Levius Andronicus and Plautus, who wrote fanciful plays about love, or a slight mocking of the upper classes, and incorporated slapstick humour and music into their works. During the reign of Julius Caesar, audiences also enjoyed mimes. Eventually, large spectacles and shows replaced traditional tragedies and comedies in the Roman Empire.

English drama can trace its origins to Rome. The popularity of drama lessened after the fall of the Roman Empire until about the tenth century. Two factors contributed to this decline. Firstly, the early Christians and the infant Church condemned play-acting because drama was associated with pagan ritual. Secondly, non-Christian invaders throughout Europe kept indigenous forms of theatre from flourishing because of the uncertainty of life due to war and invasions. As a result, there are few records of early Christian plays that are still extant. The absence of documents makes it impossible for us to know which types of plays were performed. It is likely that travelling players went from town to town, entertaining the public. These travelling players told their tales through song, acting, or mime.

By the twelfth century, these players had become so popular that the Church, which had condemned drama as a pagan tradition, started using it for its own purpose. Drama became a means for promoting religious activities. Liturgical plays (dramatisations of prayers and Bible stories) were performed at Easter and Christmas time. Other biblical stories, such as the story of Creation and the birth of Christ, were acted as well, and became precursors to non-devotional drama.

In addition, the miracle play (stories of miracles) developed from liturgical drama and led to the creation of the morality play. In morality plays, different characters represent abstract qualities. The most famous morality play is *Everyman* (c.1500), the story of a character by that name who meets Death and finds that his friends forsake him. Only his friend Good Deeds follows Everyman on his journey to meet Death. Morality plays show the progression from the earlier liturgical plays, which were wholly religious in theme, to those that were less religious and more didactic and political.

> ***All the world's a stage,***
> ***And all the men and women merely players;***
> ***They have their exits and their entrances;***
> ***And one man in his time plays many parts..."***
>
> — William Shakespeare, *As You Like It*

By the sixteenth century, drama had adopted realism and was concerned with humanistic themes. Humanism emphasises the ability of people to reason, and evaluates the place of humankind in the universe. It was a movement that developed in northern Italy in the fourteenth century when Petrarch (1304-1374), a theologian and man of letters, created an educational system emphasising the study of classical literature such as poetry, grammar, rhetoric, and history. The sixteenth century also popularised two forms of the theatre that had roots in classical traditions: the tragedy and the comedy. Tragedy was influenced by the Roman writer Seneca, (4? B.C.-65 A.D.) who lived around the time of Nero, while comedy was influenced by two Roman writers, Plautus (254?-184 B.C.) and Terence (190?-159 B.C.). The first comedy to develop along the lines of classical theory was *Ralph Roister Doister* (1553-1554) by Nicholas Udall. Another form that gained popularity was the chronicle play (a popular presentation of history), among which was *The True Chronicle of King Leir* (1594, 1604) a predecessor to Shakespeare's *King Lear*.

Elizabethan England marked a flowering of drama. It was the time of the great play-wrights Thomas Kyd, who wrote *The Spanish Tragedy* (c. 1587); Christopher Marlowe (1564-1593), whose most famous play was *Dr. Faustus* (1588); and of course, William Shakespeare (1564-1616). Much has been written on Shakespeare, considered to be one of the greatest writers of all time. Shakespeare wrote both tragedies and comedies. His tragic heroes are men of great character whose weaknesses lead either to their corruption or to encounters with impossible situations. His comedies revolve around love. Shakespeare's earliest extant play is Henry VI (c.1588). His plays have withstood the test of time. They have been produced on stage throughout the centuries, and in modern times most, if not all of his plays such as *Romeo and Juliet*, *King Lear*, *The Tempest*, and *Hamlet*, to name just a few, have also been adapted to television and film.

While theatre flourished during the time of Elizabeth I, by the time Charles I (1600-1649) came to the throne in 1625, theatre was seriously threatened. This was largely due to a new religious climate in England of the time called Puritanism, one form of worship within the confines of Protestantism. Puritans believed that excess ceremony or ritual in religion was wrong. They believed that the extravagances of the Catholic Church, which relied heavily on ceremony, were evil and thus they abolished all rites and rituals in their system of worship. Puritans were a powerful and influential group in England at that time.

Charles I had many conflicts with Parliament, largely composed of Puritans. When he tried to impose the Anglican or Church of England liturgy that had some amount of ritual and ceremony over England and Scotland, there was a large public outcry. Other problems such as money caused him to have more conflict with Parliament and eventually led to Civil War. Charles was beheaded in 1649 and the monarchy was not restored until 1660. In the interregnum, English government was run by Parliament. Life was very strict for the general population during these years. The Puritans banned all forms of entertainment, or amusement, especially theatre, because they considered it to be the work of the devil and to be disrespectful of political figures.

After the renewal of the monarchy in 1660, a period known in English history as the Restoration, theatre re-developed, but was often obscene and raucous as a counter-reaction to the period of the ban. Drama eventually developed into two branches during this period: heroic plays and comedies of manners, the latter of which took a cynical and witty look at court life and was greatly influenced by the French playwright Molière. In England, John Dryden (1631-1700) was perhaps the most important playwright of this time, writing many comedies, heroic plays, and tragedies.

The period from the eighteenth century to the mid-nineteenth was a quieter era. Certain forms, like the drama of sensibility, as well as parodies and burlesques, were prominent. Important playwrights of this period included Henry Fielding, author of *Tom Thumb* (1730); John Gay, who wrote *The Beggar's Opera* (1728), a ballad-opera play; and Oliver Goldsmith, who wrote the comedy *She Stoops to Conquer* (1773).

The second half of the nineteenth century experienced another revival of the theatre. Two of its greatest representatives were Oscar Wilde (1854-1900) and George Bernard Shaw (1856-1950). Wilde wrote comedies such as *An Ideal Husband* (1895) and *The Importance of Being Earnest* (1895). Shaw criticised social evils such as prostitution, in *Mrs. Warren's Profession* (1894). In *Arms and the Man* (1894), he was concerned with the romantic image of the soldier, and his *Man and Superman* (1901) and *Pygmalion* (1912), though both comedies, were social commentaries.

The twentieth century was rich in new and traditional forms of theatre. Dramatists expressed social concerns and dealt with poverty, realism of war and its effect on the general population, political issues, the fast pace of changing technology, and the individual's ability to adapt. Some famous playwrights include Somerset Maugham, who wrote *Caesar's Wife* (1919) and Noel Coward, *Private Lives* (1930), both known for their sophisticated comedy of manners; T.S. Eliot, who wrote *Murder in the Cathedral* (1935); and W.H. Auden, who experimented with verse form in *The Ascent of F6* (1936).

English-language drama traditions of the twentieth century also developed rich traditions outside of Great Britain. Here is a list of some playwrights from different countries:

*Australia:* Kylie Tennant, Ray Lawler, Patrick White, Hal Porter, Douglas Stewart, David Williamson

*Canada:* James Reaney, George Ryga, Drew Hayden Taylor, Robert Lepage, Carol Bolt, Sharon Pollock, Betty Lambert, Joanna Glass, Judith Thompson

*South Africa:* Athol Fugard

*United States:* Arthur Miller, Tennessee Williams, David Mamet, Lanford Wilson, Sam Shepard, Ntozake Shange, Marsha Norman, Beth Henley, Tina Howe, Wendy Wasserstein, August Wilson

### WARM-UP

▸1 Match the terms in column A to the definitions in column B.

| A | B |
|---|---|
| 1. Mime | a) long speech in drama by one character |
| 2. Play | b) a light piece of satire |
| 3. Sketch | c) performance of a story on stage |
| 4. Improvisation | d) dramatic expression without speech |
| 5. Monologue | e) spontaneous expression of speech and actions to present a story |
| 6. Pantomime | f) farcical drama performed with mimicry |
| 7. Skit | g) a short play, often musical |
| 8. Oration | h) a drama with exaggerated emotions and a happy ending |
| 9. Melodrama | i) formal speech |
| 10. Soliloquy | k) talking without regard to listeners |

▸2 Which do you prefer to see, a film or a play? Explain your answer.

UNIT 4.1

# TRIFLES

## CHAPTER CONTENTS

- **READING:** structure of a Play; Trends of the Times: The One-Act Play; biographical information; *Trifles* by Susan Glaspell
- **LITERARY ELEMENTS:** mood; setting; symbolism; characterisation; irony; dramatic structure; theme
- **WRITING:** paragraph practice; a literary essay

The first play in this section was written early in the twentieth century. Its plot concerns the investigation of a rather strange murder.

## ABOUT THE AUTHOR

SUSAN GLASPELL was born in 1876 in Davenport, Iowa. She wrote short stories and articles, but she was especially well known as a playwright. She and her writer husband, George Cram Cook, founded the Provincetown Players, a theatre group that experimented with new trends. The group moved to New York in 1916 and in that year staged two one-act plays by Eugene O'Neill, as well as Glaspell's own work *Trifles*. The productions were a great success. Glaspell's works reflected her own interests in women's issues. *Trifles* provides a good example of her interest in women's lives. Her other works include *The Outside* (1918), *Woman's Honor* (1918), *Bernice* (1919), *The Inheritors* (1921), and *The Verge* (1921). Glaspell won the Pulitzer Prize for drama in 1931, for her play *Alison's House* (1930).

## STRUCTURE OF A PLAY

In traditional drama, such as the tragedies of William Shakespeare, a play is divided into five acts, each of which has several scenes. Acts often last from thirty minutes to an hour, whereas scenes might last as little as a few seconds or as long as thirty minutes. An entire performance can take from two to three hours. In contemporary times, most plays have fewer acts and do not last as long as Shakespeare's (although Robert Lepage's seven-act *The Seven Streams of the Ota River* actually lasts seven hours and has two intermissions, including an hour-long meal break!).

Scenes are made up of dialogue (the actors' lines or speeches) and stage directions (instructions to the actors and the director about the set, gestures, entrances and exits, etc.).

The plot (dramatic structure) of a traditional play, or tragedy, follows a similar structure to that of a traditional short story, rising in action to a climax in Act III, then falling until the final dénouement at the end of Act V. In the first parts of the play, the life and fortunes of the leading character (who can be a tragic hero or protagonist) would go well, and then a conflict would arise, leading to a climax and tragedy, usually with much loss of life, including the protagonist's, by the end of the play.

A narrator is usually not present. This does not limit the possiblity of a narrator, but usually there is no narrator because the action is meant to unfold in the presence of an audience. We analyse drama using many of the same literary terms found in the analysis of short stories and novels: theme, plot, setting, characterisation, irony, foreshadowing, imagery, dialogue, and so on. Review these terms in the literary elements section at the beginning of the book.

The short play became popular in the eighteenth century as an after-show diversion. Its real purpose was often to entice latecomers to theatrical productions for reduced admissions prices. By the nineteenth century, the one-act play changed its objective and became the curtain raiser or the pre-show entertainment to the main theatre attraction. Commercial theatre owners used short plays as a means to entertain the audience as it waited for latecomers to be seated.

Moreover, by the late nineteenth century repertory or non-commercial theatres — places that encouraged experimental forms in drama and poetry — grew rapidly. By the early twentieth century, many playwrights such as Eugene O'Neill, Susan Glaspell, and George S. Kaufmann used sketches and one-act plays as an opportunity to stage their works in repertory and small community theatres. Furthermore, vaudeville theatre, consisting of variety entertainment that included music-hall sketches, songs, dances, and famous actors, developed as another popular form of entertainment in the early twentieth century. Great actors used one-act plays as vehicles to show their talents in variety theatre.

The one-act play is not just a shortened version of a full-length play, but can indeed stand up in its own right as a complete literary work. The one-act play may be defined as a single and uninterrupted short dramatic presentation. Like the short story, it has a unified structure that captures and develops a single episode in a character's life. In addition, like the short story that must have a unity of effect, the one-act play must also conform to a logical sequence in time, place, and plot. The problem is quickly exposed and resolved. The one-act play continued to be a successful and popular dramatic form throughout the twentieth century.

### Warm-Up Discussion Topics

▸1 With what sorts of things do you associate the word *trifles*, the title of the play?

▸2 If someone learns that another person did something really terrible, should the first person inform the authorities no matter what the circumstances?

**INITIAL READING** ▸ ***Reading a play involves different reading strategies than reading a novel or a short story. Plays are meant to be performed by the players and seen by the audience. Every aspect of the performance — the set, the costumes, the physical appearance of the characters, and their gestures — are as important to the meaning of the play as are the actual words spoken. Therefore, when reading a play, it is important that the reader pay careful attention to the characters' physical descriptions, their physical actions, sound effects, props such as furniture or other items seen on the set, and any other explanations or directions given by the playwright.***

As you read the following play for the first time, try to imagine the setting as well as the characters and their voices. You may wish to read the play aloud with other students to add realism and enjoyment to your experience.

1917

# TRIFLES

SUSAN GLASPELL

Scene: *The kitchen in the now abandoned farmhouse of John Wright, a gloomy kitchen, and left without having been put in order — unwashed pans under the sink, a loaf of bread outside the breadbox, a dish towel on the table — other signs of incompleted work. At the rear the outer door opens, and the Sheriff comes in, followed by the County Attorney and Hale. The Sheriff and Hale are men in middle life, the County Attorney is a young man; all are much bundled up and go at once to the stove. They are followed by the two women — the Sheriff's Wife first; she is a slight wiry woman, a thin nervous face. Mrs. Hale is larger and would ordinarily be called more comfortable looking, but she is disturbed now and looks fearfully about as she enters. The women have come in slowly and stand close together near the door.*

**COUNTY ATTORNEY** *(rubbing his hands)*. This feels good. Come up to the fire, ladies.

**MRS. PETERS** *(after taking a step forward)*. I'm not — cold.

**SHERIFF** *(unbuttoning his overcoat and stepping away from the stove as if to the beginning of official business)*. Now, Mr. Hale, before we move things about, you explain to Mr. Henderson just what you saw when you came here yesterday morning.

**COUNTY ATTORNEY.** By the way, has anything been moved? Are things just as you left them yesterday?

**SHERIFF** *(looking about)*. It's just the same. When it dropped below zero last night, I thought I'd better send Frank out this morning to make a fire for us — no use getting pneumonia with a big case on; but I told him not to touch anything except the stove — and you know Frank.

**COUNTY ATTORNEY.** Somebody should have been left here yesterday.

**SHERIFF.** Oh — yesterday. When I had to send Frank to Morris Center for that man who went crazy — I want you to know I had my hands full yesterday. I knew you could get back from Omaha by today, and as long as I went over everything here myself —

**COUNTY ATTORNEY.** Well, Mr. Hale, tell just what happened when you came here yesterday morning.

**HALE.** Harry and I had started to town with a load of potatoes. We came along the road from my place; and as I got here, I said, "I'm going to see if I can't get John Wright to go in with me on a party telephone." *[People in the country had to share a telephone line; in other words, they could listen to the conversations of all the people sharing the line]*. I spoke to Wright about it once before, and he put me off, saying folks talked too much anyway, and all he asked was peace and quiet — I guess you know about how much he talked himself; but I thought maybe if I went to the house and talked about it before his wife, though I said to Harry that I didn't know as what his wife wanted made much difference to John —

**COUNTY ATTORNEY.** Let's talk about that later, Mr. Hale. I do want to talk about that, but tell now just what happened when you got to the house.

**HALE.** I didn't hear or see anything; I knocked at the door, and still it was all quiet inside. I knew they must be up, it was past eight o'clock. So I knocked again, and I thought I heard somebody say, "Come in." I wasn't sure, I'm not sure yet, but I opened the door — this door *(indicating the door by which the two women are still standing)*, and there in that rocker — *(pointing to it)* sat Mrs. Wright. *(They all look at the rocker.)*

**COUNTY ATTORNEY.** What — was she doing?

**HALE.** She was rockin' back and forth. She had her apron in her hand and was kind of — pleating it.

**COUNTY ATTORNEY.** And how did she — look?

**HALE.** Well, she looked queer.

**COUNTY ATTORNEY.** How do you mean — queer?

**HALE.** Well, as if she didn't know what she was going to do next. And kind of done up.

**COUNTY ATTORNEY.** How did she seem to feel about your coming?

**HALE.** Why, I don't think she minded — one way or other. She didn't pay much attention. I said, "How do, Mrs. Wright, it's cold, ain't it?" And she said, "Is it?" — and went on kind of pleating at her apron. Well, I was surprised; she didn't ask me to come up to the stove, or to set down, but just sat there, not even looking at me, so I said, "I want to see John." And then she — laughed. I guess you would call it a laugh. I thought of Harry and the team outside, so I said a little sharp: "Can't I see John?" "No," she says, kind o' dull like. "Ain't he home?" says I. "Yes," says she, "he's home." "Then why can't I see him?" I asked her, out of patience. "'Cause he's dead," says she. *"Dead?"* says I. She just nodded her head, not getting a bit excited, but rockin' back and forth. "Why — where is he?" says I, not knowing what to say. She just pointed upstairs — like that *(himself pointing to the room above)*. I got up, with the idea of going up there. I talked from there to here — then I says, "Why, what did he die of?" "He died of a rope around his neck," says she, and just went on pleatin' at her apron. Well, I went out and called Harry. I thought I might — need help. We went upstairs, and there he was lying' —

**COUNTY ATTORNEY.** I think I'd rather have you go into that upstairs, where you can point it all out. Just go on now with the rest of the story.

**HALE.** Well, my first thought was to get that rope off. I looked... *(Stops, his face twitches.)*... but Harry, he went up to him, and he said, "No, he's dead all right, and we'd better not touch anything." So we went back downstairs. She was still sitting that same way. "Has anybody been notified?" I asked." "No," says she, unconcerned. "Who did this, Mrs. Wright?" said Harry. He said it business-like — and she stopped pleatin' of her apron. "I don't know," she says. "You don't *know?*" says Harry. "No," says she, "Weren't you sleepin' in the bed with him?" says Harry. "Yes," says she, "but I was on the inside." "Somebody slipped a rope round his neck and strangled him, and you didn't wake up?" says Harry. "I didn't wake up," she said after him. We must 'a looked as if we didn't see how that could be, for after a minute she said, "I sleep sound." Harry was going to ask her more questions, but I said maybe we ought to let her tell her story first to the coroner, or the sheriff, so Harry went fast as he could to Rivers' place, where there's a telephone.

**COUNTY ATTORNEY.** And what did Mrs. Wright do when she knew that you had gone for the coroner.

**HALE.** She moved from that chair to this over here... *(pointing to a small chair in the corner)*... and just sat there with her hand held together and looking down. I got a feeling that I ought to make some conversation, so I said I had come in to see if John wanted to put in a telephone, and at that she started to laugh, and then she stopped and looked at me — scared. *(The County Attorney, who has had his notebook out, makes a note.)* I dunno, maybe it wasn't scared. I wouldn't like to say it was. Soon Harry got back, and then Dr. Lloyd came, and you, Mr. Peters, and so I guess that's all I know that you don't.

**COUNTY ATTORNEY.** *(looking around).*

I guess we'll go upstairs first — and then out to the barn and around there. *(To the Sheriff).* You're convinced that there was nothing important here — nothing that would point to any motive?

**SHERIFF.** Nothing here but kitchen things.

*(The County Attorney, after again looking around the kitchen, opens the door of a cupboard closet. He gets up on a chair and looks on a shelf. Pulls his hand away, sticky.)*

**COUNTY ATTORNEY.** Here's a nice mess. *(The women draw nearer.)*

**MRS. PETERS** *(to the other woman).* Oh, her fruit; it did freeze. *(To the Lawyer).* She worried about that when it turned so cold. She said the fire'd go out and her jars would break.

**SHERIFF.** Well, can you beat the women! Held for murder and worryin' about her preserves.

**COUNTY ATTORNEY.** I guess before we're through she may have something more serious than preserves to worry about.

**HALE.** Well, women are used to worrying over trifles. *(The two women move a little closer together.)*

**COUNTY ATTORNEY** *(with the gallantry of a young politician).* And yet, for all their worries, what would we do without the ladies? *(The women do not unbend. He goes to the sink, takes dipperful of water form the pail and, pouring it into a basin, washes his hands. Starts to wipe them on the roller towel, turns it for a cleaner place.)* Dirty towels! *(Kicks his foot against the pans under the sink.)* Not much of a housekeeper, would you say, ladies?

**MRS. HALE** *(stiffly).* There's a great deal of work to be done on a farm.

**COUNTY ATTORNEY.** To be sure. And yet... *(with a little bow to her)* ...I know there are some Dickson county farmhouses which do not have such roller towels. *(He gives it a pull to expose its full length again.)*

**MRS. HALE.** Those towels get dirty awful quick. Men's hands aren't always as clean as they might be.

**COUNTY ATTORNEY.** Ah, loyal to your sex, I see. But you and Mrs. Wright were neighbors. I suppose you were friends, too.

**MRS. HALE** *(shaking her head).* I've not seen much of her of late years. I've not been in this house — it's more than a year.

**COUNTY ATTORNEY.** And why was that? You didn't like her?

**MRS. HALE.** I liked her all well enough. Farmers' wives have their hands full, Mr. Henderson. And then —

**COUNTY ATTORNEY.** Yes — ?

**MRS. HALE** *(looking about)*. It never seemed a very cheerful place.

**COUNTY ATTORNEY.** No — it's not cheerful. I shouldn't say she had the homemaking instinct.

**MRS. HALE.** Well, I don't know as Wright had, either.

**COUNTY ATTORNEY.** You mean that they didn't get on very well?

**MRS. HALE.** No, I don't mean anything. But I don't think a place'd be any cheerfuller for John Wright's being in it.

**COUNTY ATTORNEY.** I'd like to talk more of that a little later. I want to get the lay of things upstairs now. *(He goes to the left, where three steps lead to a stair door.)*

**SHERIFF.** I suppose anything Mrs. Peters does'll be all right. She was to take in some clothes for her, you know, and a few little things. We left in such a hurry yesterday.

**COUNTY ATTORNEY.** Yes, but I would like to see what you take, Mrs. Peters, and keep an eye out for anything that might be of use to us.

**MRS. PETERS.** Yes, Mr. Henderson. *(The women listen to the men's steps on the stairs, then look about the kitchen.)*

**MRS. HALE.** I'd hate to have men coming into my kitchen, snooping around and criticizing. *(She arranges the pans under sink which the Lawyer had shoved out of place.)*

**MRS. PETERS.** Of course it's no more than their duty.

**MRS. HALE.** Duty's all right, but I guess that deputy sheriff that came out to make the fire might have got a little of this on. *(Gives the roller towel a pull.)* Wish I'd thought of that sooner. Seems mean to talk about her for not having things slicked up when she had to come away in such a hurry.

**MRS. PETERS** *(who has gone to a small table in the left rear corner of the room, and lifted one end of a towel that covers a pan)*. She had bread set. *(Stands still.)*

**MRS. HALE** *(eyes fixed on a loaf of bread beside the breadbox, which is on a low shelf at the other side of the room. Moves slowly toward it)*. She was going to put this in there. *(Picks up loaf, then abruptly drops it. In a manner of returning to familiar things.)* It's a shame about her fruit. I wonder if it's all gone. *(Gets up on the chair and looks.)* I think there's some here that's all right, Mrs. Peters. Yes — here; *(Holding it toward the window.)* this is cherries, too. *(Looking again.)* I declare I believe that's the only one. *(Gets down, bottle in her hand. Goes to the sink and wipes it off on the outside.)* She'll feel awful bad after all her hard work in the hot weather. I remember the afternoon I put up my cherries last summer. *(She puts the bottle on the big kitchen table, center of the room, front table. With a sigh, is about to sit down in the rocking chair. Before she is seated realizes what chair it is; with a slow look at it, steps back. The chair, which she has touched, rocks back and forth.)*

**MRS. PETERS.** Well, I must get those things from the front room closet. *(She goes to the door at the right, but after looking into the other room, steps back.)* You coming with me, Mrs. Hale? You could help me carry them. *(They go into the other room; reappear, Mrs. Peters carrying a dress and skirt, Mrs. Hale following with a pair of shoes.)*

**MRS. PETERS.** My, it's cold in there. *(She puts the cloth on the big table, and hurries to the stove.)*

**MRS. HALE** *(examining the skirt)*. Wright was close. I think maybe that's why she kept so much to herself. She didn't even belong to the Ladies' Aid. I suppose she felt she couldn't do her part, and then you don't enjoy things when you feel shabby. She used to wear pretty clothes and be lively, when she was Minnie Foster, one of the town girls singing in the choir. But that — oh, that was thirty years ago. This all you was to take?

**MRS. PETERS.** She said she wanted an apron. Funny thing to want, for there isn't much to get you dirty in jail, goodness knows. But I suppose just to make her feel more natural. She said they was in the top drawer in this cupboard. Yes, here. And then her little shawl that always hung behind the door. *(Opens stair door and looks.)* Yes, here it is. *(Quickly shuts door leading upstairs.)*

**MRS. HALE** *(abruptly moving toward her)*. Mrs. Peters?

**MRS. PETERS.** Do you think she did it?

**MRS. PETERS** *(in a frightened voice)*. Oh, I don't know.

**MRS. HALE.** Well, I don't think she did. Asking for an apron and her little shawl. Worrying about her fruit.

**MRS. PETERS** *(starts to speak, glances up, where footsteps are heard in the room above. In a low voice)*. Mr. Peters says it looks bad for her. Mr. Henderson is awful sarcastic in speech, and he'll make fun of her sayin' she didn't wake up.

**MRS. HALE.** Well, I guess John Wright didn't wake when they was slipping that rope under his neck.

**MRS. PETERS.** No, it's strange. It must have been done awful crafty and still. They say it was such a — funny way to kill a man, rigging it all up like that.

**MRS. HALE.** That's just what Mr. Hale said. There was a gun in the house. He says that's what he can't understand.

**MRS. PETERS.** Mr. Henderson said coming out that what was needed for the case was a motive; something to show anger or — sudden feeling.

**MRS. HALE** *(who is standing by the table)*. Well, I don't see any signs of anger around here. *(She puts her hand on the dish towel which lies on the table, stands looking down at the table, one half of which is clean, the other half messy.)* It's wiped here. *(Makes a move as if to finish work, then turns and looks at loaf of bread outside the breadbox. Drops towel. In that voice of coming back to familiar things.)* Wonder how they are finding things upstairs? I hope she had it a little more red-up up there. You know, it seems kind of sneaking. Locking her up in town and then coming out here and trying to get her own house to turn against her!

**MRS. PETERS.** But, Mrs. Hale, the law is the law.

**MRS. HALE.** I s'pose 'tis. *(Unbuttoning her coat.)* Better loosen up your things, Mrs. Peters. You won't feel them when you go out. *(Mrs. Peters takes off her fur tippet, goes to hang it on hook at the back of room, stands looking at the under part of the small corner table.)*

**MRS. PETERS.** She was piecing a quilt. *(She brings the large sewing basket, and they look at the bright pieces.)*

**MRS. HALE.** It's log cabin pattern. Pretty, isn't it? I wonder if she was goin' to quilt or just knot it? *(Footsteps have been heard coming down the stairs. The Sheriff enters, followed by Hale and the County Attorney.)*

**SHERIFF.** They wonder if she was going to quilt it or just knot it. *(The men laugh, the women look abashed.)*

**COUNTY ATTORNEY** *(rubbing his hands over the stove)*. Frank's fire didn't do much up there, did it? Well, let's go out to the barn and get that cleared up. *(The men go outside.)*

**MRS. HALE** *(resentfully)*. I don't know as there's anything so strange, our takin' up our time with little things while we're waiting for them to get the evidence. *(She sits down at the big table, smoothing out a block with decision.)* I don't see as it's anything to laugh about.

**MRS. PETERS** *(apologetically)*. Of course they've got awful important things on their minds. *(Pulls up a chair and joins Mrs. Hale at the table.)*

**MRS. HALE** *(examining another block)*. Mrs. Peters, look at this one. Here, this is the one she was working on, and look at the sewing! All the rest of it has been so nice and even. And look at this! It's all over the place! Why, it looks as if she didn't know what she was about! *(After she has said this, they look at each other, then start to glance back at the door. After an instant Mrs. Hale has pulled at a knot and ripped the sewing.)*

**MRS. PETERS.** Oh, what are you doing, Mrs. Hale?

**MRS. HALE** *(mildly)*. Just pulling out a stitch or two that's not sewed very good. *(Threading a needle)*. Bad sewing always made me fidgety.

**MRS. PETERS** *(nervously)*. I don't think we ought to touch things.

**MRS. HALE.** I'll just finish up this end. *(Suddenly stopping and leaning forward.)* Mrs. Peters?

**MRS. PETERS.** Yes, Mrs. Hale?

**MRS. HALE.** What do you suppose she was so nervous about?

**MRS. PETERS.** Oh — I don't know. I don't know as she was nervous. I sometimes sew awful queer when I'm just tired. *(Mrs. Hale starts to say something, looks at Mrs. Peters, then goes on sewing.)* Well, I must get these things wrapped up. They may be through sooner than we think. *(Putting apron and other things together.)* I wonder where I can find a piece of paper, and string.

**MRS. HALE.** In that cupboard, maybe.

**MRS. PETERS** *(looking in cupboard)*. Why, here's a birdcage. *(Holds it up.)* Did she have a bird, Mrs. Hale?

**MRS. HALE.** Why, I don't know whether she did or not — I've not been here for so long. There was a man around last year selling canaries cheap, but I don't know as she took one; maybe she did. She used to sing real pretty herself.

**MRS. PETERS** *(glancing around)*. Seems funny to think of a bird here. But she must have had one, or why should she have a cage? I wonder what happened to it?

**MRS. HALE.** I s'pose maybe the cat got it.

**MRS. PETERS.** No, she didn't have a cat. She's got that feeling some people have about cats — being afraid of them. My cat got in her room, and she was real upset and asked me to take it out.

**MRS. HALE.** My sister Bessie was like that. Queer, ain't it?

**MRS. PETERS** *(examining the cage)*. Why, look at this door. It's broke. One hinge is pulled apart.

**MRS. HALE** *(looking, too)*. Looks as if someone must have been rough with it.

**MRS. PETERS.** Why, yes. *(She brings the cage forward and puts it on the table.)*

**MRS. HALE.** I wish if they're going to find any evidence they'd be about it. I don't like this place.

**MRS. PETERS.** But I'm awful glad you came with me, Mrs. Hale. It would be lonesome of me sitting here alone.

**MRS. HALE.** It would, wouldn't it? *(Dropping her sewing)*. But I tell you what I do wish, Mrs. Peters. I wish I had come over sometimes she was here. I — *(Looking around the room.)* — wish I had.

**MRS. PETERS.** But of course you were awful busy, Mrs. Hale — your house and your children.

**MRS. HALE.** I could've come. I stayed away because it weren't cheerful — and that's why I ought to have come. I — I've never liked this place. Maybe because it's down in a hollow, and you don't see the road. I dunno what it is, but it's a lonesome place and always was. I wish I had come over to see Minnie Foster sometimes. I can see now — *(Shakes her head.)*

**MRS. PETERS.** Well, you mustn't reproach yourself, Mrs. Hale. Somehow we just don't see how it is with other folks until — something comes up.

**MRS. HALE.** Not having children makes less work — but it makes a quiet house, and Wright out to work all day, and no company when he did come in. Did you know John Wright, Mrs. Peters?

**MRS. PETERS.** Not to know him; I've seen him in town. They say he was a good man.

**MRS. HALE.** Yes — good; he didn't drink, and kept his word as well as most, I guess, and paid his debts. But he was a hard man, Mrs. Peters. Just to pass the time of day with him. *(Shivers.)* Like a raw wind that gets to the bone. *(Pauses, her eye falling on the cage.)* I should think she would 'a wanted a bird. But what do you suppose went with it?

**MRS. PETERS.** I don't know, unless it got sick and died. *(She reaches over and swings the broken door, swings it again; both women watch it.)*

**MRS. HALE.** She — come to think of it, she was kind of like a bird herself — real sweet and pretty, but kind of timid and — fluttery. How — she — did — change. *(Silence; then as if struck by a happy thought and relieved to get back to everyday things.)* Tell you what, Mrs. Peters, why don't you take the quilt in with you? It might take up her mind.

**MRS. PETERS.** Why, I think that's a real nice idea, Mrs. Hale. There couldn't possibly be any objection to it, could there? Now, just what would I take? I wonder if her patches are in here — and her things. *(They look in the sewing basket.)*

**MRS. HALE.** Here's some red. I expect this has got sewing things in it *(Brings out a fancy box.)* What a pretty box. Looks like something somebody would give you. Maybe her scissors are in here. *(Opens box. Suddenly puts her hand to her nose.)* Why — *(Mrs. Peters bend nearer, then turns her face away.)* There's something wrapped up in this piece of silk.

**MRS. PETERS.** Why, this isn't her scissors.

**MRS. HALE** *(lifting the silk)*. Oh, Mrs. Peters — it's — *(Mrs. Peters bend closer.)*

**MRS. PETERS.** It's the bird.

**MRS. HALE** *(jumping up)*. But, Mrs. Peters — look at it. Its neck! Look at its neck! It's all — other side to.

**MRS. PETERS.** Somebody — wrung — its neck.

*(Their eyes meet. A look of growing comprehension of horror. Steps are heard outside. Mrs. Hale slips box under quilt pieces, and sinks into her chair. Enter Sheriff and County Attorney. Mrs. Peters rises.)*

**COUNTY ATTORNEY** *(as one turning from serious thing to little pleasantries)*. Well, ladies, have you decided whether she was going to quilt it or knot it?

**MRS. PETERS.** We think she was going to — knot it.

**COUNTY ATTORNEY.** Well, that's interesting, I'm sure. *(Seeing the birdcage.)* Has the bird flown?

**MRS. HALE** *(putting more quilt pieces over the box)*. We think the — cat got it.

**COUNTY ATTORNEY** *(preoccupied)*. Is there a cat? *(Mrs. Hale glances in a quick covert way at Mrs. Peters.)*

**MRS. PETERS.** Well, not now. They're superstitious, you know. They leave.

**COUNTY ATTORNEY** *(to Sheriff Peters, continuing an interrupted conversation)*. No sign at all of anyone having come from the outside. Their own rope. Now let's go up again and go over it piece by piece. *(They start upstairs.)* It would have to have been someone who knew just the —

*(Mrs. Peters sits down. The two women sit there not looking at one another, but as if peering into something and at the same time holding back. When they talk now, it is the manner of feeling their way over strange ground, as if afraid of what they are saying, but as if they cannot help saying it.)*

**MRS. HALE.** She liked the bird. She was going to bury it in that pretty box.

**MRS. PETERS** *(in a whisper)*. When I was a girl — my kitten — there was a boy took a hatchet, and before my eyes — and before I could get there — *(Covers her face an instant.)* If they hadn't held me back, I would have — *(Catches herself, looks upstairs, where steps are heard, falters weakly.)* — hurt him.

**MRS. HALE** *(with a slow look around her)*. I wonder how it would seem never to have had any children around. *(Pause.)* No, Wright wouldn't like the bird — a thing that sang. She used to sing. He killed that, too.

**MRS. PETERS** *(moving uneasily)*. We don't know who killed the bird.

**MRS. HALE.** I knew John Wright.

**MRS. PETERS.** It was an awful thing was done in this house that night, Mrs. Hale. Killing a man while he slept, slipping a rope around his neck that choked the life out of him.

**MRS. HALE.** His neck. Choked the life out of him.

*(Her hand goes out and rests on the birdcage.)*

**MRS. PETERS** *(with a rising voice)*. We don't know who killed him. We don't know.

**MRS. HALE** *(her own feeling not interrupted)*. If there'd been years and years of nothing, then a bird to sing to you, it would be awful — still, after the bird was still.

**MRS. PETERS** *(something within her speaking)*. I know what stillness is. When we homesteaded in Dakota, and my first baby died — after he was two years old, and me with no other then —

**MRS. HALE** *(moving)*. How soon do you suppose they'll be through, looking for evidence?

**MRS. PETERS.** I know what stillness is. *(Pulling herself back)*. The law has got to punish crime, Mrs. Hale.

**MRS. HALE** *(not as if answering that)*. I wish you'd seen Minnie Foster when she wore a white dress with blue ribbons and stood up there in the choir and sang. *(A look around the room)*. Oh, I wish I'd come over here once in a while! That was a crime! That was a crime! Who's going to punish that?

**MRS. PETERS** *(looking upstairs)*. We mustn't — take on.

**MRS. HALE.** I might have known she needed help! I know how things can be — for women. I tell you, it's queer, Mrs. Peters. We live close together and we live far apart. We all go through the same things — it's all just a different kind of the same thing. *(Brushes her eyes, noticing the bottle of fruit, reaches out for it.)* If I was you, I wouldn't tell her her fruit was gone. Tell her it ain't. Tell her it's all right. Take this in to prove it to her. She — she may never know whether it was broke or not.

**MRS. PETERS** *(takes the bottle, looks about for something to wrap it in; takes petticoat from the clothes brought from the other room, very nervously begins winding this around the bottle. In a false voice)*. My, it's a good thing the men couldn't hear us. Wouldn't they just laugh! Getting all stirred up over a little thing like a — dead canary. As if that could have anything to do with — with — wouldn't they laugh! *(The men are heard coming downstairs.)*

**MRS. HALE** *(under her breath)*. Maybe they would — maybe they wouldn't.

**COUNTY ATTORNEY.** No, Peters, it's all perfectly clear except a reason for doing it. But you know juries when it comes to women. If there was some definite thing. Something to show — something to make a story about — a thing that would connect up with this strange way of doing it.

*(The women's eyes meet for an instant. Enter Hale from outer door.)*

**HALE.** Well, I've got the team around. Pretty cold out there.

**COUNTY ATTORNEY.** I'm going to stay here awhile by myself *(to the Sheriff)*. You can send Frank out for me, can't you? I want to go over everything. I'm not satisfied that we can't do better.

**SHERIFF.** Do you want to see what Mrs. Peters is going to take in? *(The Lawyer goes to the table, picks up the apron, laughs.)*

**COUNTY ATTORNEY.** Oh I guess they're not very dangerous things the ladies have picked up. *(Moves a few things about, disturbing the quilt pieces which cover the box. Steps back.)* No, Mrs. Peters doesn't need supervising. For that matter, a sheriff's wife is married to the law. Ever think of it that way, Mrs. Peters?

**MRS. PETERS.** Not — just that way.

**SHERIFF** *(chuckling)*. Married to the law. *(Moves toward the other room.)* I just want you to come in here a minute, George. We ought to take a look at these windows.

**COUNTY ATTORNEY** *(scoffingly)*. Oh, windows!

**SHERIFF.** We'll be right out, Mr. Hale.

*(Hale goes outside. The Sheriff follows the County Attorney into the other room. Then Mrs. Hale rises, hands tight together, looking intensely at Mrs. Peters, whose eyes take a slow turn, finally meeting Mrs. Hale's. A moment Mrs. Hale holds her, then her own eyes point the way to where the box is concealed. Suddenly Mrs. Peters throws back quilt pieces and tries to put the box in the bag she is wearing. It is too big. She opens box, starts to take the bird out, cannot touch it, goes to pieces, stands there helpless. Sound of a knob turning in the other room. Mrs. Hale snatches the box and puts it in the pocket of her big coat. Enter County Attorney and Sheriff.)*

**COUNTY ATTORNEY** *(facetiously)*. Well, Henry, at least we found out that she was not going to quilt it. She was going to — what is it you call it, ladies!

**MRS. HALE** *(her hand against her pocket)*. We call it — knot it, Mr. Henderson.

**(CURTAIN)**

## Reader's Response

▸1 Discuss your opinion about the ending of the play. Did the women do the right thing?

▸2 In your opinion, could the events in this play — which was written in 1916 — happen in contemporary society? Explain your answer.

## Close Reading

▸1 Reread the following lines. They are the description of the opening scene. Underline all the descriptive adjectives, nouns, and verbs that create the mood of the setting. Then in your own words describe the setting (where and when the story takes place) and the mood (atmosphere or ambiance) of the scene.

Scene: The kitchen in the now abandoned farmhouse of John Wright, a gloomy kitchen, and left without having been put in order — unwashed pans under the sink, a loaf of bread outside the breadbox, a dish towel on the table — other signs of incompleted work. At the rear the outer door opens, and the Sheriff comes in, followed by the County Attorney and Hale. The Sheriff and Hale are men in middle life, the County Attorney is a young man; all are much bundled up and go at once to the stove. They are followed by the two women — the Sheriff's Wife first; she is a slight wiry woman, a thin nervous face. Mrs. Hale is larger and would ordinarily be called more comfortable looking, but she is disturbed now and looks fearfully about as she enters. The women have come in slowly and stand close together near the door.

▸2 List all the major characters and tell their relationship to each other.

| Characters | Relationship to Each Other |
|---|---|
| | |
| | |
| | |
| | |
| | |

▸3 What is significant about the rocking chair?

▸4 Why did Mr. Hale initially go to the farmhouse?

▸5 What do we understand to be Mr. Hale's opinions of John and Minnie Wright as he is talking to the Sheriff?

▸6 What was Mrs. Wright's emotional state when Mr. Hale found her? State directly Mrs. Wright's words and gestures to prove your point.

▸7 What had happened to Mr. Wright?

▸8 Describe Mrs. Hale and Mrs. Peters' relationship with Mrs. Wright.

▸9 How had Mrs. Wright's personality and lifestyle changed since her marriage?

▸10 Describe the relationship between Mrs. Hale and Mrs. Peters. Does it change throughout the play?

## WRITER'S CRAFT

### *Symbolism*

▸1 What is suggestive about Mrs. Wright's messy kitchen?

▸2 John Wright does not want a telephone. What does this indicate about Wright?

▸3 The quilt is a blanket that is made up of small pieces of cloth sewn together to create a design. Explain how the quilt symbolises the discovery of the motive by Mrs. Hale and Mrs. Peters.

▸4 Many symbols reveal the nature of the Wrights' personalities and that of their marriage. Write an interpretation for each symbol below.

**a)** Minnie Wright's girlhood clothes and her present clothes

**b)** the dead canary

**c)** the deterioration in the sewing of the quilt

▸5 Find two other symbols that the author uses to develop characterisation of the other characters in the play.

**a)**

**b)**

▸6 What is the significance of the title of the play?

## Characterisation: Male/Female Roles

▸1 What is the purpose of the male characters at the farmhouse?

▸2 Why are the female characters at the farmhouse?

▸3 Why does Mr. Hale say, "Well, women are used to worrying over trifles."

▸4 Cite three examples from the play that show the men's attitude of superiority over the women.

▸5 How do the women react to the men's condescending attitude? Give two examples.

Verbal response

Physical response

▸6 What is ironic about Mrs. Hale's words, "We call it — knot it, Mr. Henderson," at the end of the play?

## Dramatic Structure

▸1 What information does the exposition of the play reveal?

▸2 What part of the play is the rising action? What information does it provide?

▸3 What is the climax of the play?

▸4 Give three examples of how the characters' reactions or their descriptions create moments of tension in the play.

▸5 In your opinion, what is the theme of the play?

## Paragraph Practice

▸1 Write a short paragraph on John Wright's personality.

▸2 Write a paragraph on the ironic symbolism of Mrs. Wright's name.

## WRAP-UP DISCUSSION OR WRITING ACTIVITIES

- ▸1 Write a literary essay discussing how this play exposes male-female stereotypes and gender biases.
- ▸2 Write a literary essay discussing the effectiveness of the stage directions on keeping the tension throughout the play.
- ▸3 Explain how the character of Minnie Wright is developed throughout the play.
- ▸4 Discuss the significance of symbolism and imagery in the play.
- ▸5 Discuss the dramatic structure of the play.
- ▸6 Research further background about the author and write a literary essay using the biographical approach.
- ▸7 Examine the moral dilemma of this play and discuss its impact on the theme.
- ▸8 Discuss the pertinence of the play's title.
- ▸9 Read another play by Glaspell and compare it to *Trifles*.
- ▸10 Write a literary essay using a feminist perspective.

# References

### INTERNET

**BIOGRAPHICAL AND BACKGROUND INFORMATION ON SUSAN GLASPELL (*TRIFLES*)**

http://itech.fgcu.edu/faculty/wohlpart/alra/glaspell.htm
http://www.nagasaki-gaigo.ac.jp/ishikawa/amlit/g/glaspell20.htm
http://www.spartacus.schoolnet.co.uk/Jglaspell.htm
http://www.vcu.edu/engweb/eng384/trifles.htm
http://www.scribblingwomen.org/sbbio.html

**LINKS**

http://www.bedfordstmartins.com/litlinks/drama/glaspell.htm

UNIT 4.2

# THE WORLD OF MARY HUNTER

## CHAPTER CONTENTS

- **LISTENING:** *The World of Mary Hunter* by Martin Kinch
- **READING:** biographical information; Trends of the Times: Radio Plays; characteristics of radio drama
- **LITERARY ELEMENTS:** sound devices; dramatic structure; narrative structure; imagery
- **WRITING:** paragraph practice; literary essay; critical review

In this chapter, you will listen to an engaging, half-hour-long radio drama that was part of a series broadcast in the mid-1990s.

## ABOUT THE AUTHOR

MARTIN KINCH was born in England in 1943. He has had a long and multifaceted career connected with the theatre, first in England, then in Canada, as director, producer, and author. He is a two-time Chalmers Award-winning author for his plays *Me?* and *April 29, 1975*. He also worked at the CBC (Canadian Broadcasting Corporation) as a drama producer and director in the 1980s. In 1994, Kinch moved to Vancouver where he became a freelance writer and director. During this period, he wrote the "Becker" series (of which *The World of Mary Hunter* is episode 2) for CBC radio.

He presently divides his time between Vancouver where he sits on the board of Playwrights Theatre Centre, and Grenfell College at Memorial University of Newfoundland where he regularly teaches and directs. He continues to write for the theatre.

## TRENDS OF THE TIMES: RADIO PLAYS

Radio plays have been very popular with English-speaking listeners since the first production, featuring scenes from Shakespeare, was broadcast by the British Broadcasting Company (BBC) on February 16, 1923. With a crystal set and headphones, many early listeners had to struggle to hear over the crackling noises of poor reception. At first, popular stage plays such as J.M. Synge's *The Playboy of the Western World* (1907) and Maeterlinck's *The Blue Bird* (1908) were adapted for radio performances. It wasn't long, however, before dramatists on both sides of the Atlantic began to write plays exclusively for the new medium. The very first, *Danger* by Richard Hughes, was broadcast by the BBC on January 14, 1924.

About a decade later in the United States, Orson Welles and the Mercury Theater of the Air were busy producing many radio plays that reached high levels of artistic achievement. Their *War of the Worlds*, perhaps the most well-known radio play, was broadcast in the United States on October 30, 1938. Orson Welles' dramatisation of the short story by H.G. Wells about an invasion of Martians on earth created major havoc. Welles transformed the original story into a radio play with a setting in New Jersey, in the eastern United States. His production simulated a music program that was interrupted by interviews and news bulletins. Six million listeners had tuned into the program on October 30, but many did not hear the opening announcement about the production being just a play. Audiences thought the newscasts were real. Over one million people panicked as they tried, in various ways, to escape destruction at the hands of the Martians. Although many shocked people later called for stricter regulations for broadcasting, none ever materialised.

Radio drama was also very popular throughout the thirties, forties, and fifties in Great Britain and Canada. *The Archers*, a British soap about country folk which began on January 1, 1951 and still continues today, is the longest-playing radio drama. Many well-known writers, such as Dylan Thomas, Samuel Becket, Hal Pinter, Tom Stoppard, Carryl Churchill, Arthur Miller, David Mamet, and Archibald MacLeish to name but a few — as well as others such as Giles Cooper (sixty radio plays) and Rhys Adrian (thirty-two plays) — have written excellent plays for radio. The genre is still widely ignored in academic circles.

Despite the advent of television in the late forties and its almost instant popularity, many people continue to enjoy listening to radio drama. At the turn of the twenty-first century, the BBC was producing more than twenty-two hours weekly, while European producers were broadcasting well over a hundred hours of radio drama that reached over seventy-five million listeners.

The radio play you will listen to in this chapter was produced by the Canadian Broadcasting Company in 1994, a public corporation that continues weekly broadcasting of the excellent radio plays for which it has been renowned for many decades.

### Warm-Up Discussion Topics

▸1 People listen to the radio for different reasons. Some listen to the news; others listen to talk shows and informative programs; and still others turn it on as background music. What is your principal reason for listening to the radio? About how many hours do you listen per week?

▸2 Media guru Marshall McCluhan divided media into two categories: hot and cold. He classified TV as a cool medium (due to more sensory involvement of the user — through vision and hearing) and radio as a hot medium (less sensory involvement of the user — only hearing is involved). Do you agree with his assessment? Why or why not?

**INITIAL LISTENING ▸ You are about to listen to a play that is an example of the detective fiction genre. In detective fiction or a "whodunit" (i.e., "Who committed the crime?"), there is always a puzzle to be solved. The protagonist carefully tries to piece together the mystery but is often faced with *red herrings* or clues that lead in the wrong direction or to a dead end.**

**As you listen to the play for the first time, settle into a comfortable chair and enjoy the story. See if you can figure out who committed the murder and what motivated the crime as the tale unravels. In a real-life situation, you would likely hear a radio play only once and then it would be gone forever. However, for the purposes of literary analysis, we will ask you to listen to it a second time.**

**Before you get started, here are two pieces of background information. Banff is a very popular resort town and artistic center in the picturesque Canadian Rocky Mountains. Desdemona is the wife of Othello in the Shakespearean tragedy of the same name. Although devoted to him and innocent, she is murdered by her husband in a fit of jealousy.**

**Now listen to the play on the audio CD accompanying the textbook.**

# The World of Mary Hunter

### Listener's Response

▸1 Which character did you enjoy the most? Why?

▸2 Did you enjoy this play? What were its strengths? What were its weaknesses?

▸3 In one sentence, summarise the plot.

**CLOSE LISTENING ▸ Before listening to the play a second time, read the following section about the characteristics of radio drama. Then listen closely, focusing carefully on the aesthetic and literary qualities of the play and its production.**

### *Characteristics of Radio Drama*

Radio plays require attentive listening by the audience as there are no visual clues to help listeners follow the story line. Like a stage performance or a music concert, once the play starts, it continues uninterrupted to the end. Then it is over, leaving the audience with only memories and impressions. However, unlike with a stage performance, the listener must imagine all the visual aspects, such as the characters' actions and appearances, and the various scenes and props.

To help listeners follow the action and imagine the characters and setting, many aural clues are given. These clues are presented hierarchically in a fictional soundscape; in other words, the most important ones are louder and seem closer, and the less important ones are quieter and seem farther away. The dialogue, which carries the story, is the most important aural element of the play, so it is usually in the foreground (i.e., it is fairly loud). Dialogue can be interrupted by narration that serves to change the time frame and to change the scene. Each character usually has a distinct voice (pitch, intensity), vocabulary, and accent so that the audience associates it immediately with a particular person. Moreover, other vocal sounds — sighs, laughter, shouts, breaths, and so on — and hesitations also serve to heighten the drama and characterisation.

Then there are a series of sound effects and music that either add to the context of the action in the foreground or serve as background atmosphere. Sound effects include engines revving, tires squealing, rain falling, cutlery rattling, dance music playing, voices talking, gun shots reverberating, and so on. The sounds appear closer or farther away, and none are redundant. In other words, each sound must have significance. Moreover, the sounds are discrete and irregular in order to add rhythm, "colour," and variety. Since the mid-1970s, stereo production has added another dimension to sound.

Sometimes a certain type of music will indicate a change in scene; this is called signposting. Signposting is usually accompanied by dialogue, too, to make sure that the reader follows the action. Many radio dramas consist of a sequence of rapid scenes that build to a narrative climax in a structure similar to the traditional dramatic structure of a short story. By their very nature, radio plays have a very linear quality to them because of their sequencing in real time. The story unfolds to the listener who, in following the events and interactions between the characters, often connects in an emotional way to them.

Now, please complete the following exercises and questions.

▸**1** Match the character with the role.

| | |
|---|---|
| **1.** Becker | **a)** a fading movie star |
| **2.** Mary Hunter | **b)** Mary Hunter's niece |
| **3.** Hannah | **c)** Mary Hunter's former lover |
| **4.** François Martel | **d)** the hotel detective |
| **5.** D.D. King | **e)** the hotel cook |
| **6.** Robert "Bobby" Defoe | **f)** the movie producer |
| **7.** Raina Cantrel | **g)** Mary Hunter's assistant |
| **8.** Hickey | **h)** the hotel manager |

▸2 Describe the setting of the play.

▸3 Who narrates the story?

▸4 What accusation does Mary Hunter make against the hotel's chef?

▸5 Why does Mary Hunter think that D.D. King would like to get rid of her?

▸6 What was the most perfect moment of Mary's career?

▸7 Which drug did the glass of water contain?

▸8 Why does Raina consider Hanna (Mary Hunter's assistant) to be a troll?

▸9 What was used as the murder weapon?

▸10 Why was Mary Hunter murdered?

## WRITER'S CRAFT

### *Sound Devices*

▸1 What kind of "sound" is used to create atmosphere and to portray the general time frame of the drama?

▸2 List three different sound effects (not dialogue) that are used to portray specific settings for different scenes.

▸3 How do you know immediately that François is speaking in the first dialogue?

▸**4** What distinctions between the other male characters do you hear (when they speak) that help make them more identifiable?

▸**5** **a)** Which background sounds are used for portraying an important element in the character of Robert "Bobby" Defoe, the leading man?

**b)** What do they show about him and how is this important to understanding what happened between Mary and Raina?

## Dramatic Structure

▸**6** What is the purpose of Becker's opening speech?

**a)** to explain the nature of his job

**b)** to engage in a dialogue with hotel guests

**c)** to describe the setting

**d)** to introduce the major characters

▸**7** How does the use of dialogue throughout the play serve to make the story very actual for the listener? (Hint: in what time frame — present, past, or future — does the action seem to be taking place during the dialogues?)

▸**8** What purposes do the narrated sections between the dialogues serve?

**a)** They indicate changes in scene.

**b)** They are used to compress time, i.e., to summarise certain events in the story.

**c)** They serve to show how Becker is conducting his investigation and to reveal what he suspects and concludes.

**d)** They help move the action along.

**e)** They provide variety. Just dialogue, or just narration, would be less interesting.

▸**9** How does the author use a series of clues as key elements in the dramatic structure of the play?

▸**10** In what ways does the story of Desdemona (a story-within-a-story and repeated references to it) add to the dramatic structure of the play and help Becker solve the mystery?

▸**11** How does the narrator personally involve the listener at the end of the play?

▸**12** Are the plot and dramatic structure of this play classical (using exposition, complication/conflict, rising tension, climax, falling tension, dénouement or resolution) or more modern and experimental?

### *NARRATIVE STRUCTURE*

▸**13** Explain how Mary Hunter's role of Desdemona is an example of both a flashback and foreshadowing.

▸**14** Who says, "I wonder how it feels to die? Like a soft pillow descending over your face..." and what literary device are these lines an example of?

### *IMAGERY*

▸**15** In the lines below, spoken by D.D. King to Becker, what kind of figure of speech are the images of the lemon and the turkey? Explain what each image refers to.

"...*Mountain Love* is a last ditch attempt to squeeze a few more drops out of the lemon before it dries up completely. The best thing she could do for me is really get poisoned The publicity just might sell this turkey."

lemon: __________

turkey: __________

▸▸▸ ***Note how D.D. King's speech here and elsewhere is peppered with familiar language and clichés ("last ditch attempt," "squeeze... lemon," "turkey"). By contrast, Bobby Defoe speaks a very cultured, more formal language although he uses a swear word here and there. Radio dramatists manipulate the level of language (vocabulary), accent, enunciation, intonation, and pace to help distinguish characters and reveal their personalities.*** ◂◂◂

▸**16** **a)** What kind of figure of speech is used in this line spoken by François: "She nibbled the vegetables a bit, like a rabbit."

**b)** What general connotations does a rabbit have?

**c)** Why would the author use repeated images of a rabbit in connection with Mary Hunter? What does this imagery lead the listener to believe about her?

## WRAP-UP DISCUSSION OR WRITING ACTIVITIES

▸1 How is sound (music, sound effects, voices) used for signposting and for creating atmosphere in this play?

▸2 Describe how the dramatist creates a particular soundscape for this play by using a hierarchy of sounds (louder/closer and softer/farther away).

▸3 Discuss the characterisation in the play, paying particular attention to the techniques required by the medium of radio.

▸4 Discuss how dialogue and narration are used in this play. Explain the role of the narrator.

▸5 Explain how point of view in this play is related to dramatic effect and to the listener's enjoyment.

▸6 Describe the dramatic structure of the play.

▸7 Explain the importance of the setting to the dramatic structure of the play. How is the setting revealed?

▸8 After reading a newspaper review of a play, write a critical review of *The World of Mary Hunter.*

▸9 Research the characteristics of the detective story (or "whodunit") genre. Is this play a classical "whodunit"? Explain.

▸10 Dramatise a scene from one of the short stories that you have read for radio.

▸11 Write a one-act radio play.

▸12 Listen to Orson Welles' *War of the World* and write a critical review of this play.

# References

## PRINT

Benson, Eugene, ed. *The Concise Oxford Companion to Canadian Theatre.* Toronto: Oxford University Press, 1990.

Benson, Eugene and L.W. Conolly. *English-Canadian Theatre.* Toronto: Oxford University Press, 1987.

Bordman, Gerald Martin. *The Oxford Companion to American Theatre.* New York: Oxford University Press, 1992.

Brocket, Oscar G. *History of the Theatre*. Boston: Allyn & Bacon, 1968.

Brown, John Russell. *What is Theatre?: An Introduction and Exploration*. Woburn, MA: Focal Press, 1997.

Hartnoll, Phyllis, and Peter Found, eds. *The Concise Oxford Companion to the Theatre.* Oxford : Oxford University Press, 1992.

Kruger, Loren. *The National Stage: Theatre and Cultural Legitimation in England, France, and America.* Chicago: University of Chicago Press, 1992.

## INTERNET

**Biographical Information about Martin Kinch (*The World of Mary Hunter*)**
http://www.canadiantheatre.com/k/kinchm.html
http://www.nextlevel.com/ozone/martink.htm
http://www.theatrebc.org/M2000/scenedevbios.htm#MARTIN KINCH

**Detective fiction genre**
http://www.mysteryguide.com/classic-whodunit.html

**Listening to radio plays: fictional soundscapes**
http://interact.uoregon.edu/MediaLit/FC/readings/Listentoradio.html

**Samuel Beckett's radio plays: music of the absurd**
http://www.geocities.com/Paris/7127/thesisfaeces/title.html

**Understanding the radio play**
http://www.scribblingwomen.org/understanding.htm

**BBC Radio 4s — The Archers, as postmodern drama**
http://www.reflect.demon.co.uk/Linda/thesis.html

**Radio Drama Project Group**
http://www.ebu.ch/rdo/drm_pgr1.html

**Excerpts of New American Radio Drama**
http://www.somewhere.org/NAR/Work_Excerpts/Excerpts.htm

**How to write radio drama**
http://home.sprynet.com/~palermo/mtr_radi.htm

**International radio drama**
http://www.irdp.co.uk/radiodrama.htm

**Orson Welles' production of *War of the Worlds***
Script: http://web2.airmail.net/lgroebe/waroftheworlds.htm
Recording: http://www.earthstation1.com/wotw.html

**Picture of CBC sound effects studio**
http://www.radio.cbc.ca/facilities/drama.html

**Lists of links**
http://listen.to/playtime
http://www.irdp.co.uk/page8.htm

**Broadcasting — related web sites**
http://www.baycadd.com/~radio/bcast2.htm
Radio Theatre on the Web: http://www.mtn.org/~jstearns/Radiodrama.html

**Pictures and movies**
http://www.cphotels.ca/cp.asp?loc=banff/
http://www.cmhhike.com/banffspr.htm

**Pictures**
http://www.compusmart.ab.ca/mcgregor/Pictures/Banff/
http://www.banffnationalpark.com/

# Glossary of Literary Terms

**Action** — events taking place in a dramatic or narrative work

**Acts** — divisions of a play that usually last from thirty minutes to an hour

**Alliteration** — repetition of same consonant in a series of words

**Antagonist** — person who opposes the main character in a narrative or dramatic work

**Assonance** — repetition of same vowel sound in a series of words

**Atmosphere** — the emotional mood of the text

**Blank verse** — meter but no rhyme scheme

**Character** — all persons found in a dramatic or narrative work

**Climax** — the point of maximum conflict of the story

**Comparison** — looking at similarities and differences between two or more items

**Complication** — conflict in the story

**Conflict** — the opposition of different characters or forces in a dramatic or narrative work; may be either internal or external

**Connotation** — the secondary level of a meaning or association of a word

**Consonance** — repetition of consonants in a series of words

**Couplet** — two lines that rhyme

**Denotation** — the literal or dictionary meaning of a word

**Denouement** — the conclusion of the story

**Dialogue** — conversation in written form

**Dramatic structure** — the beginning, middle, and end of a dramatic or narrative work

**Essay** — short written composition on a single subject

**Exposition** — what happens at the beginning of the story

**External action** — action that happens outside the body of the characters in a narrative or dramatic work

**Fiction** — all written works that are created in the imagination of the author

**First-person narrator** — the story told through the perspective of an "I"

**First-person plural narrators** — the story told through different narrators such as the "I" or "We"

**Flashback** — an event that happened before the story takes place

**Flat character** — a minor character who does not develop throughout the narrative or dramatic work

**Foreshadowing** — clue as to what will happen in the future of the narrative or dramatic work

**Formal speech** — language of the educated, standard usage of language; more regimented rules of language

**Free verse** — poetry that does not conform to any fixed pattern (in either rhyme or rhythm)

**Hyperbole** — an exaggerated statement

**Iamb** — a poetic foot containing an unstressed followed by a stressed syllable

**Iambic pentameter** — five poetic feet consisting of alternating unstressed followed by stressed syllables

**Imagery** — descriptions that create mental images aroused by the perception of the five senses: sight, sound, smell, taste, and touch.

**Informal speech** — language which is more familiar; less regimented

**Internal action** — action that happens in the minds of the characters in a narrative or dramatic work

**Intrusive point of view** — third-person point of view which is judgmental

**Irony** — the opposite of that which is expected

**Limited point of view** — third-person point of view which narrates from the perspective of one character

**Metaphor** — describing one thing as if it were something else

**Meter** — rhythmical pattern of words in poetry based on the accented and non-accented syllables of speech.

**Mood** — the emotions of a narrative or dramatic work

**Narration** — recounting of a sequence of events in a narrative work

**Narrative structure** — the way in which the sequence of events in a narrative or dramatic work is ordered; they can be chronological or non-chronological

**Nonfiction** — prose works that are not fiction, such as biographies, historical accounts, scientific articles, etc.

**Novel** — a long work of prose fiction with many characters and plots

**Objective point of view** — third-person narration from a non-judgemental point of view

**Octave** — stanza of eight lines

**Omniscient point of view** — third-person narration that is all-seeing and all-knowing; describes thoughts and actions of all characters

**Onomatopoeia** — words that resemble sounds associated with the object

**Oxymoron** — a figure of speech containing contradiction

**Persona** — the voice or character of the speaker (or narrator) in a literary piece

**Personification** — gives human qualities to non-human objects or animals

**Play** — a story written for the stage; story performed on stage

**Plot** — what happens in the story

**Poem** — a poetic work

**Poetry** — literary genre that is qualified by its rhythmic language

**Point of view** — the eye and voice through which a story is told

**Prose** — ordinary speech or writing with no specific rhythmical pattern (meter), as opposed to poetry

**Protagonist** — the main character in a narrative work; does not have to have heroic qualities

**Quatrain** — a stanza containing four lines of sometimes alternating rhymes

**Refrain** — a line, phrase, or stanza that is repeated at intervals throughout a poem or song

**Repetition** — a sound, word, sentence or image seen over and over throughout a narrative or dramatic work

**Rhyme** — repetition of stressed sounds in words usually found at the end of lines of verse

**Round character** — usually a major character who changes or develops in a narrative or dramatic work — one of the major genres of fiction; one play

**Scenes** — sections of acts in a play that can last from a few seconds to thirty minutes

**Sestet** — last six lines of a sonnet

**Setting** — where and when the story takes place

**Short story** — compact narrative fiction; usually can be read in one sitting

**Signposting** — music or sound that indicates a change of scene in a radio drama

**Simile** — a comparison using "like" or "as"

**Slang** — language that is not accepted as the standard

**Sonnet** — a poem of Italian origin with 14 lines in iambic pentameter

**Stage directions** — instructions to the actors and the director about the set, gestures, entrances and exits, etc.

**Stanza** — group of lines (usually four) which rhyme

**Static character** — a secondary character; one who does not change

**Stereotypes** — character who is ordinary; a type or mould

**Style** — the way in which a narrative or dramatic or poetic work is written; the types of words, sentences, and structures used for an overall effect

**Symbol** — a particular word or idea that may represent something else

**Syntax** — the grammatical order in which sentences are organised

**Tercet** — three lines that rhyme; a triplet

**Theme** — the central concept in a narrative, dramatic, or poetic work

**Third-person narrator** — story told through a "he" or "she" who is not part of the events

**Tone** — the technique in which an attitude is revealed

**Voice** (or persona or narrator) — the person who speaks in a literary piece

# Glossary of Grammatical Terms

**Clause** — a group of words containing a subject and a verb, but not necessarily expressing a complete idea

**Comma Splice** — incorrect use of comma; substitution of a comma for a period

**Complex Sentence** — one independent clause and at least one dependent clause

**Compound Sentence** — two independent clauses joined by a coordinate such as "and," "but," "or" etc.

**Compound-Complex Sentence** — two independent clauses and at least one dependent clause

**Co-ordinating Conjunction** — words such as "and," "but," "or," "so," "yet"

**Co-ordination** — joining of two or more ideas of equal importance

**Dependent or Subordinate Clause** — clause which expresses an incomplete idea

**Direct Quotation** — repetition of the exact words a person has said or written using double quotation marks

**Homographs** — words that are spelled the same but pronounced differently and with different meaning

**Independent clause or principal clause** — clause that expresses a complete idea

**Indirect quotation** — stating indirectly what someone else has said

**Paragraph** — a group of sentence with one main idea

**Parallel Construction** — refers to the use of similar grammatical structures

**Paraphrasing** — restating in your own words someone else's ideas or texts

**Prefix** — additions affixed "in front of" root word in order to give particular meanings to root word

**Principal or main clause** — see independent clause

**Relative pronouns** — words such as "who," "whom" "whose," "which" and "that," which are used to show subordination

**Run-on sentence** — at least two independent clauses with no punctuation or too many conjunctions (and, but, or) between them

**Sentence** — a group of words containing a subject and verb and expressing a complete idea

**Sentence Fragment** — an incomplete idea; part of a sentence but punctuated as if it were a sentence

**Simple Sentence** — one independent clause

**Subordination** — shows relation between ideas having different degrees of importance; less important idea is subordinated to a more important idea

**Subordinating Conjunction** — words such as "because," "when," "since," etc. (See unit 2 for complete list.)

**Suffix** — additions affixed "after root word" in order to give particular meanings to root words

**Supporting Details** — facts, examples, or statistics that give further information on the central idea of a paragraph

**Thesis Statement** — a sentence that contains the essential opinion or gist about the subject of an essay

**Topic Sentence** — introduces the subject of the paragraph and contains an opinion about the subject

**Transitionals** — words and expressions that make connections between sentences and paragraphs in order to link ideas such as "furthermore," "moreover," etc. (See unit 2 for complete list.)

# INDEX

The index lists key words and expressions pertaining to literary terms or periods, authors featured in the book or on the website, and writing or grammatical terms. Page numbers printed in bold indicate that this is where the word or expression has either been defined or has received its fullest treatment.